The Spirit of Chinese Philanthropy; a Study in Mutual Aid

STUDIES IN HISTORY
ECONOMICS AND
PUBLIC LAW

EDITED BY

THE FACULTY OF POLITICAL SCIENCE

OF COLUMBIA UNIVERSITY .

VOLUME FIFTY

New York

COLUMBIA UNIVERSITY

LONGMANS, GREEN & CO., AGENTS

LONDON: P. S. KING & SON

1912

CONTENTS

248641

1

THE SPIRIT OF CHINESE PHILANTHROPY

STUDIES IN HISTORY, ECONOMICS AND PUBLIC LAW

EDITED BY THE FACULTY OF POLITICAL SCIENCE
OF COLUMBIA UNIVERSITY

Volume L]   [Number 1

Whole Number 125

THE SPIRIT OF CHINESE PHILANTHROPY

A Study in Mutual Aid

BY

YU-YUE TSU, Ph.D.

New York
COLUMBIA UNIVERSITY
LONGMANS, GREEN & CO., AGENTS
LONDON: P. S. KING & SON
1912

THIS VOLUME

IS DEDICATED TO

DR. F. L. HAWKS POTT

PRESIDENT OF ST. JOHN'S UNIVERSITY
SHANGHAI, CHINA

PREFACE

In this monograph the writer has endeavored to describe Chinese Philanthropy and to interpret its characteristics and ideals as he understands them. The subject is greater than can be adequately treated in a work of the present scope, but it is hoped that no injustice has been done to the subject and that further study of it may be stimulated by this presentation.

The writing was begun before the change of government in China took place. Some parts of the monograph, touching the political organization of the country may not therefore exactly fit the new conditions, but as they are true representations of conditions that obtained in the immediate past and went far into a remote past, we have allowed them to stand, as first written.

The problem of population in China in its intimate relation to social wellbeing and progress is of vital interest not only to China but also to the world. The writer's interest in it was first aroused by Professor A. A. Tenney's lectures at Columbia University. Professor E. A. Ross' book, *The Changing Chinese*, contains an illuminating study of it, perhaps the most thorough one that bears upon present conditions in China. The problem will repay further study.

The writer wishes to record his indebtedness to Professor F. H. Giddings, Professor Friedrich Hirth, Dr.

7]   7

R. M. Binder and Mr. Parker Vanamee, for valuable
suggestions in the preparation of the monograph, and
to Professor E. R. A. Seligman, for assistance in putting it through the press.

Y. Y. T.

CHELSEA SQUARE, NEW YORK CITY. *April, 1912.*

CONTENTS

CHAPTER VI

CONCLUSION : RISE OF NATIONAL SELF-CONSCIOUSNESS AND SOLIDARITY

INTRODUCTION

In his great standard work *The Middle Kingdom* (Rev. Ed., 1904, vol. ii, p. 265) the late Professor S. W. Williams says with regard to the benevolent institutions of the Chinese: "In large towns voluntary societies are found, having for their object the relief of suffering, which ought to be mentioned, as the *Chinese have not been fairly credited with what they do in this line.*"

It has also been maintained in the early days of our relations with China that the native efforts in the matter of public charity are not worth much and that the spirit of benevolence was not an originally Chinese virtue. There may not be many who hold such views nowadays, but it appears that, to convince skeptical critics, the truth has to be traced back to the most ancient literature to show how, far from being introduced and fostered by western missionaries, as some feel inclined to assume, the spirit of charity to one's neighbor has originated and developed on Chinese soil itself. To prove this, it seems, there was nobody better qualified than a patriotic Chinese whose education might be expected to do justice to every side of the question. Such is Mr. Andrew Yu-Yue Tsu, the author of this essay, who combined researches in Chinese literature, carried on in seminar work under the Department of Chinese with western methods studied in the Departments of Sociology and Social Economy.

FRIEDRICH HIRTH,
Professor of Chinese.

DEPARTMENT OF CHINESE,
  COLUMBIA UNIVERSITY,
    NEW YORK, *May 10, 1912*

CHAPTER I

The Study of Philanthropy.—Philanthropy has been defined as "universal good-will," or "spirit of active good-will towards one's fellow-men, especially as shown in efforts to promote their welfare."[1] As a social phenomenon, philanthropy had originated in sub-human gregariousness and mutual aid, but its wonderful development has been achieved in human society through human consciousness. The process whereby philanthropy has reached its present status may be traced by pointing out its several stages. As an ideal, philanthropy was first regarded as a personal virtue, a quality of the pious soul, and as such received tremendous encouragement and development by a close alliance with religion. But at present, philanthropy shows a tendency to dissociate itself from religion and to occupy an independent position. The conception of it as a personal virtue is being merged into the larger conception of it as a social virtue. As a social virtue, philanthropy seems coextensive with consciousness of kind. From a narrow ideal, coinciding with family, clannish, tribal and national limitations of sympathy, philanthropy is tending toward universalism *pari passu* with the growth of sympathy. In practice, philanthropy began as a palliative for distress, as alms-

[1] *Webster's New International Dictionary* Reference History edition, 1911

giving, grew into institutional charity, and finally became a science, variously known as scientific philanthropy or social economy.   It began with emphasis upon the individual; it now seems to be laying more and more emphasis upon the social environment.   Instead of aiming to improve the condition of the poor and destitute directly, it aims to do so indirectly by the improvement of such social conditions as cause poverty and destitution.   It has adopted as its goal the total elimination of the causes of poverty and misery in society.[1]   In adopting such a goal, and working toward its realization, the philanthropist joins hands with the sociologist, the economist, the ethicist, the statesman and other workers in other fields of human effort for progress toward a perfect society.[2]

I. PHILANTHROPY IN CHINESE THOUGHT

Philanthropy as a virtue: As a virtue philanthropy has been highly exalted by the Chinese moralists of all ages. Both Confucius and Mencius regarded it as the distinguishing characteristic of man,[3] as one of the fundamental constituents of nobleness and superiority of character.[4]   Asked by one of his disciples about philanthropy, Confucius replied. 'It is to love all men.'[5]

Philanthropy natural to man: High and noble as the virtue of philanthropy is, it is nevertheless conceived of

[1] Devine, *Principles of Relief*, p. 181

[2] Spencer, *Principles of Ethics,* vol ii, pp 432-3 Giddings, *Principles of Sociology*, pp. 420-2.

[3] *Analects of Confucius*, tr. Legge, '*Chinese Classics*', vol 1, p. 405; *Mencius*, tr Legge, '*Chinese Classics*', vol. ii, p. 485

[4] *Analects*, p. 320.

[5] *Ibid*, p 260

as lying naturally within the capacity of every person. Thus it is written in the *Classics:*

The feeling of commiseration belongs to all men, so does that of shame and dislike ; and that of reverence and respect ; and that of approving and disapproving. The feeling of commiseration implies the principle of benevolence ; that of shame and dislike, the principle of righteousness ; that of reverence and respect, the principle of propriety ; and that of approving and disapproving, the principle of knowledge. Benevolence, righteousness, propriety, and knowledge, are not infused into us from without. We are certainly furnished with them. . . . Hence it is said "Seek and you will find them. Neglect and you will lose them." Men differ from one another in regard to them ;—some as much again as others, some five times as much, and some to an incalculable amount :—it is because they cannot carry out fully their natural powers.[1]

The spontaneity of sympathy in man is set forth in the following lines :

All men have a mind which cannot bear to see the sufferings of others. . . . My meaning may be illustrated thus ; If men suddenly see a child about to fall into a well, they will without exception experience a feeling of alarm and distress. They will feel so not as a ground on which they may gain the favor of the child's parents, nor as a ground on which they may seek the praise of their neighbors and friends, nor from a dislike to the reputation of having been unmoved by such a thing. From this case, we may perceive that the feeling of compassion is essential to man.[2]

Acquirement and development of philanthropy: Apparently opposed to this view of human nature, yet not

---

[1] *Mencius*, tr. Legge, *op. cit.*, pp. 402-403.

[2] *Ibid.*, pp. 201-2.

really so, is the view of another school of ethicists, whose chief representative is Hsin-tse. His contention is that all social qualities and sentiments, which we attribute to human nature, are not original but acquired ones. Thus he says :

Man's nature is radically evil or egotistic; when it is good or altruistic, it is the product of art. . . . By nature a man when hungry desires to eat, when cold, to clothe himself, when tired, to rest. Yet to-day, a man seeing his father or brother in the same condition will desist from self-gratification in deference to his father or brother. Such action or rather inhibition from action is against his nature, but it is in accordance with the principles of a dutiful son or of an affectionate brother and with the established morals and rights. Following nature there will be no self-restraint or deference to others.[1]

Like the other powers, the power of philanthropy is capable of development through exercise. Thus after saying that the four principles of benevolence, righteousness, property and knowledge are natural and essential to man, Mencius continues :

Men have these four principles just as they have their four limbs. When men, having these four principles, yet say of themselves that they cannot develop them, they play the thief with themselves, and he who says of his prince that he cannot develop them, plays the thief with his prince. Since all men have these four principles in themselves, let them know to give them all their development and completion, and the issue will be like that of fire which has begun to burn, or that of a spring which has begun to find vent. Let them have their complete development, and they will suffice to love and protect all within the four seas. Let them be denied that devel-

[1] Hsin Tzŭ, *Essay on Human Nature.*

opment, and they will not suffice for a man to serve his parents with.[1]

State and philanthropy: Ancient ethico-political thinkers have always thought of ethics and politics as closely allied. The state is regarded as existing for the promotion of human happiness; the best government is one which is truly benevolent in its solicitude for the welfare of the people. Hence the term 'benevolent government' occurs frequently in the Chinese Classics.

Once Mencius was consulted by King Hwuy of Leang regarding Government. The king complained that in-spite of his efforts for the good of his people, he failed to attract them to himself, and he wanted to know the reason for it. Mencius, knowing that the cause of the failure was the luxury of the court and its indifference to the real needs of the people gave the following pointed reply:

Your dogs and swine eat the food of men, and you do not know to make any restrictive arrangements. There are people dying from famine on the roads, and you do not know to issue the stores of your granaries, for them. When people die, you say, "It is not owing to me; it is owing to the year." In what does this differ from stabbing a man and killing him, and then saying; "It was not I; it was the weapon"? Let your Majesty cease to blame on the year, and instantly from all the empire the people will come to you.[2]

Goal of state philanthropy: The benevolent office of the state must be for the elimination of material destitu-tion among the people, and the realization of economic sufficiency, as its first duty, for without economic suf-

---

[1] *Mencius*, tr. Legge, *op. cit.*, p. 203.
[2] *Ibid.*, p. 132.

ficiency, there would be no possibility of spiritual progress. The picture of economic sufficiency among the
people is thus depicted :

Around the homestead with its five mow, the space beneath
the walls was planted with mulberry trees, with which the
women nourish silk-worms, and thus the old were able to
have silk to wear. Each family had five brood hens and two
brood sows, which were kept in their breeding seasons, and
thus the old were able to have flesh to eat. The husbandmen
cultivated their farms of hundred mow, and thus their families
of eight mouths were secured against want.[1]

Opposition to philanthropy: Just as philanthropy is
exalted by Confucius and Mencius as the distinguishing characteristic of humanity and as a virtue to be
cherished by all, so it is denounced by Chuang-Tzŭ, the
Taoist, as a false outgrowth of human nature and as a
disturbing factor in human wellbeing. In his writings,
there is an account of an imaginery interview between
Confucius and Lao Tzŭ, the founder of Taoism, in which
the principle of philanthropy is made to appear in the
light above described:[2]

When Confucius was going west to place his works in the
Imperial library of the House of Chow, Tzŭ Lu counselled
him, saying, "I have heard that a certain librarian of the
Cheng department, by name Lao Tan, has resigned and retired into private life. Now as you, Sir, wish to deposit your
works, it would be advisable to go and interview him."

"Certainly," said Confucius ; and he thereupon went to see
Lao Tzŭ. The latter would not hear of the proposal ; so
Confucius began to expound the doctrines of his twelve
canons, in order to convince Lao Tzŭ.

[1] *Mencius,* tr. Legge, *op. cit.,* p. 461.

[2] *Chuang Tzŭ, Mystic, Moralist, Social Reformer,* tr H. A. Giles,
pp. 165-167.

"This is nonsense," cried Lao Tzŭ, interrupting him. "Tell me what are your criteria."

"Charity," replied Confucius, "and duty towards one's neighbor."

"Tell me, please," asked Lao Tzŭ, "are these part of man's original nature?"

"They are," answered Confucius. "Without charity, the superior man could not become what he is. Without duty to one's neighbor, he would be of no effect, These two belong to the original nature of a pure man. What further would you have"?

"Tell me," said Lao Tzŭ, "in what consist charity and duty to one's neighbor?"

"They consist," answered Confucius, "in a capacity for rejoicing in all things; in universal love, without the element of self. These are the characteristics of charity and duty to one's neighbor."

"What stuff!" cried Lao Tzŭ. "Does not universal love contradict itself? Is not your elimination of self a positive manifestation of self? Sir, if you would cause the empire not to lose its source of nourishment, there is the universe, its regularity is unceasing; there are the sun and moon, their brightness is unceasing; there are the stars, their groupings never change; there are birds and beasts, they flock without varying: there are trees and shrubs, they grow upwards without exception. Be like these; follow Tao, and you will be perfect. Why then these vain struggles after charity and duty to one's neighbor, as though beating a drum in search of a fugitive. Alas! Sir, you have brought much confusion into the mind of man."

Philanthropy unnatural to man.—Chuang Tzŭ's view of human nature is therefore diametrically opposed to Confucius and Mencius. To try to make men charitable is as much destruction of his nature and so injurious as it is to try to lengthen the legs of a duck or to shorten those of a crane. In either case, there is an attempt to

go against what has been foreordained by natural providence, and the result is suffering, physical for the one and
moral for the other. All is well with nature, Chuang
Tzŭ would say; nature is self-sufficient, let it evolve itself
undisturbed by human artifice; this is the royal road to
complete contentment and happiness of life. Thus he
says:

Intentional charity and intentional duty to one's neighbor are
surely not included in our moral nature. Yet what sorrow
these have involved. . . . And the charitable of the age go
about sorrowing over the ills of the age, while the non-charit-
able cut through the natural conditions of things in their
greed after place and wealth. Surely then intentional charity
and duty to one's neighbor are not included in our moral
nature. Yet from the time of the Three Dynasties downwards
what a fuss has been made about them!

Those who cannot make perfect without arc, line, com-
passes and square, injure the natural constitution of things.
Those who require cords to bind and glue to stick, interfere
with the natural functions of things. And those who seek to
satisfy the mind of man by hampering with ceremonies and
music and preaching charity and duty to one's neighbor,
thereby destroy the intrinsicality of things.

. . . And just as all things are produced, and none can tell
how they are produced, so do all things possess their own
intrinsic qualities and non can tell how they possess them.
From time immemorial this has always been so, without varia-
tion. Why then should charity and duty to one's neighbor
be as it were glued or corded on, and introduced into the
domain of Tao, to give rise to doubt among mankind? [1]

Destruction of the natural integrity of things, an order to
produce articles of various kinds—this is the fault of the artisan.
Annihilation of Tao in order to practice charity and duty to
one's neighbor—this is the error of the Sage. [2]

[1] *Chuang Tzŭ*, tr. Giles, pp 101-102   [2] *Ibid*, p 108

In concluding this discussion of philanthropy in Chinese thought, we may say that the Chinese nation has always considered Confucianism orthodox and Taoism heretical. In spite of the beauty and vigor of his philosophy and his language, Chuang Tzǔ has not succeeded in breaking the influence of the teachings of Confucianism upon the nation and its civilization.

II. CHINESE PHILANTHROPY IN PRACTICE

Historical Notices.—Chinese history has been written not as a history of a people, but as a chronicle of kings and emperors. Hence while giving detailed accounts of royal lives, deeds and reigns, it gives meagre notices of the lives and activities and conditions of the people, and the latter, in fact, only where illumined by contact with royalty. This being so, we find that the practice of philanthropy, so far as recorded, has been contemplated as originating with the rulers, as a function of the state, as imperial paternalism flowing downwards to benefit the people, while practically nothing is said of initiative and practice in philanthropy on the part of the people themselves. Such a representation becomes the historians of the court, whose function is the preparation of the historical archives of the reigns and dynasties for the glorification of dead kings and emperors. We are not therefore to infer from historical notices that the people have been nothing else than receivers of Imperial charity. As we shall see in the following chapters, popular initiative and participation in philanthropy seem to be so prevalent in reality as to overshadow whatever Imperial initiative and participation there is in the same.

Ancient Old-Age Pensions: The earliest rulers, known as the Five Rulers (2255–2205 B. C.), were described as setting the example of nourishing the aged of the nation for later rulers:

The lord of Yü, nourished the aged (who had retired from the service) of the state in (the school called) the higher hsiang, and the aged of the common people (and officers who had not obtained rank) in (the school called) the lower hsiang. The sovereigns of Hsia nourished the former in (the school called) the hsü on the east, and the latter in (that called) the hsü on the west. The men of Yin nourished the former in the school of the right, and the latter in that of the left. . . .[1]

We may regard this as the earliest instance of Old Age Pension System sanctioned by the state.

Poor Relief : The poor are described as of four classes :

One who while quite young, lost his father was called an orphan ; an old man who had lost his sons was called a solitary. An old man who had lost his wife was called a pitiable widower ; an old woman who had lost her husband was called a poor widow. These four classes were the most forlorn of Heaven's people, and had none to whom to tell their wants ; they all received regular allowances.

The dumb, the deaf, the lame, such as have lost a member, pigmies and mechanics, were all·fed according to what work they were able to do.[2]

They received the emperor's bounties, as he ordered his officers periodically to open his granaries and vaults and distribute their contents to the poor and friendless and the needy.[3]

Beginnings of Institutional Charity and Social Legislation: During the Chow dynasty (1122–255 B. C.), the state periodically gave relief to orphans in spring and summer, and during the Han dynasty (206 B. C.–25

---

[1] *Li Ki,* tr J. Legge, in *Sacred Books of the East,* ed. F. Max Muller, vol. xxvii, pp. 242, 466

[2] *Ibid.,* pp 243-244.

[3] *Ibid.,* p. 264.

A. D.), an emperor ordered state support of neglected children and children of poor families with supply from the public granaries. During the Sung dynasty (960–1260 A. D.) public lands were devoted to the cultivation of grains, which went to fill public granaries established in all districts; buildings were erected for the reception and care of cast-away children.[1] An emperor of the Yuan dynasty (1260–1368 A. D.) in 1271 ordered alm-houses to be built for the shelter of the poor.[2] In 1659, Emperor Sun-chi issued an edict in which desertion or destruction of infants was severely condemned. He ob-served therein that it seemed strange to him that while the beasts of the field and the fowls of the air cherished their young, rational beings should want to destory their daughters; that the destruction of infant life was a blacker crime than robbery, for all creatures were or-dained of Heaven to live.[3] In 1711, Emperor Kang Hsi ordered the establishment of foundling hospitals through-out the empire. A private hospital that was established two years after this date at Shanghai survives to this day.[4] In 1724, a government almshouse was opened at Canton; and in 1739, Emperor Kien Lung ordered it to feed 4,676 destitute persons.[5] In 1783, the same Em-peror reprinted the edict of 1659, condemning persons committing infanticide to be punished with 100 blows and exile for a year and half.[3] In 1805, (9th year of Kia King) a private charities society, at Shanghai, the

---

[1] *Chinese Repository*, vol. xiv, p. 184.

[2] H. C. Chen, *Economic Principles of Confucius and His School*, vol. ii, p. 298.

[3] J. R. Grey, *Walks In The City of Canton*, p. 571.

[4] *Chinese Repository*, vol. xiv, p. 180.

[5] *China Review*, vol. ii, p. 91.

Hall of United Benevolence, was formed;[1] since then, it has had an unbroken career. In 1873, a proclamation encouraging care and preservation of infant life was issued by the provincial authorities of Hupeh.[2]

The above account of the beginnings of institutional charities and social legislation is far from being a complete statement of what took place during the years mentioned; it is intended only to serve as an indication of the development of practical philanthropy in China.

The poor law of China: The law of China recognizes the right to relief of those dependent persons, who may be classed as the ' worthy poor.'   This right is contained in the following law :

All poor destitute widowers and widows, the fatherless and children, the helpless and the infirm, shall receive sufficient maintenance and protection from the magistrates of their native city or district, wherever they have neither relations nor connections upon whom they can depend for support. Any magistrate refusing such maintenance and protection, shall be punished with 60 blows.

Also when any such persons are maintained and protected by government, the superintending magistrate and his subordinates, if failing to afford them the legal allowance of food and raiment, shall be punished in proportion to the amount of the deficiency, according to the law against an embezzlement of government stores.[3]

The law not only recognizes the right to relief, but also stipulates that the relief should be sufficient, and that the negligent magistrate must be punished.

Ineffectiveness of the law: Good as the law is, there

[1] *Chinese Repository*, vol xv, p 402 *et seq*

[2] Grey, *op. cit*, p. 575.

[3] *Ta Tsing Leu Lee*, tr. G. T Staunton, p 93

are serious defects in its administration. In the first place, its enforcement would require poor-law administrative machinery, but no such provision is made by the Imperial Government, and so its provisions merely impose additional duties upon magistrates already burdened with other functions. In the second place, supposing poor relief were seriously contemplated by the magistrate, he is met by another difficulty: he must find his own funds for it, from the same source that he usually gets his official emoluments, from the land tax   Theoretically, he is expected to find funds for all kinds of undertakings from this source, but because of his own insignificant official salary, of his need of paying the government employees in his district as well as of furnishing fixed revenue for the Provincial and Imperial Administrations, practically he is unable to find much left for poor relief. In the third place, to increase taxation is out of the question, so long as there remains Imperial sanction that the land tax is forever fixed, and so long as the people are without voice or vote in the government.[1]

Legal Status of Popular Philanthropic Institutions: For these reasons, the excellent law has remained practically a dead letter on the statute-book.   There are government reliefs and charities, but their number is insignificant compared with those philanthropic institutions that have been organized by the people themselves and are controlled by them.   These popular institutions being under the law, of necessity, are nominally under the supervision of the civil authorities, in whose jurisdiction they are placed.   There is some form of legal incorporation, whose chief elements are approval of the institutions by the civil authorities and their

[1] For further discussion of this point, see chap v, *infra*

promise to protect (and sometimes, financially to assist) them.   But the real control of the institutions is not in the hands of the civil authorities, but in those of the people, and their support is derived almost entirely from voluntary sources rather than from official ones.

Relative Efficiency of State and Popular Control: The popular character and control of philanthropic institutions cannot be too strongly advocated. First, popular institutions give the people opportunity to be interested in social work; they are incidentally educative agencies for the development of social responsibility in the minds of the people.   A government institution is not as interesting to the people, for it is apparently far removed from their participation therein.   Secondly, popular institutions supported by the public are more responsive to criticism, whether approving or disapproving, by the people, and so tend more to efficiency, than government institutions whose support is only indirectly and remotely derived from the people.   Thirdly, the management of philanthropic institutions of the people is generally entrusted to the hands of the most public-spirited and esteemed persons of the locality, for the people like to see their interests promoted; whereas, if philanthropic institutions were under state control they would generally be regarded as a part of mere official routine work at one extreme or as a part of a spoils system at the other extreme.   For these reasons, it has been fortunate that most social and philanthropic works in China have been initiated and controlled by the people themselves.   This does not suggest enmity between the people and the government, but it suggests the practical democracy of the nation.

Present organization of philanthropy in China: Every city or district or town has its own philanthropic institutions, supported by the inhabitants and administered by their representatives. There is usually one institution in every place which is larger than any of the rest, and this institution serves as a central organization for the place, corresponding, in position, but only partly in nature to charity organization societies in the cities of America and Europe. Thus, we have the Hall of United Benevolence at Shanghai, the Practical Benevolent Society at Ningpo, the Hall of Sustaining Love at Canton, the Hall of Benevolence at Chefoo, *et cetera*, all of which are composite organizations with special departments or forms of activity varying from five to seventeen in number.

Scope and Character of Chinese Philanthropy: In illustration of the activities of central charities societies, such as we have mentioned in the preceding paragraph, we may cite those of the Hall of Benevolence of Chefoo:[1] The seventeen forms of activities are (1) Non-interest loans to the poor; (2) Burial facilities for the poor; (3) Waste-paper collection; (4) Assisting ship-wrecked persons; (5) Fire protection; (6) Aid to widows, (7) Reception of deserted infants; (8) Free supply of books to the poor who are desirous of reading; (9) Free education for poor children; (10) Orphanage; (11) Industrial school for poor girls; (12) Refuge for the cure of opium-habit; (13) Refuge for the homeless sick; (14) Hospital work; (15) Refuge for the poor in winter; (16) Free kitchen; (17) Vaccination.

Chinese philanthropy may be divided into three general groups: I. Charity, in the strict sense of the word, meaning disinterested aid to the poor; II. Mutual Benefit, or the method of relief and protection by reciprocal

[1] *Decennial Report*, 1882-1891. *China· Imperial Maritime Customs Report. I. Statistical Series*, no 6, first issue, p 60.

efforts; III. Civic Betterment, or the promotion of public welfare through voluntary co-operation on the part of the inhabitants.   There are other activities which are benevolent in nature, such as the humane treatment of animals, which cannot be included in the above division. But as far as the human content is concerned, Charity, Mutual Benefit and Civic Betterment succinctly describe the character and scope of Chinese Philanthropy.

CHAPTER II

POPULATION AND SOCIAL WELL-BEING

Incipient Poverty: Poverty is known to exist extensively in China. It is not obtrusive poverty, but pervading incipiency toward poverty, that obtains there. It is expressed in the smallness of capital, in the easy precipitation of persons from frugality into destitution in adverse times, in the lowness of wages, and in the scarcity of luxury and comforts of life. The chief cause of this incipient poverty, we agree with Professor Ross, lies in the over-pressure of population upon means of subsistence. He says:

Most of the stock explanations of national poverty throw no light on the condition of the Chinese. They are not impoverished by the niggardliness of the soil, for China is one of the most bountiful seats occupied by man. Their state is not the just recompense of sloth, for no people is better broken to heavy, unremitting toil. The trouble is not lack of intelligence in their work, for they are skilful farmers and clever in the arts and crafts. Nor have they been dragged down into their pit of wolfish competition by wasteful vices. . . . They are not victims of the rapacity of their rulers, for if their government does little for them, it exacts little. In good times its fiscal claims are far from crushing. With four times our number the national budget is a fifth of ours. The basic conditions of prosperity—liberty of person and security of property— are well established. . . . Nor is the lot of the masses due to exploitation. . . . There are great stretches of fertile agricultural country where the struggle for subsistence is stern and yet the cultivator owns his land and implements and pays tribute to no man. . . For a grinding mass poverty that cannot be matched in the Occident there remains but one general cause, namely, the *crowding of population upon the means of subsistence.*[1]

If the elimination of poverty is the fundamental problem of philanthropy, then the study of population is of paramount importance. Our conviction is that the solution of the problem lies in the healthy equilibration of population with the supply of subsistence and wealth, according to some worthy standard of living, through social regulation of population, on the one hand, and promotion of economic prosperity on the other.

The Population of China : No one knows exactly what is the population of China, although the Chinese government has from time to time made estimates, more or less accurate, from returns of taxation units and from enumeration of families. Probably the estimate of E. H. Parker (385,000,000) is the most reliable.[2] Similarly, the exact density of population is unknown, although as to the fact of denseness there seems to be no question. Smith says that for the plain of north China, the probable density for the more sparsely populated districts is 300 persons to the square mile, and for the more thickly-settled regions, from 1,000 to 1,500 persons per square mile.[3] F. H. King, formerly professor of agricultural physics in the University of Wisconsin, who went to China to study Chinese farming, writes that whereas in the United States land and population are

[1] E. A Ross, *The Changing Chinese*, pp. 95-96.

[2] *China, Past and Present*, p. 30; see H. B Morse, *Administration and Trade of China*, p. 203.

[3] A. H Smith, *Village Life in China*, p. 19

in the ratio of 20 acres to one person, in China they are in the ratio of one acre to one person, and of that one acre half is arid and unproductive. Of the real density of cultivated land in China, America and Japan, the following summary is gathered from Professor King's book:[1] Shantung Province has 1,783 people, 212 cattle or donkeys and 399 swine, or 1,995 consumers and rough-food transformers per square mile of farm land ; America's rural districts in 1900 had 61 persons and 30 horses and mules for one square mile of improved farm land; Japan in 1907 had 1,922 persons and 125 horses and cattle per square mile; Chungming Island at the mouth of Yangtse River, China, in 1902 had according to official census, 270 square miles of land, with 3,700 persons per square mile.

Causes of Density : We know but dimly the historic process whereby China became populated and densely populated as time went on. It is certain that the Chinese people are not indigenous inhabitants; they came from without the land. They were first heard of moving from the north and west down the valley of the Hwang Ho (Yellow River), and spreading thence to the other parts of the country along natural water-courses.[2] From the very first they were described as cultivators of the soil. In their progress they both assimilated the inhabitants already there and drove many tribes into refuge among the mountains of the northwestern part. We may conclude that both congregation and genetic aggregation[3] had operated to make China populous. The fertility of the land, combined with its accessibility, attracted immigration and settlement, and the fertility

[1] F. H. King, *Farmers of Forty Centuries,* pp 3-4

[2] Parker. *China. Her History, Diplomacy and Commerce,* p. 5 *et seq*

[3] Terms as defined in Giddings, *Principles of Sociology,* pp 89, 91.

combined with the art of agriculture enabled people to obtain abundant subsistence, and was thus conducive to rapid reproduction. But whatever the historic process whereby China has become one of the most populous nations of the earth, we may mention some causes of prolific reproduction to-day.

Present Causes of Prolific Reproduction : 1. Rural Conditions : The population of China is largely rural, having agriculture as its main occupation. "By far the larger part of the most numerous people on the globe live in villages. . . . The traveler will be impressed with the inconceivably great number of Chinese altogether outside of the great centres of urban population.[1] For the farmer, the circuit of food-getting or the relation between labor and subsistence is the simplest, since he is able to feed himself and his family without recourse to third parties. We believe that this facility in food-getting tends to encourage the rearing of many children. Moreover, the unchanging and monotonous rural life, lacking the distracting influences of urban life, tends to confine the farmer's interests to his immediate family and thus to intensify his fondness for children. Finally, the desire for children is also strengthened by need for farm helpers, and by the wish to see one's land pass down to posterity without going out of the family.

2. *Ancestor worship*: Ancestor worship puts a premium on male progeny, since only male descendants are eligible for religious and sacrificial services before the *manes* of the departed. Naturally this tradition creates in the parents the desire to have male children, in order that their posthumous welfare may be assured. From this, perhaps, began the association of family prosperity

[1] Smith, *op. cit*, p. 15

with male progeny and is, perhaps, the basis of the crav-
ing for progeny, the cause for creation of large families.

3. *Early marriage*: Ancestral worship and the patriarchal family encourage early marriage. Sons live with
their parents even after coming of age; they hold no
private property until the death of the head of the family.
Marriages are arranged for by the parents, who often find
themselves under the necessity of supporting their sons'
families. Hence, the financial check upon early marriage
among the young is absent. Moreover, the dependence
of women upon men, the absence of self-support on the
part of women, facilitates early marriage. Early marriage
causes rapid multiplication of population.

Effects of surplus population: The Malthusian theory
of the growth of population maintains that there is an
intimate relation between population and food-supply.
This relation may be called the equilibration between
population and food-supply. In order to present clearly
the process as it seems to be in operation to-day in
China, its effects will be considered under four aspects.
Those extraordinary ways whereby population is usually
relieved of its surplus, such as famines, pestilence, wars,
and so forth, which Malthus emphasized, will be ignored
and more attention directed to the conditions of living,
consequent upon congestion of population.

Four Aspects of Equilibration:

1. *Population and Tillage of the Soil:* The main
source of food-supply is the soil; hence labor spent in tillage becomes the principal means of support. The increased demand for food because of the increase of population may be met in two ways, (1) intension cultivation of
lands already under service, and (ii) extension of the area
of cultivation. Both ways have been used in China. It

has been observed that, whereas there are 20 acres of land for one person in America there is only one acre for one person in China, and of this one acre, half is arid and unproductive. But severe intensive cultivation has enabled one sixth of an acre of good land to support a man.[1] The continuous struggle for food has made the Chinese expert agriculturists without the aid of science.

But intensive cultivation is limited by the law of diminishing returns; it will not go beyond the point where labor fails to get its requisite compensation. New lands must therefore be sought in order to keep up with the demand for food-supply. Professor Ross witnesses that land is utilized in China as perhaps it has never been elsewhere. All available productive land is under cultivation, and there is little waste land or pasturage. He draws a vivid picture, as follows:

To win new plots for tillage, human sweat has been poured out like water. Clear up to the top the foothills have been carved into terraced fields. On a single slope I counted forty-seven such fields running up like the steps of a Brobdingnagian staircase. And the river bed, five hundred feet below, between the thin streams that wander over it until the autumn rains cover it with a turbid flood, has been smoothed and diked into hundreds of gem-like paddy fields green with the young rice. In the mountains, where the mantle of brown soil covering the rocks is too thin to be sculptured into level fields, the patches of wheat and corn follow the natural slope and the hoe must be used instead of the plough. Two such plots have I seen at a measured angle of forty-five degrees, and any number tilted at least forty degrees from the horizontal. From their huts near the wooded top of the range half a mile above you, men clamber down and cultivate Lilliputian

[1] F. H. King, *Farmers of Forty Centuries*, p 194

patches of earth lodged in pockets among the black, naked rocks. . . . . . .

Nowhere can the watcher of man's struggle with his environment find a more wonderful spectacle than meets the eye from a certain seven-thousand-foot pass amid the great tangle of mountains in West China that gives birth to the Han, the Wei and the rivers that make famed Szechuan the "Four-river Province." Save where steepness or rock-outcropping forbids, the slopes are cultivated from the floor of the Tung Ho valley right up to the summits five thousand feet above. In this vertical mile there are different crops for different altitudes—vegetables below, then corn, lastly wheat. Sometimes the very apex of the mountain wears a green peaked cap of rye. The aerial farms are crumpled into the great folds of the mountains and their borders follow with a poetic grace the outthrust or incurve of the slopes. . . . .

The heart-breaking labor of redeeming and tilling these upper slopes that require a climb of some thousands of feet from one's cave home is a sure sign of population pressure. It calls up the picture of a swelling human lake, somehow without egress from the valley, rising and rising until it fairly lifts cultivation over the summits of the mountains. In June these circling tiers of verdant undulating sky-farms are an impressive, even a beautiful sight; yet one cannot help thinking of the grim, ever-present menace of hunger which alone could have fostered people to such prodigies of toil.[1]

Incidentally, deforestation must result from extension of cultivation, and because of lack of knowledge of the physiographic consequences of deforestation, there has been little attempt at reforestation. To the deforestation of hillsides is due the innumerable floods of the rivers, which have caused untold suffering among the people of China.

II. *Population and Migrations:* That migrations of

[1] *The Changing Chinese,* pp. 72-74.

peoples have been caused almost entirely by physical conditions affecting food supply seems to be a well-recognized etiological fact.[1] From very ancient times, there have been recorded movements of population in China from one part to another to relieve congestion.[2] There must be considerable movements of population within the Chinese empire following the destructions of population in certain parts during rebellions, famines and floods, but of such intra-migrations we have no statistical knowledge.

Emigration from China to other countries has been a more conspicuous phenomenon. Probably ten millions[3] of Chinese are now residing in foreign lands, mostly in the islands of the East Indies and in America. This number, large as it is, is insignificant compared with the 400,000,-000 in China, but is most significant of the intense struggle for food, when taken along with the fact that the Chinese people are not strong in migratory instincts, but deeply attached to their homeland.

III. *Population and Plane of Living.:* Where the command over means of subsistence remains practically the same, a surplus of population results in general impoverishment. Each inhabitant must work harder for his living and receive less compensation for his labor; and the final result is the reduction of comforts of life, and the lowering of the plane of living. The real cost of an intense struggle for life does not end here, but in the deprivation of leisure time and surplus energy, which are all-essential for material and spiritual progress. May it not be that the arrest of civilization in China, of cultural, artistic, philosophical and scientific development, in which

[1] E. Huntington, *Pulse of Asia.*

[2] H. C Chen, *Economic Principles of Confucius*, vol. ii, p. 301.

[3] Ross, *op. cit.,* p 106

ancient China was so renowned, has been largely due to
this deprivation of leisure time and depletion of surplus
energy, because both have been absorbed in the struggle·
for life?

IV. *Population and Physical Energies:* A further result of the intense struggle for life is the impoverishment
of vital energies, due to a combination of conditions, such
as the heaviness of labor, low plane of living, insuffi-
ciency of nourishment, child-labor, unsanitary conditions,
et cetera. An indirect witness of this impoverishment of
vital energies is the habit of opium-smoking, which but
yesterday claimed 25,000,000[1] as its slaves in China.
Following an investigation, Mr. S. Merwin wrote:

While passing through an iron-smelting village, I noticed that
the black-smiths who beat up the pig iron were regular living
skeletons. They work from about five in the morning until
about five in the evening, stopping twice during that time for
meals. When they leave off in the evening after a hasty meal,
they start with their pipes and go on until they are asleep. I
do not know how these men can work. I presume that it was
the hard work that made them take to opium smoking.[2]

A similar picture is given in the Philippine Opium
Commission report, quoted by Professor Ross:

Absolute dullness and dreariness seem to prevail everywhere.
As these two demons drive the Caucasians to drink so they
drive the Chinese to opium. . . And the poor who have no
leisure? They often have no food, or so little that any drug
which removes first the pangs of hunger, and later the healthy
cravings of appetite, seems a boon to them. . . . The life of
the indigent Chinese coolie is pain caused by privation.[3]

[1] Ross, *op. cit*, p 141.
[2] *Drugging A Nation,* p 63
[3] *The Changing Chinese,* p 142

Closely following exhaustion of vital energies must be early senility and high mortality. There have been various estimates regarding the death rate of adults and infants, and the average length of life in China, but until reliable census statistics are obtained, the matter remains one of conjecture. There seems to be no doubt, however, that the average length of life in China is less than in the prosperous nations of the West.

Regulation of Reproduction: Having seen the results of the equilibration of population and means of subsistence, we ask: Is there not some way whereby population and means of subsistence can be equilibrated without the attending evils, above described? Our answer to this question is conscious regulation of reproduction, on the one hand, and promotion of economic prosperity of the country, on the other.

Indirect Methods: Spencer has made clear that the multiplication of a race tends to decrease as we rise in the scale of evolution,[1] that is, in inverse ratio to the ascending individuation of its members. Applying this law of multiplication, we may reasonably expect that with the advance of civilization in China, there will be a corresponding decrease of reproductive fertility. Translated into the life of the masses, this law operates through popular education. Education increases their intelligence, which in turn multiplies their interests and wants, and so raises their standard of living. Between an over-numerous family and a high standard of living, intelligence has always decided for the latter. The maintenance of a high standard of living and of cultural achievements tends to delay the age of marriage, since the preparation of life would become more laborious and

[1] H. Spencer, *Principles of Biology*.

energy-absorbing. Especially effective in controlling reproduction and in delaying the age of marriage would be the education of girls. Education would fire them with ambitions they have never felt before, would increase their interests in the multiform activities of life, would individualize them, and would create in them the consciousness that they are more than mere sex creatures. They would not be hopelessly dependent upon men for their livelihood, and so would enter marriage as a free partner of life's sacred compact rather than be driven into it by necessity. When they have a home, they will make it not a mere feeding and breeding place, but a place for comfort, happiness and refinement.

Direct Methods: With this indirect method, there should be direct and explicit education of the people on matters pertaining to population, reproduction and social well-being. Much can be done toward the formation of sound social standards and judgments with regard to these matters through publicity agencies, such as the newspaper, public lectures, and societies. The people have not realized the importance of the problem of posterity and the heritage that is in their power to give. The motto should be implanted in the mind of every adult and parent, that quality is before quantity.

Complementary to this regulation of population is the promotion of economic prosperity, the introduction of new industries, the development of scientific agriculture and of natural mineral resources, the building of railways, the extension of commerce, the increase of industrial and political efficiency, and so forth, all of which are having splendid beginnings, so that there will be created a greater supply of economic goods at the command of the people, a greater reserve of surplus energy, and leisure time for advancement of civilization and individuation.

CHAPTER III

Causes of Dependence: Dependence and destitution are due to causes for which a person may be responsible or not. A person suffering from the consequences of accidents of birth, such as parental desertion, congenital deformity, mental degeneration, is not responsible for his misfortune because the causes are entirely beyond his control. In the same way, perhaps in less degree, a person is not responsible for the results of natural, accidental and social causes of dependence, such as old age, sickness, incapacity by accidents, unemployment and social prejudices. By social prejudices we mean for example such conventional habits of thought as that which prevents a woman from seeking to support herself in the economic world. Some causes of destitution, which may be distinguished from the above-mentioned by being designated personal and immoral, such as laziness, evil habits, inebriety, *etc.*, are causes for which a person is responsible. And yet, enlightened thought is coming more and more to regard even these so-called personal causes as dependent upon impersonal factors and conditions.

The Care of the Poor: It is the expression of the sense of social solidarity, whether conscious or unconscious, which urges the bearing of the burden of poverty of the few members by the community as a whole. Traditionally, there are four dependent classes in China, who are recognized as the worthy poor, and for whose benefit charity is largely instituted. They are the aged, the orphans, the widows, and the sick. It seems that the preference of these four classes of dependence to others as objects of public charity and care is based upon definite social judgments. The care of the aged is motivated not only by humanitarian ideas, but also by the customary regard for age which is strong in the patriarchal society of China. The care of the orphans is motivated not only by the recognition of their helplessness, but also by the value of children, engendered by ancestral worship. The care of widows is motivated not only by purely chivalrous ideas but also by the social ethic which demands that widows should neither be remarried nor earn their living independently.

Present Stage of Charity in China; In regard to relief of the dependent classes, Chinese philanthropy has reached the stage of systematization and institutionality, of adequate relief, but not of scientific prevention of destitution. For instance, charity is ever ready to take in its care deserted infants or foundlings, and spends much energy in bringing them up; but it has not sought to correlate the social phenomenon of infant desertion with other social phenomena, such as fecundity, as cause and effect. Charity has sought to alleviate the sufferings of the sick, but has not done much for the elimination of sickness-producing conditions and causes. But the scientific stage is bound to be reached, for the principle of adequate relief must inevitably point to that goal.

1. CARE OF AGED MEN

Attitude Toward the Aged : The attitude of a civilized community toward its worthy aged is one of deep respect and of readiness to assist in their need. For those who

in their younger days have rendered public service to the
nation or community, pensions, decorations and other
honors are their reward.   For the indigent aged there
are almshouses, workshops, and homes, provided by state
and private munificence.   In these ways society shows
its appreciation of services rendered by individuals,
whether in the distinguished form of military and civil
duties, or in the unrecorded form of daily work in honest
pursuit of livelihood.   Both forms of services benefit society, and entitle the individuals who grow old therein
to the care of society, when that is needed for their comfort and happiness.

In China the aged have always received respect and
deferential treatment, for filial piety is the central feature
of ethics and religion, of the family and the state.   The
providing for the comfort of the aged who are unable
to earn their living, and must depend upon the support of others, is a very ancient custom.[1]   Occidental
sojourners in China have observed that the faces of
China's old men have the most beneficent, calm and benign expression, and have remarked that it is due to the
absence of worry, since the care for aged parents is
considered a sacred duty.[2]   The extremely limited economic surplus of individuals leaves men in old age almost
entirely dependent upon the support of their children,
and were it not for this deep-rooted consciousness which
regards nourishing the aged the sacred duty of the
young, extensive suffering would have happened to most
aged people.

Public Institutions: Private support is usually spontaneous and generous, but public institutions are neces-

[1] See chapter i.
[2] *Cf.* Ross, *op cit*, p 64

sary for supplementing relief in behalf of poor families. Public aid takes the form of home aid or institutional care, both of the governmental and of the popular kind.

Home Aid : In home aid, the Hall of United Benevolence at Shanghai is doing an extensive work. Care of the aged is one of the five principal departments of this institution. The aged remain at their own homes, and receive monthly 600 coins. The method of administration of this aid is to have officers of the institution recommend cases of indigency, or to stand as guarantee for genuineness of reported cases, to have the cases carefully investigated into, and after the genuineness of a case is ascertained, to issue a ticket in favor of the applicant. The beneficiary must be over 60 years of age, and enjoys his benefit during good behavior until his death.[1]

Home for the Aged: At Canton, Kuangtung, there is a government old men's Home, which according to its records kept on stone-tablets and bronze bells is of early origin, having been organized in 1724. Two bells within the precincts of the institution are dated respectively 1723 and 1724.[2]

The institution was described as being situated a short distance from the East gate of the city, adjoining the parade ground, built in rows, one story high, with plenty of open air and space for moving about. There were in 1873, 310 inmates, five or six persons living in one room. Besides the inmates, this institution supported partially 978 non-resident persons.[2]

The inmates must be above 60 years of age to be admitted. An admittance fee is charged which entitles the applicant to the privilege of having his lodging there for

[1] *Chinese Repository*, vol xv, pp 406 *et seq*

[2] *China Review*, vol ii, pp 88 *et seq*

life.   Each inmate receives 30 catties (40 lbs.) of rice and
330 coins per month.   Every three years a suit of winter
garments is distributed to the inmates.[1]

The fund for maintaining the institution came from
the Commissioner of Land Tax of the province of
Kuangtung, or Liang Tau, and the two magistrates of
Canton were trustees; but the immediate management
of the institution was said to have been farmed out.[1]

A Monastic House for the Aged: An interesting institution for aged men was maintained by the abbot of a
monastery in Nankin in 1812 A. D., according to
Chinese Records.[2]

It had a comprehensive and admirable regulation.
Men were admitted above 70 years of age, provided they
were without other means of support.   The capacity of
the institution was for 160, and it was said to be full all
the time.   An inmate must strictly observe the institutional life.   Once a month they were given a day to leave
the house and visit friends outside; but their other ab-
sences could not be more than once or twice a month.

Four persons lived in one room; and they were responsible for its cleanliness.   Each person was provided
with bedding and clothing, the use of which was regulated according to the seasons.   In winter months, fire
for warming the feet was supplied.   The inmates rose in
the morning with sunrise and retired with the nightfall.
As a precaution against fire no lamps were allowed in
the rooms.

The inmates had three meals a day of vegetarian diet,
this being in accord with monastic life.   The meals were
served in a large dining hall.   The superintendent struck

[1] *China Review*, vol. ii, pp. 88 *et seq.*
[2] *To-i-lu*, bk. iii, sec. v.

a wooden bell,—another sign of monastic life,—and the
inmates assembled and together partook of their common
meal, and when the superintendent got through with the
meal the whole assembly was expected to rise and leave
the room.   One of the regulations of the institution was
that the inmates being quite old, their food should be thoroughly cooked.   On festival days extra food and gifts
were distributed.   Besides all the necessities of life freely
distributed, each inmate was given 100 coins a month as
pocket money.   The kitchen fire was kept aglow at all
hours, so that hot tea could be had when needed.

The dead of the institution were buried in the cemetery
of the monastery and their names were recorded on
scrolls and remembered in religious services.   For the religious worship of the inmates themselves an ancestral
hall was built, where the inmates could establish their
own family shrines and worship there.

It is natural to infer from the above description that
the life of the inmates of the institution must have been
a happy one.   We could imagine of the group of buildings by the side of the monastic establishment in the
midst of quiet and beautiful surroundings,—as is generally the case with locations of monasteries,—possibly
nestling at the foot of some hill, surrounded by tall pines
and waving bamboos, embosomed in an atmosphere undisturbed by the noise and jostle of the market-places,
but filled with the notes of singing birds, with the sweet-
smelling incense that waft hither from the altars of the
gods in the temple, and with the distant chanting of the
monks in their rounds of daily exercise; and we could
imagine the benign, calm and serene faces of the white-
haired men of seventy and more in their rooms, in the
court-yard, in the garden, conversing, reading, dreaming,
or watching the flowers, the birds, the bees, contented

and friendly with all nature and all men, spending the twilight of their life in peace.

II. CARE OF AGED WOMEN AND WIDOWS

Status of Woman and Civilization : The status of woman gauges the civilization of a people. In the advanced nations of the West, man and woman have each recognized the value of the other sex. Disabilities, hitherto imposed upon women are being removed. Since the beginning of the Nineteenth Century, women have come forward abreast of men, and reclaimed one after another their rights and privileges. They have the right to education, not with the expectation better to please men, as Rousseau and the 18th Century thought, but on the ground of their own satisfaction and self-development. They have free choice of professional careers and self-support; even married women hold property in their own names. They enter into marriage out of freewill; and they have the right of initiating divorce proceedings as men do. In advanced states, political suffrage has been granted to them, and they are vigorously applying their newly gained power for social betterment. Thus, step by step, the advancement of civilization is marked by the rise of the status of woman in society.

Woman in Early Times : But we need not go far back in the past to find that women were helplessly subject to masculine rule. It was not until 1848, that the married women of New York could hold property on their own account and independently of their husbands.[1] It was in 1801, that the first divorce demanded by a woman was granted in England.[2] In primitive society, woman from

[1] E. A. Hecker, *A Short History of Women's Rights*, p. 163.
[2] *Ibid.*, p. 137.

her lack of physical strength and other disabilities of sex was at a disadvantage in competition with man. She required his protection, and in return she became his slave-worker. She was a slave before the institution of slavery, as Bebel says.[1]   Physical superiority became superiority in all respects.

Widowhood : Man, having assumed authority over woman, has for ages been the dictator of what woman should be. The status of widows is a pertinent illustration of man-made ethics. Legouvé says:

In the past, this title of widow represents only the abasement of the wife, the annihilation of all personality, slavery, condemnation, death. In our day, widowhood is freedom and equality with man. In ancient times, every wife saw her destiny so closely sealed to the lot of her husband, that though a widow she still belonged to him. The tie that death had broken for him, seemed to be drawn closer around her, and the shade of the dead husband hovered over and subdued the oriental woman, to drag her to the funeral pile; on the Jewish woman it imposed a second husband; the Christian woman it condemned to seclusion; the feudal woman it delivered up to the guardianship of her son; the very law which left them life refused them all power as mothers, all independence as women.[2]

Status of Woman in China : In China, the low status is a survival of the past, a black spot upon its civilization which has only recently begun to be wiped away. Not that Chinese women are naturally inferior to men, but the imperturbable customs have deprived them of freedom and development. Without going further into the life of women, we will study the ideas of widowhood, current in China even to this day.

[1] *Woman, Past, Present and Future*
[2] *Moral History of Women,* bk iv, ch. vi

There is a book in the Chinese language, known as the *Lives of Virtuous Women*, written by Liu Hsian. It is a compilation of biographies illustrating the feminine virtues of such noted women in history as have been traditionally esteemed. For centuries this book has been considered the best text-book for young girls and young women in their preparation for their life and position in society. The first paragraph of the book quotes Confucius as saying that a woman observes in her whole life a triple dependence: at home, dependence upon the father; in wedlock, dependence upon the husband; in widowhood, dependence upon the son, there being no time when she is free of masculine supervision. Concerning widowhood, it is said that "a man has the privilege of a second marriage, but a woman never." The book abounds in stories exalting the virtue of perpetual widowhood. Two examples are here given:

In the Kingdom of Liang there was a widow, who was beautiful and virtuous. Since the death of her husband many a noble suitor had come and sought her hand; but to them all, she turned a deaf ear. Finally the King's envoy came bearing royal wish to marry her. The widow replied, I have learned about a woman's virtue; she follows one and never changes her allegiance. If she forgets her dead and puts aside her virtue in order to seek life and happiness for herself, how could she be called faithful? Thereupon the widow took a knife and mutilated her beautiful face, saying, Thus have I punished myself; I have not followed my husband on account of the child. The King hearing of this, rewarded her with gold, and called her the Virtuous Widow.

In Wei, a Lady Wong was married to a King Yu. He died, and she fearing that she might be urged to remarry, on account of her youthful age, marred her features. In her room, there came one summer, a pair of swallows and made

their nest. Later, the male bird died ; but the female bird
would not leave the place, and formed the habit of perching
upon the arm of Lady Wong. Lady Wong was deeply
touched by the bird's loneliness, and in order to identify it,
fastened a little bit of silk thread upon its leg. The next
summer, the same bird came to the house, but it came alone.
Thereupon, Lady Wong wrote the following : Last summer
you lost your mate, this summer you come alone ; Human
fidelity must not be less than this.

Such devotion and self-sacrifice is worthy of the
highest praise and honor in the pages of history, such
noble characters are worthy of imitation by later generations. But what more wrong use of these records can
be made than as instruments to inculcate in young girls
and women self-effacement and submission to men. What
greater injustice is there than that of forcing upon widows
the limitations of perpetual sacrifice for men, without
demanding proportionate reciprocation on the part of
widowers. Then, because widows must live in seclusion, it becomes necessary to provide for their maintenance. In the light of the above statement, charity to
widows becomes a means whereby society cultivates
those sentiments in and conditions of women, which are
most advantageous to men only, and so is injustice to
womanhood.

Honor for Female Virtue : But we must not think that
masculine selfishness is the only motive behind charity to
widows. There is honor to women in China. The innumerable records in the pages of history, describing the
fidelity, the heroism, the filial piety, the nobility, and the
wisdom of women, as rulers, as mothers, as wives and as
daughters are conscions acknowledgments of the nation's
indebtedness to its women. In the same spirit, society
assiduously provides for the comfort and happiness of

widows during life and erects in their honor memorial arches after death.

Public Aid : Private care of aged women, as we have seen of aged men, is spontaneous.   The same filial piety which considers the care of aged fathers a sacred duty considers in a far greater degree care of mothers a sacred duty.   As to the widows, their families would not willingly neglect their care, since virtuous widowhood is an honor to the families cherishing it.   But public aid must supplement private care on account of the limited resourcefulness of most families, as well as of the justice of the community participating in the responsibility for maintaining its own widows.

In every community, there can be found small societies or clubs whose object is to relieve widows either of the community in general or of certain groups, such as widows of scholars, widows of the laboring men, and so forth.   These organizations are usually of limited operation.   Besides them, there are incorporated charitable institutions, which aid widows and aged women. Of the latter, we may mention the Widows Aid department of the Hall of United Benevolence at Shanghai. In 1843, it had eighty-seven women and widows under its care;[1] in 1908, 351 persons, and in 1909 362 persons.[2] The women are divided into four classes: I. Widows who have vowed perpetual widowhood; II. Widows who are primarily poor; III. Aged women of the city; IV. Aged women of other cities.   Of Class I, we found that the average age of its 100 widows is 43 years; but this number is considerably raised by a few very elderly members.   The average age at which they came under

[1] *Chinese Repository,* vol xiv, pp 418-420.
[2] *Annual Reports.*

institutional care was 28; but the youngest was 20 and the eldest 76. Regarding the number of years they have received aid from the institution, one member who is 84 years old, has been receiving aid continuously for 58 years, another for 51 years, another for 49 years, another for 44 years, two for 43 years. The average number of years is 11.5.

In the regulations of the Hall of United Benevolence, there is a paragraph which indicates the public honor to women, spoken of previously:

If among the women there be any example of extraordinary chastity or extreme distress attended with unusual circumstances, such as the supporting of relatives, or the supporting of orphans, thereby maintaining the family, and if there be no depreciatory accounts among the villagers and neighbors, then shall a particular statement of the case be made, in order to its being recorded, in preparation for the record of merit for the prefecture and districts where it will be preserved, to the honor of chastity and filial piety.[1]

' Homes are provided for aged women and widows. For example, the Home of Aged Women at Canton was reported as housing 340 inmates in 1874, besides non-residents numbering in all 1062 individuals under its care.[2] Of the internal regulation of resident institutions for women, that of the "House of Pure Widowhood," contained in *Tō-ı-lu*,[3] is most interesting, as it shows clearly the social customs in regard to the status and care of widows in particular and of women in general.

House of Pure Widowhood: This institution at Soochow is of the nature of a cloister. It is for young

---

[1] Report in *Chinese Repository*, vol. xv, p 406.

[2] Grey, *Walks in City of Canton*, pp 525-526; Dr. J G. Kerr in *China Review*, vol ıı, pp. 88 *et seq.*

[3] Bk ıiı, sec ıı

widows who have taken the veil of perpetual widowhood. It provides quiet, seclusion, and sociability for the
inmates. It receives not only poor widows, but also
widows from well-to-do families who prefer its quiet
life to that of their own homes. Once within the walls
the inmates are supposed never to leave the institution
again, nor to see any man, not even near relatives.

To enter the House, a woman must be a widow for at
least a hundred days. This period of time is allowed in
order that the widows may complete their funeral services to their dead. The candidate must vow never to
marry again or to leave the House, and never to see men,
except her parents and parents-in-law at the three festival days of the year. Any violation of this vow is followed by immediate dismissal from the House.

But the financial aid which the House gives to its inmates may be extended to those non-resident widows,
who desire but cannot adopt the cloistered life, either because they have their mothers-in-law at home, who in
old age need their services, or for some equally weighty
reason.

The House is built in two sections. The inner section
is the living quarters of the inmates, separated from the
outer section by a wall, with a gate guarded by two old
maids. Into this inner section no outsider is allowed to
go. The public does not know what is contained in the
outer section for the outer section is separated from the
outside world by another wall, which has a gate watched
by two old men.

To permit communication between the inmates and the
gate-keepers, who act as errand-runners, but at the same
time to obviate direct personal meeting and to avoid the
inmates being seen by outsiders, a contrivance is built in
the outer wall, consisting of a wooden box, like a dumb-

waiter box, which is fixed and turns upon a vertical axis, so that a message placed in it by the inmates may be received by the watchmen outside by a turn of the box. This illustrates with what care seclusion of the inmates is preserved. It reflects an ancient ceremonial law, which goes as follows:

The men should not speak of what belongs to the inside of the house, nor the women of what belongs to the outside. Except at sacrifices and funeral rites, they should not hand vessels to one another. In all other cases when they have occasion to give and receive anything, the woman should receive it in a basket. If she have no basket, they should both sit down, and the other put the thing on the ground, and she then take it up. Outside or inside, they should not go to the same well nor to the same bathing house. . . . . They should not ask or borrow anything from one another. . . Things spoken inside should not go out, words spoken outside should not come in.[1]

The house supplies all the necessaries of life, such as food, lodging, bedding, furniture, clothing, small sums of money, medical care, and so forth. All these are matters of thorough regulation. In case of death, the remains are buried in the cemetery of the House, and the name of the dead is inscribed upon a scroll in the temple of the cemetery.

The children of the inmates, if any, are taken care of by the House. Girls live with their mothers, but boys live with their tutors. Girls are married on coming of age at the expense of the House; should they remain unmarried, they are treated as regular inmates. Boys are educated in the school which is attached to the

[1] *Li Kî*, tr J Legge, in *Sacred Books of the East*, ed. F. Max Muller, vol xxvii, pp. 454-455.

House, and should any show aptitude for a learned profession, he is specially prepared for that profession, while the rest are sent out at 14 for apprenticeship in trades.

Concluding Remarks: Although we have no exact knowledge of the number of widowed women in China, both young and elderly, we believe that it is considerable. An interesting question to ask is whether, upon the introduction of modern civilization into China and the adoption of female education and the rise of the consciousness of social justice between the sexes, the old customs regarding widowhood in particular and the status of women in general will survive or be modified. The question seems to admit of but one answer: The ·status of women, including widowhood, will be changed for the better. Already the traditional restrictions upon woman's work are being cast aside, because of new fields opened and demanding women. Year by year the number of young women who step out of the family circle, hitherto the only sphere of female labor, to teach in schools, to nurse in hospitals, to serve as secretaries, to work in factories, is increasing. This social change suggests a new field wherein widows may devote their time and energy: social service. As far as we know, the Christian Church invented the utilization of widows in social service. It seems to us that it is a beneficent invention both for the widows and for society. For social service, the widows in China may be trained and developed; then, instead of wasting themselves away, behind self-imposed walls of seclusion and solitude, they may go forth into society, to turn their energies of love and sympathy upon a world that sorely needs the ministry of women.

III. CARE OF DEPENDENT CHILDREN

Desertion of Infants : There are no statistics to indicate
the extent of desertion of infants in China.[1] That it does
exist there, there seems to be no doubt. It seems to be
a social problem more serious in some parts of the
country than in other parts, in some years than in
others. It has been observed that infanticide and desertion are more common in the southeastern provinces
than in the others, and after years of bad crops than after
years of good ones. We may say that the chief causes
of infant desertion are poverty and congestion of population. An official proclamation issued by the provincial
authorities of Hupeh in 1873 is an illuminating document, giving the ordinary causes of this social problem.
In part, it is as follows:[2]

In ancient times, the girl Ty-ying begged His Majesty Wen
to permit her to sacrifice her liberty in order that her father,
who was in official disgrace might be released from bondage.
In another case, the girl Mulan wished to serve as a soldier in
order to take upon herself the liability of her old father to
serve in the wars. These instances show with what filial instincts girls of old were imbued. At the present time, we too
apprehend there is no lack of daughters equally ready to sacrifice themselves to their parents or to render the names of
their family as illustrious by filial acts of devotion. Such
being the case, how comes it that the female infant is looked
upon as an enemy from the moment of its birth, and no sooner
enters the world than it is consigned to the nearest pool of
water? Certainly, there are parents, who entertain an affection for their female infants, and rear them up, but such number scarcely 20 or 30 *percentum*. The reasons are either
(first) that the child is thrown away in disgust because the

---

[1] For discussion, see E. H. Parker, *China, Past and Present*

[2] Grey, *Walks in City of Canton,* pp 565-567

parents have too many children already, or (secondly) that it is drowned from sheer chagrin at having begotten none but females, or from the apprehension that the mother will not conceive again readily enough if she has to suckle the child, or lastly, in the fear that the poverty of the family will make it difficult to devote the milk to her own child, when the mother might otherwise hire herself out as wetnurse.

Now all these are the most stupid of reasons. People seem to be ignorant of the fact that no men are born from heaven without some share of its blessings, and that hunger, cold or bodily comfort are matters of predestination; so also with sons and heirs, who are even in a greater degree dependent upon the destiny of heaven, and cannot be forcibly coaxed out of it.

All that those have to do, who are unable, through poverty, to feed their children, is to send them to the foundling hospital, where they will be reared up until they become women and wives, and where they will always be sure of enjoying a natural lifetime.

With regard to the question of money or no money in the bridal casket, means or no means of bringing up a family, why, the bare necessaries of life for such children, in the shape of the coarsest gown and head-gear do not cost much. There are cases enough of poor lads not being able to find wives all their lives long but we have yet to hear of a poor girl, who cannot find a husband, so that there is even less cause for anxiety on that score.

But there is another way of looking at it. Heaven's retribution is sure, and cases are common where repeated female births have followed those where the infants have been drowned, *i. e.*, man loves to slay what Heaven loves to beget and those perish, who set themselves against Heaven, as those die who take human life. Also they are haunted by the wraiths of the murdered children and thus not only fail to hasten the birth of a male child but run the risk of making victims of themselves by their behavior.

The real reasons why girls suffer the consequences of poverty more than boys do are, (1) girls, being forbidden by custom to be wage-earners, are a heavy liability to their families, while boys are an asset in the economic struggle; (2) girls will leave their own homes and become members of outside homes, while boys remain members of their own homes and hand down the family-heritage; (3) ancestor worship requires male officiates, and so boys only can satisfy the religious demands of filial piety. In short, girls are more negligible than boys, because their social value is less than that of boys. This is a vicious judgment, born of medieval thought, and the social ethics of to-day demands its eradication.

Public Care of Dependent Children : Public care of dependent children consists of partial aid for children in poor families, and institutional care of foundlings. The first method is always preferred, wherever possible, for it preserves the home and the natural parental and filial sentiments. The next preferred method in the case of foundlings is to provide for as much home life as possible by placing them out among different homes. This is not adoption by these homes, for the children are still in the possession and care of the institutions placing them out, and it becomes adoption only after due legal transfer of right of possession from the institutions to the homes. The last method to mention is institutional care, where a number of foundlings live together with wetnurses under one roof.

Home Aid : Partial home aid is undertaken by voluntary societies in a community. Its objects are to help poor families bear the burden of their children, and thus obviate breaking up homes, and to remove the necessity of mothers working without a sufficient period of convalescence after child-birth. The amount of aid depends

upon circumstances. Ordinarily monthly supplies of food
and money are given for five months after the birth of a
child. It is argued that the first five months constitute
the most trying period for poor parents to keep their infants. By the end of the five months there will have developed the tie of affection between the parents and the
infants, too strong to be easily broken. In extraordinary
cases special aid is given. Such cases are: (1) children
upon whom the continuation of the family name depends;
(2) children whose mothers die at their birth; (3) children
adopted when very young by outside families. In such
cases the aid continues for three years. Societies for
protection of infants have definite areas of operation, corresponding to those of villages or wards of towns and so
forth. In this way local spirit or neighborhood feeling
is utilized. This point is illustrated in the following
statement, made by a founder of a local society:

In the 23rd year of Tau Kwang (1843), I discussed the matter
with residents within a radius of ten miles, urging the formation of an infants protection society to counteract the misery
of poverty. Since the formation of the society, we have
successfully prevented infant desertion within the district.
Monthly aids are given in every case of need for five months.
Each member of the society not only pays a membership
share of 360 coins a year, but also makes the promise never
to desert infants. The society has existed for ten years and
each year there were from seventy to a hundred cases taken
care of. But the moral effect of such a society is far greater
than the material aids.[1]

Placing-out System : The Foundling Hospital of Shanghai[2] receives foundlings, but instead of keeping them in

[1] *To-i-lu,* bk ii, sec 1, p. 13; *cf.* F Hirth, *Ueber gemeinnützige
Anstalten in China,* p 19

[2] Report in *Chinese Repository,* vol xiv, pp 177-195.

one public institution sends them out to the homes
of wetnurses for care.   At the headquarters of the
institution, foundlings are received, examined and registered.   The points specified in the registration are:
(1) name and date of birth,—this being known from
written information attached to the foundlings, which
parents are usually anxious to give; (2) physical condition, such as conditions of health or disease, perfectness
or defects of the limbs, the senses, etc.; (3) lines and
fashion of the finger marks, for identification; (4) the
clothing in which the foundlings are received.   A ticket
is next made out for each foundling, and the infant is
then assigned to a wetnurse.   The placing-out system
requires vigilant inspectors of the infants placed-out
and of the wetnurses, and so the institution provides as
follows: [1]

One of them to take charge of the records and registers, the
receiving of infants, the allotment of nurses, the giving out
the children's tickets, and the receiving and dispensing of
money.   It is requisite that all these be recorded minutely
and carefully.   The other, to make investigations, daily to
give out the things which may in turn be requisite, and taking
in his hand the infants' record, to go around to the place appointed for each; first to examine the child's ticket, then to
take cognizance of the nurse's diligence or neglect, and
whether the child be fat or thin, which is upon the spot to
be entered into the record, in readiness for the First and
Fifteenth days of the month, when the directors shall examine
and verify, and dispense praise or blame.

The choice of wetnurses, which is deemed very important is thus regulated.

[1] *Op cit*, p 184.

The most important thing in the nourishing of the infants is the hiring of wetnurses. . . If there be any one who wishes to take this function, either her own husband can come to the office and announce her name, or a relative or neighbor must come and be security for her. The officers of the Hall must then examine whether she really is properly qualified for the function or not, and shall then enter her name upon the record; when infants come, they are to be distributed successively to the nurses.[1]

Serious negligence on the part of nurses is treated as a criminal offence.

Adoption of Foundlings: Approximately three fifths of the foundlings live, and the rest die either when received or afterwards. Of the living, three fourths ultimately are adopted into homes, and one fourth remain under institutional care. Concerning adoption, the institution provides as follows:

In the transfer of children, it is only requisite with regard to the boys that they legitimatize into some family; beyond this there is no further need for anxiety. But as regards the girls, there is great fear of their being bought as concubines, or bought and sold again with other similar abuses.[2]

Hence adoptions must be accompanied by sufficient guarantee of good faith and done through legal form:

The tickets or documents for the adopted children shall be drawn out in duplicate. The one shall be the bond for the receiving of the child, which shall be laid by in the institution, and the other the agreement of the transfer, which shall be given to the family adopting the child. These shall be stamped with the official seal of the Sub-prefect.[3]

Concerning the disposal of those who are not adopted

[1] *Op. cit.*, p. 185.   [2] *Ibid*, p. 187.   [3] *Ibid*, p. 186

by families, our information is limited to a general rule, which runs as follows:

When a child has reached the age of three years, it is then able to eat and drink, to run and walk by itself and if, as hitherto, it is unadopted by any one, the said child shall receive a ticket, and be again taken into the institution, where there shall be hired nurses to take charge thereof.[1]

Administration : From the history of the institution, it seems that the officers were originally elected by the subscribers, and approved or authorized by the civil officers. Those persons were elected, who had shown themselves most energetic promotors or were most able financially to be promoters of the interests of the institution. These were positions of trust and honor. As the business of the institution became exacting and voluminous, executive officers were selected who could give entire time to the work, while the honorary officers became the directors and examiners of the records of the institution. The directorate seems to be self-perpetuating. The honorary offices descend from father to son, and from friend to friend of one's own choice. This policy seems to have been adopted on account of its practical advantages. It insures the continuity of the institution and promotes its efficiency, since neither sons nor friends would willingly abuse the honor and trust by neglecting the responsibilties of the offices. There are recorded cases in which sons unable to receive the offices that had descended from their fathers, were relieved of their responsibilities.[2]

Finances : The efficiency of management of philanthropic institutions may be illustrated in the methods

[1] *Op. cit.,* p. 187.   [2] *Ibid.,* pp. 180-182.

used for raising money.   One of the commonest methods
is known as the benevolent ticket:

It is now decided that one benevolent ticket shall be valued
equal to 360 coins, and that these shall be collected according
to the four seasons.   One person may write several tickets, or
several individuals may join together for one ticket, or all the
members of a household, both the family and domestics, may
subscribe to a corresponding number of tickets, or may call
and invite friends and relations to join in any number of
tickets. . . . According to the seasons, the tickets shall be
taken and the money called for, the period of three years com-
pleting the term.[1]

The tickets are authorized by the civil officials, and
are of the following form:[2]

Having received the sub-prefect's order to take charge of the
Foundling Hospital, we have agreed to raise a subscription,
and now beg to request you (naming the person) dwelling at
(place of residence) for a voluntary subscription of (number
of) tickets, the aggregate amount of which will be (amount
in coins).   Year, date.

Accompanying the invitation to subscribe is an essay of
moral persuasion, of the following nature:

If, for the extension of kindness to our fellow-creatures and
to those poor and destitute who have no father and mother,
all the good and benevolent would give one coin, it would be
sufficient for the maintenance of the foundlings one day.   Let
no one consider a small good unmeritorious nor a small subscription of no avail.   Either you may induce others to subscribe by the vernal breeze from your mouth or you may yourself nourish the blade of benevolence in the field of happiness,
or cherish the already sprouting bud.   Thus, by taking your

[1] *Op. cit.*, p 190.   [2] *Ibid*, p. 191.

endeavors to accomplish your object, you may immeasurably
benefit and extend the institution [1]

The merit of the 'benevolent ticket' system is that it
puts the participation in philanthropy within the capacity
of the ordinary people, who have little surplus to spare,
while at the same time it places no limit to the gener-
osity of the more capable.   It democratizes philanthropy.
Thus, during one year, 4586 tickets were subscribed by
1272 persons, of whom the 26 largest subscribers took
half of the number of tickets, and the remaining 1246
persons the other half.[2]

State Encouragement: Realizing the value of philanthropic institutions, the Government of China is in the
habit of encouraging their efforts by public recognition
of their services and by awards.   The following is an
example: [3]

Yung-ching, 2nd year, 4th Intercalary month, 28th day.   The
following edict was issued to the Prefect and Sub-prefect officers of Shun-tien Fu:

Outside the Kwang-ning gate of the capital there has heretofore been the Pu-Tsai-Tang, or Hall of Universal Benevolence, where all aged, diseased and destitute persons might find
an asylum.   Those who had the control of the work, invariably
delighting in virtue, well merited commendation, and His Majesty Kang Hsi gave them an inscribed tablet in order to lead
onwards the love of virtue.   You who have the official charge
of the place, ought also constantly to give them commendation
advice in order to stimulate and excite them. . . .

And we have heard that within the Kwang-kin gate there is
a foundling hospital, where all those infants and children, who
cannot be nourished and brought up are received during a
course of ten years; it has reared and settled many.   The

[1] *Op cit*, p. 191.   [2] *Ibid*, p. 192   [3] *Ibid*, p. 177.

nourishment of the young and the maintaining of orphans being an exaltation of virtue of a similar nature with the supporting of the infirm, and compassionating of the aged, and a thing which in common practice of the world is difficult, we both praising and delighting in it, have especially granted a door-tablet and also make a gift of money, in order to manifest our own inclinations and to commend and lead the way in pecuniary aid to its support by our people. . . .

Institutional Care: As an illustration of institutional care where the dependent children are housed in one place we may describe the Foundling Hospital at Canton.[1] As this is a state institution light will be thrown upon others of its kind at the same time.

The institution was described as being situated a short distance from the city of Canton, built upon somewhat elevated and rolling grounds. The buildings were one story high and arranged in rows with alleys between, opening into a central street. Each row of rooms was supervised by a woman overseer. The whole group of buildings was surrounded by a wall. At one time it was said to have employed 980 wetnurses, of whom 200 resided in the institution, and the rest were non-resident. About ten or twelve infants were received every day. To dispose of its charges, the institution would daily exhibit the children for the inspection of persons who wished to adopt them. The adoption fee would be divided among the wetnurses and the other servants of the institution. The institution derived its funds from the provincial treasury, and was under state supervision and management.

Modern Methods: In recent years modern methods have been introduced into Chinese philanthropy. Of

[1] Dr J G Kerr, "Native Benevolent Institutions of Canton," in *China Review*, vol ii, pp 89-91.

the newer type of institutions, the Home for Orphans at Shanghai is an example. It has been in existence for about ten years, and has recently moved into its new home in a suburban village. It receives boys and girls of all ages up to 16 years, and is equipped with farms, orchards, school-rooms, workshops and play-grounds. It teaches the boys farming, horticulture, fruit-raising, care of trees, carpentry, furniture-making, printing, photography, and other manual trades, and the girls, machine-sewing, tailoring, embroidery, laundry, music, kindergarten work, and so forth. At the time of its last report there were ninety-nine boys from five to nineteen years of age, and thirty-seven girls from six to sixteen years of age. It has an enlightened aim, to make out of the children men and women independent and useful in society.[1]

IV. CARE OF THE DESTITUTE SICK

Public Health : The presence of sickness in a com-munity can generally be accounted for by the unsanitary condition of life, overtaxation of physical energies, and lack of proper medication, For the individual, an added factor exists, that is, the chance of communication. For the eradication of sickness, therefore, prevention by the improvement of sanitation and restoration of life-energy is more important than mere medicinal remedy; and social effort rather than individual effort alone is power-ful enough to accomplish it. But prevention depends upon scientific knowledge of the causal relation of sani-tation and health, and of the origin, communication and cure of diseases. The impetus behind sanitary move-ments and preventive measures, which obtains to-day in

[1] Report of Home for Orphans, 1910.

Occidental nations is largely based upon this scientific knowledge, and the seeming apathy toward sanitation and toward diseases in the past is largely a reflection of helpfulness on the part of society to cope with them, the lack of confidence of conquering them due to ignorance of their causation, communication and cure.

Public Responsibility : In China, social responsibility of public health is sufficiency recognized but the importance of sanitation is inadequately realized because there is lack of scientific knowledge on the matter. The consciousness of social responsibility for health is shown in the existence of public hospitals for the care of the destitute sick, the distribution of medicine to the poor, public aid in the event of deaths of the needy. To the poor and the laboring class, sickness, unless temporary, is ruinous. They lack the means to command efficient medical treatment, they lose their time and health which are their most valuable possessions. A prolonged sickness may cause unemployment or neglect of the fields and plunge them into destitution. Thus, the directors of a public dispensary at Shanghai, after speaking of the sickness-begetting conditions of the fields in which the laboring men have to work in the summer and the unhealthy conditions in which they usually live said in a report:

The well-to-do get their own doctors, but if the laboring and the poor be exposed to pernicious influences and become sick, they are unable to procure medical aid, and their diseases speedily become severe. This state of things having come to the knowledge of several benevolent individuals has excited their compassion and sympathy . . Now it is more meritorious and praiseworthy to attend to persons while they are alive than to afford coffins for them when they are dead. . . . [1]

[1] Report of the Public Dispensary, in *Chinese Repository*, vol xvii, pp 193-199

The free Dispensary: The public dispensary is the common form of relief. It is open daily or on appointed days, throughout the year or for appointed seasons. It is supported by voluntary contributions. Those dispensaries which are open for appointed days and seasons are generally able to obtain the voluntary services of the doctors while those requiring resident doctors, have to pay for their services. A subscription appeal sent out by a Public Dispensary at Shanghai furnishes some information about its work:

We respectfully notify the subscribers (that the public dispensary is attached to the Hall of United Benevolence, that it was open for three months during the last summer, that for each appointed day, it treated more than a thousand patients, that it is entirely dependent upon voluntary subscriptions, that for the present year's work it is again appealing to the merchants and scholars who delight in the works of charity). We respectfully request the lovers of virtue and promoters of benevolence to open their purses and afford relief to the sick poor and by accumulating grains of sand we shall form a pyramid. Thus whitened bones will be clothed with flesh and the well-nigh dead restored to life, the sick will be healed and immeasurable happiness diffused abroad.[1]

Sick Asylums: There are asylums where stranger who have fallen ill are sheltered. Admittance is free, but the asylum is legally free from responsibility for the inmates whatever should happen. For this purpose, a written agreement is made by the person who sends the inmate to the asylum, as follows:

We, the undersigned, having discovered at .... of the city a stranger, who is sick and destitute, on the .... day of the month, and having ascertained him to be a native of ......,

[1] *Op cit*, p 197

aged . .., without relations in this city, and having received the permit of the magistrate, send the person to you to be cared for. We fill this blank and promise to take the person away, should he get well, so that the Asylum may not be held responsible.[1]

Isolation of the Diseased : Persons suffering from contagious diseases, so far as known, are isolated. This is the case with leprosy in the southern part of China. Lepers live in colonies by themselves.[2] But isolation is not absolute. For example, in the colony, the inmates are allowed to marry and beget children. By reproduction the colony eventually becomes a centre of population, and so an economic unit, and as such could hardly be completely isolated with the rest of the economic world. Thus it is said that the members of the colony made ropes, twine, sandals and other articles of daily use and offered them for sale in the cities, in order to make a living and feed the children. We do not know whether leprosy is an inheritable disease, but it is an obnoxious idea to think that lepers should be allowed to reproduce themselves, and thus perpetuate the colony. But the description applies to the situation forty years ago. Conditions may have changed.

Care of the Defective : As regards persons suffering congenital defects, such as the blind, the deaf, the dumb, the feeble-minded, the insane, and so forth, it seems that very little is done for them through public institutions. There are here and there institutions that receive them and give them a bare living, and there are workhouses, where they are engaged in profitable industries.[3] Ac-

[1] Record of the Asylum for Strangers, Shanghai, in *To-i-lu,* bk. iv, sec vi.

[2] Grey, *Walks in the City of Canton,* pp. 688-691

[3] *Ibid ,* p 523

cording to an Occidental observer, the probable reason
of inaction is that the Chinese labor under an impression
that all blind persons have either in the present, or in a
former state of existence committed sins of heinous
nature, and for which by the deprivation of sight they
are undergoing a well merited punishment.[1]   Hence the
lack of sympathy for their sufferings.   There is, perhaps,
some such mythological thinking in the minds of some
people when they meet a blind man deprived of his sight,
or a lame man limping with crutches, or a dumb person
manipulating his fingers, or a mental defective acting in
a silly manner, or an insane person raving as if possessed
of the devil.   But we believe that there is a more fundamental reason to account for the apathy toward these
unfortunate classes, than mere superstition.

It is ignorance.   It is ignorance of what to do with the
blind, the deaf, the dumb, and the insane that discourages
charitable activity on their behalf.   For a normal person
in distress, there is hope and reasonable expectancy that
some day a self-respecting, independent and desirable
person will be made by environmental aid.   This hope
prompts charitable activity.   Abnormal persons, whether
defective in outer limbs or inner organs are thought to
be hopeless cases, and so little is done for them.

The remedy for this apparent but not real apathy toward these unfortunate classes of abnormal and defective
persons is to be sought in the introduction of scientific
knowledge concerning them, their treatment and care.
On the one hand, society needs to know that many congenital and mental defects are inheritable and constitute
real degeneration of the racial stock.   The earlier they
are eliminated the better for the race; and the elimina-

[1] Grey, *op cit*, p 523

tion may be accomplished with kindness to the unfortunate persons, and without hurting the moral sensibility of society.   On the other hand, society needs to be informed that the care of the defectives is far from being a hopeless work.   By special methods of training and supervision they may be made to earn their own living, and so reduce the burden of care upon the community, and may be given a happier and fuller life than their handicaps would otherwise have allowed them to enjoy.

Free Burial: Closely allied with the care of the destitute sick is the free burial of the poor and the distribution of free coffins.   It is a very active form of charity. The Hall of United Benevolence in the twelve months of 1908 distributed 578 coffins for adults and 867 coffins for children, and at a branch office in the same city, 631 coffins for adults and 158 coffins for children.   In its free cemetery it buried during the same twelve months 1506 adults and 3796 children.[1]   There may be various reasons to account for this activity, such as religious awe of death, superstition concerning the repose of the spirits of the dead, and other mythological reasons, but the proximate reason is the practical necessity for the work.

Need of a National Health Campaign : A much-needed campaign in China is for sanitation and positive pursuit of health.   To show what powerful social effort is available in China, we need only cite the present crusade against opium-smoking.   Thus, Professor Ross writes,

When Pekin allowed ten years for the cleansing of the land from the opium habit, it little dreamed of the enthusiastic response its initiative would call forth or of the rising spirit of patriotism that would come to its aid.   The accomplishment of the last five years elapsed has surpassed all anticipations.

[1] Report of the Hall, 1909

The production of opium in China has certainly been cut down sixty or seventy per cent, and the reform leaders even insist on eighty per cent. Millions of smokers are breaking off because the price of the drug has risen clear out of their reach.

A national conscience is beginning to show itself and the slave of the pipe is put to the blush. It is now worth while to make the smoker carry his purchased opium in his open hand and wear his permit on a big wooden tablet that he cannot conceal. No one has a greater horror of " losing face " than the Chinese, and there is hope that the rising generation will shrink from opium as they shrink from a cobra. [1]

The virility of the opium crusade is clearly due to publicity given to the matter, exposure of the evils, and the consequent formation of a sound constructive public opinion and aggressive policy. The agitation for sanitation and health will be equally virile, given similar conditions.

[1] Ross, *The Changing Chinese,* pp. 169, 171

CHAPTER IV.

Mutual Benefit and Social Consciousness: Mutual
benefit is an essential factor in Chinese philanthropy.
There is a readiness among the people to combine in
in order better to relieve one another's burdens in distress,
a tendency to co-operate in dealing with want and misfortune and other adverse conditions, which constitutes
a distinct social habit. Undoubtedly the tendency to
co-operate in philanthropic undertakings is re-inforced
by the habits of co-operation engendered in economic
activities, such as the trades guild, and by consciousness
of kind developed within particular groups, such as the
clan or community. Thus men of the same clan or
community more readily enter into association for
mutual benefit than men of different clans or communities, and in the same way, members of the same
trade more readily enter into association for mutal benefit than members of different trades. In other words,
mutual benefit in philanthropy is an expression of social
consciousness, and the degree and extent of the former
is determined by the intensity and extent of the latter.
If we conceive of social consciousness within a society
as unevenly distributed and concentrating around numerous points which represent the numerous interests
and objects for which people associate themselves, and if
we conceive of it as ever tending to spread outward
from these points, through friendly social interaction and

74   [74

co-ordination among the different minor social groups and interests until it permeates society generally, then we can think of mutual benefit as at first limited within definite areas such as the clan, the village, the particular trade-guild, and so forth, but as finally overflowing the limitations, and spreading throughout the nation.

Value of Mutuality : The value of mutuality in philanthropy cannot be overestimated. It alone may not be a sufficient agent in the elimination of distress and want, but it is a constructive agent because it recognizes the principle of justice, and utilizes the consciousness of social solidarity. Although it is a corporate functioning, mutual benefit cannot swamp individual responsibility. Although it is a charity, it does not compromise personal dignity; and although it is giving of aid, it does not pauperize the receiver.

To study this important phase of Chinese philanthropy, we will examine its clearest expressions in the clan organization, in the village community, in the voluntary associations for mutual benefit, and in the trades and crafts guilds.

I. The Clan Organization

What it is : The clan is a consanguinity group, observing patronymic descent. The families of the clan acknowledge a common male ancestor or ancestors, whether real or adopted, and are thereby held together and known by the common family name. Genealogical records are carefully kept in order both to substantiate claims of clan privileges, and to regulate the degree of kinship.

Clans send out off-shoots in the manner of trees. The larger branches trace their origin to the trunks, and the smaller branches trace their origin to the larger branches and only indirectly to the main trunks. But the ambition of a clan is to trace its ancestral line as far back as possible, terminating it in some well-known personage in history, and to locate its original home, to which it may look back with pride.

Localization : A clan tends to localize, that is, to strike root in the ground which it occupies. The localization is initiated by acquirement of estate. Time strengthens the bondage to the locality through burial of the dead, presence of ancestral tombs, establishment of ancestral halls, maintenance of ancestral worship, identification of economic interest with the locality, and the weight of tradition.

As conditions are more favorable for these achievements in rural than in urban districts,—*e. g.*, a rural district offers greater possibility for complete identification of economic interest with locality than an urban district,—and as the relatively unchanging conditions of a rural district offer less disturbance to the process of localization than the relatively changing conditions of an urban district, we find clans better localized in the rural than in the urban districts. Localization is conducive to complete organization, and so we find clans retain their solidarity as long as they remain in rural districts, but begin to disintegrate when subjected to urban influences. But a clan organization seldom disintegrates completely as long as there are living members. It is kept up by the establishment of a rural home, where the ancestral hall is built, and clan burial ground laid out. To this home members return for reunions, usually on special occasions for worship of ancestors.

The Social Value of Clan Organization : Whatever the intrinsic value of a clan organization, we find it rendering distinct services for social well-being in China, owing to the presence of peculiar political conditions.

One such service is the maintenance of law and order in the country. The political government of China hitherto has been generally weak and unaggressive in the maintenance of law and order in the land, and were it not for the completeness of the organization of the people into clans, there would have existed conditions different from those that have hitherto existed in the country. The traditional law-abiding nature of the people, despite the apparent absence of governmental machinery, is explained by clan solidarity, working itself out in a system of legal responsibility of members of a family for one another.

Another service, which the clan renders is its promotion of co-operative spirit in social life. The clan trains the members to think of personal welfare in terms of social welfare, and inculcates in them the consciousness of social responsibility. The training may be narrow, but it is thorough; and in the absence of social training through national functioning, as has been the case in China until recently, the clan mode of life has been the only sphere which offered preparation for true social life, by the formulation of social habits and ideals.

There is some disadvantage to the nation in clan organization for its tendency to produce a narrow spirit of clannishness, which may prevent the development of national consciousness, and so weaken national solidarity. But this influence is much exaggerated. In the first place, clans have never been so completely isolated as to produce excessive intolerance. Trades and industries draw men from different clans, and so tend to counteract exclusiveness, by the creation of new bonds through economic interest. Urban conditions have created common civic interests among inhabitants, without regard to clan affiliations, thus tending to neutralize clannishness. The innate business instinct of the people has caused the members of different provinces and cities to travel widely and to settle in strange provinces and cities. This extends sympathies, and wears off provincialism. The system of Imperial literary examinations which were held until recently at regular and frequent intervals, at important provincial and national centers, brought together scholars from widely separated localities, and their common profession easily facilitated intercourse and exchange of ideas, and thus helped to create nation-wide sympathies and consciousness. Further, we may say that whatever clannishness and provincialism there has been in China may be as much due to geographical isolation and absence of easy communication between different parts, and to the immediate consequence of diversification of dialects and customs, as to the clan organization itself, and perhaps more due to the former than the latter.

Clan Charities: A clan possesses an estate in common. Because the estate is common property it is inalienable. It may have been handed down from some generous ancestor, or acquired by public subscription. It consists usually of grain-producing land; the rentals and grains produced therefrom are for the support of public interests, such as the maintenance of the ancestral hall and worship. Further, the common property serves as a store of wealth which in time of bad years is distributed or loaned to families to relieve them from want, and may also be used during ordinary times to help unfortunate members, widows, and poor scholars. We have the historic record of a case of clan charities, that of the Van Clan, which dates back as far as 1064, and presumably survives to this day. Such continuity through long periods is not uncommon, as clan records are carefully kept and relationships religiously maintained. We recall the survival of the clan of Confucius to this day, without break through 75 generations, that cover a period of 2462 years,[1] the larger part of which is still residing around the original home; and we also recall the survival of the clan of Mencius, originating with Mencius, in 372 B. C.

. *The Van Clan Estate :*[2] The records show that there was an ancestor of the Van Clan, who purchased 1000 mow of land (about 210 acres) in order to feed his own folks. This man's father had worked toward this end but it was the son who realized the plan and secured state recognition for the establishment of his estate. This was in 1064. Regulations were drawn up for the administration of the estate; but further additions and changes were frequently made as years went by, owing to the increase of the clan population. Thus there is on record this statement:

According to ancient custom, distribution of rice was equal, with extra gifts for marriages, education of children and Imperial literary examination. Later, there was reduction of land, increase of taxation and large growth in the number of descendants. For each individual in the beginning, there are 30 individuals now. Hence per-capita distributions have to be reduced, and the extra gifts discontinued. Other causes for the addition and change of regulations are the variations in the profits from the estate, and the changes of abode of the clan population.

The Van Clan estate consisted of farm lands, farming implements, a granary, and some living houses. The lands were rented to farmers, who retained a fixed percentage of the annual produce and returned the rest to the estate. The farmers were given the use of the public

---

[1] E. H Parker, *Studies in Chinese Religion*, p. 176.
[2] *Tu-i-lu*, bk i, sec i.

implements of cultivation. The produce, largely consisting of grain, was stored in the public granary. The
houses were rented to farmers at moderate rates, and in
the case of poor families, rental was free. For the repair
of these houses, whenever necessary, the families occupying them were held responsible, unless they were poor.
No destruction or alienation of public property was per-
missible.

Objects: The objects of having the clan estate were to
relieve the clan-members from poverty and destitution,
to encourage the education of the young, to reward virtue, such as filial piety and virtuous widowhood, and to
maintain the solidarity of the clan, comprising both the
dead and the living.

Administration: The first administration was appointed by the founder of the estate. Whether this administration became self-perpetuating, or whether it was
coincident with eldership in the clan or with a part of it,
so that there would be no doubt as to who should have
the control of the administration in succeding generations, we are not informed. In all probability the latter
was the actual arrangement, judging from consensus of
custom.

The officers of administration seem to have held their
offices subject to the approval of the clan. A rule of
1083 provided that they could be impeached in case of
suspected abuse of authority or dishonesty; and a rule
of 1095 provided that this impeachment should go
through legal channels, with its entire technique, such
as evidence, witnesses, *etc.* Nevertheless, while in office,
the administration exercised absolute power, with which
even the right of eldership could not interfere; and the
personal right of officers, even under impeachment, could
not be reduced in any way. These rules indicate recog-

nition of the personal immunity of officers, the unlimited character of delegated powers, and the responsibility of the administration to the clan. On the other hand, if the administration showed good management, through the annual and semi-annual reports, the officers were rewarded with gifts of rice. Public business meetings were called at the Spring and Autumnal sacrifice.

Distribution of Aid: Regular distribution according to the earliest rules (1050) consisted of rice and cloth for every individual in the clan. An adult received a quart of rice per day and a roll of cloth every year. The head of each family submitted a monthly estimate of its proper share to the managers of the estate, who after verifying it would give the desired amount. Of the minors, the absentees and the servants, there were special rules. A rule of 1050 stated that a child over five years of age should receive an adult's share of rice, but that between the ages of five an ten his share of cloth should be half that of an adult. A servant above the age of fifty, having to support children at home under 16, was to receive a full share. One full share of rice was also allowed for each family for the care of its other domestics.

The rules of 1095 provided that a person not resident within the locality could receive no grants, but one returning home before the fifth day of the month was to receive his share (1098). For the support of servants and slaves, no matter how many there might be in a family, no more than five shares were to be given; but bachelors could not claim any shares for servants.

In 1098 the age limit for children was taken away, and any child, two months after birth, could be registered together with his mother's name and be counted as a member of the family.

In 1689 it was provided that children should receive

an adult share only after reaching the age of an adult—
i. e., sixteen.   At this age a boy would be brought to
the ancestral temple accompanied by his father, elder
brother, and elders of the immediate family, and there
he would be initiated into full membership in the clan.
This always took place at the spring or autumnal sacrifices.

Special Grants . Certain persons in the clan received
special grants under certain conditions.   They were:
students pursuing or preparing for a literary career,
aged persons, and widows.

Young men inclined toward a literary career, and
thus on the road to governmental preferment and Imperial honors, were greatly encouraged in their preparation, because their preferment and honors would reflect
glory upon the clan which produced them.   The rules of
1073 made several provisious for the scholars attending
the Imperial examinations, and those engaged in the
teaching professions.   The rules of 1689, amplified these
rules and arranged gifts in grades according to the
literary progress of the scholars.   Those who did not
need gifts were permitted to refuse them in favor of
the more needy.

Persons over sixty years of age, according to the
rules of 1689, were given an extra share of support; over
seventy, two extra shares; at eighty, three extra shares;
at ninety, four extra shares; and if without descendants,
an added share.   The total number of shares for a person could not exceed five.   This provision shows the
reverence for age which is in full accordance with the
mores of patriarchal society.

A widow having passed her third year in widowhood
was registered and received on her own account a full
share of support.   At the fifth year of her widowhood

she received an extra share; at the tenth, two extra
shares; at the fifteenth, three extra shares; at the twentieth, four extra shares. Beyond this there was no increase. Upon remarriage support was withdrawn.

For special occasions, such as funerals and marriages,
families were assisted by the clan estate.

Conclusion: The custom is not uncommon for persons of much wealth to devote their benevolences to their
clans, in the distribution of goods or in the founding
of useful institutions, such as schools, or in the construction of public works, such as roads and bridges.
But an extensive system such as that of the Van Clan is
rare. A commoner system is one in which mutual benefit operates more directly. The Clan store consists
of voluntary contributions of grain from individual
farmers during harvest seasons, and is used for the
relief of distress in poor years. Such a system is both
prevalent and ancient; Chu-tse, the great editor of
the Confucian Classics, was said to have founded one for
his home town in 1181 (Sung dynasty).[1]

II. THE VILLAGE COMMUNITY

Local Spirit: We have considered the operation of
mutual benefit, based upon the clan, or consanguinity;
we will now consider its operation based on local spirit.

We may regard clan consciousness, *i. e.*, consciousness
of kind based upon consanguinity, as the simplest expression
of what we know as social consciousness in its
broadest meaning. It is the simplest because it is elementary and primary; it appeared earliest in social evolution, and has always been an important element in the later
development of social consciousness. The next simplest
expression of social consciousness is what we may call

[1] *To-i-lu,* bk v, sec. i.

"local spirit" or localism. It is an attachment to a locality primarily, and secondarily attachment of members of the locality to one another.

We have already referred to the tendency of clans to localize. But in the complexities of migration localities become settled by families of more than one clan, and finally by many families representing many clans, perhaps with no single clan numerically preponderant. A fair-sized village is of this description. In such a village community, the members are conscious of an attachment for the place, created and strengthened perhaps by generations of residence, by associations of childhood, and by identification of economic interests. The occupation of a common locality becomes a basis upon which the members build their social intercourse. Solidarity may be strengthened by intermarriage among the different clans, by division of labor in local industries and by the recognition of community interests, which are symbolized in the worship of local deities.

The Village Government: The village is a self-governing group, although it is politically under the district magistrate, who has jurisdiction over all the villages within his district. In self-government and in its relation to the political organization of the country, the village has been said to resemble the early New England communities, with their town-meeting government.[2] The headmen of the village are elected by the members of the village, and have delegated powers to control its affairs and to promote its interests. Their services may or may not be paid for,[2] and they remain in office during good behavior. Their public duties consist in the main-

---

[1] Morse, *Trade and Administration of the Chinese Empire*, p. 47.

[2] Williams, *Middle Kingdom*, vol i, p. 482.

tenance of roads, supervision of fairs, building and up-keep of public edifices, sinking of wells, engagement of theatrical companies, policing of the place, *etc.*[1]

In the cultural, economic and industrial life of the village, co-operation is expressed prominently in the conduct of markets and fairs, in the communal "village hunts," in the associations for the watching and gathering of crops, in the communal education of the young, and in public maintenance of religious worship and theatricals.[2]

Village Charities: For charitable purposes there are local societies for the care of foundlings, poor families and their children,[3] mutual loan associations, and mutual providential associations.

Mutual Loan Societies: Of the reason for the formation of mutual loan societies, Smith says:

Every Chinese has constant occasion to use money in sums which it is very difficult for him to command. The rate of interest is always so high that a man who is compelled to borrow a considerable amount, upon which he must pay interest at two and a half, three, or even four per cent a month, will not improbably be swamped by the endeavor to keep up with his creditors. . . . By distributing the payments over a long period, and by the introduction of an element of friendship into a merely commercial transaction, the Chinese is able to achieve the happy result of uniting business with pleasure[4]

Concerning the operation of these mutual loan societies, the following description contains the essential elements:

[1] Smith, *Village Life in China*, p 227

[2] Smith, *ibid, passim.*

[3] See Chapter III, Charity.

[4] Smith, *op. cit*, p 152.

The simplest of the many plans by which mutual loans are effected is the contribution of a definite sum by each member of the society in rotation to some other one of their number. When all the rest have paid their assessment to the last man on the list, each one will have received back all that he put in, and no more. . . . The man who is in most need of money invites certain of his friends to co-operate with him, and in turn to invite certain of their friends to do the same. When the requisite number has been secured, the members assemble and fix the order in which they each shall have the use of the common fund. This would probably be decided by lot. Unless the amount in question is a very trifling one, every meeting of the members for business purposes will be accompanied by a feast attended by all the partners, and paid for either by the one for whose benefit the association was organized, or by the person whose turn it is to use the common fund.[1]

Various other elements enter into these mutual loan transactions, such as the payment of interest for the use of the common funds; and the size of the membership in the society and the period of its existence are quite variable.

Mutual Providential Associations: Families and individuals of moderate means provide for special drains upon their resources occasioned by such events as weddings and funerals by co-operation. Societies for such purposes follow the model of mutual loan societies, with special memberships, *i. e.*, those who have either the family functions above mentioned on hand, or expect their occurrence in the near future with reasonable certainty.[2]

Mutual providential associations usually operate with the least display of commercialism. The following regulation of a society for funerals is an illustration. It provides for a membership of 32, divided into four depart-

[1] Smith, *ibid*, p 153   [2] *Ibid*, pp 189-190

ments, presumably corresponding to the residences of
the members, east, west, north and south. Each department has an elected head, through whom business is
transacted. In case a death occurs in the home of any
member of the society, the four departments contribute
money voluntarily and forward it to the bereaved family
through the four departmental heads. The family is not
expected to make any formal acknowledgment. The
members attend the funeral and assist in its arrangements.[1]

III. Provincial and District Clubs[2]

The Basis of Association: In large trading cities and
towns of China there are always present more or less
people from distant cities, who have come for trade,
travel, and sometimes for fulfilling official appointments. These people, while mixing freely with the natives of the place, are inclined to segregate into separate
groups according to their several provinces or cities.
They form what are known as provincial clubs. It is
natural for fellow-provincials and fellow-townsmen to
feel drawn toward one another while residing among
strangers. The attachment with one's native place is not
easily dissolved; in fact, it is apt to be strengthened by
absence. The custom of reckoning one's birthplace by
that of one's grandfather, which obtains in China universally, tends further to prolong the attachment with
one's native place. This attachment for a common native place is the ground of association among the co-
provincials.

The number of provincial and district clubs in any one
city is varied according to the importance of the place as

[1] *To-i-lu*, bk viii, sec i.
[2] Morse, *Gilds of China*, pp. 35-48.

a trading centre. The city of Shanghai, in the province of Kiangsu, had a Chinese population of 488,000 in 1910, of which 232,982 were natives of 17 outside provinces. One province alone sent out 168,761 individuals, while the smallest number from a single province was 407. There must be therefore as many provincial clubs as there are provinces represented, and probably many more. A much smaller city, Chingkiang, is reported to have at least twelve such clubs,[2] composed of members from eight outside provinces.

Functions of the Clubs: *Social and Charitable*: These district and provincial clubs are called Hwei-Kwan.[3] They exist for mutual protection and aid and social and business intercourse. The membership of a Hwei-kwan consists of all reputable natives of the home province or district. The government of the club is vested in the hands of one or more managers, elected by the members. The income of the club is derived from assessment upon the members, initiation fees and rentals of real estate.

The club naturally serves as an agency for the practice of philanthropy both among its own members and others. It takes care of transients from the home province or district, assists needy members, provides free transportation or burial of poor co-provincials, helps needy students, co-provincials, who come to the place for their Imperial examinations, and helps members in the redress of wrongs. It becomes, moreover, a convenient channel through which members may be reached

---

[1] Population for the " Port Settlement " only, 1910, in *China Mission Year Book*, 1911.

[2] *Imperial Maritime Customs, Decennial Report*, 1892-1901, vol. i, p 461.

[3] Morse, *op cit.*, pp. 35-38.

by appeals for subscription to charitable works of the
·place where they are.

IV TRADE AND CRAFT GUILDS [1]

The Basis of Association: Association in trade and
craft guilds is based upon community of interests, industrial, professional and commercial.   The guilds are
societies, with specific objects in view, and the consciousness of kind among members is based upon neither
considerations of consanguinity nor of locality in itself,
although the latter must necessarily affect guild formation, but upon common ecnomic and cultural interests.

The number of guilds is unlimited, for there are possible as many kinds of guilds as there are trades, professions and forms of labor.   And so there are bankers'
guilds, tea guilds, druggists' guilds, fishmongers' guilds,
millers' guilds, wheelbarrow guilds, physicians' guilds,
and so on.   They are known as Kung-so, or Public
Offices.[2]

Functions of the Guilds: Trade and Charity: The
guilds exist primarily for the promotion of the interests
of the specific trades, crafts, *etc.*   They therefore exercise control of the trades, fix wages and prices, regulate
supplies of professional services, and exercise other functions pertaining to the interests they represent.   The
government and support of the guilds follow the general
lines described in connection with provincial clubs.

In matters of social relief, these guilds become mutual
benefit agencies.   Members assist one another and their
families in misfortune, their association being the
ground for co-operation in relief.   Moreover, just as
provincial clubs are convenient channels through which
to reach their members for subscriptions to charitable

---

[1] Morse, *ibid.,* pp 9-34.   [2] Morse, *ibid ,* p 9

works, so these craft and trade guilds are equally convenient channels through which to gain the support of shop-keepers, business establishments, professional and labor bodies for charitable works. This method of raising funds is commonly resorted to by philanthropic institutions. It is a fruitful method, as the guilds are able to unite the trades and make them contribute as corporations for such objects. Thus, the Hall of United Benevolence at Shanghai systematically appeals to various guilds for their support. The following is a sample of such an appeal:

At the establishment of the institution in the 9th year of Kiaking, it comprised the four departments of relief of widows, support of the aged, dispensing of coffins and burial of the poor. They were afterwards extended by the support of a free school, a fund for sparing animal life, the supply of water buckets and padded clothes for assisting in case of fire, funeral expenses, the relief of starving strangers, wayside deaths and casualties by drowning, all involving a great expenditure. We have been constantly favored, Worthy Gentlemen, by your donations, annual subscriptions and contributions, besides the voluntary 10 cash coffin-tickets, voluntary vagrant-tickets, and voluntary padded-coat-tickets; you have opened your purses and cheerfully aided the effecting of all those objects. In the first month of the present year our magistrate opened a refuge for the board and lodging of destitute sick and infirm. This necessarily involved us in a large amount of expenditure and the income was not sufficient to meet the outlay. We have been led to consider how that which is raised by many is easily supported, and how the joining of many small pieces will soon make a whole skin. Therefore, as at our instance, the honorable guild of the bean merchants increased their voluntary impost, we respectfully solicit the honorable guilds of the cloth merchants here and in the south of Tsz'-ki in Chekiang to follow the same plan pursued by the bean merchants and to send us in a regular subscription. Thus by the conscientious assistance to so worthy an object it will be perpetuated.[1]

Voluntary Assessment for Charitable Purposes : The guilds have the practice of making assessments upon their members for charitable purposes based upon the volume of business they enjoy. These assessments are arranged by the managers of the guilds and are made known by public proclamations. The following is a sample of such a guild-enactment:[2]

The worthy scholars of Shanghai, in consequence of the subscription purchase of the free burial-ground by Tang, the former magistrate of this city, agreed upon adopting the name of Tung-Jin Tang (United Benevolence Hall), and with noble elevation of mind purchased several halls and rooms for a public place of the institution. At the commencement of the 9th year of Kiaking it was determined to do good by the effecting of four objects. The spirit of United Benevolence is very wide, and it is difficult to say where it should begin and where end. As it is, the support of the aged, relief of widows, with the procuring of coffins and burial are four objects affecting the greatest amount of misery of the living or of the dead, and which are also most striking to the eye and wounding to the heart. It is therefore imperative that with unremitting efforts these should be made their first business. But for such undertakings the necessary expenditure is very large. Benevolent purposes should be universally upheld. We, of this branch of trade, therefore, fearful lest at any time our resources for subscriptions should be limited, conceived that nothing could be better than to subscribe small sums according to the supply of commodity, which would be a plan for the perpetuation of a continual contribution. We, accordingly, came to a public determination that from the middle of the first month of the

---

[1] *Chinese Repository,* vol xv, p. 417.

[2] *Ibid ,* vol xv, pp 414-415

present year, with the exception of rice, every description of bean, wheat, pulse, *etc.*, should for every 100 piculs pay a sub- scription of 14 cash and the bean-cakes 7 cash for every 100 piculs   This subscription is to be paid into the hands of the monthly treasurer, according to the monthly supply of the trade, for the public fund of the Tung-Jin-Tang.   There may not be the slightest concealment or diminution which would at once destroy the invariable principle of justice on which we wish to act, and if any discovery of fraud should hereafter take place, it is determined that a heavy fine and forfeiture shall be the penalty.

But as our trade has been gradually flourishing and the ob- jects of the institution demand of us to supply the deficiency from our surplus, and since also the operations of the institu- tion are daily extending, it is our humble opinion that the promotion of good and bestowal of blessing tends to increase the prosperity of our trade.

The enforcement of the enactment by one trade-guild resulted in enlisting 75 stores which were members of the guild to contribute regularly to the charity fund by voluntary assessment.   We may therefore regard the guilds as not only promoting the welfare of their own members, but also as being powerful agencies for the sup- port of outside charities.

Conclusion : From the foregoing considerations it ap- pears that the social organization of the Chinese people is such as greatly to facilitate not only the cultivation of co-operation and mutual aid, but also to render easy the application of these principles in the field of practical philanthropy.

CHAPTER V

CIVIC BETTERMENT

Philanthropy as Promotion of Social Welfare: In the foregoing chapters we have described two phases of philanthropy as understood and developed among the Chinese, *viz.*, charity for the dependent classes of society, and mutual benefit. It remains for us to describe the third phase of Philanthropy, namely, Civic Betterment. In including this last phase within the field of philanthropy, we are understanding the term in its broadest significance, that is, Promotion of Social Welfare.

According to Chinese conception and practice, civic betterment is a legitimate department of philanthropy and it is a legitimate field in which one may devote one's altruistic energies. Thus one person may found a free school for the education of youth, another may open his private park to the public, and thus provide general opportunity for esthetic and cultural enjoyment, and a third person may contribute toward building a bridge or maintaining a free ferry service. All would be called philanthropists or social benefactors.

The inaction of the Government toward social welfare has been such that the problem of civic betterment has fallen almost entirely upon the shoulders of the people themselves. To show the attitude of Government toward the social welfare of the people, and the freedom with which the people are allowed to undertake the work by themselves, we will briefly describe the political organization under which the people find themselves both in theory and in practise.

The Chinese Government, in Theory and in Practise: The Imperial Government of the Chinese Empire has been generally known as an Absolute Oriental Monarchy. It is so in theory at least. The Emperor rules by divine right; the people are his subjects. His will is the state; and disobedience is treason. He governs the empire with the assistance of his ministers, who together with other high officials form what is known as the Metro-·politan Administration, and with the service of civil and military officials appointed and sent by the throne to their posts throughout the empire. The people are supposed to have no share in the government. But this absolute monarchy is true only in theory. In practise it is far from being absolute. If we study closely the political organization of the country, we find that the Imperial Government has been founded on a principle, more in accord with Spencer's view of minimum state authority than with an imperialist's conception of state authority.

For administration the country is divided into provinces, the provinces divided into prefectures, and the prefectures into districts, which are the smallest administrative units.[1] The districts are governed by magistrates, the magistrates are supervised by prefects, the prefects are under the jurisdiction of the governors of the provinces, and the provinces stand in a relation of quasi-independence to the Central or Metropolitan Administration. The Central Government appoints all the officials of the empire and exercises power of removal of the same, makes laws and levies taxes, and employs

[1] There are 183 prefectures in the 18 provinces of China proper, and 1,443 districts

the provincial and subordinate officials to enforce the laws and collect the taxes.   Beyond these minimum requirements for administrative purposes and a general disciplinary oversight by the Central government, the provinces are left largely to their own control.   Hence it has been said, "the government of China is an autocratic rule superposed on a democracy."[1]

The District Municipality: The Imperial Rule comes into contact with the people through the District Magistrate, who is the appointed official and representative of the Government for the smallest political division, the District.   His jurisdiction extends over a walled city and the surburban and rural territory lying around it as far as the boundaries of neighboring Districts.   The District is the civic, political, judicial and fiscal unit, whereby the people of China are divided.   The District is consequently the most important unit of social and political organization, and the Magistrate, the most important Government official so far as the people are concerned.

Paternalism: The District Magistrate is the holder of a very large number of offices and he performs many functions.   He is the Mayor of the District, the police Magistrate of the city, the Court of first instance in all civil cases arising in the District, the Registrar of the landed property of the inhabitants, the Tax collector for the Provincial and Metropolitan Administrations, the Poor Relief Commissioner, the Commissioner of Public Works and Buildings, and the Guardian of the Morals and Physical well-being of the people of his jurisdiction. In short he is everything, and so metaphorically is known as the "Father and Mother" of his people.[2]

[1] Morse, *Trade and Administration of Chinese Empire*, p. 46.

[2] Morse, *ibid*, pp 69-72.

Defects In Administration: In theory therefore, the social welfare of the people is a well recognized function of the Government and is amply provided for by law. But in practise, there are serious defects in Public Finance and Administrative organization which prevent the District Magistrate from carrying on his functions for social welfare, or oblige him to undertake only an indispensable minimum of the work. These defects are as follows: (1) The District Magistrate has no proper funds at his disposal, specifically designated for his various functions and offices; he must find the funds himself. (2) The Magistrate is given an insignificant official salary, a sum entirely inadequate as compensation for his duties and responsibilities, for maintaining the dignity of his office and for maintaining his subordinates. He is expected to derive his real compensation from emoluments of his office. (3) The chief source for funds to carry on the District Administration is the land-tax. But the Magistrate is also the tax-collector for the Provincial and Metropolitan Administrations. That is to say, the income of the tax is not all retained for local purposes. Out of what may be retained for local purposes, the Magistrate finds the funds for his administration, and the salaries for his subordinates, and for himself. But the tax has been fixed by tradition; and there is no possibility of increase, without antagonizing the people, since in the utilization of the revenue the people have no voice. Under these circumstances, no motive arises to prevent the Magistrate from appropriating as much as possible from the official revenue both for himself, and for his friends in office, or from neglecting the local needs of the people excepting the absolutely unavoidable. Rarely do Magistrates impoverish themselves in order to be the "Father and Mother" of their people.

What is called official corruption in Chinese Government is therefore due not merely to human weakness in the officials but also to defects in the organization of the Government itself. Reform in the organization of the Government is therefore more needed than reform in the individual officials.

State Neglect: The result is a government with a well-meaning paternalism and a theory of existing for the well-being of the people, but in reality impotent to promote their interests, and so estranged from their sympathies. The District municipality becomes like the other political divisions of the country merely an administrative unit of the Central Government, and not an organ for the satisfaction of local needs of the people, as it should be. The hundred and one undertakings, such as roads, street-lights, removal of rubbish, water-supply, school system, police, fire-protection, *etc.*, which people of the West are accustomed to regard as functions of a municipal government are, with a few exceptions of recent date, never undertaken by the proper Government officials. For these, the people are left to work out their own salvation in perfect freedom. Thus, the Government of China as far as the well-being of the people is concerned resembles a temporarily set-up tent, fastened to the national soil with a few pegs and propped up with a few poles here and there, rather than a permanent building of stone and mortar firmly grounded on national foundations.

Practical Democracy: One condition which has made the people tolerate a government estranged from their lives is its permitting them to live in perfect freedom and autonomy, provided the minimum taxation is paid and the moral principles of the Penal Code are observed. What the people everywhere desire is unhampered freedom for pursuing their livelihood, and this the Chinese have in abundance. A keen American observer, Hon. Holcombe, writes thus:

In point of fact the Chinese are governed less than almost any nation in the world. So long as they pay their taxes and violate none of the requirements of the moral code, they are not disturbed by the authorities. A thousand and one official inspections, exactions and interferences, common enough everywhere in America and Europe are quite unknown in China.[1]

Dr. Coolidge, author of *Chinese Immigration*, says: " If the Chinese Government be regarded from the top it appears to be a centralized autocracy; if from the bottom, a pure democracy."

Popular Co-operative Undertakings: The government's neglect is the people's opportunity. We have shown the relative part taken by the Government and the people respectively in charities: that the Governmnnt takes a relatively insignificant part in the relief of the dependent classes, and that the people have the work almost entirely in their own hands. We have also shown how the factor of mutual aid among the people enters into the whole fabric of social organization. We will now show how, in the absence of an aggressive Governmental pursuit of social welfare, the people themselves have undertaken the necessary philanthropic work by co-operative measures grouped under the title of Civic Betterment.

I. FREE EDUCATIONAL OPPORTUNITIES

Government Education: Until the institution of Hioh Pu, or Board of Education by the Metropolitan Admin-

---

[1] *Real Chinese Question*, p 4.

istration in 1903, there was no national system of education. Prior to that date, there had existed for upwards of ten centuries the Imperial Literary Examinations. But these were concerned more with tests for civil service, rather than with the actual education of the people. The latter has almost entirely been in the hands of the people themselves. Since the institution of the Educational Board, the Government has inaguarated a system of public education which intends eventually to cover the empire with free educational opportunities as completely as in any modern country. In 1910 there were already 42,650 new educational institutions of all grades in China; but it is a note-worthy fact that the public and private institutions out-numbered Government institutions.[1]

Free Charity Schools : Charity organizations have entered into the field of providing free educational opportunities for the poor. The Hall of United Benevolence reported maintaining a free school;[2] and the Hall of Sustaining Love at Canton reported the maintenance during 1872 of 19 schools with twenty teachers, and 15 schools with 16 teachers in 1873.[3] We have already referred to school work for children of widows, and provision by clans for the education of their own young people.

Public Lectures : Another instrument for popular education is free lectures. The reports of the Hall of Sustaining Love showed that in 1872, the society engaged the services of three lecturers, for a total of 16 months. In 1873, it engaged three lecturers for a total of 18 months.[4] There are also voluntary societies which

[1] *China Mission Year Book,* 1911, p 79
[2] Report in *Chinese Repository,* vol xv, pp. 402 *et seq.*
[3] *China Review,* vol iii, pp 108 *et seq*
[4] *China Review,* vol. iii, pp 108 *et seq*

take up the work of lecturing. *Tö-i-lu* contains the record of a society founded in 1755, which besides distributing books, posters, songs and pictures, conducted lectures. The method was to have a lecturing team consisting of earnest and eloquent speakers spend the first three days of a month at the club house, and then spend the other seven of the first ten days in the month in visiting different sections of the city.

The lectures are almost always concerned with morals, it being the belief that the morals of the people are the foundation of national prosperity. The following sample is on record in *Tö-i-lu*[1] :

This society teaches men to be good. Those who come to hear must have the elements of good already in them. They have the good intention to come and so they will have good words to hear. One good word stimulates one good thought, and the man is good for life: do not depreciate this sentence. In this way daily dangers may be turned into advantage, and death itself into life.

Everyone has parents: let him serve them;

Everyone has elders: let him respect them;

Everyone has nighbors · let him be at peace with them;

Everyone has children · let him teach them properly;

Let everyone do his duty: If he does it not, but what he ought not to do, he becomes a criminal. Note how criminals are invariably discovered and brought to justice. See what miserable end do the squanderer and the gambler always come to When they founder in trouble, then they envy the lot of the common laborer who toils in the street earning his honest livelihood with diligence and in freedom. The good people are always honored by their neighbors, and prized by their parents and elders, and blessed by Heaven with prosperous and numerous progeny. They shed honor upon the name of

[1] Bk. i, sec. ii, p 19.

their parents and ancestors. This is true filial piety and worthier than sacrifices. Let everyone who hears start the day with a good thought. Those who have been already good, be steadfast; those who are not good, repent; it is never too late to reform.

Literary Censorship : Another function along educational lines is the suppression of indecent literature and a censorship of popular plays and songs. This is generally undertaken by reputable publishers who agree to buy up the indecent literature and destroy their plates. The movement is enforced with fines for recalcitrant publishers.[1]

Other activities, along educational lines, are distribution of tracts, useful information, songs, pictures and posters calculated to improve public morals; and the collection and burning of waste printed matter to inculcate respect for letters. In some cities there are owners of private parks equipped with libraries, zoological sections and aquariums, who open them for the enjoyment of the public, admission being either free or by payment of a nominal fee.

II. PUBLIC SAFETY AND PROTECTION

Under this heading there are several forms of activity engaged in by charity societies and voluntary associations, such as life-saving on water, pilot-boats and fire protection. They are agencies for safety and protection of lives and property.

The Life-saving Station at Wuhu ·[2] This association came into existence before the Tai-ping rebellion, *i. e.*, before the middle of the nineteenth century. It has its

---

[1] Nevius, *China and the Chinese,* p. 221.

[2] Report of the Association in *China Review,* vol. vi, p 277, *et seq*

offices along the shore, and its object is to render assistance to persons and boats in distress on the river. Its equipment consists of life-boats, administration offices, rooms for the rescued persons and burial ground for the drowned.

Life-boats: The boats are manned by crews that live on board all the time. Each boat has a helmsman and four sailors. On account of the importance of their duties the crews are carefully selected and disciplined. The regulations read in part:

Men wishing to serve in the life-boats should come to this office with their securities when an agreement will be made out and signed. The Association will not be responsible for accidents met with in their service, such as slipping overboard or being lost in stormy weather. All it can do in such cases is to provide a coffin; it will not listen to claims for compensation.

The crews are required to live on board the boats, and may not absent themselves without leave. Should any be called away on account of urgent business, he must find his own substitute. Gambling, drinking and opium-smoking are forbidden; criminals may not be sheltered on board nor contraband goods received thereon. For light offenses, dismissal from employment is the punishment, but for heavy offenses the offender is handed over to the penal authorities for punishment.

The boats must always be in readiness. Whether in day or in night, in storm or in rain, the boats must put out to render assistance to boats or persons in distress, at the summons of the alarm-drum. For the encouragement of the crew, they are, besides their regular wages, rewarded for their diligence. For saving one life the reward is 1000 coins; for a corpse recovered the reward is 500 coins; and during nights the sums are doubled.

In case of an accident, human life must receive first attention, and only after all possible help has been given for rescue of life may attention be turned to the recovery of lost goods. The life-boats must proceed to save life, and after having ascertained that everybody on board the wrecked vessel is accounted for, convey the rescued persons to the station. Should there be anyone missing, search must be made on all sides, and dead or alive every individual must be found before the cargo is attended to.

When a person is saved, he is brought to the office and lodged in the rooms prepared for such transients for three days, during which time he is cared for and clothed by the Association. In the case of a woman refugee, the local constable is notified and he must find her suitable lodging with some married woman of elderly years. With a man, no matter how distant his destination may be, traveling expenses are given him and he is sent away after the third day. But a woman is not sent away until her relatives come to claim her, or at least until her family is notified of the fact.

Careful records of the persons saved, together with their names, home addresses, and the dates are kept at the office. Unclaimed bodies of the drowned are buried by the association. In one year (1876) 52 lives were rescued and 46 corpses recovered on the river. Assistance was given also to many vessels in hardship. Goods recovered are brought to the administration office, where they await reclaiming by the proper owners.

Management and Finances: Association business is taken care of by a salaried Committee of 12 men, who occupy the offices in groups of four at a time. As to the duties of the Committee-men, it is required that they shall always keep in touch with one another, and co-operate heartily, for "it is by co-operation that the good cause can be best furthered."

The finances of the association are derived from several sources. A part of the funds comes from civil officials, but the major part from voluntary contributions. Publicity is rigidly maintained through monthly and annual reports. Of the annual reports, it is recorded, one copy is kept at the association office, another copy goes to the District magistrate, and a third is solemnly burned before the local god.

At this religious performance, all the officers of the Association must be present, and together they make the following declaration:

We, the managers of the Life Saving Association venture to come before thee, O God, and humbly represent that owing to the vastness of the waters and the raging of the billows in the rivers of Wuhu, a sudden squall striking the passing craft and taking the sailors unawares will cause ship-wreck and loss of life.

· Though we are aware that the term of a man's life is already decreed and that Heaven's power may not be opposed, yet such sights grieve the heart. Thus it is that we have sought means to save life, and that persons have come together to form a Life Saving association, supported entirely by voluntary contributions. Premises have been erected and boats built with the object of affording security from danger, ensuring a safe passage in stormy weather. A public cemetery has been opened for the burial of the dead and coffins are kept ready for use Thus are good deeds done, afloat and ashore A statement of receipts and disbursements has been prepared and in this work of humanity we have been faithful to the trust reposed in us by the benevolent subscribers.

We pray Thee to examine our conduct, and to mete out

justice to us. May we be punished if we have sacrificed the public good to our private ends, and if we have been laborers unworthy of our hire, if we misappropriated public funds, or if we have caused subscribers to fall off by spreading false reports. While on the other hand, may we be recompensed if we have discharged our duty with all fidelity sparing neither trouble nor fatigue. This we pray to the end that good deeds may endure forever. Humbly we submit our statement of accounts for the year now ended.[1]

Public declaration before the gods is obviously prompted by a utilitarian motive: to gain the confidence of the people and to satisfy the supporters of the honesty of the administration. The utilization of the religious propensities of the people may not be disadvantageous in winning support for charitable undertakings, and we find many a charitable institution having patronage deities and religious observances.

Other riparian cities have similar life-boats, such as Ching-Kiang, Nanking, and Ichang. The boats of the last city are known as Red-boats on account of the color of their paint. Here the boats were first managed by a co-operative society, but later were taken over by the Government because of the importance of the service to the trade of the place.

The "Red-Boats" of Ichang :[2] Ichang is a city situated at a place along the Yantse River, where the stream enters a ravine between high mountainous shores and where there are treacherous rapids. Before the establishment of the Red-boats Service, the dangers of the river, although known, were avoided with difficulty, much loss of lives and property often occurring. At first the

[1] *China Review*, vol. vi, p. 283

[2] *Imperial Maritime Customs, Decennial Report*, 1892-1901, vol i, pp 201-204

fishing boats in the neighborhood were paid small sums to enlist them in the work of rescue. But the plan did not succeed, because it often happened that at the time of a wreck no fishing boat was near enough to the scene of disaster to render any assistance. In 1854 a prosperous merchant, by name Li Yun-kuei, collected subscriptions from the traders whose junks passed through the rapids, and with the money thus raised he built three boats after the pattern of the fishing boats, but distinguished from the latter by being painted red, to be engaged exclusively in the life-saving and piloting work. The society formed to manage the boats was called K'ang Chi T'ang. Later the number of boats was increased to 27. The Government, recognizing the value of the service, subsidized it, and finally caused it to be transformed into a Government service and it has since been managed by the Government with special officials in charge.

Fire Protection : Chinese municipalities do not have fire departments, and so for protection against fires, the people must band themselves together in co-operative associations. These associations usually conform to the streets or wards into which a city is divided. The result is a net-work of fire brigades and stations covering the whole city. In some places the administration of these brigades is taken care of by the charity societies. Thus the Hall of United Benevolence at Shanghai has a fire protection department.[1] It maintains eleven stations throughout the city. Each station is provided with equipment for fighting fires, such as engines, lanterns, firemen's uniforms, *etc.* Each station has ten men under a headman. These men are paid for their services after each occurrence of fire.

[1] *Chinese Repository,* vol xv, pp 409-410

III. FREE PUBLIC SERVICE

In free public service we include not only agencies of transportation, such as ferries, but also means of communication, such as roads and bridges, maintained by voluntary subscription to serve a public free of charge or for a nominal fee. Thus it has been observed by foreign travelers in China:

> It is also worthy of remark that most of the roads and fine archbridges, as well as the public buildings of China, are constructed by voluntary donations. In connection with these public works, it is very common to see stone tablets erected, containing the names of the donors and the amounts of their subscriptions.[1]

Such undertakings are usually entrusted to local charity societies and sometimes to special societies.

Lights and Bridges: The Hall of United Benevolence maintains lights at four places along water-ways around Shanghai, and pays for the services of four men engaged in taking care of the lights. It repairs roads and pavements, cleans sewers, and keeps up the bridges. During 1909, besides miscellaneous repairing, it paid for 574 yards of road-paving, replaced a bridge-railing, and repaired eight bridges.[2]

Free Ferry Service: The Life Saving Association at Wuhu ran a free ferry across the river, according to its report[3] for 1875. It possessed six boats for this service, two having a capacity of 60 passengers each, two forty passengers each, and two ten each. The boats were manned according to their sizes. For the large ones,

---

[1] J. L. Nevius, *China and the Chinese*, p 224.

[2] Report of the Hall for 1909

[3] *China Review*, vol. vi, pp 277-283.

there was a helmsman and four sailors; for the middle-sized, a helmsman and three sailors, and for the small ones, a helmsman and two sailors.

On both sides of the river there were landing stations and ticket offices. A flag raised upon a pole indicated the period during which the service was in operation. It was limited to the day-time. In the night and in severe storms, the boats would not run and the flag was not hoisted up.

Each passenger went aboard with a ticket. When the full number of tickets was collected, the boat proceeded for the other shore. But for special parties, such as a funeral party, a physician in his professional visitation, a marriage party, the boats would cross the river without the full number.

These boats were maintained by voluntary subscriptions. As an inducement, a subscriber for a certain sum of money would be given a ferry pass, if he had use for one, which entitled the holder to prompt service.

IV. MUNICIPAL SELF-GOVERNMENT BY THE PEOPLE

Its Evolution: The work of the philanthropic and co-operative associations for civic betterment, as described above, belongs to the class of municipal functions and has been undertaken by the people themselves because of neglect by the Government authorities, as we have already pointed out. Beginning in voluntary co-operation for mutual benefit, these undertakings gradually become established by custom and finally are recognized as public institutions, both by the people and the civil authorities. At first scattered and uncoördinated, the agencies for these undertakings gradually coalesce and consolidate into one system. Thus results what is virtually municipal self-government by the people.

Instead of the civil authorities protesting against the encroachment on their authorities, they encourage this development of popular self-rule by giving it full recognition and freedom of action.

The Case of the Newchwang Guild: An early case illustrating this evolution is that of the Local Guild of Newchwang, Manchuria, recorded in the *Decennial Report of Imperial Maritime Customs* for 1882–1891.[1] The Local Guild is made up of the principal native merchants of the city, and practically combines in itself the duties of a municipal council and those of a chamber of commerce. It maintains order in the streets, takes care of the roads, drains and reservoirs, controls public lands, administers poor relief, subsidizes charitable institutions, controls banks, regulates exchanges of trade, marts and transportation. It finances its activities by taxation upon transactions between merchants not natives of the city but residing and doing business therein, by collecting bridge-dues upon carts transporting goods, and shop dues; for all of which the guild has the authorization of the local civil officials. The authority of the guild and its method of administration is shown in the proclamations it issues. The following is one concerning bridge-dues:

It is generally understood that living traffic is a sure sign of a town's prosperity. To encourage traffic, therefore the public thorough-fares must be kept in good repair

A former president of the Guild built bridges across the streams and tidal creeks in the vicinity of Ying-tsu for public use, but as nothing was done to keep them in repair, the strong current gradually undermined the supports, so that many bridges were in danger of collapsing.

[1] Pp 34 *et seq*

The roads, too were the cause of universal complaint.

A subscription was consequently raised from the resident merchants to defray the annual outlay for repairing the roads and bridges in the neighborhood of the port.

During the Summer of the second year of Emperor Kuang Hsu (1876) continued rains did much harm to the public thoroughfares, suspending thereby a great deal of the cart traffic. This state of affairs coming to the ears of the Taotai, he issued orders to the Guild that the roads and bridges were to be promptly put in thorough repair. This was done at great expense, and the ordinary subscription not proving sufficient to meet the unusual outlay, a plan was devised to tax all carts carrying merchandise. Permission having been received from the Tartar General and the Civil Governor at Moukden, through the influence of the Taotai, a tax was then instituted, which has been continued up to the present time.

The Guild now informs the public that beginning with to-day, the First of the Ninth Moon and ending with the First of the Third Moon of the following year, bridge-dues will be levied on all carts laden with produce of any kind at the following rates: [1]

Local Self-Government, A Growing Movement: During recent years, local self-government by the people is developing in many cities and towns. It is distinctly encouraged by the Imperial Government as a step in the preparation toward Constitutional Parliamentary Government. A short time ago the writer sent out some questions to his friends at Shanghai in regard to municipal self-government in that city. The replies are significant. They show that self-government is directly sanctioned by the local civil officials and indirectly by the Imperial Government; that local government is in the hands of the franchised citizens of the city, who elect the officers of the

[1] *Ibid.*, p. 37

local administration, but that the district magistrate acts
as a director and advisor and that it practically takes over
all the functions of a municipality, including the powers
of taxation and police. The new local self-government
supervises the educational institutions, opens free schools,
undertakes sanitation, street-cleaning, public works, light-
ing, police, traffic regulation, supervision of commercial
amusements, inspection of food-markets; it makes its
own laws and enforces them, and collects taxes. The
taxes are called Public Welfare Taxes, and consist of
house and shop tax, license of vehicles and of boats, tax
on advertisement spaces, commercial amusements, and
food-markets. An interesting fact is that the budgets
of the Shanghai Municipal Self-government contain an
estimate of the yearly incomes and expenditure of the
charitable institutions of the city, indicating that the
municipality is aiming at including among its functions
supervision and support of these hitherto voluntary and
independent institutions. The new self-government administration does not displace the old civil government of the city. That is to say, the magistrate who is
the appointed representative and agent of the provincial
and imperial administrations still retains his office, collects the land taxes and forwards them to the higher administrations. There is a division of labor. The magistrate takes care of the city as far as it is an administrative
unit of the empire; while the new local government takes
care of the city as such for the satisfaction of its local
needs.

The New Political Régime · In the famous constitution
of 1908 promulgated by the Imperial Government, local
self-government is fully instituted and defined. In
principle it aims to preserve the functions and powers
which the district magistrate now exercises intact, and

to superadd upon the existing régime, the new organization for local self-government, along the lines we have already described in connection with the local self-government of Shanghai city.

It is thus apparent that by successive and almost imperceptible gradations, what was, in the beginning, mere voluntary co-operative measures on the part of the people for mutual protection and civic betterment on the occasion of official omission in a political organization, wherein popular franchise was unknown, has become one of the fundamental features of a new order of political life, wherein popular franchise and self-government are the essential features. The outward suddenness, apparently suggested by the promulgation of the new Constitution and the transition from an Absolute Monarchy to a democratic form of government is therefore more apparent than real. Silent causes have been working for generations under the shadow of the old régime, and the new régime is their natural consummation.

CHAPTER VI

Conclusion: Rise of National Self-consciousness and Solidarity

Chinese Philanthropy, the Product of National Genius: Chinese Philanthropy is a product of the genius of the Chinese Nation. It is organically related with the life, tradition and ideals of the nation, and from them has derived its energy, its guiding principles and characteristics. It is an expression of Chinese civilization.

Democratic Foundation: The notable characteristic of Chinese Philanthropy is its democratic foundation. Instead of being a state institution, it has been more a popular one; instead of being fostered under the paternalism and direction of the state, it has been developed by the co-operation and initative of the people.

Esprit de Corps of Minor Social Groups: The spirit of Chinese Philanthropy indicates a developed social consciousness in the hearts of the people. There is a strong sense of social solidarity, which shows itself in the many sharing the burden of the poverty, want and misfortune of the few, in the readiness to give mutual aid, and in the voluntary co-operative undertaking for civic betterment. The sense of social solidarity is strongest in the *esprit de corps* of the minor social groups within the nation, such as the clan, the village, the District, the Province, and the guilds.

Absence of National Consciousness in the Past: Until the beginning of the present century, there had not been a national self-consciousness and solidarity comparable in strength with the spirit and solidarity of the minor social groups.. This is attributable both to the presence of unfavorable conditions, and to the absence of favorable conditions for the development and sustenance of the spirit of nationalism. The gigantic territory of the empire, the want of convenient and rapid means of communication between widely-separated parts, · the resulting effect in the diversification of local dialects, and to a less extent of local customs, and the absence of a powerful, aggressive, centralized national Government have been some of the conditions which deterred the rise of national consciousness and solidarity in the people.

Geographical Isolation and Absence of Conflict : But there was a condition, whose presence in the national experience of China exercised an even greater influence than the above-mentioned conditions in the determent of the rise of national consciousness and solidarity, namely, geographical isolation. During historic times since the occupation of the empire in its present dimensions in the second century B. C. and until the last century A. D., China was practically cut off from intercourse with the other historic peoples of the world by physical barriers, the oceans and the mountains. The only important people with whom China came into hostile contact for any considerable number of times during the 2000 years down to the middle of the nineteenth century were the Tartars from the north and northwest. Geographical isolation has meant, therefore, absence of international conflict. History seems to show that conflict between nations is the chief, potent condition for the rise of national consciousness and solidarity.

Governmental Decentralization : The absence of international conflict also furnishes a reason for the non-appearance of a powerful, aggressive, centralized national government. So long as China remained an isolated country, having enough productive land and possessions to satisfy its political ambitions, and having the natural physical barriers to protect it from foreign attack, it did not need a very strong, aggressive and centralized national government. There was need only for so much of organized government as would insure the primary conditions of social well-being within the realm, such as peace, order, security of property, safety of life, and freedom for lawful pursuit of livelihood. For the assurance of these primary conditions of social well-being, decentralization of government may be just as favorable a policy as centralization, and moral authority may be more successful than authority of force, if socialization is sufficiently advanced and the social population sufficiently homogeneous. Decentralization and moral authority would be preferred both for their economy and their compatibility with the purpose of organized government in such a country. The final picture of the country would be something as follows: the country would be divided into administrative units, such as provinces, prefects and districts; each political division would be held responsible to the next higher division for the fulfilment of certain administrative duties, but otherwise It would be semi-independent; the central government would be an organ for balancing the works of the various political units, rather than be their taskmaster; the laws of the land would be little more than the crystallization of the customs of the nation; the people would be given great freedom and opportunities of self-government; the government would utilize some popular national ethical system or religion as the means of ruling the people and keeping them in their legitimate spheres of life and activity.

Such has been actually the case with China until recently. Mayers, writing in 1878 says, "the central government of China, so far as a system of this nature is recognized in the existing institutions, is arranged with the object rather of registering and checking the action of the various provincial administrations, than that of assuming a direct initiative in the conduct of affairs."[1] As to the practical freedom and democracy of the Chinese nation, we have already indicated it in Chapter V.

The New National Consciousness and Solidarity: International Relationships: But since the beginning of the 19th century, the conditions of the national life of China have undergone great change. Geographical isolation has disappeared on the advent of ocean steamers; China has become part of the world system of commerce and international relationships; she has measured strength with other peoples, and has compared her civilization with theirs; and so through these international, inter-racial and inter-cultural contacts, the Chinese nation has attained self-consciousness, and the national government is being consolidated and centralized. Thus Morse says: "The hammering of twenty years has welded the Empire together, and the Imperial Government was compelled, in its foreign relationships, to act as a ruler and not as a mere supervisor, and to adopt a more centralized policy."[2]

Improved Internal Communication: Besides, new means of communication have been introduced into the country, such as railroads, steamships, and the telegraph; and the distant parts of the empire are brought closer

[1] Morse, *Trade and Administration of the Chinese Empire*, p. 53.
[2] *Ibid.*, p. 55

to one another and to the national center, the Capital; and so there is better intercourse and intelligence among the people in the different provinces and districts. Again quoting Morse:

In the old days, too, the communication was slow, and two or three months might elapse before the authorities at Canton could receive a reply to their request for instructions, with the result that much must be left to the man on the spot. The introduction of steamers brought Canton, Nanking and Hankow, the seats of the most important viceroyalties, within a week of the Capital; and the extension of the telegraphs which directly resulted from the Russian difficulty of 1880, brought the most remote of the high provincial authorities into immediate touch with the central administration, and furthered the centralization which had already become established; and now the Empire is ruled from Pekin to an extent unknown while China still played the hermit.[1]

The New Education: There is yet another factor, which is directly fostering the growth of the spirit of nationalism. Speaking of this new factor, as awakening the people to a sense of their citizenship in the nation, Professor Bevan says:

There are two forces that are welding the Chinese people and their government into a single nation, one from without and one from within. Contact with foreign nations has compelled the Chinese nation to assert itself as the actual governing power throughout the whole empire. Increase of knowledge and the birth of a new education have brought the people to a real and truer self-realization; and this realization of self is driving the people to demand a civilization similar to the civilizations which they have discovered around

[1] Morse, *op. cit*, p. 56.

them. On the one side, there is a movement in the direction of strengthening the central authority and drawing closer the ties between the central administration and the administrations of the constituent parts of the empire, while on the other side there is a demand that the people shall have a share in the making of the laws and in their carrying out when made. The central power is attempting to govern either immediately by itself, or indirectly through its agents more directly and more closely responsible to itself. The people is trying to make its voice heard in the government councils; they are making a distinct attempt to obtain for themselves a share in the legislative and administrative functions of the empire. The Constitution is an effort to combine these two forces.[1]

The Nation-Wide Basis of Philanthropy . With the rise of national self-consciousness and solidarity, philanthropy will acquire a nation-wide basis of operation.   On the one hand, the extension of social consciousness throughout the whole nation, uniting the people in all parts of the empire will extend the field of philanthropy, and facilitate its application; on the other hand, the centralization of the Government, the assumption of definite responsibilities and powers by it will ultimately mean a more active participation of the Government in social welfare. Already we find the people of all sections of the country responding to appeals for aid of some particular section in times of misfortune with greater readiness than was obtainable ten or twenty years ago. Already, we see the Government taking up the problem of public education, and initiating other reforms. Furthermore, whereas there was estrangement between the Government and

[1] "The New Chinese Constitution," in *China Mission Year Book,* 1911.

the people formerly, there seems to be a conscious co-operation between the two now, such as has been shown in the co-operation for public education and for the suppression of opium, because it has been for the first time clearly realized that the Government and the people have identical and not variant interests. In other words, the Government is logically bound to assert itself in the promotion of the social welfare of the nation. But in so doing, it will not be so unwise as to discourage the people's activities along the same lines. Rather the Government will co-operate with the people by under-taking those works which lie beyond the power of private voluntary institutions and associations, or beyond that of particular cities, and localities, because of juristic and financial conditions, and by further developing existing undertakings of the people through financial assistance and legislative standardization. This seems to be the new ideal that is actuating the conscience of the people and the government to-day.

A New National Personality : And so a new era in China's life has begun. The social consciousness which was in the past confined within the limits of minor social groups and associations and political divisions has broken forth and merged into the larger consciousness of the nation. The loyalty which people in the past gave un-conditionally to their immediate clans, localities, guilds, and provinces, has now found its proper subordination in the new alignment of allegiance to the nation. In this transition from the old to the new era, there is, therefore, a readaptation of the habits of mutual aid and co-opera-tion, trained in the social functioning and experiences of smaller associations, for the functioning and experiences of the larger association, the nation. As a historical fact, and not as a mere figure of speech, the Twentieth Century B. C. witnessed the birth of the Ancient China, and the Twentieth Century A. D. is witnessing the birth of the New China,—the evolution of a new National Personality through new national experiences.

BIBLIOGRAPHY

A partial list of publications cited

L. R. O. Bevan. Article: "The New Chinese Constitution," in *China Mission Year Book* Shanghai, 1911.

H. C. Chen. *Economic Principles of Confucius and His School.* N. Y., 1911.

China Review. Vols. II, III, VI. Shanghai, 1873-1875, 1877-1878.

Chinese Repository Vols. XIV, XV, XVI, XVII. Canton, 1845-1848.

Chuang Tzŭ, Mystic, Moralist and Social Reformer. Tr. H. A. Giles. London, 1889

Decennial Reports, 1882-1892; 1892-1901. *China, Imperial Maritime Customs.* Shanghai.

E. T. Devine. *Principles of Relief* N. Y., 1904.

F. H. Giddings. *Principles of Sociology.* N. Y., 1896.

J. H. Grey *Walks in the City of Canton.* 1875.

A. E. Hecker. *A Short History of Women's Rights.* N. Y., 1910.

Hsin Tzŭ. *Essay on Human Nature*

E. Huntington. *Pulse of Asia* Boston and N. Y., 1907.

F. H. King *Farmers of Forty Centuries.* Madison, Wis, 1911.

E. Legouvé *Moral History of Women.* Tr. from 5th Paris Ed. by J. W. Palmer. N. Y., 1860

Lî Kî Collection of Treatises on the Rules of Propriety or Ceremonial Usages Tr. J. Legge, in *"Texts of Confucianism," Sacred Books of the East,* ed. F. Max Muller. Vols. XXVII, XXVIII Oxford, 1885.

Liu Hsian *Lives of Virtuous Women.*

Mencius. Tr. J. Legge, in *Chinese Classics.* 2nd Ed. Rev. Vol. II. Oxford, 1895.

S Merwins. *Drugging a Nation.* N Y., 1908.

H. B. Morse. *Gilds of China.* N. Y., 1909

—— *Trade and Administration of the Chinese Empire.* London, 1908.

J. L. Nevius. *China and the Chinese.* N Y., 1869.

E. H. Parker. *China, Her History, Diplomacy and Commerce.* London, 1901.

—— *China, Past and Present.* London, 1903

—— *Studies in Chinese Religion* N Y, 1910.

E. A. Ross. *Changing Chinese.* N Y, 1911.

A. H. Smith. *Village Life in China. A Study in Sociology.* N. Y., 1899.

H. Spencer. *Principles of Biology.*

—— *Principles of Ethics.* N. Y., 1904.

Ta Tsing Leu Lee, Being the Fundamental Laws and a Selection from the Supplementary Statutes of the Penal Code of China. Tr. G. T. Staunton. London, 1810.

Tö-i-lu Rules and Regulations of Benevolent Institutions. Wu-si, 1869

2

THE STATUS OF ALIENS IN CHINA

STUDIES IN HISTORY, ECONOMICS AND PUBLIC LAW

EDITED BY THE FACULTY OF POLITICAL SCIENCE
OF COLUMBIA UNIVERSITY

Volume L]   [Number 2

Whole Number 126

THE STATUS OF ALIENS IN CHINA

BY

VI KYUIN WELLINGTON KOO, Ph.D.,

English Secretary to the President of China

New York
COLUMBIA UNIVERSITY
LONGMANS, GREEN & CO., AGENTS
LONDON: P. S. KING & SON
1912

TO

MY FATHER AND MOTHER

WHO HAVE EVER BEEN GENEROUS AND ATTENTIVE IN THE

EDUCATION OF THEIR CHILDREN FOR PUBLIC SERVICE

THIS MONOGRAPH, THE FIRST FRUIT OF

TWENTY YEARS OF SCHOOLING

IS GRATEFULLY AND AFFECTIONATELY DEDICATED

PREFACE

THE chapters which are herein presented, with the exception of the concluding one, were originally intended to form an introductory part of a treatise on alien claims against China, which is still in the course of preparation. After they were written, however, it was found that they constituted, both as to the substance which they embodied and as to the arrangement of the topics which they included, a fairly complete whole in themselves. It was therefore decided, with the concurrence of a number of professors in the Faculty of Political Science at Columbia University, that they might advantageously be left to stand in a separate form by themselves; hence the appearance of the present volume.

In deciding upon this plan of publication I was also influenced by a consideration of the timeliness of the subject to which the studies embraced in this volume are devoted. Commerce, religion, travel and other interests are drawing increasing numbers of foreigners into China, and the question of their precise status, while residing or being within her territory, becomes to-day, not only one of enhanced interest, but one of growing practical importance. The multifarious and sometimes complex problems which arise out of their intercourse with the Chinese people depend for their prompt solution primarily upon an accurate knowledge of the rights, privileges and immunities which they are entitled to enjoy under laws and treaties, and of the limitations and restrictions, arising from the same sources of sanction, upon such rights, privileges and immunities. The need of this knowledge is all the more pressing by reason of the fact that foreigners in China enjoy judicial extra-territoriality.   Although in recent years several mono- graphs have appeared which treat of the position, (gen- erally a few phases of it), of foreigners of a particular nationality in China, I am not aware of any work in existence which considers the status of aliens in China as a class, or from the Chinese point of view.   The pres- ent treatise is an attempt in these directions.

My profound thanks are due, first of all, to John Bassett Moore, Hamilton Fish Professor of Inter- national Law and Diplomacy in Columbia University, for his sound instruction in the principles of the law of nations, for his inspiring direction in the preparation of this work and for reading over the manuscripts and sug- gesting invaluable corrections, which were without ex- ception accepted and incorporated in the work. I am also deeply indebted to Professor Charles A. Beard, of Columbia University, who very kindly accepted charge of the printing of this monograph after I sailed from New York for Peking, and who made arrangements for the verification of the references, the preparation of the index and the reading of the proof sheets.

V. K. WELLINGTON KOO.

LONDON, *April 16, 1912.*

CONTENTS.

PART I

THE PRE–CONVENTIONAL PERIOD (A. D. 120–1842)

PART II

THE CONVENTIONAL PERIOD (SINCE 1842)

PART I

THE PRE-CONVENTIONAL PERIOD
(A. D. 120–1842)[1]

---

[1] During this period two treaties of peace, boundary, and land trade were concluded between China and Russia, viz., the treaty of Nerchinsk, August 27, 1689, and that of Kiakhta, October 21, 1727, amended by the convention of October 18, 1768. These treaties, however, were very limited in their operation, and did not provide any comprehensive system of trade intercourse and consular jurisdiction as did those beginning with the treaty of Nanking, August 29, 1842; hence for the purposes of this study, the year 1842 is considered more suitable to mark the commencement of China's broad treaty relations with foreign powers The French, English, Chinese, Russian and Latin texts of the treaty of 1689; the French, Chinese, Russian and Latin texts of the treaty of 1727; and the French and Russian texts of the supplementary convention of 1768 are all found in *Treaties between China and Foreign States* (Shanghai, 1908), vol. I.

CHAPTER I

HISTORY OF THE ENTRANCE OF FOREIGNERS INTO CHINA

EVIDENCES of the fact abound in Chinese history that the presence of the alien in China dates back to time nearly immemorial. Embassies from the neighboring countries; commercial missions disguised as bearers of tribute; daring explorers on land and at sea; missionaries of the Sacred Book of Buddha, the Koran and the Bible; and refugees from persecution—these visited the imperial capital or its outlying provinces, lived there and in some cases died there in days as old as written records. Putting aside legendary notices altogether, which make mention of visitors to the Chinese Empire as far back as in the reign of Hwangti (2697 B. C.), the Hebrews, for instance, fleeing from persecution in Egypt, began to migrate into the western parts of the Empire long before the beginning of the Christian Era, and established a colony of their own, which still exists to-day in Kaifung Fu, the capital of Honan Province.[1] In A. D. 120, a little more than two centuries after the first Chinese embassy was despatched to Parthia, the king of Shan, a country southwest of China, sent to the son of Heaven a tribute-bearing mission with musicians and jugglers from Ta-tsin, which is now known to have been the Roman Orient.[2] Half a century later, in 166, the repre-

[1] Sir J. F. Davis, *China* ("History of Nations" series, 2 vols), vol I, pp. 23-25.

[2] Professor Friedrich Hirth summarizes the results of his researches

sentatives of Emperor Marcus Aurelius Antoninus arrived in Loyang with ivory, rhinoceros horns, and tortoise shell as presents to the Chinese Throne.[1]

Indeed the Romans would have opened up direct intercourse with China, for once at least, much earlier than they did but for the fact that their missions hitherto accredited to the Chinese Empire had been persistently and successfully obstructed in the progress of their journey by the merchants of Parthia. The cause of this obstruction is not difficult to explain. The Parthians had been the sole dealers in the *Serica vestis*, which was either a silken or cotton fabric, between its Chinese producers and its Roman consumers; they had, frequently, and under great hardships, journeyed to China to purchase new stock, and had for generations reaped large profits from the monopoly. If the Romans should have succeeded in establishing direct relations with China it would have meant to the Parthians the entrance of undesirable competition in their trade, and perhaps the ruin of their lucrative business. As a matter of fact, these apprehensions were unnecessary; for even the mission of 166, though it was able to reach the Chinese capital and was received with courtesy and kindness, failed, as most attempts of the kind in subsequent days did, to inaugurate definite commercial or diplomatic relations between the two greatest empires in the world.[2]

into old Chinese records in the following words: "My interpretation of these records leads to the conclusion that the ancient country of Ta-tsin, called Fu-lin during the Middle Ages, was not 'the Roman Empire with Rome as its capital, but merely its oriental part, viz., Syria, Egypt and Asia Minor; and Syria in the first instance." *China and the Roman Orient* (Shanghai, 1885), p 6. For an account of the audience accorded this mission, see *ibid*, pp. 36-37.

[1] *Ibid.*, Translations E3, H5, O2, Q36, R21.

[2] S. W. Williams, *A History of China* (New York, 1901), pp. 58-60.

The failure of the first Roman embassy in accomplishing its ulterior objects, however, did not put an end to the influx of foreigners into the Celestial Kingdom. Though not disposed to enter into formal relations with distant countries, the Chinese Emperor entertained no objections·to the coming of their subjects into his realm. The Parthians continued to visit China, followed by the Greeks, the Persians, the Nestorians, the Buddhist pilgrims, and the Arabs clear down to the end of the so-called Dark Ages in the West. The great stimulus which urged these adventurers to undertake long journeys and suffer hardships was the trade in the natural and artificial productions of China and India, which had already become considerable in extent and value by the middle of the ninth century. Abu Zaid, one of the two noted Arab travelers of that time, speaks in his narrative (A. D. 877) of the sack of the city of Canfu, then the port of all the Arabian merchants, in which one hundred and twenty thousand Mohammedans, Jews, Christians, and Magians, or Parsees engaged in traffic, were destroyed.[1]

Among the mediaeval travelers to the Chinese Empire many have since become well known for the knowledge of Central Asia which their wanderings gave to Europe; and particularly of this class are the papal nuncios sent out from Rome in the thirteenth century. At that time the irresistible onslaught of the Mongols under Genghis and his successors, with its attendant ravages, was inspiring terror in the minds of the Europeans. Pope Innocent IV, with a view to exhorting the invaders to be more humane, prepared a papal message and sent John of Plano Carpini, a Franciscan monk, to deliver it

[1] Williams, *op. cit.*, p. 62.

to the king of the Tartars in 1246. To the admonitions and exhortations of the Bishop of Rome, the Mongol king made a terse, vigorous and arrogant reply. One passage of that document reads:

The series of your letters contained that we ought to be baptized and to become Christians; we briefly reply, that we do not understand why we ought to do so. As to what is mentioned in your letters, that you wonder at the slaughter of men, and chiefly of Christians, especially Hungarians, Poles, and Moravians, we shortly answer, that this too we do not understand. Nevertheless, lest we should seem to pass it over in silence, we think proper to reply as follows: It is because they have not obeyed the precept of God and of Genghis khan, and, holding bad counsel, have slain our messengers;[1] wherefore God has ordered them to be destroyed, and delivered them into our hands. But if God had not done it, what could man have done to man? But you, inhabitants of the West, believe that you only are Christians, and despise others; but how do you know on whom he may choose to bestow his favor? We adore God, and, in his strength, will overwhelm the whole earth from the east to the west. But if we men were not strengthened by God, what could we do?[2]

Nearly twenty years later, in 1274, Pope Gregory X sent another mission to the Chinese Emperor, composed of the two Polo brothers, Matteo and Nicolo, and accompanied by Marco Polo, the latter's son. However, both these missions failed in their object, namely, the promotion of the Roman Catholic faith in China. For this reason a third embassy was sent out by Pope Nich-

[1] Allusion is here made to Tartar ambassadors, whom the Russians murdered before the battle of Kalka.

[2] Murray, *Marco Polo*, p. 49; passage quoted and notes given in Williams, *The Middle Kingdom* (3d ed., 2 vols, New York, 1851), vol. 2, p. 425.

olas IV in 1288 with John De Corvino at its head, and this time the wishes of the pope were fully carried out in Peking.   To complete the list of noted travelers in the Celestial Empire, there must be mentioned the names of Rubruk, who entered the boundaries of the Empire in 1253; Friar Odoric, who made a tour in China in the first part of the fourteenth century, and Ibn Batuta, the Moor, who visited it about 1342.

CHAPTER II

PRIVILEGES AND PROTECTION OF ALIENS

IT is thus seen that throughout the ancient and middle ages there was almost a continuous flow inward and outward of foreign subjects in China. The question arises, What treatment did they receive from the Chinese Government? From the records of what they did in China and from the narratives which they wrote of their experiences in the course of their travel therein, it appears that they enjoyed many privileges and ample protection. In the first place, during this period there was evidently no policy of seclusion. and confinement in China: her doors, both on her land frontiers and her coasts, were kept widely open to receive whoever chose to enter. Travelers who went to China by water, such as Friar Odoric (1286–1331) and Ibn Batuta (1342), and those who like Carpini journeyed on land, appear to have encountered no difficulty at all in gaining admission at her portals. Nor were there laws in existence restricting the free circulation of foreigners within the Empire. Alien visitors who made tours of the country as Odoric did, visiting one city after another, hardly faced any official obstruction. It seems to be true that a certain kind of passport was necessary to travelers in the country, but, as will be seen later, these were designed to facilitate and protect, rather than to hinder and restrict, them in their travel. Similarly, foreign merchants must have enjoyed the same freedom in entering the country; for this alone could account for the prosperity of com-

18   [140]

merce in the Provinces of Kwangtung, Chekiang, and Fukien during the period under consideration. Foreign trade had so developed, even in 990 B. C., as to make it worth while to levy a duty on imported goods in that year. "During the Tang dynasty (A. D. 618–907) a regular market was opened at Canton and an officer was sent thither to collect the government dues on sales."[1]

There being no permanent diplomatic officers accredited to the Chinese Empire at that time, except, possibly, the papal legate John de Marignolli, who as the representative of Pope Benedict XII, resided in Peking for four years from 1338, the protection of the aliens in the country was left entirely to the Emperor. Those who went to China then were allowed to travel or reside therein, not by right, but simply on sufferance, and could have been easily subjected to restrictions and even discriminations without thereby giving ground for a rightful protest. But the alien merchants and travelers in China of that time implicitly confided to the Emperor the security of their lives and property within his dominion; and it may now be said that their confidence was not at all misplaced. The Imperial Government placed the aliens practically on the same footing as its own subjects: it opened to them public employments and extended to them the fullest protection. Olopum, one of the Nestorians who entered China in the Tang dynasty, was raised to the rank of high priest and national protector by Emperor Kautsung. Marco Polo, though a Venetian by birth and allegiance, was appointed to the office of Prefect of Yangchow, which he held for three years. John de Corvino, a Romish missionary, was given an imperial audience and allowed to build a

[1] R. K. Douglas, *Europe and the Far East* (Cambridge University Press, 1904), p. 2.

Catholic church with a steeple and bells, preach the gospel, and baptize, even in the capital of the Empire. In their travel from one part to another in the country the same passports insuring the protection of the local authorities were issued to foreigners and natives. A passage found in the narratives of Ibn Wahab about his experiences in China shows at once the measure of protection taken in the Tang dynasty in behalf of travelers and the want of discrimination against aliens. The Arab adventurer observes :

If a man would travel from one province to another, he must take two passes with him, one from the governor, the other from the ennuch (or lieutenant). The governor's pass permits him to set out on his journey and contains the names of the traveller and those also of his company, also the ages of the one and the other and the clan to which he belongs. For every traveller in China, whether a native or an Arab, or other foreigner, cannot avoid carrying a paper with him containing everything by which he can be verified. The ennuch's pass specifies the quantities of money or goods which the traveller and those with him take along; this is done for the information of officers at the frontier places where these two passes are examined. Whenever a traveller arrives at any of them, it is registered that such a one, son of such a one, of such a calling, passed here on such a day, month, and year, having such things with him. The government resorts to this means to prevent danger to travellers in their money or goods; for should one suffer loss or die, everything about him is immediately known and he himself or his heirs after his death receive whatever is his.[1] . .

[1] Reinaud, *Relation des voyages faits par les Arabes et les Persons dans l'Inde et à la Chine dans le IXme Siècle de l'ère Chrétienne* (2 vols, Paris, 1845), Tome I, p. 41; quoted by Williams, *A History of China*, p. 73.

CHAPTER III

ADOPTION OF THE "CLOSED-DOOR" POLICY

WITH the beginning of the sixteenth century a marked change took place in the attitude of the Chinese Government toward the foreigners within its territory. Instead of continuing to treat them liberally, the Emperor, from that time down to the middle of the last century, pursued, as a rule, increasingly vigorous measures of surveillance, restriction, and, to a large extent, exclusion in his dealings with the alien merchants and missionaries in his empire. However, when the circumstances and conditions of the time are examined into it will be found that the adoption of this new and apparently retrogressive policy on the part of China was neither unnatural nor unreasonable.

First of all, reports of the conquest of the East Indies and of the forcible occupation of parts of India and the Malay Peninsula by Portuguese adventurers at the commencement of the sixteenth century, as an immediate outcome of the discovery by Vasco da Gama of the maritime route from Europe to Eastern Asia around the Cape of Good Hope, naturally awakened suspicions in the minds of Chinese rulers as to the ulterior motives of those foreigners who were flocking in increasing numbers to the shores of their dominions. The report from the Sultan of Malacca that the Portuguese had by force of arms captured his island-territory in 1511 further alarmed the Emperor, who, influenced by a subject of the Sultan, at once ordered steps to be taken to check the advance of the first Portuguese mission to China, which was then on its way to Peking, and appointed a court to examine its character. Satisfactory credentials were demanded of Thomé Perez, the chief emissary, and his colleagues, but they failed to produce them; thereupon they "were adjudged to be spies and sent back to Canton to be detained till Malacca was restored." In September, 1523, Perez and others died under circumstances not yet definitely ascertained.[1] The aggressions of the Spanish in the Philippines in 1543 were likewise known to the Chinese; and undoubtedly it was a sense of fear inspired by this knowledge that such deeds might be duplicated on their own coast which led them peremptorily to refuse the admission of a party of Spanish Augustine friars in 1575 and again in 1579, and caused them to imprison at Canton in 1580 Martin Ignatius, the envoy of Philip II of Spain.

In this connection it is to be remembered also that toward the end of the sixteenth and during the first part of the seventeenth century the internal conditions of China were such as to make it very desirable to raise a bolt across her doors. The life of the Ming dynasty under its effete and supine rulers was then already at its

---

[1] Of the precise circumstances under which these Portuguese emissaries died, authoritative writers on China give varying versions. To the clause quoted above from *A Short History of China,* p. 77, Williams adds this statement: "This not being done, he and others suffered death in September, 1523; other accounts lead to the inference that he died in prison." Davis, in *China and the Chinese,* vol. I, p. 16, says: "Perez, on his arrival [at Canton] was robbed of his property, thrown into prison, and ultimately, it is supposed, put to death." Douglas, in *Europe and the Far East,* p. 11, appears, however, to be quite sure of the point, as he writes: "These [credentials] having been found to be faulty, Perez was thrown into prison and, together with other Portuguese offenders, was finally beheaded."

ebb; the spirit of rebellion was rife in most parts of the Empire; the Manchus were harassing the northern provinces; in short, the country was then in a hopeless state of defence against the advent of a foreign foe, as indeed she always had been in every previous period of her transition from one dynastic rule to another. It was therefore natural that the rulers of the time should be peculiarly sensitive to any appearances of foreign aggression, and keenly apprehensive lest the strangers from the West might take advantage of China's weakness and resort to schemes of occupation and conquest.

But the apprehensions of attack by designing westerners from without, aggravated as they were by the unsettled conditions within, were not the only reasons for the enforcement of a stringent policy toward aliens in the country. There was a more cogent argument; there was a necessity for the changed attitude. The atrocious conduct of the Portuguese and others appeared to be a just cause for taking precautions to prevent their gradual usurpation of sovereignty over the southern provinces.

As early as 1506 the foreign traders began to be unscrupulous and resort to lawlessness for the purpose of gaining admission into China. A Chinese work records:

During the reign of Chingtih (1506), foreigners from the West, called Fah-lan-ki (or Franks), who said they had tribute, abruptly entered the Bogue, and by their tremendously loud guns, shook the place far and near. This was reported at court, and an order returned to drive them away immediately, and stop the trade.[1]

In 1518, only shortly after his brother Ferdinand suc-

[1] Quoted by Williams in *The Middle Kingdom*, vol. 2, p. 432.

ceeded with difficulty in obtaining the permission to
trade at Canton, Simon Andrada seized the island of
Shong-Chuan (also called St. John's) with his squadron,
erected a fort there, committed acts of piracy on the
native trading-vessels, and engaged in open hostilities
with a Chinese naval force, which however, succeeded
finally in dislodging him from his ill-gotten stronghold.[1]
Twenty years later, in 1537, the Portuguese again clandestinely took possession of several islands in the vicinity
of Canton. "Macao was commenced under the pretext
of erecting sheds for drying goods introduced under the
appellation of tribute, and alleged to have been damaged
in a storm."[2] At Ningpo and Chinchow where they
established a trading factory in 1518, their presence was
hardly less objectionable and they suffered accordingly.
One sinologue writes:

There the conduct of the foreigners had been infamous. They
outraged every law and set the feelings of the people at defiance. They refused to submit to the native authorities, and
on one occasion in revenge for one of their number having
been cheated by a Chinaman they sent an armed band into a
neighboring village and plundered the natives, carrying off a
number of women and young girls. By such deeds they
brought down on themselves the vengeance of the people,
who rose and massacred eight hundred of the offenders and
burnt thirty-five of their ships. At Chinchow in the province
of Fukien they invited disaster by similar misconduct.[3]

The subjects of the king of Portugal were, however,

[1] Davis, *China*, vol. 1, p. 30.

[2] Williams, *A History of China*, p. 76. The subsequent dispute between the countries as to which is the real sovereign over the territory
has been a subject of perennial negotiations, and to-day it still awaits a
final settlement

[3] Douglas, *Europe and the Far East*, p. 11.

not the only disturbers of peace and order in the
Empire. The Dutch were scarcely less violent in making their début on Chinese territory. They commenced
their intercourse with China by the forcible occupation
of the Pescadores, coercing the residents there to build
forts for them, and expelling them from the islands when
they refused to obey the order. They evacuated their
new possessions only when they saw that they stood a
very slim chance of overcoming the 5000 Chinese troops
that were approaching to dislodge them; and then they
retired only to seize Formosa, their occupation of which
gave occasion in 1662 for a war with the Chinese, which
ended with their definitive expulsion from it. The violent
entry of the Dutch on Chinese territory was evidently
still remembered in 1655 when the Dutch East India
Company, having found forcible measures not to be ad-
vancing their commercial aspirations, resorted to the
humbler means of sending a mission to Peking to petition
for the liberty to trade; and after obsequiously performing as ordered, every kind of humiliating ceremony and
homage before the Emperor, the Dutch representatives
obtained nothing but the meagre privilege of sending
an embassy with four ships of trade once in eight years.
The two subsequent missions, in 1664 and 1795 respectively, brought forth no better results.

Ruder still was the manner in which the Englishman
was introduced to the Chinese nation. In the summer
of 1637 Captain Weddel, at command of a fleet of five
ships belonging to the British East India Company, appeared before Macao; but meeting with nonchalance, if
not active obstruction, at the hands of the Portuguese,
he sailed up to Canton and arrived in the neighborhood of
the forts. The authorities at Canton were about to negotiate with the English Captain as to the conferring of

commercial privilege on his compatriots when their minds succumbed to the evil influences of the Portuguese, who "so beslandered them [the English] to the Chinese, reporting them to be rogues, thieves, beggars, and what not, that they became very jealous of the real meaning of the English."[1] Accordingly, the Bogue forts fired upon one of the barges in search of a waterboat, in order to compel the departure of the English vessels. But the latter, taking umbrage at the conduct of the Chinese, displayed their bloody ensigns, attacked the forts with their broadsides, and in a few hours compelled the Chinese garrison to take flight. About one hundred men from the fleet landed, took possession of the forts, and hoisted the British colors. They also seized the ordnance and captured two Chinese junks. In the face of *force majeur* the authorities at Canton, of course, sued for peace, and the English ships were supplied with cargoes after they restored the captured guns and vessels to the rightful owners. But no further trade was carried on by the English at Canton. until 1684; and though in the meantime several attempts were made at Amoy, Ningpo, and Chusan, they resulted in great losses by reason of the heavy tolls levied on the privilege by the local authorities.

Being thus already suspicious of the designs of the aggressive westerners in general, and highly dissatisfied with their manner of conducting intercourse with them, the Chinese people had yet another reason for considering the presence of the foreign traders in their community as undesirable. The bloody contests of mercantile avarice, the conspiracy and intrigue, to which the Portuguese, the Dutch and the English did not blush to

---

[1] Quoted by Davis in *China*, vol. 1, pp. 49-50.

resort for the purpose of excluding one another and thereby securing a monoply of trade, tended also to breed a contempt in the minds of the Chinese rulers for foreign commerce and for those who were thus attempting to promote it. Allusion has already been made heretofore to the misrepresentations which were made by the Portuguese before the Chinese authorities at Canton in 1637 as to the character and motives of the British, and which resulted in a clash of the forces of the two countries then altogether unacquainted with each other; but this was not the only case that occurred. In 1619 the English and Dutch Companies entered into a strange alliance of defence, "arranged after much diplomatic negotiation on the part of their government," [1] for the purpose of forcing the Chinese to trade with them and them alone. Article 10 of the supplementary convention provided:

Touching the question where and in what place ships of defence shall be first employed, . . . the defence shall be employed for the gaining of the trade to China. And to that end the fleet shall be sent to the Philippines, there to hinder and divert the Chinese that they shall not traffic with any others but with us.[2]

"But the Dutch, after fortifying the Pescadores with the aid of the allied fleets, appropriated the trade to themselves, regardless of the protests of the agents of the English Company at Batavia [3]" Three years after the formation of this alliance the Dutch appeared off Macao

---

[1] A. J. Sargent, *Anglo-Chinese Commerce and Diplomacy* (Oxford, 1907), p. 3.

[2] Quoted in *ibid.*

[3] *Ibid.*

with a fleet of seventeen vessels carrying their national colors. The Portuguese at once attacked them and inflicted upon them the loss of their admiral and three hundred men. The defeated squadron withdrew and the Portuguese trade interests were thus successfully protected for the time being.

These examples perhaps suffice to show that the conduct of the alien traders in China during the sixteenth and seventeenth centuries was far from being such as to make a favorable impression on the Chinese Government or to convince it of the desirability of maintaining foreign commercial intercourse. It is, therefore, not surprising that as time went on China began to restrict more and more the conditions under which trade might be prosecuted; that she gradually turned a deaf ear to the repeated petitions, presented by imposing embassies, for an extension of the trading privileges; that by the middle of the eighteenth century Amoy and Ningpo were closed to commerce and the liberty to trade was confined to the single port of Canton; and that even the people, who were always conscious of the benefits of international commerce and desirous of promoting it in spite of the strong disinclination of their rulers toward extensive trading, became finally willing and glad to abide by the imperial policy of non-intercourse, and thereby forego their gains from unlimited foreign trade.

There was, however, yet another chain of circumstances which, though quite different in character from the unsatisfactory conditions born of foreign commerce along the coasts, equally necessitated the pursuance of a more restrictive policy in the treatment of aliens. These were the circumstances developed by the early complete toleration of Christian evangelization by foreign missionaries throughout the empire. For instance, their elevation to high rank tended to make the Catholic priests self-conscious, ostentatious and arrogant, thereby arousing not only jealousy but often deep animosity against them in the minds of Chinese officials. Even Peking was not spared the experience of friction between these two classes of servants of the Chinese Government. Adam Schaal, a distinguished German Jesuit, who was appointed president of the Board of Astronomy by Emperor Shunchi and was his favorite minister, was promptly impeached on the accession of Emperor Canghi on the ground that he and his associates were seducers announcing to the people "a false and pernicious doctrine;" and accordingly they were all banished to Canton, where Schaal died in prison in 1665.

But the dissensions among the various orders of Catholic missionaries were far more dangerous to the well-being of the state, for they tended to weaken the authority of the Emperor over his territory and his subjects. Matteo Ricci, a sensible and broad-minded Jesuit, who arrived in China in 1582, considered ancestral worship as a civil rite and allowed Chinese Christians to continue observing it; and the whole Jesuit order upheld his views. Their opponents, the Dominicans and Franciscans, took exception to this opinion and considered ancestral worship as idolatrous. Another line of cleavage between the orders formed on the meaning of the word Thien or Heaven in Chinese; the Jesuits interpreting it to mean the true God, but their opponents considering it to denote only the material universe devoid of all holiness. The disputes were referred to the Bishop of Rome. Innocent X condemned the Jesuit views but Alexander VII later approved them. When Clement XI ascended to the headship of the Catholic Church he took steps to enforce his views, which were those of the

Dominicans and Franciscans. He interdicted the worship of either ancestors or Thien, and through his representative in China enjoined the Chinese Catholics not to disobey his decree. Emperor Kanghi, who in 1700 had declared in an edict that Thien meant the true God and that ancestral worship was a civil institution, taking offence at this invasion of his sovereign power, issued in retaliation an edict, tolerating those who preached the doctrine of Ricci but declaring his resolution to persecute those who followed the opinions of Maigrot, the original propounder of the Dominican and Franciscan views.. From that time on Christian missionaries fell rapidly into disfavor with the Throne; until in 1723 Emperor Yung Chung in an edict denounced all of them, and in 1737 Emperor Kienlung, conscious of the fact that the mischievous priests were laboring in secret to subvert his authority over his own subjects, and perhaps recalling at the same time that the leader and organizer of the most inveterate anti-Manchu party, which seized Fukien and Formosa and defied the Manchu rulers at Peking for decades after they had ascended the throne of China was a Catholic, ordered the vigorous persecution of Christians and Christian missionaries everywhere except Peking. The decree was so loyally executed by the provincial authorities that by 1810 there were only 29 European priests left in all China, with about 200,000 converts.[1]

Thus it seems clear that the policy of non-intercourse, adopted at the beginning of the modern era and enforced with increasing vigor in the following three centuries, was but an outcome of the unsatisfactory condi-

[1] Davis, *China*, vol. I, pp. 37-41; Douglas, *Europe and the Far East*, pp. 13-19.

tions bred by 'foreign intercourse in its commercial and religious aspects during that period. It was not espoused and pursued by China without cause or reason. As viewed by her rulers of the time, it was at once a wise and necessary measure: it was intended to be both a remedy for the ills which foreign trade and foreign religion had already produced on their territory and on their subjects and a preventive against the dangers to the safety of their nation which appeared still latent in them.

CHAPTER IV

A SURVEY OF THE EFFECTS OF THE NEW POLICY

LIKE many other remedies and preventives, the application of the "closed-door" policy gave rise to new ailments, which soon developed into maladies, quite as serious as those which it was intended to cure and prevent, in the constitution of the Chinese State. For the attempt taken by the Government practically to exclude foreign religion and trade bred a spirit of discontent in the minds of the westerners resident in the empire. The dissatisfaction was especially keen on the part of the foreign merchants; the missionaries, who occasionally succeeded in penetrating into the inland to carry on their proselytizing work, being willing to submit to the will of the local authorities. These merchants were far from being contented to have their mercantile activities confined to the single city of Canton under any circumstances. If the duties levied on commerce by the officials in that southernmost provincial capital were oppressive, they wanted to remove their trade to some place where they hoped it might be carried on under less onerous conditions; if on the other hand, the trade at Canton was profitable, they wanted to extend it to other ports of the Empire so that their gains might be proportionally augmented. It was evidently this "spirit of mercantile avarice" which induced them to send expensive missions one after another to Peking to petition for more and more commercial privileges; which, so far as their practical object was

32   [154

concerned, always failed. And the repeated failure of
these missions tended only, on one hand, to aggravate
the grievances of the western merchants and make them
more insistent on their demands and, on the other, to
increase the arrogance of the Chinese authorities and to
all appearances confirm their belief that foreigners could
not live without trade with China.

The foreign merchants and the Chinese authorities thus
drew farther apart from each other; they gradually ranged
themselves on opposite sides; and their respective interests became more and more irreconcilable. Suspicions
arose on the part of the traders as to the good faith of
the Celestial officials in protecting foreign persons and
property, and defiance of their authority soon became the
order of the day. On the other hand, the Chinese rulers,
as they found the foreign subjects to be increasingly recalcitrant, applied to them with greater industry and
persistence the policy of discrimination and exclusion.
Hence arose between the foreign residents and the Chinese authorities during the last half-century of the Pre-
conventional Period a constant friction, which eventually
resulted in open war between China and Great Britain,
in the consequent abolition of the precarious régime of
foreign intercourse, and in the creation of another artificial system for the conduct of the relations between the
Chinese and the westerners. The evidences of friction
were most clearly reflected in those phases of intercourse
which related to foreign trade, to the government and
protection of the aliens, and to the question of jurisdiction over them. A review of these problems in the
order mentioned is necessary to a due appreciation of
the significance of the changes affecting the status of
aliens in China, brought about by the treaty of Nanking
of August 29, 1842.

CHAPTER V −

ORGANIZATION, REGULATION, AND PROTECTION OF FOREIGN TRADE

As has already been indicated, after the foreign merchants made a number of attempts to evade the oppression of monopoly and official extortion at Canton by seeking a less trammeled trade in Amoy, Ningpo, and Chusan, and failed on account of the more onerous conditions required of them there, they were finally compelled to return to the port, from which they sought to escape, by an imperial edict of 1757, which closed all the other places in the empire to foreign commerce. From that year to 1842 Canton, the southernmost city in China, was, therefore, the only seat of trade and intercourse open to the foreigner. The restriction as to the place of foreign trade was preceded by a more inconvenient one as to the persons with whom it might be conducted. In 1702 there was appointed the "Emperor's Merchant," in whose hands was concentrated the entire trade, and through whom alone foreigners were allowed to sell their imports and purchase native products for export.[1] The introduction of this "monster in trade," as he was called by the mercantile community, was vigorously objected to, and he soon disappeared. His place was filled by a combination of Chinese merchants formed in 1720 for the purpose of regulating prices in

[1] H. B. Morse, *The International Relations of the Chinese Empire* (London, 1910), p. 64.

tea and silk in the interest of their own purses.[1] The
Cohong, as the organization was called, was formally
given a charter by the authorities in 1760 to carry on a
monopoly of the trade, but its career was brief; for by
reason of its insolvency it was dissolved by order of
the government in 1771. Trade, however, was not much
benefited by this stroke of official regulation, for its
immediate result was the creation of a new monopolistic
association, of at first twelve, and later thirteen Chinese
merchants, known under the old name of Cohong.[2]
This body, like its predecessor, was granted the exclusive
privilege of trading with foreigners, the retail dealers
in imported goods being able to carry on their trade
only on its sufferance, and subject to suppression by the
authorities at its instance. In return for the valuable
monopoly the Cohong had, however, to perform onerous
duties, political or diplomatic as well as commercial and
fiscal. It was responsible for the customs dues on the
whole trade, whether prosecuted by individuals or
organized companies, and also for the good behaviour
of the entire foreign population in the factories and on
board vessels lying in the port. It was the sole intermediary between the Chinese official and the foreigner,
and was always bound to transmit communications between
the two. Where the local authorities or the Imperial
Government had issued orders and decrees in regulation
of the commerce or conduct of the foreigner, it must
see to it that they were obeyed: and if obedience was
not secured it must bear the consequences of official
wrath, though no special authority was given to it to
enforce such obedience. The only weapon at its disposal,

[1] Morse, *op cit.*, p. 65.
[2] *Ibid*, pp. 67-68.

in such a case, was the threat to stop trading altogether, which proved in most instances sufficiently terrible to coerce the foreign traders to act in conformity with the will of the authorities.[1]

On the side of the foreign traders there was no such compact and exclusive organization as the Cohong. They represented some twelve nationalities[2] and carried on their trade independently of one another not only as between the merchants of different nations but, with one or two exceptions, as between those of the same nation. The exceptions were the two East India Companies, the British and the Dutch, of which the former, by reason of its power, wealth, and organization as well as on account of the early exit of its rival from the scene, was by far the more important factor in the history of foreign trade and intercourse at Canton. By virtue of its charter granted by Parliament the British East India Company was entitled to a monopoly of the trade between China and Great Britian, and in enjoyment of that right it maintained in Canton a large force of employees and a permanent agency. Besides, it exercised an effective authority and control over all British subjects and Indiamen trading in China through the power of granting and revoking licenses without which they could

---

[1] Sargent, *Anglo-Chinese Commerce and Diplomacy*, pp 15-17.

[2] These included all the great powers of the West except Russia. One of her subjects, Krusenstern, the circumnavigator, sailed to Canton in 1806, but while he succeeded in selling his goods and reloading his ship, an imperial edict was soon issued, condemning his enterprise and prohibiting the renewal of similar attempts in the future. The ground of the prohibition was that the treaties of 1689 and 1727 did not provide for trade and intercourse anywhere except across the northern frontiers of the empire See the edict of Emperor Kia-King on the case, January, 1806. Sir George Staunton, Bart. F. R. S., *Penal Laws of China* (London, 1810), p 518

not trade there at all. The select committee of supercargoes, which was at the head of the Company's establishment in Canton, "had wide power of arrest and
seizure both of persons and ships contravening the Acts
of Parliament under which they enjoyed their privileges."[1]

By reason of these advantages accruing from its organized power the Company, as compared to the individual
trader, stood in a privileged position in Canton. It
enjoyed with the Chinese authorities a prestige and
influence which no other body of foreign merchants
shared. The local officials recognized its representatives
as a kind of responsible governors of all the foreign
factories and negotiated and communicated with them
about matters pertaining to the regulation of trade and
the government of the foreign traders. Thus in 1715,
for instance, the Hoppo, collector of customs, entered
into an agreement of 8 articles with the supercargoes
of the Company conferring upon British merchants a
number of privileges.[2] Such privileges, once obtained
by the Company, were at once enjoyable by all other
foreign traders without a separate grant on the part of
the authorities. For this reason the western merchants
looked for protection against official oppression and the
misconduct of the Cohong, not to their own consuls,
who were, after the fashion of the time, themselves merchants, and who "not being credited by the Chinese
Government, came and went, hoisted or lowered their
flags, without the slightest notice from the authorities,"[3]

[1] Sargent, *Anglo-Chinese Commerce and Diplomacy*, p. 17 n.; citing
26 Geo III, cap 57; 33 Geo III, cap 52; 53 Geo. III, cap. 155.

[2] Peter Auber, *China An Outline of its Government, Laws, and
Policy, and of the British and Foreign Embassies to, and Intercourse
with, that Empire* (London, 1834), pp. 152-155

[3] Williams, *A History of China*, p. 100.

but rather to the Company, which was the actual bulwark of their privileges and their security. Nor was the Company slow in turning its influence and power to account; it was always ready to protect not only British interests but all foreign interests. In the words of a competent authority:

It was the only representative foreign body and, as such, was compelled by its traditions to champion the cause of foreigners in general.[1]

Under these circumstances the trade with the Cohong was not necessarily disadvantageous to the foreign merchants. The rule permanently adopted in 1754,[2] which required every foreign ship to offer a security merchant selected from among the hong merchants, was a measure designed to increase the responsibility of the Cohong for the amount of customs revenue due upon its cargo and for the peaceful conduct of its crew rather than one intended to place a hardship upon the traders; and this was all the truer because seldom would a hong merchant refuse to act as security for a trustworthy captain or supercargo. In the actual process of trading,[3] which consisted mostly in the bartering of foreign commodities for native products, as Indian opium and English cotton goods for Chinese tea and silk, the Cohong had no more power to dictate prices than the Company or the individual traders; an attempt to extort easy terms on imports in the hands of the foreigner would be met by a

[1] Sargent, *Anglo-Chinese Diplomacy*, p. 20.

[2] Auber, *China*, pp 168-169

[3] For an account of the various steps required by the Regulations to be taken before a foreign merchantman could unload, see J. W. Foster, *American Diplomacy in the Orient* (Boston, 1903), pp 33-35; Morse, *International Relations*, pp. 74-76.

like demand in respect of the export cargo in the possession of the hong merchant. Besides, every trader was at liberty to reship his cargo from Canton if he could not find a hong merchant willing to accept his terms. In short, "monopoly was met by monopoly."[1] In the words of another authority:

The Cohong system, monopolistic though it was, was one which, on the whole, worked with little friction. The foreign traders enjoyed the practical monopoly assured to them by their distance from the home market and the difficulty of communication, while the East India Company, still holding a monopoly of the trade with England, paid the dividends on their stocks in these years solely from the profits of their China trade.[2]

Nor did the foreign traders suffer much from the system of the Cohong in other respects. The opportunity, enjoyed by the hong merchants and sometimes utilized in their own interest, of first reading themselves the communications addressed by the factories to the authorities, as a result of their being the sole intermediaries between the two, was taken away from them in 1814 when Sir George Staunton, as a representative of the Company's select committee at Canton, obtained from the Viceroy among other concessions the permission "to address the government in Chinese through the Hong merchants without the contents being inquired into."[3] In 1831 the privilege was robbed of all its value to the hong merchants when the concession was made that if they intercepted letters and refused to transmit them,

[1] Sargent, *Anglo-Chinese Commerce and Diplomacy*, p. 20.
[2] Morse, *International Relations*, p. 85.
[3] Auber, *China*, p. 250.

two or three foreigners might go to the city gate and give them to the guard for delivery to the authorities.[1]

As against the misconduct of the Provincial authorities the foreign trader had but few remedies. The power of regulating the trade, aside from the few imperial edicts in general terms, rested mainly with the officials at Canton and in their hands it was jealously guarded against encroachment. In 1829 when the representatives of the East India Company insisted on the reduction of the heavy port-charges on shipping and threatened to stop the trade altogether, the Viceroy replied:

As to commerce, let the said nation do as it pleases; as to regulations, those that the celestial empire fixes must be obeyed.[2]

But there were ways of seeking relief from the hostile attitude of the authorities toward foreign interests which, though few, were not always ineffective. In 1715 the supercargoes of the Company laid their grievances before the Hoppo in a conference, and the result was a satisfactory agreement of eight articles, one of which was:

8th: That the Hoppo would protect them from all insults and impositions of the common people and Mandarins, who were annually laying new duties and exactions which they were forbidden to allow of.[3]

When thirteen years later, in 1728, a surtax of 10 per cent was levied on all goods sold to foreign merchants,

[1] Morse, *International Relations*, p. 70.

[2] J. F. Davis, *China and the Chinese* (2 vols., London, 1857), vol. 1, p. 99

[3] Auber, *China*, pp. 153-154

the latter at once set up a campaign of protest and agitation in order to have it removed. Their complaints finally reached the Court in Peking and in 1736 Emperor Kienlung upon his accession to the throne issued an edict abolishing the extra duty.[1]

Direct appeals to the Throne over the head of the Provincial authorities constituted another remedy against their cupidity and abuse of power. These took the form and character either of an impressive embassy or of a memorial by a humble individual. As an instance of the latter kind may be cited the case of Mr. Flint, who, as an agent of the East India Company, went up to Tientsin in 1759 and there sent a petition to the Emperor, praying for relief from the extortions of the Hoppo at Canton. While the petitioner was subsequently tried and imprisoned for his adventure, his efforts to safeguard the foreign trading interests were not fruitless. As the result of his memorial an imperial commissioner was dispatched to Canton to inquire into the complaints made against the collector of customs and settle the matter. After holding a court of investigation and trial the commissioner assembled before him the traders of all nations and announced to them that the corrupt Hoppo was degraded and that all duties paid over the regular six per cent on goods, the perquisites of two per cent to the customs officer, and the tonnage dues on ships should be remitted.[2]

The expedient of sending embassies to Peking in order to lay before the Throne the grievances of the foreign merchants and pray for their redress proved less successful in accomplishing the immediate purposes of

---

[1] Auber, *China*, pp 158-162.

[2] Williams, *A History of China*, pp 97-98, Davis, *China and the Chinese*, vol. 1, pp. 48-50.

their promoters, as shown in the mission of Lord Macartney in 1783 and in that of Lord Amherst in 1816. Yet, the very fact of their being sent to Peking to appeal over the head of the Provincial authorities necessarily produced a wholesome effect upon the foreign commercial interests, for it tended to place a check upon the corruptions or excesses of such authorities.

However, the most effective means in the possession of the foreign factories to compel the authorities to hear their complaints and regard their wishes was the threat to stop trading. Just as the Cohong frequently used this weapon to enforce obedience on the part of the foreign community, so the latter, too, knew how to wield it for the purpose of exercising a restraint on the conduct of the Chinese officials, who, though always pretending to be indifferent to the maintenance of trade, were in fact as unwilling as the merchants to have it cease, the two practical reasons being that they were responsible to the Peking Government for the customs revenue, and that they derived their incomes mainly from this source.

There was another danger, born of the peculiar conditions under which foreign trade was conducted at Canton, from which the alien merchants sought protection. This was the occasional insolvency of one or more of the hong merchants, with whom alone they were permitted to trade. Attracted by high rates of interest, which ranged from two to five per cent a month, money entered Canton freely, especially from India.[1] During the seven years beginning with 1774 the total amount of debts incurred by seven hong merchants and some shopkeepers

[1] Hunter, *Fau-Kwai*, p. 39; cited in Morse, *International Relations*, p. 68.

who traded through them reached $4,296,650.[1] A ma-
jority of the creditors, who were resident in India, applied to the Indian Government for assistance in seeking
a recovery, and accordingly, Sir Edward Vernon, admiral on the station, dispatched a frigate to Canton bearing
a remonstrance to Isontock, the Chinese Viceroy.[2] In
view of this display of force the Viceroy memorialized
the Throne on the subject, and in response the Emperor
sent him an edict ordering the liquidation of the debts
by the entire body of hong merchants, and renewing the
interdiction, proclaimed in 1760, against borrowing from
strangers. The whole amount of indebtedness, after
making a reduction, was ultimately paid with funds
which " were provided by a surtax on the foreign trade:
Tls. 1·200 a picul on green tea, Tls. 0·620 on black tea,
and Tls. 6 on silk." [3]

After 1782 the Cohong was given the administration
of the so-called Consoo fund, raised by a direct levy of
three per cent on the foreign trade, and available to meet
any liability for debts, fines, losses, etc.; [4] and at the same
time its joint responsibility for money obligations owing
to foreigners was confirmed. The burden thus thrust
upon the Cohong was an onerous one. From 1793 to
1810, $3,550,000 were paid by it in liquidation of debts
due to foreign traders, including the East India Company, from Chinese merchants. In the period from 1823
to 1829 the amount of foreign indebtedness on the books
of insolvent Chinese was $2,960,066, and the hong mer-
chants as a body again liquidated it.[5] In 1836 one of the

[1] Morse, *International Relations*, p. 161.

[2] Auber, *China*, pp. 182-183; Davis, *China and the Chinese*, vol 1, p 56

[3] Morse, *International Relations*, pp 161-162

[4] *Ibid*, p. 68.   [5] *Ibid.*, p. 162

hong members, the Hingtai firm, became insolvent to the amount of $2,261,439, which sum was ascertained by a joint committee of three Chinese and three foreign merchants. On April 21, 1837, the Cohong, at the instance of the foreign creditors, petitioned the Viceroy for the order that the debtor firm should liquidate its indebtedness; but the Viceroy informed the petitioners that "they were held jointly responsible—the property of the foreigners cannot be left without an ultimate guarantee for its safety."[1] An examination of the accounts was ordered, but no satisfaction was obtained. At the same time the firm of Kinqua, another member of the Cohong, also became insolvent to the sum of $1,000,000, all due to foreign merchants. The two claims were amalgamated, and after an attempt made by the creditors to negotiate a settlement with the Cohong failed on account of a difference of opinion as to the period in which liquidation should be effected, the matter was referred by some in a memorial to the British Government and by others in a petition to the Viceroy at Canton. While this two-sided representation was respectively engaging the attention of the authorities in both countries, an agreement was concluded between the creditors and the Cohong, whereby the debts of two firms were to be paid by annual instalments, those of Hingtai in eight and a

---

[1] *Corr. Rel. China,* 1840, p. 262; quoted in Morse, *International Relations,* p. 163.

According to Davis, the Cohong was, after the settlement of 1829, released from joint liability for the debts of its individual members. "The eyes of the government," says he, "were, however, opened to the mischievous consequences of the regulation which obliged the corporation of Hong merchants to be answerable for the debts of any member of the Consoo, however improvident or dishonest; and it was enacted that from henceforth the corporate responsibility should cease." —*China and the Chinese,* vol. I, p. 97.

half years, without interest, and those of Kinqua in ten years, with simple interest at six per cent. The instalments due on the two debts for the years 1838 and 1839 had already been paid when war broke out toward the end of the latter year; from that time on further payments were suspended, and the question was finally made the subject-matter of article 5 of the treaty of Nanking, August 29, 1842, in which China was bound to pay the round sum of $3,000,000 in settlement of the debts.[1]

[1] Morse, *International Relations*, pp. 162-165. It is interesting to note here that while debts owing by the Chinese were generally liquidated, those due from British merchants after 1834 often evaporated, as in 1835 and 1837, through the ready absconding of the debtors and the powerlessness of the superintendents to compel satisfaction. See 25 *Br. and For. State Papers* (1836-1837), pp. 390, 395.

CHAPTER VI

LEGAL CONTROL OVER FOREIGNERS

In the second quarter of the nineteenth century the problem of maintaining a control over the foreign population in Southern China became increasingly difficult. The number of " people from afar " grew steadily: at Canton there were 165 foreign residents in 1832 and 307 in 1836.[1] Macao in 1830 was the home of 3351 white persons with 1129 slaves.[2] Among these were British,[3] Indians, Parsees, Americans, Portuguese, Germans, Dutch, Swedish, Danish, French, Spanish and Italians. While these diverse foreigners lived together and constituted a community of their own, they had no common organization over them. There were indeed consuls in Macao and Canton: England in 1699 sent a commission to Mr. Catchpool, the East India Company's chief supercargo, to be "king's minister or consul for the whole Empire of China and the adjacent islands[4]; the United States Congress in 1786 appointed Major Samuel Shaw as consul at Canton[5]; and the French tricolor was

---

[1] Morse, *International Relations*, p. 72.   *Ibid.*, p. 46

[2] " For several months in the year there are not less than two thousand of Her Majesty's subjects at Canton, Whampoa, Macao, and the immediately adjacent anchorages" Cap. Elliot to Vt. Palmerston, Sept. 26, 1837, 25 *Br and For. State Papers* (1836-1837), 397

[4] Williams, *A History of China*, p. 94.

[5] Foster, *Am. Dipl. in the Orient*, p 32. This office was purely honorary, " for there were neither salary nor perquisites annexed to it." *Ibid.*

hoisted in 1802[1]; but all these representatives were themselves merchants, neither accredited to the Chinese Government nor recognized by it as official agents of their nations or nationals. The control of the foreign residents was naturally and properly left to the Chinese authorities.

The Chinese notion of territorial sovereignty and jurisdiction, as entertained, though at times vaguely, by the officials of the Empire in the early days, was not essentially different from that which is maintained by modern international jurists. Within the territory of the Empire the imperial laws were supreme; foreigners who went there were permitted to stay only on sufferance; they were under the same obligation as the Chinese subjects to obey them and subject to the same penalties enacted to punish their violation. This notion was vigorously followed by the Chinese rulers in their intercourse with the westerners. The exercise by them of the absolute power to regulate commerce within their dominions has already been shown.[2] When Commissioner Lin Tseh-su undertook to suppress opium importation and opium smoking the right of regulation was again exercised. When Captain Elliot, British Superintendent of Trade, refused to accept on behalf of British subjects his proposition that any vessel bringing opium into China in future should be confiscated, and that the guilty persons should submit themselves to the penalties of Chinese law, the commissioner asked him this question: "How can you bring the laws of your nation with you to the Celestial Empire?"[3] And in practice, he followed his

[1] Douglas, *Europe and the Far East*, p 57

[2] See *supra*, pp 34 ff.

[3] Sargent, *Anglo-Chinese Commerce and Diplomacy*, pp 75-76.

views unhesitatingly. Among the measures which he enforced on foreign merchants in order to effect a complete suppression of opium were those of search in the factories, confiscation, imprisonment, and expulsion. He apparently felt sure that in applying these methods of constraint to vindicate the laws of the Empire he was only exercising a right appertaining to a sovereign and independent nation, and conferred on him under imperial sanction.

It was also in exercise of the rights flowing from territorial sovereignty that the Chinese rulers placed the government of foreigners in the hands of their own deputies. "In the Hong merchants' factories," to quote the language of the Viceroy at Canton, "where foreigners live, let them be under the restraint and control of the Hong merchants."[1] Regulations were made and adopted from time to time for observance by the traders and other foreigners. Thus they were required to return from Canton to their home or to Macao when the trading season was over; they were prohibited to walk about in the streets of their own accord, row on the river, or ride in sedan chairs; to bring women, guns, spears, or other arms to the factories.[2] These regulations were enforced upon the foreigners under the penalty of deportation for the offenders or of the stoppage of trade for the whole foreign community. In 1830, for instance, the prohibition of trade was threatened to compel the departure of three women on visit from Macao to the English factory, and later in the year the threat was again employed for the same purpose in the case of a visit by some American women.

[1] Morse, *International Relations*, p. 70.
[2] *Ibid.*, pp. 69-71.

CHAPTER VII

ALIENS SUBJECT TO CHINESE CRIMINAL JURISDICTION[1]

WITH regard to their criminal jurisdiction over the alien, Chinese rulers of the time were even more jealous in guarding it against infringement than in keeping intact their control over him in civil matters. The rule of policy pursued by them was that crimes committed on Chinese territory should be punished according to Chinese laws. Section 34 of the Penal Code, which was in full force before the system of extraterritoriality was formally introduced by treaty, provided: " In general, all foreigners who come to submit themselves to the government of the Empire, shall, when guilty of offences, be tried and sentenced according to the established laws." The seeming deviations which they are sometimes said to have allowed on their own part in practice are more apparent than real, apart from the observation which may be made that even if they constituted true exceptions they would only all the more prove the rule.

Thus take a few examples. In the agreement of 1715 entered into between the Chinese Hoppo and the supercargoes of the East India Company there was an article

[1] The question of jurisdiction in civil suits between Chinese and foreigners did not arise in this period, as they were readily settled by direct negotiation between the parties themselves. " Business disputes between foreigners were never brought to the knowledge of the Chinese, and this was quite in accord with the Chinese practice of settling civil suits through the guild, or by arbitration—never by appealing in the courts." Morse, *International Relations*, p. 96.

which provided in part "that if their English servants
should commit any disorder or fault deserving punishment, the Chinese should not take upon them to punish,
but should complain to the supercargoes, and they would
see them sufficiently punished according to the crime."[1]
This provision as well as the other seven in the compact
was assented to by the Chinese customs collector at
Canton, but "there is no evidence that they were ever
carried out."[2] Moreover, even if the authorities had
followed the provision in practice, still they can hardly
be considered to have thereby assented to the principle
of extraterritoriality, as it is now understood; for their
practice would have been in accord with the international
usage of the time, which survives to this day in the principal maritime states except Great Britain, allowing to
the seamen of foreign vessels lying in port a considerable
measure of exemption from the territorial laws.

Again, in 1810, a Chinese was found dead in a boat at
Whampoa and the murderer was believed to have been
an English seaman of the *Royal George*, one of the
Company's ships, though no evidence was adduced to
identify him. The Chinese authorities at first refused to
give clearance papers to the British vessels unless the
offender was surrendered, but they finally issued them
on condition that the culprit, when discovered, should
be punished agreeably to the laws of England.[3] Undoubtedly the acceptance of such a condition by the
local authorities, might on first thought be deemed as a
surrender of their jurisdiction over territorial crimes ;
but when viewed closely in the light of the circumstances,

[1] Auber, *China*, p. 153.
[2] Morse, *International Relations*, p. 65.
[3] Auber, *China*, pp. 237-238.

the act of acceptance, it would seem, signifies no more
than the adoption of the most convenient way of terminating an impasse brought on by the Chinese themselves
in holding all the English ships responsible for the acts
of a criminal whose identity was not known to them.
There was, therefore, no real ground upon which to base
an inference that the settlement of the case in that way,
was intended to establish a precedent showing the concession on the part of the Chinese rulers of the important principle of territorial jurisdiction.

Still less pertinently could a case of direct settlement
between the parties, such as that of the death of a Chinese
woman in 1821 alleged to have been caused by the negligence of the Company's ship *Lady Melville*, in which
the relatives of the deceased agreed not to bring the
matter before a court but consider it as closed in consideration of the payment of an indemnity by the ship,
be interpreted as a relinquishment of plenary jurisdiction
by the Chinese authorities; for such a composition for
crimes was then fully recognized by the Chinese law, the
theory of it being that the governmental machinery was
maintained to preserve the public peace and order, and
that so long as a crime was committed by one individual
upon another without disturbing the state of public
tranquillity, the officials were not bound to take cognizance of it unless the injured party or his family peti-
tioned them for their intervention and redress.

It has been suggested that the supplementary treaty
of Kiakhta concluded with Russia on October 18, 1768,
amending article 10 of the "Treaty of the Frontier,"
October 21, 1727, relative to the suppression of brigandage and other disturbances along the conterminous
frontiers, may be considered as forming a veritable
exception to the rule of plenary jurisdiction maintained

by China within her territory.[1] The amended article
provided that armed persons who crossed their own
boundary line and committed acts of brigandage on the
foreign side should be arrested and detained in order to
be jointly examined by the local authorities, and that
if they were Chinese subjects, they "shall be delivered
up, without distinction of persons, to the tribunal which
governs the outlying provinces, and shall be punished
with death: the subjects of Russia shall be delivered up
to their senate, to suffer the same penalty;" adding that
"the murderers shall be brought to and executed at the
frontier."[2]   This stipulation, which was, by its terms,
strictly reciprocal, far from establishing the principle of
extraterritoriality, seems to have involved nothing more
than an application, in exceptional circumstances, of the

---

[1] Morse, in his *International Relations of the Chinese Empire*, p. 60,
states that the treaty of August 27, 1689, "introduced the first elements
of the principle of extra-territoriality; if any of either nationality
committed acts of violence on the foreign side of the frontier, they
were to be sent to their own side of the frontier and delivered to the
officers of their own nation, 'who will inflict on them the death penalty
as punishment for their crimes.'" This opinion appears to be based on
the English translation of the Russian text alone, for the Latin and
Chinese texts of the same treaty (to be found respectively in *Treaties
between China and Foreign States*, i, pp. 1 and 2) do not, on a close
examination, seem to support it. The language of the Latin text, as
respects article 2, is vague and ambiguous, while that of the corresponding article, numbered 4, of the Chinese text appears to confirm
rather than impair the principle of territorial jurisdiction. A considerable amount of uncertainty of expression characterizes the treaty of
October 21, 1727, also. In fact, the various texts of the two treaties
show not only a want of agreement in their meaning and purport, but,
as in the case of the first treaty, a lack of correspondence in the numer-
ical designation of the articles The ambiguity of the meaning of the
treaty of 1689 led to the negotiation and conclusion of that of 1727,
and again the vagueness of the provisions in the latter, particularly on
the subject of punishment of crimes along the frontier, gave birth to
the supplementary treaty of 1768.

[2] *Treaties between China and Foreign States*, i, p 18.

principle of personal law, which is found in the criminal jurisprudence of substantially all civilized nations to a greater or less extent. The situation with which the two governments were dealing was that of a boundary line which, although adjusted in principle, was in many places actually uncertain. The country was sparsely settled, and the jurisdiction within which an offence was committed would often be difficult to determine. In these circumstances the two governments, in order to suppress brigandage, which had more than once caused serious controversies and put in jeopardy their friendly relations, agreed that in case of violent crimes along the frontier, the offenders should be handed over to their own authorities for punishment. Examples of similar arrangements, designed to meet similar conditions, may be found in treaties between other countries. The United States and Mexico have, for instance, agreed to the crossing of the frontier by the armed forces of either country in pursuit of hostile Indians.

But while the exceptions, it is thus seen, are more apparent than real, the rule is exhibited in sharp relief in a great number of cases. In Canton, for instance, aside from the cases occurring respectively in 1689, 1722, 1807, and 1824, in each of which the alien defendant was sentenced to pay a fine, there arose a number of those in which death sentence was executed by Chinese authorities on foreign criminals. In 1780 a French seaman of the licensed ship *Success* killed a Portuguese sailor of the *Stormont* of the East India Company, it was said, in self-defence. The criminal took refuge in the French consulate, but on demand of the local authorities he was given up by the consul and publicly strangled by order of the governor of the province.[1]   Four years

[1] Morse, *International Relations*, p. 102. "This was the first instance

later, in November 1784, a gunner on the licensed ship
Lady Hughes, in firing a salute, wounded three Chinese
boatmen, one of whom died the following day from the
effect of the injury. The foreign factories attempted to
shelter him from arrest, but the Chinese officials demanded his surrender and, not obtaining it, arrested and
kept in custody the supercargo of the ship, evidently to
bring pressure to bear upon the alien traders. This
measure proved successful, for on November 30, in
order to secure the release of the supercargo, the gunner
was given up by the factories to the Chinese authorities,
who caused him to be strangled on January 8, 1785, in
execution of a judgment received from Peking.[1]   Again,
on September 23, 1821, Francis Terranova, an Italian
sailor on board the American ship *Emily,* threw down
an earthern jar on a Chinese woman, who was selling
spirits and fruits in a boat alongside of the ship, and
thereby caused her death. The Chinese authorities held
a trial of the accused on board the vessel in the midst of
some forty Americans and ordered him to be put in irons
and delivered up. On the captain's refusal to hand him
over, the American trade was stopped. A week later,
on October 25, the prisoner was, however, brought into
the city, given a second trial, again adjudged guilty, and
strangled on the public execution ground.[2] It was
stated that at the trial on board the *Emily* the American
merchants said to the Chinese judge: "We are bound
to submit to your laws while we are in your waters, be
they ever so unjust. We will not resist them."[3]

of an European being executed for the murder of another in China, and
was considered to form a dangerous precedent." Auber, p. 181.

[1] Davis, *China and the Chinese,* vol. 1, pp. 57-59; Auber, *China,* pp
183-188.

[2] Williams, *A History of China,* p 108; Davis, *China and the Chinese,*
p. 90; Foster, *American Diplomacy in the Orient,* pp. 40-41.

[3] *North American Review* (January-June, 1835), 58, 66.

. Even in Macao, a place leased to Portugal for an annual rental of 500 taels, which was paid regularly until 1849, there had always been a Chinese officer to sit in judgment of all criminal cases. In 1749 certain alleged criminals took refuge in the convent of Nossa Senhora do Amparo, and the Portuguese refused to deliver them up; but as soon as the Chinese authorities cut off their supplies and ordered other traders to leave the city, they yielded and accepted a convention, the fifth article of which "provided that, in case of homicide, the Chinese official at Casa Branca should go to Macao to sit as coroner, and that he should transmit the evidence to Canton for final judgment."[1] In 1773 an Englishman, Francis Scott, was charged with the killing of a Chinese at Macao, and he was arrested, tried, and acquitted by the Portuguese authorities; but the Chinese authorities insisted upon, and finally obtained, his surrender to them, retried him, and executed him.[2] In fact the criminal jurisdiction in Macao was exercised by Chinese rulers not only in cases wherein a Chinese was concerned, as plaintiff or defendant, but also in those between foreigners.[3] "In cases of murder," states a contemporary writer, "though it should happen that an European killed another in Macao, the Portuguese government was not, at an early period at least, suffered to try the cause. The Chinese mandarins judged, condemned, and executed the criminal, and that even within the walls of the city."[4]

Jealous as the Chinese authorities were in preserving intact their rightful jurisdiction over territorial crimes, they do not appear, on the other hand, to have evaded the responsibility of protection, which is the complement

---

[1] Morse, *Intern. Rel*, p. 45.
[3] *Ibid*, p. 100.
[2] *Ibid.*, pp. 101-102.
[4] Auber, *China*, p. 85.

of the right of jurisdiction. In 1721 an officer of the
Hoppo accidentally died near Whampoa, and a Chinese
Mandarin having the command of 1,000 soldiers forthwith arrested two mates and four inferior officers of the
Cadogan, as they were walking near the factory at Canton fourteen miles from where the customs officer died.
The arrest, though undoubtedly occasioned by the incident at Whampoa, was nevertheless made without probable cause, and therefore upon the supercargoes' representation for redress, the commander who committed
the affront was degraded and dismissed from his office,
and a promise was also given that he would be bambooed
and rendered incapable of being again admitted into the
Emperor's service.[1] Where murder or assault was
committed on foreigners by Chinese subjects,[2] the
culprits were punished by the authorities with equal
rigor and promptness. As was recorded by a chronicler
of the time, "the Chinese have no desire to screen their
countrymen from punishment when guilty, but that the
inquiry must be carried on according to their own forms
and usages."[3]

[1] Auber, *China*, pp. 155-156

[2] A summary of the cases in which Englishmen were assaulted or
killed by Chinese is given in Morse, *International Relations*, pp. 107-108.

[3] Auber, *China*, p. 310.

PART II

THE CONVENTIONAL PERIOD (since 1842)

CHAPTER VIII

THE NEW RÉGIME

To all intents and purposes the treaty of Nanking, August 29, 1842, which was the first sequel of the Opium War, confers for the first time a definite status on the alien in China. Heretofore he had no legal standing before the Chinese authorities; he traded and resided in the Empire—in Canton and Macao—purely on their sufferance; but now he enjoys these privileges as rights guaranteed by imperial agreements. Subsequent treaties with other nations as well as with Great Britian have enlarged the scope of the alien's rights and multiplied them in number. Thus take a few examples. The general regulations of July 22, 1843, made in pursuance of the treaty of Nanking expressly provide for the punishment of Englishmen committing crimes in China by English laws, thus placing them under the recognized protection of extraterritoriality. Again, the treaty of Tientsin with the United States, June 18, 1858, secures for the Christian missionary in China not only toleration in the exercise of his religion but the liberty quietly to teach it. Once more, the treaty of June 26, 1858, with Great Britain enables British subjects under passports to travel, for pleasure or for purposes of trade, to all parts of the interior; and that of October 8, 1903, with the United States recognizes the right of missionary societies to rent and to lease in perpetuity, as their public property, buildings, or lands in all parts of the Empire. From their very nature, however, the rights of the

alien in China have their limitations, and both these
must be sought, in the first and last analysis, in the
treaties concluded between China and foreign states.
Usage forms the basis neither of the one nor of the
other. Unlike Turkey, China has conceded nothing
which is derogatory of her sovereign rights, beyond
what she has voluntarily surrendered in written compacts;[1] prior to her entering into the successive treaties
and agreements with the powers, beginning with that of
August 29, 1842, she always claimed the full measure of
her sovereignty and jurisdiction within her territory,

[1] "The system of extraterritoriality in China, and formerly in Japan,
is built on another basis than that on which extraterritoriality in Turkey
has been placed. In Turkey it is based on custom and usage, while in
China it rests solely on treaty." Mr. Bayard to Mr. Straus, April 20,
1887, Appendix to 3 *Wharton's Digest of International Law,* p. 854,
sec. 68a. That, in the absence of treaty stipulations to this effect, the
privilege of extraterritoriality is not enjoyable by any foreigners in
China would seem necessarily to follow, by analogy, from the decision
in the case of the *Maria Luz.* This was a Peruvian bark. In 1872 it
put into the port of Kanagawa, Japan, with a cargo of coolies from
China to Peru, under stress of weather. The Japanese Government, on
being apprized of cruelties inflicted on the coolies by the master, ordered
an investigation. Some Chinese coolies on board were summoned to
appear as witnesses, but they, once on shore, refused to return. The
master of the bark demanded that they be restored, but the Japanese
authorities informed him that he might sue for their restoration on
their contracts with him. The court, to which the suit was brought,
refused, however, either to decree specific performance of the contracts
or to grant damages. Subsequently, the Peruvian Government presented claims against Japan in behalf of the master; but the Emperor
of Russia, to whom the case was referred by the two governments to
be arbitrated, decided that in the absence of formal stipulations there
could not be "placed upon the Japanese Government the responsibility
of action which it has not wittingly provoked, and of measures which
are in conformity with its own legislation," hinting at the same time
that to avoid similar misunderstandings in the future, evidently about
the question of jurisdiction, special treaties might be made with Japan
with a view to making reciprocal relations more precise. See 5 Moore,
International Arbitrations, 5034.

and generally enforced her claim in practice; after the establishment of her treaty relations, she naturally and rightly looked upon her own express engagements as the sole guide in her treatment of the alien within her Empire; the custom that may be tolerated by the authorities of a given locality not being accepted by her as either to expand or limit the provisions of treaties conferring rights on him. In short, what is not expressly conceded by China in treaties with foreign powers remains as part and parcel of her unyielded sovereignty. This point is necessary to be noted here, because, if it is overlooked, the status of the alien in China, which will be outlined in the following sections of the chapter, cannot be accurately and fully appreciated.

CHAPTER IX

ORIGIN OF THE EXTRATERRITORIAL JURISDICTION IN
CHINA.

§ 1. *Essence of Judicial Extraterritoriality and its
intricate genesis in China.*

Extraterritoriality in China has a more intricate origin
than that commonly attributed to it. Unlike the so-
called extraterritoriality of diplomatic officers, the abnormal system is legally constituted by two concurrent
conditions, namely, the exemption, partial or complete,
of aliens from the territorial laws and the application to
them to the same extent, by their representatives within
the territory, of the laws of their own country; but
historically the first condition may have existed without
legal authorization, thus leaving an interval, so to speak,
of lawlessness, and this is practically what happened in
China. No exemption, either plenary or limited, from
the operation of the local laws was accorded aliens by
Chinese authorities prior to the conclusion of the first
treaties with Great Britain; on the contrary, and as was
shown in a preceding section, the rulers of the time,
conscious of their rights, were very jealous in preserving
their sovereignty and jurisdiction from infringement, and
in general, they succeeded in carrying out their national-
istic policy; what is meant here is that the alien traders,
particularly the British, early began to withdraw themselves, by open defiance, from the operation of the
local laws, and that to a considerable degree, they were

62   [184

successful in pursuing their course of sheer contumacy.
Likewise the assertion and exercise by Great Britain of
jurisdiction over her subjects in China were commenced
nearly a decade before China's consent to such questionable procedure was obtained, though, it is true, considerably later than the adoption on the part of the
traders of the attitude of non-submission to the local
laws. Indeed, when hostilities broke out in 1839 between the two countries over the opium question, extraterritoriality in China, as far as the British subjects were
concerned, may be said to have already traversed a persistent, though slow and irregular, course of development; to have fought many battles with the Chinese
authorities for its own existence, undergone several
stages of experimentation, and begun to assume an
aspect of stability and appear as the inevitable, in spite
of the vigorous and continued efforts of the Chinese
rulers to oppose and subvert it. What Great Britain
succeeded, therefore, in wringing from China at the end
of the expensive and ignoble war in 1842, in respect of
the question of jurisdiction over British subjects in
China, was merely an official recognition of what had
already been brought into being and engrafted on her,
in practice, without her consent or countenance.

§ 2. *General attitude of defiance on the part of aliens in
early days towards Chinese authority*

That this is a historically correct statement of the
evolution of the extraterritorial system in China will be
clearly seen when it is fully considered how the Chinese
law relaxed its hold on the aliens, how the British law
and court were introduced and gradually extended over
British subjects in China, how her recognition of the

artificial system was extracted, and finally how the system itself was immediately improved upon and placed upon a permanent footing by the British Government.

As to the first of these questions, it is to be observed that a want of regard for Chinese laws characterized the foreigners who went to China in the seventeenth and eighteenth centuries. They were either adventurous or desperate characters, and with the exception of a few missionaries, they were all animated by the sole desire to seek fortune in a new land. It mattered little what the territorial laws required and what they prohibited; they came on a mission to replenish their purses and were prepared to leave as soon as their object was accomplished; in their opinion, it would have been disloyal to themselves to allow their conduct to be shackled by laws of which they knew nothing, and about which they did not care to know anything. A small number of them, endowed with an inquiring turn of mind, indeed manifested an interest in Chinese laws and acquired a knowledge of them; but then, they observed, China was such a different country from their own, particularly in religion, that they considered it impossible to obey her laws without at the same time humiliating themselves and disgracing their own country. To govern themselves by laws with which they were familiar, was equally impossible; there was no common organization in existence over them, nor could they recognize any one of their own class assuming to restrain their conduct in China and regulate their intercourse with the Chinese people.

Under these circumstances it is not surprising that they considered themselves as exempt from all laws, Chinese and other, and that they lived in China "very much in what the lawyers called 'a state of nature,' that is governed by no rule but their own passions or interests."[1] And violence naturally became the favorite means of attaining their ends, however illegitimate they were. Thus in 1831, for instance, several European opium-smuggling boats shot a number of innocent Chinese in order to clear their way of obstructions to the prosecution of their illicit trade. In 1833 another party of foreign traders organized an armed attack on a Chinese village for the same reason. Another case of equal significance and interest, as illustrating the attitude of the alien traders of the time, occurred in the same year. A licensed English merchant, James Innes, one afternoon at 2 p. m. demanded of a security merchant the arrest before sunset of Chinese who had wounded him in the arm, and threatened to burn down the Chinese customs house in case of non-compliance with his demand within the alloted space of time. As this was not done by the Chinese merchant, "I bought rockets and bluelights," as he subsequently declared before the select committee of the East India Company, "and by eight p. m. the Mandarin's house was on fire."[2] The conduct of the western people in Canton could easily be imagined from the candid declaration of one of the witnesses examined in May, 1840, presumably about the opium traffic. "We never paid any attention," he said, "to any law in China that I recollect."[3]

This attitude of defiance toward Chinese laws was necessarily aggravated by the difficulty of enforcing them on foreigners caused by the transient character of the trade in which they were engaged, and by the inability of the Chinese officers to understand their language and to distinguish their identities one from another. For-

[1] Davis, *China and the Chinese*, vol. I, p. 100.
[2] Auber, *China*, pp 364-366.
[3] Davis, *China and the Chinese*, vol. I, p. 126 n.

eigners remained in Canton only during the trading season; when it was over, they usually left, as they were indeed required to until a very late period, for places outside the dominions of China. Even if they had remained in Canton or gone to other parts of the country, it would have been difficult for the Chinese authorities to apprehend the alien offender in a given case of breach of local laws without the aid of his own countrymen.[1] The combined result of these two circumstances was that foreign criminals could easily escape from justice, and foreign debtors abscond without encountering serious obstructions on their way to other parts of the world. And this impunity of the guilty and the dishonest naturally served as encouragement to those who already had only too little regard for the territorial laws, to persist in, if not actually to carry to a still more objectionable point, their chosen course of resistance to authority.

Nor was this attitude confined solely to individual traders; the select committee of the East India Company likewise considered itself and its employees as being exempt from the obligation of observing the local laws, and it endeavored to defend its position on two grounds. First, it argued thus: "Nations in general must be admitted to possess the right of regulating their commerce according to their separate views of policy; but China forms an exception to civilized countries,

---

[1] "As the native officers of government do not understand the language of the foreigners, it has always been the practice to order the chiefs of the respective countries to find out the murderer, and question him fully, and ascertain distinctly the facts, and then deliver him up to the government, after which a linguist is summoned, the interrogatories translated, and the evidence written down, and the prosecution conducted to a close."—Canton Viceroy's memorial on the Terranova Case, 1821, Staunton, *Notices of China*, p. 419.

where trade is regulated by treaties."[1] It was in pursuance of this view that it arrogated to itself, as has
already been pointed out heretofore, the rôle of cham-
pioning the cause of foreigners in Canton in opposition
to the authorities. Secondly, it considered itself as
possessing "unlimited power over every British subject
and vessel in this Empire;"[2] and accordingly it contended that British subjects and their property in China
were subject to its exclusive control.

It may perhaps be thought that the occasional visits
of British naval representatives to the dominions of the
Chinese Emperor must have produced, both by their
moderate views and by their exemplary conduct, a salutary effect upon the exotic lawless elements, particularly
upon their own countrymen. But unfortunately this does
not seem to have been the case, and the influence which
their presence exerted appears to have been altogether
in the opposite direction, the reason being that their
views were intemperate and their conduct was far from
exemplary. A few cases will probably suffice to illustrate
the statement. In 1741 Commodore Anson of H. M. S.
Centurion, forcibly brushing aside all opposition, entered
Canton and constrained the Chinese to furnish him with
supplies; after which he left the port, captured a Spanish
galleon from Acapulco, and ignoring the protest of the
local authorities, re-entered Canton with his prize.[3] In
1802 and 1808 British marine forces, under orders from
the British Government, were landed in Macao to occupy
the place in order to prevent attack by the French, without even giving notice to the Chinese authorities.[4] In

---

[1] Quoted in Sargent, *Anglo-Chinese Commerce and Diplomacy*, p.
40 n.

[2] *Ibid*, p. 46. [3] Davis, *China and the Chinese*, vol. 1, pp. 44-45.
[4] *Ibid.*, pp. 65-66, 73-77.

1814 the British frigate *Doris* seized. two American vessels lying in the Canton river, and "considerably within the admitted range of Chinese neutrality,"—an incident which "was considered by the Chinese not merely as a national affront, but as actually connected with some ulterior schemes for an hostile invasion of their territory."[1]

§ 3. *British resistance to the exercise of jurisdiction over them in criminal cases*

But it was in cases of homicide and wounding committed by their countrymen in Canton that the British traders resisted most openly and persistently the exercise of authority and jurisdiction over them by the Chinese rulers,—a fact which more than any other led to the subsequent inauguration of the British extraterritorial system in China. In any case of offence committed by a foreigner it was common for his factory chief, or the supercargo of his vessel in port, to refuse the demand of the local authorities for his delivery for trial and make a show of resistance at the outset; but while the subjects of all other nations usually yielded in the end and allowed the Chinese law to take its own course, the British, with the organized strength of the East India Company behind them, generally persisted to the last in their defiance to authority.

In pursuing this course the English merchants must have found a renewed impetus in the case of a Frenchman who killed a Portuguese sailor in December, 1780. Prior to that year, although cases of homicide perpetrated by foreigners had occasionally occurred in Canton, as in 1689, 1722 and 1754, yet in none of them had the offender been executed, he having been either freed on payment of a fine or an indemnity, or sentenced to

[1] Davis, *op. cit.*, 78; Morse, *Intern. Rel*, p. 55.

imprisonment.[1] In the case of 1780 the accused was actually put to death by the authorities in pursuance of a judicial sentence passed on him. The feeling which the execution awakened in the minds of Englishmen at Canton, with their peculiar propensity to disregard the local laws, may be inferred from the statement recorded by an English chronicler of the time: "This was the first instance of an European being executed for the murder of another in China, and was considered to form a dangerous precedent."[2] Then, four years later, occurred the gunner's case, "which led to the adoption of extreme measures of defence on the part of the Select Committee, and to those of equal determination to enforce the laws on the part of the Chinese."[3] On November 24, 1784, information reached Canton that a gun fired from the country ship *Lady Hughes*, while saluting, had wounded three Chinese, one of whom died the following day. Chinese deputies were at once sent to the president of the English factory to demand, in accordance with the laws of the Empire, that the man who fired the gun should be given up for public examination. They were, however, informed by the Select Committee that in all probability the gunner had absconded and that the committee had no power over country ships, but that the supercargo of the *Lady Hughes* would be induced by every means to produce the man, if the Chinese would consent to have his examination held in the factory

[1] At Macao, foreign offenders in such cases had been executed by the Chinese authorities, notably in that of Francis Scott, an Englishman, in 1773—a case, by the way, which was characterized by an English writer on China as "a most atrocious act of sanguinary injustice," "stamping indelible disgrace on the Portuguese of that place."—Davis, *China and the Chinese*, i, p. 52.

[2] Auber, *China*, p. 181.

[3] *Ibid.*, p. 183.

—"a stipulation which," according to Davis, "was founded on the recollection of what occurred in the Frenchman's case."[1] The deputies declared that the trial must be before the Fooyuen in the city. The following morning the supercargo, who had been dispatched by the Select Committee to Canton "for the purpose of explaining the circumstances," was "decoyed away and conveyed into the city under a guard of soldiers with drawn swords."[2] The committee took alarm, and in concert with the other factories, ordered up the boats of the several ships, manned and armed "as a guard to the committee's persons, in case any violence should be intended, as well as to manifest, in the strongest manner, the view which they took of the conduct of the local authorities."[3] The Chinese rulers, not knowing the object of the bellicose preparations on the part of the foreign factories, took similar measures of precaution for themselves, and appeared determined, as on previous occasions, to enforce the law of the land. At the same time they requested a deputation from the factories to visit the supercargo in their custody, apparently to convince them that he was well taken care of. The emissaries on their return reported that "his behaviour was much agitated, and it was evident he would be glad to get handsomely out of the business."[4] As a matter of fact, he had been very civilly treated, as he subsequently declared after his release.[5] But the Select Committee

---

[1] China and the Chinese, i, p. 57   [2] Auber, p 184

[3] Ibid.   [4] Davis, China and the Chinese, i, p. 58.

[5] In the proceedings of the select committee it was recorded. "In about an hour after [the surrender of the gunner] the supercargo arrived at the factory, and gave a very satisfactory account of the treatment he met with and the civilities he received from the several mandarins, most of whom visited him and sent him presents."—Auber, China, p. 185.

apparently had great misgivings as to the fate of the supercargo in the hands of the authorities, and accordingly, at his request, they gave up the gunner to the Chinese officials with a recommendation in his favor, signed by the representatives of the foreign community. The supercargo was immediately liberated, and the gunner was tried, convicted and imprisoned pending a final decision from the Throne. On January 8, 1785, an order was received from the Emperor, in pursuance of which the gunner was strangled.[1]

The outcome of the gunner's case keenly disappointed the British traders at Canton including the select committee, although years before, in 1754, they had demanded of the local authorities with equal insistence the most condign punishment of a French sailor who had killed one of their countrymen in an affray;[2] for thereafter they pursued an unvaried course of lasting opposition to the surrender of any English criminal for trial before a Chinese court of justice. A brief review of the cases of homicide or wounding involving Englishmen, which arose during the period from the settlement of the gunner's case to the termination of the rule of the East India Company at Canton, will illustrate the policy of the British subjects in China.

On February 11, 1800, the officer of the watch on board H. M. schooner *Providence*, sent from Lintin to Whampoa by H. M. S. *Madras*, having hailed a boat which had been at the schooner's bow for some time, and receiving no answer, fired into her, under a convic-

---

[1] Auber, *China*, p. 187.

[2] Davis, *China*, 1, p. 47. In this case the viceroy, at the demand of the English, stopped the French trade until the offender was given up. The latter was thrown into prison after conviction, but released the following year by order of the Emperor on occasion of a general act of grace.

tion that the parties were attempting to cut the vessel's
cable.   The shot wounded a Chinese, and another fell
overboard and was drowned.   The local government
demanded of the select committee that the offender,
who had meanwhile been kept in custody by the lieutenant of the schooner, should be given up for examination and be confronted with his Chinese accuser, who
charged him with having in a struggle occasioned the
other to fall overboard.   Captain Dilkes, of the *Madras*,
admitted the act of wounding but made some counter
charges of theft and declared that he could not allow the
seamen in his ship to be examined at Canton without
his being present.   The negotiations had already lasted
for a month when the discovery by the authorities of
the fact that the man who was drowned threw himself
overboard, together with the circumstances that the
wounded Chinese had recovered from his injury, brought
the matter to an uneventful conclusion.[1]

A more significant case occured in 1807.   On February 24, some sailors of Company's ship *Neptune* went
on shore and, while under the influence of ardent spirits,
entered into a quarrel with some Chinese.   Thereupon
the commander and officers interposed and secured their
men within the factory: but the Chinese followed them
in great numbers and continued the disturbance in spite
of the efforts of the mandarins and security merchants
to disperse them.   Toward the close of the day, the
sailors eluded their officer, rushed out to renew the
fight, and although they were brought back again, they
wounded several Chinese, one of whom died three days
afterwards.   The usual demand on the part of the local
officials for the surrender of the offenders for trial was

---

[1] Auber, *China*, pp. 203-206.

made to the select committee, but, of course, in vain. There was also some difficulty in discovering the person who struck the mortal blow in the affray. Investigations were conducted on board the Neptune by the British, and an offer of $20,000 was made by a Chinese security merchant as a reward for the discovery of the offender. Trade was meanwhile stopped by the local government. To extricate themselves from the predicament, the select committee proposed an examination of the fifty-two men of the *Neptune* to be held in the British factory, which proposal the authorities at first rejected, and afterward accepted. The trial which took place was described in the following terms:

Although the forms and solemnities of a Chinese court of justice were observed, an important concession was made in favor of the Committee, seats being provided for Captain Rolles of his Majesty's Ship *Lion*, the members of the Committee, and for Sir George Staunton, and two of Captain Rolles' marines with fixed bayonets were allowed to remain sentries at the door of the factory during the whole of the examination.[1]

No evidence was produced by the Chinese but Captain Buchanan, of the *Neptune*, admitted that eleven of the men had been most violent, hoping that some punishment against these men would have satisfied the demand for justice. The authorities, however, appeared determined to ascertain, if possible, the man who struck the blow. The discovery of the principal offender being apparently impossible, it was finally arranged that one of the eleven whom the mandarins considered as the most guilty, should be detained in Canton in the custody of

[1] Auber, *China*, p 226.

the select committee, obviously to await a decision of
the Emperor on the case. Edward Sheen was accordingly named. But soon after, the committee attempted
to bring Sheen with them to Macao, and this evoked
strong objections from the authorities. Captain Rolles,
of H. M. S. *Lion*, now intervened : he declared that he
felt it to be utterly impossible to allow Sheen to remain
at Canton, and threatened to take him to the *Lion* if the
Chinese persisted in refusing to allow him to go to
Macao. In the face of this coercion they acquiesced in
the plan of the committee. An imperial edict[1] of January, 1808, adjudged Sheen to be guilty of accidental
homicide, and he was accordingly released from deten-
tion on payment of the sum of 12.42 taels (about 4
pounds sterling) to the family of the deceased, as prescribed by the Chinese law for such cases.

Before leaving this case, however, it is interesting to
quote here what the secretary to the Court of Directors
of the East India Company recorded about the settlement of the affair, as showing that in pursuing the policy
of obstructing the course of Chinese law and justice, the

---

[1] For the text of the edict, see Staunton, *Penal Laws of China* (London, 1810), appendix xi, p. 523. A curious point in this document is
that the statement of the facts of the case made by the viceroy at Canton (probably himself a victim of the deceptions of his subordinate
officers), as embodied in the edict, is at total variance with what
actually took place—killing in an affray. In the report it was stated
that, on a certain morning, " Edward Sheen employed a wooden stick
in an oblique direction to keep open the shutter of the above-mentioned
window ; but in doing this, the wooden stick slipped and fell downwards. It happened also that Leao-a-teng, a native of China, went to
the street called She-san-hong to buy goods, and passing at the same
moment under the said upper story, was struck and wounded by the
end of the stick falling, as aforesaid, upon his left temple, and he
thereupon fell to the ground." The report added that medical assistance proved of no avail to the wounded man and that he died the following day

British subjects at Canton were also encouraged by those of their countrymen who were accustomed to practise no better principles of intercourse with a foreign people than those they observed in India:

The whole of the proceedings regarding the affair of the *Neptune* received the approbation of the Court, who expressed their entire satisfaction with the ability and firm conduct displayed by the Committee, and also the sense which they entertained of the important services rendered by Captain Rolles and Sir George Staunton. Captain Rolles was presented with £1,000 by the Court of Directors, and Sir George Staunton was appointed by the Court Chinese interpreter to the factory.[1]

The two cases of homicide, occurring respectively in 1810[2] and 1820, were terminated with no pregnant results, as regards the question now under consideration, since in each of them the real offender was not discovered, although his surrender was as usual insisted upon by the authorities and clearance papers were withheld for a while. In the latter case, the fact of a butcher on board the Company's ship *Duke of York* killing himself in a fit of insanity, was communicated by the committee to the local government "in such terms, that without a direct asseveration on the part of the committee that he was the man who caused the death of the Chinese, left the local authorities to infer such was the case."[3] The case of the death of a Chinese woman in 1821, in which the Company's ship *Lady Melville* was implicated, "was settled, as innumerable others have been, by pecuniary inducements to the relations of the deceased not to lodge complaints with the officers of government."[4]

---

[1] Auber, *China*, p. 228.   [2] See supra
[3] Auber, *China*, p. 283.   [4] See supra

In the same year (1821), the full enforcement of the Chinese law was again openly defeated in the case of H. M. S. *Topaze*. On December 15, the frigate, then at the Lintin anchorage, dispatched a barge to the island of Lintin for water and also to enable the seamen to wash their clothes. While thus engaged, they were attacked by a Chinese mob armed with clubs and bamboo spears. To cover the retreat of the seamen, the commander on board the frigate sent a party of marines in two armed cutters and at the same time fired several rounds from the big guns at the neighboring village, to keep it in check. In the clash of forces fourteen Englishmen were wounded and on the Chinese side two were killed and four wounded. On the 19th, Captain Richardson, of the *Topaze*, addressed a request to the viceroy urging him to punish the delinquents. The viceroy replied by stating that a deputy would be sent to Lintin to investigate the case, and that the wounded Englishmen should be sent on shore for examination. The captain objected to the latter proposal, and as to the former, he, apparently misapprehending the object of the viceroy's suggestion, declared that he would not allow an official examination on board the King's ship. The committee of the factory was accordingly informed by the viceroy that if the men from the *Topaze* were not sent on shore, or if the captain departed before the affair was settled, the chief of the factory should be held responsible. Meanwhile the trade was stopped, and the viceroy issued an edict, which in part reads:

Heretofore the governors have never had official correspondence with the naval officer of the said nation. On this occasion, as his representation said, natives had wounded fourteen Englishmen, I therefore deputed an officer to take with him the Hong merchants and the linguists and go to Lintin, and take an inquest of foreigners who were wounded, and prosecute. If the said man of war really had any men who had received wounds, it was incumbent on her to obey my orders and deliver them up, and wait till an inquest was taken, and proof being obtained, the matter might be examined into and justly prosecuted ; but abruptly to request the said deputed officer to go on board to hold an inquest was not only a violation of the forms of government, but a thing impossible to be done ; and then to make this a cause of obstinate resistance, excites a suspicion that the tale of fourteen men being wounded was for the most part not true.[1]

On the frigate's leaving Linton for Macao, the viceroy issued another edict declaring the chief of the English factory to be responsible, but the select committee returned an answer that it had no control over ships of war and requested him to negotiate directly with the captain. On January 5, 1822, hearing that the viceroy was about to cite the case of 1784 as a precedent, the committee, in concert with the captain, took steps "for the immediate removal of every Englishman from Canton, with the view to ulterior measures." Five days later, it notified the authorities of the Province that in view of their attitude toward the committee, the latter resolved to quit Canton with all the Company's ships. Seeing that the committee had no control over the warship, the viceroy on the 13th absolved it from all responsibility, but still forbade the resumption of trade until the seamen were given up for examination. The merchants, though still refusing to return to Canton under such circumstances, were yet anxious to renew trading, and they suggested to Captain Richardson a proposal which they thought might satisfy the Chinese

[1] Auber, *China*, p 291.

authorities. This was to the effect that inasmuch as the captain in deciding on the case could not be master, he would, on his return to his country, report the affair to his sovereign, and the parties concerned might be prosecuted according to law. The viceroy rejected the overture and reiterated his demand for the delivery of the men. The matter thus came to a deadlock. However, the frigate having sailed on February 8, after receiving a mandarin on board and giving him an account of all the circumstances connected with the Linton affair, the viceroy, on receiving assurance from the select committee that the whole case would be reported by the captain to his sovereign, permitted, by an edict of February 22, the re-opening of the trade. In November, 1823, the demand for the surrender of the men was renewed, but the matter was ultimately dropped.[1]

On his return home the first lieutenant of the *Topaze* was court-martialed but finally acquitted; and the Admiralty issued an order to the naval commander-in-chief in India that in future no vessel of war should visit any part of China, without a requisition from the Governor-General of India, or from the select committee of supercargoes at Canton. The Bengal Government was at the same time enjoined "carefully to abstain from requiring any ship in his Majesty's service to proceed to China unless in case of indispensable necessity," and the select committee was ordered likewise not to do it except when induced by "an occurrence of vital importance and of the most urgent necessity."[2]

In 1824, an accusation was made by a Chinese against a midshipman of the Company's ship the *Earl of Bal-*

[1] Auber, *China*, pp. 288-309; Davis, *China*, 1, p. 91; Morse, *Intern. Rel.*, p. 105.

[2] Auber, *China*, p. 306.

carras for having caused the death of a man in a boat alongside of the ship by throwing a billet down on him, and $3,000 was demanded as a compensation. The ship's surgeon, after examining the body, declared that the man had died from disease, and later it also appeared that the billet had not hit him at all, but that the allegation was an attempt at extortion. The matter was reported to the viceroy by the select committee and one of the Chinese was arrested, the Fooyuen declaring that the parties, if guilty, should be severely punished.[1]

The last case of homicide which occurred before the termination of the rule of the Company was that of 1833, in which a Chinese was killed in an affray at Kumsingmoon. Although an innocent Lascar was induced to declare himself the murderer and brought to Canton, he was released by order of the authorities after an exchange of correspondence with the select committee.[2]

§ 4. *Examination of the reasons assigned for the resistance.*

It is thus seen that although the number of cases of homicide and wounding in which Englishmen were involved is on the whole not at all appalling, yet the policy of the English merchants with regard to the enforcement of the Chinese criminal law upon their offending countrymen in such cases is unmistakable. The question arises, what were the reasons for such open and persistent obstruction on their part of the course of law and justice? Were it that no cause was assigned by them for their recalcitrancy, it might certainly be sufficiently explained, though not justified, on two concurrent general grounds. In the first place, the

[1] Auber, *China*, p. 310.
[2] Morse, *Intern. Rel.*, p. 107.

average human being, untrained in abstract philosophy or positive law, naturally finds the use of capital punishment, for whatever crime it may be, to be repugnant to his feelings, and the British merchants at Canton in the early days were neither all philosophers nor all lawyers. Secondly, the disrespect toward the territorial laws, predicable of foreigners in China generally, was so aggravated, in the case of the British at Canton, by the characteristic Anglo-Saxon pride and faith in the superiority of their own race and in the supremacy of their own institutions that they could not see how any of their countrymen could have committed a crime in China, and if perchance one of them was found guilty, still they could see no reason why he should sacrifice his life or freedom to vindicate the laws of a barbarous nation, alike to the humiliation of his compatriots and to the disgrace of his own civilized land. But the British merchants in China, with the wealth and organized power of the East India Company back of them, were naturally not content with leaving their conduct to be explained by posterity unaided by a word of defence from their own lips; they gave reasons for what they did, and it therefore becomes interesting to inquire whether or how far these reasons were valid or true.

One of the principal grounds assigned by the foreigners at Canton generally, and by the British in particular for opposing the course of Chinese law was the alleged "sanguinary injustice" of its provisions. Whatever accurate knowledge a handful of the wiser among them may have possessed on the subject, the prevailing notion of the foreign community at Canton was that the laws of China recognized neither distinction nor difference between wilful and accidental homicide: that in either case it was simply a question of the forfeiture of a life for a .life, admitting no excuse and no justification under any circumstances.

This belief, however, was totally destitute of foundation, as will be seen even after a very cursory examination of the pertinent provisions of the Chinese Penal Code then in force. Section 290, relative to killing with an intent to kill, and killing in an affray, reads:[1]

All persons guilty of killing in an affray; that is to say, striking in a quarrel or affray so as to kill, though without any express or implied design to kill, shall, whether the blow was struck with the hand or the foot, with a metal weapon, or with any instrument of any kind, suffer death, by being strangled, after the usual period of confinement.

All persons guilty of killing with an intent to kill, shall suffer death by being beheaded, after being confined until the usual period.

When several persons contrive an affray, in the course of which an individual is killed, the person who inflicts the severest blow or wound, shall be strangled, after the usual period of confinement. The original contriver of the affray, whether he be engaged in it or not, shall be punished at the least, with 100 blows, and perpetual banishment to the distance of 3,000 lee. The rest of the party concerned shall be punished with 100 blows each.

Section 292, relative to killing or wounding in play, by error, or purely by accident, reads:[2]

All persons playing with the fist, with a stick, or with any weapon, or other means whatsoever, in such a manner as obviously to be liable by so doing to kill, and thus killing or wounding some individual, shall suffer the punishment provided by the law in any ordinary case of killing or wounding

[1] *Penal Laws of China*, trans. by Sir G. Staunton, p. 311.
[2] *Ibid.*, p. 313.

in an affray; likewise any person who, being engaged in an affray, by mistake kills or wounds a by-stander, shall be punished in the same manner; that is to say, the person killing another in the manner above stated, shall suffer death by being strangled.   If guilty of wounding only, he shall be punished more or less severely according to the nature of the wounds inflicted. . . .

All persons who kill or wound others purely by accident, shall be permitted to redeem themselves from the punishment of killing or wounding in an affray, by the payment in each case of a fine to the family of the person deceased or wounded.

By a case of pure accident, is understood a case of which no sufficient previous warning could have been given, either directly, by the perceptions of sight and hearing, or indirectly, by the inferences drawn by judgment and reflection; as for instance, when lawfully pursuing and shooting wild animals, when for some purpose throwing a brick or a tile, and in either case unexpectedly killing any person; when after ascending high places, slipping and falling down, so as to chance to hurt a comrade or by-stander; when sailing in a ship or other vessel, and driven involuntarily by the winds; when riding on a horse or in a carriage, being unable, upon the animal or animals taking flight, to stop or govern them; or lastly, when several persons jointly attempt to raise a great weight, the strength of one of them failing, so that the weight falls on, and kills or injures his fellow-laborers; in all these cases there could have been no previous thought or intention of doing an injury, and therefore the law permits such persons to redeem themselves from the punishment provided for killing or wounding in an affray, by a fine [12.42 taels] to be paid to the family of the deceased or wounded person, which fine will in the former instance be applicable to the purpose of defraying the expense attending the burial, and in the latter, to that of procuring medicines and medical assistance.

From these sections two facts stand out clearly, in spite of the contrary notion very generally entertained by the foreigners at Canton in the early days. First, the Chinese law, like any other system of law, recognizes different degrees of culpable homicide, the punishment of death for both murder and manslaughter not being inconsistent with the fact of differentiation, inasmuch as the forms of execution in the two instances are different, namely, beheading in the one case and strangling, by which the body is not mutilated, in the other. Secondly, the same law, as has been observed by an English translator of the Code, "not only remits the punishment of death in cases of accident, but defines these cases with considerable accuracy."[1]

In fact, too, the principle of life for life, so often alleged by foreign residents in China, particularly by those who went there in the days of limited intercourse between China and western states, as underlying and controlling the Chinese law of homicide, is never allowed to modify the written laws on the subject, or to operate in any way except for the benefit of the accused in such cases. Indeed, were it otherwise, it would be altogether inconsistent with the extreme jealousy with which the Code regards and protects the person. A single illustration will suffice to explain the operation of the principle. According to section 290, in an affray contrived by several persons, resulting in the killing of an individual, the one who strikes the severest blow shall be strangled. Now if none of the participants in the affray is found to have inflicted the severest blow, the principle of life for life will never be allowed in such a case so to operate as to put any one of the accused to death, in spite of the absence of evidence proving that he struck the severest blow. It operates only in the following

---

[1] Staunton, *Notices of China,* p. 410.

case: When several persons, all participants in an affray resulting in the killing of some individual, are arrested on the charge of homicide, if one of them dies in prison before the final settlement of the case, or when being brought on his way to trial, or commits suicide for fear of a death sentence against him, then by the operation of the principle, the person who may afterwards be convicted of having struck the severest blow, will not be sentenced to death, as he surely should, if one of his co-partners in the crime had not died, but his punishment will be reduced by one degree and he will be sentenced to banishment instead.[1]

Another allegation made by the British in defence of their policy of resistance to the enforcement of Chinese laws upon them in cases of homicide was couched in the following terms:

Whatever may be the distinctions in the Chinese written laws, we see that in the practice, as far as respects Europeans, no discrimination is shown, and on the present occasion we see that the plea of self-defence is decidedly rejected.[2]

This passage is taken from the minutes of the select committee recorded in January, 1823, and the occasion referred to was the case of the *Topaze*. Remembering the real circumstances of the case, which have been stated above, it can hardly be overlooked that the statement as to the rejection of the plea of self-defence is misleading and inaccurate. In that case, as in all others, the Chinese authorities persistently demanded, and the British community, with equal obstinacy, refused, the surrender of the wounded seamen of the *Topaze* for ex-

[1] *Institutes of the Tsing Dynasty*, Digest (Ta-Tsing-Hui-Tien-Shi-Li), chap. 840.

[2] Auber, *China*, p 297.

amination, and in consequence of this unyielding resistance on the part of the British, no proceedings of any kind with a view to the determination of the guilt or innocence of the English marines were held. The seamen never appeared before a Chinese court, nor did they enter a plea of any kind. The so-called plea of self-defence was, in this case, merely the averment of an interested third party, consisting of the select committee and the captain of the Topaze, in pretended justification of certain acts committed by their countrymen. Therefore, to declare, under such circumstances, that the plea was rejected, is tantamount to an advocacy of the taking of justice into one's own hands, and to a denial of the necessity of having law, court, trial, judgment; in short, of maintaining the machinery of justice, in criminal cases.

With regard to the alleged failure of the Chinese authorities to accord foreign offenders the benefit of the distinction recognized by the Chinese law between accidental and wilful homicide, the select committee, in making the charge, gave expression not only to its own misapprehension but that of the other classes of British subjects in China. Sir John F. Davis, one time British plenipotentiary to China and governor of Hongkong, made a similar statement. After reproducing in full the "fundamental maxim of Chinese intercourse with foreigners," said to have been accurately translated by Père Premare, and invariably quoted with implicit credence by a certain class of western writers on China, Sir John Davis remarked: "It was on this principle that all the benefits of Chinese law were (before the war) denied to strangers, and that, in the case of even *accidental* homicide, they were required to be delivered up, not for trial, but execution."[1]

[1] *China and the Chinese,* i, p. 54.

These two passages reflect the general and probably sincere, but certainly erroneous, notion on the part of the foreigners at Canton that an alien charged with homicide could not expect to save his life in a Chinese court, and that Chinese judges, when they came to try him, would put aside all the principles and rules of law and justice, and hurry him to the execution-ground, whatever the facts of his case might be. It is, doubtless, true that cases had occurred in China in which death sentence was actually executed on aliens convicted of felonious homicide, in accordance with Chinese law, but this bare fact shows no more denial of justice than the innumerable cases of capital punishment taking place in all the other countries in the world. Moreover, instances were not wanting, nor even rare when compared with the total number of cases of homicide by foreigners that arose in China, in which a Chinese had been killed by an alien and the alien offender was acquitted by the Chinese authorities on the sole ground that the homicide complained of was unintentional on his part, or purely accidental. Thus in a case in 1689, in which some sailors of the Company's ship *Defence* killed a Chinese at Whampoa, the local government merely ordered them to pay an indemnity of 5,000 taels;—to which, by the way, Captain Heath objected, and after making a counter offer of 2,000 taels, and finding it to be unacceptable to the authorities, he left Canton with his ship.[1] In 1722, the gunner's mate of the *King George*, while in a boat, fired at a bird in a paddy-ground and thereby mortally wounded a boy who was reaping; but the local authorities, instead of sentencing him to death, acquitted him on payment of 2,000 taels for the benefit of the deceased's parents.[2]

[1] Auber, *China*, p. 149.   [2] *Ibid*, p. 157.

Again, the Frenchman who killed an English sailor in an affray at Whampoa in 1754 and whom the Chinese officials placed on trial before them on the most insistent demand of the British traders, though he confessed himself guilty of murder, was released the following year under a general act of imperial grace.[1] Once again, the case of Edward Sheen in 1807 constituted another notable instance of the full extension to foreign offenders of the benefit of the distinction maintained in the Chinese law between intentional and accidental homicide; for in that case Sheen, though he was admittedly the most serious offender in an affray in which two Chinese were killed, was acquitted in 1808, after paying the regular fine of 12.42 taels, on the expressly stated ground that the homicide with which he had been charged was accidental.

Besides these two allegations of indiscrimination in the Chinese law between intentional and unintentional killing, and discrimination against foreigners in its enforcement, a third count in the indictment against the Chinese law was that, even as it stood, it was too harsh and severe in the punishments which it prescribed, especially for offences against the person. As regards this charge, two observations may be made.

In the first place, the harshness of the law, as represented in the scale of punishments it embodies, is more important than real. Sir Chaloner Alabaster, at one time British consul-general in China, observes in his " Notes and Commentaries on Chinese Law: " " In regard of capital sentences, it is to be noted that the sen-

---

[1] Davis, *China*, i, p. 47. As one instance contradicting the alleged maxim of Chinese intercourse with foreigners as translated by Père Premare, it may be pointed out that after the case of 1754, as a means of preventing further disturbances at Whampoa, Dane's Island was allotted to the English, and French Island to the French sailors, for purposes of recreation *Ibid.*

tence of death, though recorded, is in innumerable cases commuted as of course to terms of penal servitude, transportation to lesser or greater distances from the offender's native place, imprisonment, or even fine."[1]   In the same work, Sir Chaloner, after a comparison of the punishments recorded in the law and those actually enforced in practice, concludes with this significant remark: "In general, then, the Chinese system may be characterized as less Draconian than our own."[2]   Sir George Staunton, who translated the Chinese Penal Code, in discussing the punishment of culpable homicide under the Chinese law, states: "When there are no circumstances of peculiar aggravation, the sentence is usually mitigated in practice one degree; and thus the murderer only suffers death by being strangled; and the offender guilty of manslaughter is banished."[3]   In his preface to the translated Code, Sir George, in enumerating the objects underlying it, remarks: "Another object which seems to have been very generally consulted is that of as much as possible combining, in the construction and adaptation of the scale of crimes and punishments throughout the Code, the opposite advantages of severity in denunciation and leniency in execution."[4]   In the same part of his work he refers to a book of drawings then just published in England under the title of "Punishments of China," and observes that "the fancy of the painter has given, in some instances, a representation of cruelties, and of barbarous executions, which it would be very erroneous to suppose have a place in the ordinary course of justice." Continuing, he states: "Thus, also, although every page

---

[1] Edition of London, 1899, p. lxv.   [2] *Ibid.,* p. lxviii
[3] *Notices of China,* p 412.
[4] *Penal Laws of China,* p. xxvii.

of the following translation may seem at first sight to bear testimony to the universality of corporal punishments in China, a more careful inspection will lead to a discovery of so many grounds of mitigation, so many exceptions in favor of particular classes, and in consideration of particular circumstances, that the penal system is found, in fact, almost entirely to abandon that part of its outward and apparent character."[1]

The second observation is that the penal laws of China, as enforced in the eighteenth and the first part of the nineteenth century, were no severer than those in force in England during the same period. Independently of Sir Chaloner's opinion, which has already been noted, that the former were in fact less Draconian than the latter, it will be interesting briefly to examine into the character of parliamentary legislation of the time on criminal matters. Blackstone, speaking of the frequency of capital punishment found in the English law of his day, made this remark: "It is a melancholy truth, that among the variety of actions which men are daily liable to commit, no less than an hundred and sixty have been declared by act of parliament to be felonious without benefit of clergy; or, in other words, to be worthy of instant death."[2] Within these 160 capital offences were included such acts as the appearance of persons armed or with their faces blacked, or otherwise disguised, in a forest, or a warren, or a high road, or a common, or a down, or a place where rabbits were kept.[3] As Stephen observes, "the legislation of the eighteenth century in criminal matters was severe to the highest degree, and

---

[1] *Penal Laws of China*, p xxvi.
[2] *4 Commentaries* (ed. of 1769), 18.
[3] Black Act, 1722, 9 George 1, c. 27.

destitute of any sort of principle or system."[1]   As late as 1827 an act of Parliament re-enacted the punishment of death for such acts as sacrilege, stealing the value of £5 in a dwelling house, and stealing horses, sheep, or other cattle.[2]   Capital punishment for letter-stealing was not abolished until 1835,[3] and for attempts to kill, not until 1861.[4]

Similarly, as to the taunt of the British merchants in China against the use of torture in Chinese courts, it may be pointed out, aside from the circumstances that no case appears in records showing the infliction of such pains on foreign culprits during the period now under consideration, that the same means of compelling confession in criminal cases was in vogue in English courts until 1722, when Parliament enacted[5] that "standing mute" should be considered as equivalent to a plea of guilty; and that, further, the presumption of innocence in favor of the accused was not introduced into the English jurisprudence until 1827.[6]

The doctrine of extensive responsibility upheld by the Chinese law in criminal matters was, too, not infrequently pointed to with a finger of scorn as another of its objectionable features, constituting in the minds of the British an added reason for their refusal to place themselves under its sway; and instances were recounted in which the trade of the entire nation had been stopped by the Chinese authorities on account of the commission of a

[1] 1 Hist. of Criminal Law of England (London, 1883), p. 471.

[2] 7 & 8 Geo. 4, c. 29; 1 Stephen, Hist. of Cr. Law, etc., p. 473.

[3] 5 & 6 Will. 4, c 81; 1 Stephen, p. 474.

[4] Consolidated Acts of 1861 (24 & 25 Viot.), ss 96-100; 1 Stephen, 475.

[5] 12 Geo. 3, c. 20; Morse, Int Rel, p 113.

[6] 7 & 8 Geo. 4, c 28, Morse, Int Rel, p. 113

criminal act by one of its subjects. In respect of this objection it may be admitted that the doctrine, as it stood, was not altogether desirable or defensible, and that the stoppage of trade had too often been threatened or enforced by the local government at Canton as a weapon to coerce the British community into submission to the rule of the Chinese law. But at the same time it will be noted that as a matter of fact no case appears to have occurred in which one British subject had been punished for a crime committed by another, nor had the whole community been punished on such a ground; the practice of suspending trade was pursued by the Chinese, not as a penalty inflicted upon the trade of the entire nation for the acts of one of its individuals, but for a wholly different purpose. . It was resorted to, not as an application of the doctrine of conjoint responsibility, but merely as a means to vindicate the honor of the law necessitated by the peculiar circumstances under which the foreign trade at that time was prosecuted, and by the still more peculiar attitude and policy pursued by the British in regard to cases in which their own countrymen were culpably involved.

Thus in the first place, the British merchants, as well as those of other nations, were segregated from the local populace, and lived in a factory. Secondly, for convenience's sake, the factory chief was always recognized by the authorities as the medium of communication in matters concerning his countrymen, just as the Cohong was made their own spokesman. Thirdly, the difficulty which the Chinese officers experienced in understanding the foreign language had developed a habit of depending upon the factory chief, in a case of offence committed by one of his nationals, for assistance in arresting the right person. Fourthly, in the case of

the British merchants, the East India Company being
known as entitled to, and actually enjoying, a monopoly
of the British trade in China, and always asserting the
privilege of controlling all the British subjects engaged
in such trade, the Chinese authorities not unnaturally
looked upon every British subject in China as an em-.
ployee or agent of the Company, and, therefore to that
extent, looked to the select committee as having an
authority over him. Finally, the attitude of the select
committee toward Chinese laws had always been defiant,
and its policy had invariably been to shelter British
offenders in China from arrest or surrender to the local
government ; and such contumacy on the part of the
committee, by reason of the power and strength behind
it, had proved more or less an insuperable obstacle in
the way of enforcing Chinese law and justice. It was
under these circumstances that the Chinese rulers frequently stopped or threatened to stop the British trade
in cases where crimes committed by British subjects
were not avenged by law; and the object of such
coercion is thus clearly seen to have been, not to punish
the entire British community for whatever offence one
of its members may have committed, as should have
been the case if the doctrine of conjoint responsibility
had been applied to it, but rather to bring pressure to
bear upon the select committee, who as a responsible
agent of the Company was necessarily interested in the
continuance of the trade, to withdraw its unlawful
support from the British culprit and surrender him for
trial in a Chinese court of justice.

Lastly, a standing objection raised by the British
merchants at Canton to the Chinese judicial system in
defence of their policy of non-submission, was the
alleged maladministration of justice in the Chinese

courts. That some irregularity existed in the Chinese courts of the time is not impossible nor improbable, as all human institutions, wherever they may be found, must, from their very nature, be imperfect. But between this admission and the inference that justice was not obtainable in China there is evidently a wide margin of difference. In the absence of evidence establishing its truth, the vague allegation may safely be considered to have been due to suspicions born of a want of familiarity on the part of foreigners generally with the process of administering justice in China, and of their well-known as well as characteristic contempt of Chinese laws, rather than to have been founded upon substantial facts. Moreover, a great many of the cases given in the preceding pages, particularly those of accidental homicide, seem to show that as a rule justice was done to foreigners wherever it was due them. Even such a severe critic of Chinese laws and institutions as Sir George Staunton saw fit, indeed, to make this observation on the Chinese judicial system :

That the laws of China are, on the contrary, very frequently violated by those who are their administrators and guardians, there can, unfortunately, be no question; but to what extent, comparatively with the laws of other countries, must at present be very much a matter of conjecture; at the same time it may be observed, as something in favor of the Chinese system, that there are very substantial grounds for believing, that neither flagrant, nor repeated acts of injustice, do, in point of fact, often, in any rank or station, ultimately escape with impunity.[1]

[1] *Penal Laws of China*, p. xxviii In the face of this statement of Sir George's alone, the following observation recorded by an ordinarily fair writer on China seems to be an unnecessarily severe stricture on the Chinese magistracy and judiciary: " With ' reason ' on their lips and the keen desire for gain in their hearts, their judgment was at the

It is thus seen that the various grounds assigned by the British at Canton in defence of their resistance to the course of Chinese law and justice were generally mistaken or exaggerated. But however invalid or insufficient the grounds may have been, the fact of their resistance to authority remains, and in tracing the origin of the extraterritorial system in China, it must be carefully noted.

As a consequence of their chosen policy of non-submission to the Chinese criminal jurisdiction, the condition of British merchants became a constantly precarious one, and their trade was frequently subjected to interruptions during the first part of the nineteenth century. As this predicament continued, feelings of embarrassment and anxiety naturally arose in the minds of the British. The interpreter of the English factory in 1813 expressed this view of the situation:

The peculiar circumstances under which foreigners are received in China, are, in fact, such that the body or nation suffers from individual offences, almost equally, whether those offences are subject to punishment, or permitted to escape with impunity. The latter event naturally tends to render foreigners objects of hatred and aversion, while the former invariably entails upon them humiliation and disgrace.[1]

And the select committee, in January, 1823, when the case of the *Topaze* was still pending a settlement, concluded the minutes of its proceeding on the matter with this pregnant observation:

The great facility which foreigners have of escaping in ships,

disposal of the long purse, but subject to their innate conviction that their countrymen, belonging to a civilized race, must be in the right as against those of rude and unlettered origin."—Morse, *Intern. Rel*, p. 112.

[1] Staunton, *Notices of China*, p. 153

and the liability of the whole trade to suspension therefrom, is a consideration of such momentous weight, that we trust that the Honourable Court will use every effort, by negotiation with the Chinese and by laws enacted at home, to put the cases of homicide on such a footing as shall prevent embarrassment to the trade.[1]

§ 5. *Establishment of a British Court of Justice for China in 1833*

So long, however, as the East India Company retained the monopoly of the British trade with China, there was no cause for serious anxiety on the part of any British resident at Canton; for the select committee as the representative of the Company, with its power and influence derived from the magnitude of its commercial dealings, was always able, on one hand to oppose the acts of the local government, as one of its agents described, " with considerable success, and in a manner which individuals, pursuing their separate interests, and unconnected by any bond of union, never could have attempted;"[2] and, on the other, by virtue of its right to control their trade, to restrain British traders from a too frequent resort to open violence. But when in 1833 the Company's charter granting a monopoly of the British trade in China, was about to expire, and vigorous opposition was offered to its renewal, Sir George Staunton, then a member for Portsmouth in the House of Commons and a veteran advocate of the Company's monopolistic interests, seeing that the hazardous experiment of throwing open the China trade to all British subjects had been irrevocably determined upon by the legislature, thought that he could not do his duty to his country better than by offering such suggestions as his experience in China had dictated, " for diminishing as much as possible that hazard.

[1] Auber, *China*, p 297.   [2] Staunton, *Notices of China*, p. *47.

and carrying out the experiment with the best prospect of success." [1]   The suggestions were embodied in a set of nine resolutions [2] which he introduced on June 13, 1833, on a motion to resolve the House into a committee on the Company's charter.   Of these resolutions the sixth reads:

That this influence of the Company acquired from the immense value of its trade being the sole existing check now in operation for the control and counteraction of the corrupt local administrators of the peculiarly arbitrary and despotic government of China, it is indispensably necessary to the security of our valuable commerce with that country, that whenever any change shall be made in the British commercial system, having the effect of putting an end to this influence, an equal or greater instrument of protection be at the same time created and substituted for it, under the sanction of a national treaty between the two countries, without which previous sanction, any attempt to appoint national functionaries at Canton for the protection of trade, would, in the present state of our relations with China, not only prove of little advantage to the subject, but also be liable, in a serious degree, to compromise the honour and dignity of the Crown.

In the seventh resolution Sir George urged that there was "no insurmountable obstacle" to the negotiation of a treaty with China by a special embassy, and in the eighth recommended, as the last resort, and in the event of a special treaty mission being found unsuccessful, the plan "to withdraw the British commerce altogether from the control of the Chinese authorities, and to establish it in some insular position on the Chinese coast, where it may be satisfactorily carried on, beyond the reach of acts of oppression and molestation, to which an unresisting submission would be equally prejudicial to the national honor

[1] Staunton, *op. cit*, p. *14
[2] 18 Hansard's *Parl. Debates* (1833), 698; Staunton, *Notices*, pp. *44-50

and the national interests of this country." The last resolution deals solely with the question of criminal jurisdiction over British subjects in China.   It reads:

That, lastly, the state of the trade under the operation of the Chinese laws in respect to homicides committed by foreigners in that country, calls for the early interposition of the Legislature, those laws being practically so unjust and intolerable that,they have in no instance for the last forty-nine years been submitted to by British subjects; great loss and injury to their commercial interests accruing from the suspension of trade in consequence of such resistance, and the guilty as well as the innocent escaping with impunity; and that it is, therefore, expedient to put an end to this anomalous state of the law, by the creation of a British naval tribunal on the spot, with competent authority for the trial and punishment of such offences.

In suggesting such a novel device as the creation of a British tribunal in a foreign state, it is probable that Sir George was as much prompted by a desire to defend the Company's policy of openly defying Chinese authority and jurisdiction in criminal cases involving British subjects as by a feeling of anxiety to protect the national honor and interests of Great Britain.   For it will be recalled that Sir George was always a loyal and able agent of the Company and that it was in appreciation of the part he played in resisting the surrender of Edward Sheen in 1807 that he was appointed by its authorities interpreter to the select committee at Canton, which marked the beginning of close connection with the Company and its interests. At any rate, the establishment of a British court in China was destined rather to increase than diminish the hazard to the British trade; for as will presently be seen, instead of removing an old source of friction which, as the result of the committee's open opposition to Chinese law, lay hidden in every criminal case wherein the offender was a British subject, it introduced a new and more permanent obstacle in the course of Chinese justice.   Moreover it also constituted itself an object of dislike equally to the Chinese and the British· to the former as a standing menace to their rightful sovereignty and independent jurisdiction, and to the latter as a symbol of unwarranted interference with their accustomed habits of life in China, cherished by them all as being essential alike to their personal freedom and their commercial prosperity.   Indeed, this flagrant act of infringement of the Chinese jurisdiction contributed no small share toward rushing the two countries into war with each other.   Bearing in mind the consequences which it brought forth, it seems clear that the institution of a British court in China, as suggested by Sir George, meant only the perpetuation of the policy of defiance to Chinese jurisdiction, and as such, it was far from being an expedient measure to relieve the British trade of interruptions by the Chinese rulers, which were as a rule deliberately invited by the select committee's persistent obstruction of the course of Chinese law and justice · The wisest step for the purpose in view would have been to do what other nations represented at Canton, such as France and the United States, had done, namely, to leave the British subjects committing crimes in China to be punished and protected by Chinese law and courts.   To say the least, the measure was not necessary, inasmuch as cases of homicide involving British subjects rarely occurred, the total number of such cases that arose in the century preceding the year 1833 not being more than half a dozen.

Reverting to the history of Sir George's resolutions in Parliament, it may be noted that they did not for the time being receive much attention; in fact they were opposed by Mr. Grant, the President of the India Board, who disposed

of them " in a summary manner," [1] for the following reasons:

> To enter into a negotiation as preparatory to the change
> which it is proposed to effect, would, I think, have a tendency
> to create much embarrassment and great difficulty in the way
> of carrying that change into operation. I think if we do not
> ourselves sound the note of alarm, the Chinese will receive
> any functionary whom we may appoint as the representative
> of the British nation at Canton, without any of the suspicion
> and distrust which the formal process of a negotiation would
> be sure to awaken in the minds of a people so sensitive and so
> jealous; and that the ordinary transactions of business between
> them and us would proceed with little or no interruption.
> Upon these grounds I am decidedly of opinion that it would
> be anything but advisable to preface the proposed change of
> system by negotiation.[2]

On the basis of this opinion, the resolutions, which had
been put by way of amendment, were negatived in the
House without a division.[3]

But when the House of Commons on July 13, 1833, resolved that " it is expedient to regulate the Trade of China
and India," [4] and ordered a special committee of five [5] to
bring in a bill, Sir George again urged his views upon the
committee, and this time he was successful, as in compliance
with his request, a provision authorizing the establishment
of British courts in China was inserted in the bill drafted
by the committee, and afterwards presented to the House
on July 1 under the title of "An Act to Regulate the Trade
to China and India." The bill passed the Commons on

[1] Staunton, *Notices of China*, p. *15.

[2] *Mirror of Parliament*, June 13, 1833, quoted in *Notices*, p. *15.

[3] 18 Hansard's *Parl. Debates* (1833), 700.

[4] 88 *Journal of H. Commons* (1833), 570

[5] Francis Baring, Charles Grant, Steward Mackenzie, Robert Gordon
and Thomas B. Macaulay.

August 13 without debate, though on the preceding day Sir
Robert Inglis expressed a doubt that the agents or consuls
provided in the proposed act would be recognized by the
Chinese Government and stated that it would be better to
have had some previous communication with it.[1]   When
it was brought before the Lords on August 20 for the third
reading, however, objections to the provision now under
consideration as well as to others were not wanting, though,
it is true, they were not fatal to the bill.   Viscount Strat-
hallan opposed the provision as establishing " a very dangerous precedent " and expressed himself as being confident
that the Chinese Government " would never suffer the establishment of Superintendents or consuls." [2]   Lord Ellen-
borough objected to the institution of a court of justice
at Canton as " wholly inapplicable to the circumstances
of the place where it was to be established.   Let the British
Legislature," he added, " arm their commissioners with
what powers for the execution of justice they might, they
would be wholly inoperative in a foreign land, even to compel witnesses to attend." [3]   Lord Auckland, in support of
the bill, replied that " as to the Courts of Justice they would
not be ordinarily resorted to, and the most effective power
was that of refusing permission to vessels to unload until
they had conformed to regulations." [4]   However, the bill
passed the Lords on August 22, though with a number of
amendments, one of which was to change the word "courts"
into " a court." [5]   The Commons agreed to the modifica-
tions and it became an act of Parliament on August 28,
1833.

As the " rule of the Company " was to terminate on
April 22, 1834, the act of August 28, 1833,[6] sought to

[1] 20 Hansard (1833), 562.   [2] *Ibid.*, 787.   [3] *Ibid*, 788.   [4] *Ibid*, 789.
[5] 65 *Journal of H. Lords* (1833), 607.

[6] 3 and 4 Will. 4, c 93; 20 *Br. and For. State Papers* (1832-1833), 256.

provide a machinery for the government of the British subjects in China.   Section 5 of the act entrusted the supervision of the British trade, hitherto controlled by the
Company, to a body of three superintendents, who were to
reside in China.   Section 6, authorizing the establishment
of a British court in China, read:

VI. And be it enacted, that it shall and may be lawful for His
Majesty, by any such Order or Orders, Commission or Com-
missions, as to His Majesty in Council shall appear expedient
and salutary, to give to the said Superintendents, or any of
them Powers and Authorities over and in respect of the Trade
and Commerce of His Majesty's Subjects within any part of
the said Dominions [of the Emperor of China]; and to make
and issue Directions and Regulations touching the said Trade
and Commerce, and for the government of His Majesty's
subjects within the said Dominions: and to impose penalties,
forfeitures, or imprisonments for the breach of any such
Directions or Regulations, to be enforced in such manner as
in the said Order or Orders shall be specified: and to create
a Court of Justice with Criminal and Admiralty Jurisdiction
for the trial of offences committed by His Majesty's Subjects
within the said Dominions, and the Ports and Havens thereof,
and on the high seas within 100 miles of the Coast of China;
and to appoint one of the Superintendents hereinbefore mentioned to be the Officer to hold such Court, and other Officers
for executing the Process thereof: and to grant such Salaries
to such Officers as to His Majesty in Council shall appear
reasonable.[1]

In section 8 it was provided that for the purpose of defraying the expenses of the new establishments in China a tonnage tax might be levied on the vessels and goods belonging
to any British subject entering any port or place where the
superintendency should be stationed.

[1] *Op. cit.*

In pursuance of the act several Orders in Council were issued on December 9, 1833.   One of them authorized the superintendency to supervise the British trade in China Another ordered a court of justice with the jurisdiction as prescribed, "to be holden at Canton, in the said Dominions, or on any British ship or vessel in the Port or Harbor of Canton;" and it further provided that "the practice and proceedings of the Court, upon the trial of all issues of fact or law, to be joined upon any indictments or informations to be therein brought or prosecuted, shall be conformable to, and correspond with the practice and proceedings of the Courts of Oyer and Terminer and Gaol delivery in England;" proper regard being given to the difference of local conditions.[1]   The third imposed a tax of 2 shillings per ton on vessels and 7 shillings for every £100 of the value of goods to be determined by their market price at Canton;[2]—which order, however, being found impracticable, was revoked by another of March 5, 1834, after which the expenses of the superintendency were to be paid one-third by India and two-thirds by Great Britain.[3] On December 10, 1833, three "Superintendents of the Trade of British Subjects in China" were appointed with William John, Lord Napier, as the chief.[4]

Thus a curious but apparently comprehensive set of machinery was provided by Great Britain for the government of her subjects in China; and it was natural on her part to expect that in providing it she had done her best, and that it ought to work well, if for no other reason than as a fair return for her labors.   But no previous consent

---

[1] 20 *Br. and For. State Papers* (1832-1833), 262.

[2] *Ibid.*, 264

[3] 22 *Br. and For. State Papers* (1833-1834), 1235

[4] *Ibid*, 1228.

to the innovations introduced into China having been obtained from the Emperor, there were in the way of putting them into operation obvious difficulties, which Lord Napier, keen and able as he was, was not especially trained to overcome. The powers which were conferred on the chief superintendent, by reason of the uncertain ground upon which they were asserted, were necessarily vague and ill-defined, and when placed in the hands of such an impetuous character as Lord Napier, a soldier by profession, they became at once an object of jealousy and a source of peril. When Lord Napier arrived in China, he at once proceeded to Canton, and reaching the city on July 25, he dispatched a letter to the viceroy, not through the recognized medium, of the hong merchants, but by a special delegation. His message was, of course, rejected; and the hong merchants, being held responsible by the viceroy for the British superintendent's conduct, urged him to leave for Macao, and follow the customary path of seeking official recognition. To this advice, the British representative replied that he would remain in the Chinese city and communicate immediately with the viceroy " in the manner befitting His Majesty's Commission and the honor of the British Nation." [1] From July 21 to 31, the chief Provincial authority issued four proclamations urging the superintendent at once to return to Macao and emphasizing the point that the great ministers of the Celestial Empire were not permitted to have private intercourse with foreigners. Considering the recognized rules of international intercourse, it seems that Lord Napier might well have accepted the viceroy's exhortation, inasmuch as his position in China was no more than what one of his contemporary countrymen states:

It is a well-understood principle of international law, that no

[1] *22 Br. and For. State Papers* (1833-1834), 1235.

public functionary sent to another state can claim the rights and privileges of his appointment till he is recognized. As a captain in the British service, though without a command, and as a British nobleman, he was undoubtedly entitled to every degree of respect and courtesy, as long as he complied with the laws and regulations of the country; but, owing to the unfortunate omission of our Government to apply for, and obtain from the Chinese authorities, in due time, his formal recognition, he had no official station, or public privilege, in China whatever.[1]

But the first British superintendent was apparently not much given to the contemplation of the refined points of international usuages, for the firm refusal of the Chinese authorities to receive him or communicate with him on an equal footing served only to remind him of the powers which he believed had been vested in him by his Government and of the profession to which he belonged. He decided to use force to compel a recognition by the viceroy of his official position. In his despatch of August 14, 1834,[2] to Viscount Palmerston, he recommended the following measures to his Government:

Looking, now, at the utter imbecility of the Government, and the favourable disposition of the People, I cannot for one moment suppose, that, in treating with such a Nation, His Majesty's Government will be ruled by the ordinary forms prescribed among civilized People. . . .

Our first object should be to get a settlement on the same terms that every Chinaman, Pagan, Turk, or Christian, sits down in England. This, no doubt, would be a very staggering proposition in the face of a Red Chop, but say to the Emperor, "Adopt this, or abide the consequences," and it is done. Now, "abiding consequences" immediately presup-

---

[1] Staunton, *Notices of China*, p. *16.

[2] 22 *Br. and For. State Papers* (1833-1834), 1241.

poses or anticipates all the horrors of a bloody war against a defenceless people. The monopolists would cry out: but I anticipate not the loss of a single man: and we have justice on our side.

The Chinese are most anxious to trade with us: the Tartar Viceroys cannot comprehend it. If the Emperor refuses our demand, remind him he is only an intruder; and that it will be his good policy to secure himself upon his throne by gratifying the wishes of his People. Remind him that the British traded to all Ports of China before his Dynasty escaped from the wilds of Tartary: and that even one of his early forefathers, not only opened all his Ports to Foreigners, but invited them to settle and spread civilization in his Empire. The Chinese all read, and are eager for information: publish among them and disseminate, far and wide, your intentions—that is, all your intentions both towards the Government and themselves. Disclaim every view of conquest, or of holding partial possession beyond a certain time; disturb not the passage of their Vessels, or the tranquillity of their Towns: only destroy their Forts and Batteries along the Coast, and on the River sides, without interfering with the People. Such annoyance to the Batteries, of course, only to be carried into effect in case of the obduracy of the Emperor. Three or four Frigates and Brigs, with a few steady British Troops, not Sepoys, would settle the thing in a space of time inconceivably short.

Such an undertaking would be worthy the greatness and the power of England, as well from its disinterestedness towards other Nations as from the brilliant consequences which must naturally ensue.

To these spirited suggestions the Duke of Wellington tersely and not unnaturally replied in February, 1835:

It is not by force and violence that His Majesty intends to establish a commercial intercourse between his subjects and China: but by the other conciliatory measures so strongly inculcated in all the Instructions which you have received.[1]

[1] 22 *Br. and For. State Papers* (1833-1834), 1263.

But before this reminder reached him, the trade had already been stopped in the August preceding,[1] and Lord Napier had put his militant notions into practice. In September he sent two British frigates up the river to awe the Provincial authorities as well as to strengthen his own foothold, but what puzzled him very much was that even force was of no avail with the Chinese on this occasion. Besides the fact that the local authorities resisted force by force, causing many to be killed and wounded on both sides, the chief superintendent's warlike experiment also elicited from the viceroy another deprecatory edict, in which it was stated:

The Celestial Empire cherishes these from afar virtuously. What it values is the subjection of men by reason; it esteems not awing them by force. The said Barbarian Eye has now again opposed the Laws, in commanding the Ships of War to push forward into the inner River: and in allowing the Barbarian forces to fire guns, attacking and wounding our Soldiers and alarming our resident People. This is still more out of the bounds of reason, and renders it still more unintelligible what it is he wishes to do.[2]

[1] The viceroy's proclamation suspending the trade in part reads: "It is an old saying, 'when you enter the frontiers, inquire respecting the prohibitions. When you enter a country, inquire into its customs.' The said Barbarian Eye having been sent by the said Nation's King from a great distance, is undoubtedly a man who understands things; but his having precipitately come to the Provincial City, without having made a full report of the circumstances and causes of coming here, was indeed a want of decorum. . . . To refer to England, should an official Personage from a Foreign Country proceed to the said Nation for the arrangement of any business, how could he neglect to have the object of his coming announced in a Memorial to the said Nation's King? or how could he act contrary to the requirements of the said Nation's dignity, doing his own will and pleasure?"—22 *Br. and For. State Papers*, 1258.

[2] *Ibid.*, p 1278

Convinced that "a continuance of the stoppage of the Trade would cause great injury to the interests of the British Merchants," Lord Napier removed the superintendency to Macao on September 26, and commercial intercourse was forthwith reopened by the Chinese authorities. But the distress occasioned by the failure of his mission, aggravated by a previous indisposition and the wearing effect of the changed climate, ultimately told on him and he died in Macao, October 11, 1834.

Sir J. Graham, speaking in the House of Commons, July 28, 1838, on the policy of the Government concerning its relations with China in 1833, summarized his observations on the career of the first British superintendent of trade in China in one sentence. He said that

it was clear, that Lord Napier leaving this country with an erroneous impression of the powers entrusted to him, did so demean himself to the Chinese authorities as seriously to endanger our commercial relations with that country, and exposed himself to such annoyances as he fully believed cost him his life.[1]

As may be inferred from what has been said, Lord Napier did not have an opportunity to put into operation the British criminal court in China appointed by the act of August 28, 1833; and the two succeeding chief superintendents hesitated to exercise a too vigorous control over their countrymen, who were accustomed to untrammeled ways of living. Sir John F. Davis, who succeeded Lord Napier, established his headquarters in Macao, while Sir George Robinson, Sir John's successor, was well satisfied with remaining on board a cutter among opium-smuggling ships, watching the progress of "this increasing and lucrative trade" and trusting to the "prudence and integrity" of the

[1] 44 Hansard (1838), 750

smugglers to avoid " any unfortunate catastrophe." Even when one Mr. Innes, a British trader, who had some of his goods seized by the custom-house for a breach of the regulations, threatened the local government with his determination to procure redress by himself by acts of reprisal against the Chinese trade, Sir George did not proceed to bring him before the British criminal court but mildly persuaded him not to carry out his threatened acts—acts which, by the way, the law officers of the Crown subsequently advised, would, if carried into effect, amount to piracy, and for which British warships " will be bound to act towards him as the Naval Instructions require Commanders of His Majesty's ships of war to act towards pirates whom they may meet "—by pledging that his case should be submitted to the consideration of the British Government, and that the recovery of his property should be made the subject of a demand on the Chinese authorities on the first occasion of the superintendent coming into formal contact with them.[1]

But even if neither opportunity nor inclination on the part of the superintendents had been wanting, still their task of deducing from their instructions a definite course of action as to the question of jurisdiction over British subjects in China would have been very difficult. With regard to civil matters the sign-manual instructions of December 31, 1833, required the chief superintendent " by the exertion of your utmost influence and authority, to adjust by arbitration, or persuasion, all disputes in which any of our subjects may be there engaged with each other, or with the Inhabitants of China, or with the Subjects or Citizens of any Foreign State; and to mediate between our said Subjects and Officers of the Chinese Government,

---

[1] 25 Br. and For. State Papers (1836-1837), 420.

in order to protect our Subjects aforesaid from all unlawful exactions or hindrances in the prosecution of their commercial undertakings." [1] In conducting such mediation the
superintendent was further required, as towards the Chinese
authorities, to "observe all possible moderation" and to
"cautiously abstain from all unnecessary use of menacing
language; or making any appeal for protection to our Military or Naval Forces," unless in cases of "the most evident necessity." [2] With regard to offenses committed by
British subjects in China, it is true that the act of August
28, 1833, and the Orders in Council of December 9 of the
same year ordered the establishment of a court of justice
and provided certain rules for the trial and punishment of
British offenders. But before these were given a trial, on
January 25, 1834, Viscount Palmerston sent the following
instructions to the chief superintendent:

With respect to questions of Law, the Order in Council appears 'to give you ample instructions; but I have to apprize
your Lordship, that, although it has been deemed advisable
at once to constitute a Court of Justice, yet it is His Majesty's
pleasure that you should not, unless in case of absolute necessity, commence any proceedings under such Order in Council
until you have taken the whole subject into your most serious
consideration. And you will, in the meanwhile, fully report
to me, for the information of His Majesty's Government, the
· result of your deliberation upon this important branch of
your duties.[3]

The obvious reason for staying the operations of the court
would seem to have been that its establishment rested on
questionable grounds and that Lord Palmerston was quite
aware of the circumstance, feeling probably in the same way

. [1] 22 *Br. and For State Papers* (1833-1834), 1229
   [2] *Ibid.*   [3] *Ibid.*, 1234.

as later did Sir J. Graham, who, speaking in the House of Commons on April 7, 1840, referred to the clause " which was inserted according to the recommendation of Sir G. Staunton, for the trial of British subjects, even in the waters of Canton," and stated that he might appeal to his honorable and learned friend, the judge of the Admiralty Court," if this clause was not at least straining beyond international law." [1]

And yet on the obligation of observing the Chinese laws, the same instructions of December 31, 1833, contain this paragraph:

And We do require you constantly to bear in mind and to impress as occasion may offer, upon our Subjects resident in, or resorting to China, the duty of conforming to the Laws and usages of the Chinese Empire, so long as such Laws shall be administered toward you and them with justice and good faith; and in the same manner in which the same are or shall be administered towards the Subjects of China, or towards the Subjects or Citizens of other Foreign Nations resident in, or resorting to China.[2]

When Captain Charles Elliot entered upon the duties of chief superintendent in 1836, he found that British armed smuggling boats landed in front of the custom-house, and accordingly he undertook to issue certain directions for organizing a police to patrol the inner waters of Canton. On April 18, 1838, he sent a dispatch to the Foreign Office in London enclosing a copy of these directions; and what was the reply he received? Lord Palmerston instructed him that the contents of his dispatch had been referred to the law officers of the Crown to determine " whether these regulations are in any way at variance with the laws of

[1] 53 Hansard (1840), 676.

[2] 22 *Br. and For. State Papers* (1833-1834), 1229.

England, or inconsistent with the territorial rights of China;" that according to their opinion, the regulations were not at variance with the laws of England, if they had been made and issued by Her Majesty according to section 6 of the act of August 28, 1833,[1] but that the superintendent had no power of his own authority to make them. Continuing, his lordship stated:

With respect to the territorial rights of China, the law officers are of opinion, that the regulations, amounting in fact to the establishment of a system of police at Whampoa, within the dominions of the Emperor of China, would be an interference with the absolute right of sovereignty enjoyed by independent states, which can only be justified by positive treaty, or implied permission from usage.[2]

In the face of this opinion, the police regulations were of course abandoned; instead, ships of war were dispatched for the purpose of maintaining order among the crews of the British merchantmen frequenting the port of Canton, but with no appreciable effect. The attitude of the British, like other foreigners, became more defiant to the Chinese authorities, and smuggling began to prosper as if under the latter's express sanction. On the conduct of the English during this period in regard to opium smuggling, one of the superintendents later recorded this observation:

The total amount of English smuggling had not only been much less during the administration of the Company at Canton, but they had the power and the means of effectually excluding it from the interior of the Boca Tigris, and confining it to Lintin and the coast. In this manner, however nefarious the nature of the traffic, and however corrupt the

[1] 3 & 4 Will. 4, c. 93
[2] 53 Hansard (1840), 686

officers of the customs, some external show of decency at least was preserved. But on the subversion of the long-established system, and the substitution of an authority whose powers were both inadequate and imperfectly defined, it was soon discovered that license was unbounded, and impunity complete.[1]

§ 6. *Proposed British Legislation of 1838*

But curiously enough, the British Government in the meantime, while hesitating obviously for want of sanction in international law to make use of one judicial institution already provided by Parliament to be established in China, urged upon the legislators in 1838, with all its strength, the creation of another with even greater powers and jurisdiction. On April 30, 1838, Viscount Palmerston introduced in the House of Commons " a bill to authorize the establishing a Court or Courts with Criminal and Admiralty and Civil Jurisdiction in China." [2]   Of this bill the first two provisions read ·

1. *Whereas* it is expedient, with a view to the preservation of good order among Her Majesty's subjects trading or resorting to the dominions of the Emperor of China, and for the purpose of promoting the amicable intercourse between such subjects of Her Majesty and the subjects of the Emperor of China, and also for the prevention of disputes by which such intercourse might be interrupted, that a British Court or Courts, with Criminal and Admiralty and Civil Jurisdiction, should be established in the said dominions, or in the vicinity thereof; Be it therefore Enacted by the Queen's most Excellent Majesty . . . That it shall be lawful for Her Majesty, by Letters Patent, under the Great Seal, to establish a Court or Courts of Justice, with Criminal and Admiralty and Civil

[1] Davis, *China*, vol. i, p. 125.
[2] 93 *Journal of H. Commons*, 476.

Jurisdiction and Authority, within any part of the dominions of the Emperor of China, or in the ports or havens thereof, or within Three Leagues of the coast, for the trial of all offences committed by Her Majesty's subjects within the said dominions, or in the ports or havens thereof, or on the high seas, within One hundred Miles from the coasts of the said dominions; and also for the deciding of all civil cases which shall be brought before such Court or Courts on any subject, matter or thing relating to trade or commerce, arising within the jurisdiction of such Courts, with right of appeal, either to Her Majesty in Council, or to any of Her Majesty's Supreme Courts of Justice in the East Indies, as Her Majesty may be pleased, by any Order or Orders in Council, to appoint; and it shall be lawful for Her Majesty to appoint a Judge or Judges, and proper Officers for such Courts, and to establish forms of proceeding in all matters criminal and civil coming under the cognizance of such Courts; and also by any Order or Orders in Council and either by reference to the provisions of any Act or Acts now in force for administering justice in the East Indies, or otherwise, as may be necessary or expedient, to make and issue any rules, regulations, directions and restrictions touching and concerning the conduct, rights and duties of Her Majesty's subjects trading or being within the jurisdiction of such Courts, and touching and concerning the exercise of such Criminal, Admiralty and Civil Jurisdiction, with a view to the enforcing such rules, regulations, directions and restrictions; and it shall also be lawful for Her Majesty, by any Order or Orders in Council, to authorize the sending out of the limits of the jurisdiction of the said Courts, any person who violate any such rules, regulations, directions or restrictions; and it shall also be lawful for Her Majesty, by any Order or Orders in Council, to impose penalties, forfeitures and imprisonment for any breach of such rules, regulations, directions or restrictions, with reference to any offences or cases triable by such Courts, which penalties, forfeitures and imprisonment shall be enforced in such manner as in the said Order or Orders in Council shall be specified; and all such Orders in Council shall have the full force and effect of laws, in the manner as if they were enacted in and made part of this Act.[1]

2. *And whereas* cases may arise within the jurisdiction of the said Courts wherein the interposition of such Courts may be required by the subjects of Foreign Powers trading to the said dominions, or by the subjects of the Emperor of China, in the determination of differences or disputes between such persons and British subjects; Be it therefore Enacted, That it shall be lawful for Her Majesty, by any Order or Orders in Council, to make and issue in the same manner as aforesaid directions and regulations for the guidance of such Courts in such Cases.

In the remaining sections of the proposal it was provided that the title of superintendent should be changed to consul, in whom should be vested all the powers exercised by the former; and that so much of the act of 1833 as gave power to the Crown to levy tonnage duties on British shipping in China to defray the expenses of the superintendency and the court should be repealed—a provision which was perhaps calculated to serve as an inducement to win the support of the Opposition for the bill as a whole.

For unstated reasons the second reading of the bill was deferred four times and the committee on the same, deferred twenty times; and it was not until July 28, that the House proceeded to resolve itself into a committee thereon. Then, on a motion made by Viscount Palmerston to that effect, Mr. Hawes left his seat and said

that he had carefully looked over the papers, the noble Lord had laid before the House, and he could not discover in them the smallest trace of the smallest consent on the part of the authorities of China to the jurisdiction proposed to be given by the noble Lord. He wished to ask the noble Lord, whether

[1] *Parl. Papers,* 1837-8, vol. I, p. I.

the authorities of China recognized this interference with their laws? The noble Lord was about to establish a court, whose authority he could not enforce. Suppose a Chinese were a defendant, and refused to appear, a verdict was given against him, what power but that of actual force could execute and enforce the jurisdiction of the court?

Here Mr. Hawes recounted a noted case of assault and battery on a Chinese by a Lascar on a ship in which the Chinese authorities took the offender into custody for inquiry and refused to comply with the demand of the chief superintendent for his surrender to be tried by English laws, and justified their refusal by appealing to the laws and usages in European countries, such as France for instance, where an Englishman would be held amenable to French laws. Continuing, Mr. Hawes said:

That proved, that the Chinese well understood their position, and the necessity of obtaining their sanction before instituting this Court. The British were admitted into the Chinese territory by sufferance, for the purposes of trade, and were bound to conform to Chinese usages, and not to attempt to force their own customs upon the Chinese. In case this measure was adopted, and attempted to be carried into effect, we should involve our commercial intercourse with China in very considerable danger. The provisions of this bill were most extraordinary. The Orders in Council—virtually, the orders of the noble Lord (Palmerston)—were to have the force of law, and were to be coextensive with the jurisdiction of the court that was to be established. The East India Company carried their trade without the aid of such powers; and the Americans conducted their commerce with China without any such powers, nay, without any salaried establishment at all; they depended on the simple principles of trading—mutual and reciprocal benefit,[1]

[1] 44 Hansard (1838), 744

The speaker concluded with moving the first of the follow-ing resolutions[1] prepared for the occasion and presented by Sir George Staunton:

That it is inexpedient to pass any Bill for the establishment of Courts of Civil and Criminal Jurisdiction within the Chinese territories, until satisfactory evidence shall have been laid on the Table of this House, that the Court of Pekin has signified its consent:

That any attempt to establish such Courts by the con-nivance, or even formal consent of the Local Authorities, would inevitably lead to the most embarrassing discussion re-specting the independence and jurisdiction of the said courts; and that it appears from the papers laid before this House, that " on the first occasion of discussion in Canton, it may be anticipated that no alternative will remain but the most re-volting submission, or removal from the port "

That British Courts of Civil Jurisdiction in China, unless distinctly recognized by the Chinese Authorities, would be, in an especial manner, injurious to the interests of British subjects trading in that country, as they would be thereby liable to be harassed by the most vexatious prosecutions on the part of Chinese plaintiffs, while they would be wholly without hope of redress against Chinese defendants:

That with a view to the prevention of recurrence of disputes in China in case of homicides committed by British subjects, it is expedient that the British Superintendent should be em-powered to summon a Special Court, to sit, in each case, on board of some British vessel in the port of Canton, or its vicinity, for the trial and punishment of such offences.

On Captain Alsager's seconding the amendment proposed by Mr. Hawes, Lord Palmerston rose in defence of the bill, stating that the resolution as moved applied rather to the act of 1833, which authorized the creation of a court of

[1] 93 *Journal of H. Commons,* 765.

admiralty and criminal jurisdiction than to the present bill; that one reason for his proposing the latter was that he thought that the court should, in addition to criminal and admiralty jurisdiction, possess civil jurisdiction, and that it was doubtful whether this could be effected under the act of 1833, in view of its apparent limitations. Nevertheless, he said he was prepared to discuss the principle of the measure he had proposed. He admitted that the present might be called an exceptional case but he excused himself on the ground that there were no diplomatic relations with China, and that another embassy to obtain them would be inexpedient. He continued:

It was alleged that the India Company had no such Courts, but that they had a power and authority which stood in lieu of it. Cases unfortunately arose, in which offences had been committed by British subjects in China, and the surrender of these subjects was required, and the Company found itself in the discreditable dilemma of either, on one hand, surrendering a British subject to be tried by courts, in which justice was openly set at defiance; or, on the other hand, refusing to deliver up the offender, and invest him with impunity for his offence. That position was full of embarrassment, and it was as discreditable to the character of the Company as it was to the character of the British nation. But such cases happened. Then came the embarrassment; if the Chinese government had chosen to assert its rights, and resented these infractions of its acknowledged jurisdiction, they would have stopped the trade, and that would have been attended with great loss. The Company, however, in more than one instance, risked the loss of trade, rather than be the instruments of committing legal murder on the subjects of this country.

He would admit to his hon. Friend that there was no consent on the part of the Chinese authorities, nor could they obtain it without that intercourse which it was impossible in the present state of things to obtain. But the question was, though the authorities of China had not given their consent, whether they would resent such an interference on the part of this country; and from the papers that had been laid on the table, he thought it clearly appeared that they would not, and that there was every probability of their being reconciled to the proposed exercise of our power.

His lordship then mentioned the name of Sir George Staunton as his authority for the statement that virtually all the Chinese laws were suspended in the case of foreigners, except in capital offences, so that there was " nothing contained in the bill which was at all inconsistent with the present practice, and the acknowledged principles of the Chinese people." Continuing, he said:

He [Sir George] further stated in his book that a foreigner who had committed an offence, if not punished, drew down the hatred of the Chinese upon the country he belonged to: and if he was punished, it led to great humiliation and disgrace to the criminal's countrymen. It was impossible for them to deliver up an offender who was sailing for China, or was resident under our protection.

Lord Palmerston referred next to one Mr. Drummond as stating " that the Chinese, in the event of a murder or homicide, would put to death any person delivered up to them whether guilty or innocent; with what the Chinese, indeed, called a regular trial, but which was, in fact, most irregular and unjust." Then he proceeded to state that—

the Chinese held the Governments of foreign countries responsible for the conduct of all their subjects in China. Sir George Staunton stated, that the Company's servants would be held responsible, not only for the conduct of the crews of all private vessels, but also for all the crews of the king's ships there. And Sir George went on to give an instance of an American, who being given up to the Chinese was put to death. This proved two things, first, that the Chinese held the entire trade of a nation responsible for all its subjects going to China, and, secondly, that the custom of delivering up persons to the Chinese tribunals in cases of homicide (a custom opposed to that which was adopted by the English) was not calculated to lead to a satisfactory conclusion. . . .

He contended, therefore, on the authority of the hon. Member for Portsmouth [Sir George Staunton] that he had clearly established the grounds upon which, not this bill, but the Act of 1833, to which the hon. Baronet opposite [Sir J. Graham] and himself were joint parties, had been passed. A due regard to British interests and to British character required that the bill should pass. If it was shown that the English Government had power to establish Courts for the trial of those greater offences, and Sir George Staunton said it did not apply to the trial of minor ones, he should like to know upon what principle that power was not to be applied to the smaller offences, which it was in fact more necessary to control and prevent, as it would be the best means of preventing that insubordination which was calculated to occasion these more grave offences. . . . Its object [of the bill] merely was to extend the powers of the existing law to the trial of civil offences.[1]

The next speaker was Sir J. Graham who began by admitting the correctness of Lord Palmerston's statement that he had taken some part in framing the measure of 1833,

but he found himself bound to say, that experience had convinced him, that the clauses were unnecessary, and he now considered, that it would be highly inexpedient to extend their operation.[2]

Sir James, however, added that he wished the bill to go

---

[1] For the full text of Lord Palmerston's speech, see 44 Hansard (1838), 745-9.

[2] *Ibid*, 749-51.

into committee, "because he approved highly of the fifth clause for the repeal of the Tonnage duties; and he therefore thought it highly desirable that so much of the bill should pass. It appeared to him, that consistently with the whole course of British policy, with international law and past experience, it would be unadvisable to pass the remainder of the bill. If some understanding were not come to on the point, he should, in the event of a division, vote against the bill."

Mr. Warburton expressed his readiness to support the bill for the repeal of the tonnage duties, but as to the other clauses, he said, they should be deferred until the House had further information on the subject.[1] At this point Lord Palmerston again obtained the floor and stated that

the right hon. Baronet had said, "Get the consent of the Chinese Government, and then come to Parliament." Did the right hon. Baronet really think that that would be the best course to adopt? Because when the Chinese Government was asked to consent, they would naturally inquire what the regulations were before they would decide. Now, the wish of the Government was, to obtain the consent of the Chinese Government to something specific, and that was all that was wanted.[2]

Another member, Mr. M. C. Lushington urged Lord Palmerston to accede to Sir J. Graham's " excellent advice ", as he felt convinced that " it would be utterly useless to attempt to get the consent of the Chinese Government to abstract regulations." [3] Then Mr. Hawes withdrew his amendment and the House went into committee on the bill.

But when clause one was proposed, Mr. Hawes rose again to move its omission, stating that as far as he

[1] *Op. cit.*, p. 751.   [2] *Ibid.*   [3] *Ibid.*

knew, no British merchants had given their assent to the measure, which was therefore to be considered as emanating exclusively from the Foreign Office. To the establishing of a court for trial of offences by British subjects, said Mr. Hawes, there could be no objection; but he protested against a court's interfering with an independent power like China.[1]

The Solicitor-General urged that the omission of the clause would place the House in a novel situation. There were, he said, two thousand of her Majesty's subjects resident near Canton, and it was necessary that there should be some means of settling the disputes which might arise. It was, according to him, for the benefit of those on the spot, that there should be some tribunal to which they might resort.[2]

Finally, Viscount Palmerston, stated that as the sense of the House appeared to be against the bill, he had " no objection to postponing it until next session." The bill was accordingly withdrawn.[3]

The proceedings on the bill of 1838 have been described above somewhat at length, not so much because they evidence the fact that it was introduced in Parliament and failed of passage, as because they elucidate certain principles which were claimed to constitute a valid ground, not only for the bill itself, but also for the act of 1833, which, as has been pointed out, was enacted at the time with little or no discussion of the principles underlying it. In the debate which took place on the bill, Viscount Palmerston, it is clear, was at once its originator and practically its sole supporter, and his speech may therefore be regarded as more important than the rest, showing the reasons he had in his mind for justifying the action of the British Government in setting up, of its own initiative and

[1] *Op. cit*, p. 751.   [2] *Ibid.*   [3] *Ibid.*

without previous consent of the territorial sovereign, an extraterritorial jurisdiction in China. It is also clear that the arguments which his lordship advanced in support of the introduction of the principle of extraterritoriality into China were not claimed by him to be original, but that he expressly stated his principal authority to be Sir George Staunton, who, as a matter of fact, was one of the avowed and most unyielding opponents to the bill, he having himself formulated and presented the set of resolutions which were calculated for no other purpose than to defeat the proposed law. Lord Palmerston's arguments as embodied in his speech may be summarized as follows: (1) that the Chinese under their own law of homicide would put to death any person delivered to them, whether guilty or innocent, thus necessitating the withdrawal of British subjects from their criminal jurisdiction, (2) that the trade of the entire nation would be held liable for the acts of one of its individuals or of its public ships; (3) that though their consent had not been obtained, the Chinese would not resent the interference of the British Government, as symbolized by the act of 1833 and the proposed measure of 1838, with their acknowledged rights of jurisdiction but that they could be reconciled to it; and (4) that the Chinese laws were suspended in the case of foreigners, except in capital offences, so that the proposed bill was not inconsistent with "the present practice and the acknowledged principles of the Chinese people."

The facts alone that not a single voice was raised in Parliament approving these arguments advanced by Viscount Palmerston in defence of his bill, but that many were lifted in refuting them, and that because of an overwhelming opposition the bill itself had finally to be withdrawn, seem to suffice to show that they cannot be either as convincing or as substantial as they may appear on initial inspection. Still it may not be altogether fruitless to examine one or two of them a little more closely. The first and second contentions, it will be recalled, have already been discussed and found to be invalid or exaggerated in connection with the consideration of the reasons assigned by the British merchants at Canton for their open resistance to Chinese law and authority; save, as to the practice of holding the entire British trade responsible for the acts of British public ships, it may be observed that in the case of H. M. S. *Topaze*, if not the only one, certainly the most prominent of its kind, the select committee was relieved by the viceroy of all imputations of responsibility as soon as he became aware that the Company's agents really had no control over the officers and crew of the vessel concerned in the case. With regard to Lord Palmerston's third proposition, it was no more than an illusory hope which, as will be presently seen, was bound to be betrayed by subsequent facts.

This brings us to the fourth and the most important contention, namely, that the Chinese authorities had voluntarily suspended Chinese laws in cases wherein foreigners were concerned, except in those of capital offences. The statement was admittedly based on an observation made by Sir George Staunton in his then recent book. In Sir George's *Notices of China*, first published in London, 1822, the author, in the chapter on "Considerations upon the China Trade," after reviewing the character of the regulations adopted by the Chinese authorities for the government of foreigners within their territory, stated: [1]

On the other hand, and as some compensation, for the imposition of such restrictions and disabilities, it appears that foreigners have, almost from the first, been admitted to be personally exempt, excepting only in cases of capital offences, from the direct operation of the penal code of the Empire.

[1] On page 131.

A footnote to this observation reads:

This exemption is expressly stated in an Imperial Edict issued in 1808, on the occasion of the trial of the British seaman, Edward Sheen: Indeed, both the law, and the excepted case, are very fully and distinctly laid down in that edict as follows: " In all cases of offences by contrivance, design, or in affrays happening between foreigners and natives whereby such foreigners are liable, according to law, to suffer death by being strangled or beheaded, the magistrate of the district shall receive the proofs and evidence thereof, at the period of the preliminary investigation, and after having fully and distinctly inquired into the reality of the circumstances, report the result to the viceroy and sub-viceroy; who are thereupon strictly to repeat and revise the investigation. If the determination of the inferior courts, upon the alleged facts, and upon the application of the laws, is found to have been just and accurate, the magistrate of the district shall, lastly, receive orders to proceed, in conjunction with the chief of the nation, to take the offender to execution, according to his sentence. *In all other instances, of offences committed under, what the laws declare to be, palliating circumstances, and which are therefore not capitally punishable, the offender shall be sent away to be punished by his countrymen in his own country.*" [1]

In the absence of the Chinese text of the edict, from which the passage was quoted by Sir George, it is of course impossible to say whether the italicized sentence is or is not an accurate translation of the original; and left in the form in which it stands, and taken alone, it does seem to convey the idea that the exemption from the territorial laws was accorded foreigners in China in cases not involving capital punishment. But the edict as represented by Sir George's own translation, which is appended by him to his " Penal Laws of China," [2] embodies much more than what was

[1] The italics are Sir George's.   [2] Page 523.

quoted by. him in the passage reproduced above, and some·
of the omitted parts of the edict, while they may not suffice
conclusively to contradict his inference as to the exemption
of foreigners from Chinese laws, appear, nevertheless, to
throw serious doubts on its finality or even its accuracy.
Thus immediately preceding his extract of the edict there
is this statement:

The foregoing having been the substance of report of the viceroy, to His Imperial Majesty, we deliberated thereon, and have
ascertained that, according to the preliminary book of the
penal code, all persons from foreign parts, committing
offences, shall undergo trial and receive sentence according
to the laws of the Empire: Moreover, we find it declared in
the same code, that any person accidentally killing another,
shall be allowed to redeem himself from punishment, by the
payment of a fine; lastly we find, that in the 8th year of Kien-
Lung (1743) it was ordered, in reply to the address of the
viceroy of Canton then in office, that thenceforward, in all
cases of offences by contrivance, etc. [here follows the extract
in question.]

And immediately following it there is this paragraph:

The case of the Englishman, Edward Sheen, opening a
window-shutter in an upper story, and the wooden stick which
supported it, slipping and falling down so as accidentally to
hit Leao-a-teng, a native, who was passing by, and by striking him to occasion his death, appears to be, in truth, one of
those acts, of the consequences of which, neither sight, hearing, or reflection could have given a previous warning; there
was, therefore, no pre-disposition to injure, as the case is evidently agreeable to the construction stated in the commentary
upon the law of accidental homicide. The said Edward
Sheen ought therefore, conformably to the provisional sentence submitted by the viceroy to his Majesty, to be allowed
to redeem himself from the punishment of death by strangula-

tion (to which he would otherwise have been liable, by the law against homicide by blows), by the payment of a fine of 12 leang 4 feu and 2 lee to the relations of the deceased, to defray the expenses of burial: and then be dismissed to be governed in an orderly manner in his own country.

From the first of these two passages it clearly appears that the amenability of foreigners to the territorial laws, whatever offence they might commit, was expressly confirmed. The second contains a judgment of sentence obviously intended to be in strict conformity with the three applicable rules of law stated in the preceding paragraph: the very fact of judging and sentencing Edward Sheen, a foreigner, at all, conforms to the first rule of the amenability of aliens in China to Chinese laws; the sentence to pay a fine in lieu of punishment is in accordance with the second rule of law as to accidental homicide; and what about the third rule contained in the italicized sentence? Instead of abstaining from exercising jurisdiction over the offender and sending him away " to be punished by his countrymen in his own country," as should have been done, if Sir George's interpretation of the rule had been correct, Sheen's offence clearly being one " committed under, what the laws declare to be, palliating circumstances," and which was " therefore not capitally punishable," the edict, after sentencing him to pay a prescribed fine, continued with this clause: " and then be dismissed to be governed in an orderly manner in his own country." The significance of the clause seems to be that, as applied by the supreme criminal court at Peking, the rule embodied in the italicized sentence in question did not, as was contended by Sir George, confer upon foreign defendants in cases of offences not capitally punishable the privilege of exemption from the territorial laws, but that it had a quite contrary purpose and effect. To the ordinary penalties prescribed by the law for such minor offences, the rule added that of expulsion from the country, where the offender was a foreigner—a provision not at all unusual in countries of the west. And this view of the purport of the rule appears also to be in harmony with the other provision in the edict of 1743, in which it originated, which was to the effect of depriving foreign offenders, capitally punishable by law and already provisionally sentenced to death by the Provincial authorities, of the benefit of a period of confinement, which the law had theretofore required to lapse in all cases between sentence and execution, in order to give the supreme tribunal in Peking time for revising the sentence in favor of the prisoner, if it saw fit Nor, again, is the distinction maintained by the edict of 1743 between offences capitally punishable and those which were not, in enforcing the added penalty of expulsion,—altogether unintelligible, since in the former case it would have been unnecessary as well as incapable of execution.

Moreover, the probable circumstance that the Chinese authorities had not taken cognizance of every case of minor offence committed by foreigners no more proves willingness or readiness on their part to exempt the alien offenders from the territorial laws than similar omissions in cases involving Chinese subjects alone can be taken as evidence of their intention to accord immunity to their own subjects from the operation of the laws. If true, the circumstance was but an incident of the principle which the Chinese conceived to underlie all human laws, namely, the preservation of the public tranquillity, and of the consequent policy on the part of the officials not to intervene in any case of offence except where such tranquillity was disturbed. Besides, it is a fact that the Chinese authorities did exercise jurisdiction over foreigners in cases of even such offences as were obviously not punishable by death according to Chinese law, assaults on Englishmen in Macao, for instance, being dealt with by the Chinese authorities as late even as 1826.[1]

It is clear, then, that what Sir George Staunton stated as to the voluntary suspension by the Chinese authorities of the territorial laws in favor of foreigners committing minor offences in China was based, to say the least, on questionable grounds; that Viscount Palmerston's repetition of it in the House of Commons on July 28, 1838, had no more sanction of accuracy than the original statement itself; and that as it was, the contention can hardly be accepted as a sound and valid argument for the introduction into China of the principle of extraterritoriality, which underlay the bill of 1838 as well as the act of 1833.

The attitude of the Chinese rulers toward the assumption by Great Britain of jurisdiction over the British subjects in China, as represented by the criminal court set up in pursuance of the act of 1833, now remains to be considered. If it had been expected, as it appears to have been by Viscount Palmerston in 1838, that the authorities of the Celestial Kingdom would not resent such interference with their rightful jurisdiction but would soon reconcile themselves to an accomplished fact, the expectation could not have been based on a correct reading of the signs of the time. The mere fact that they refused from the very outset to recognize and receive on a footing of equality the successive superintendents sent to China by the British Government, should have, it seems, sufficed to forewarn one of entertaining such a self-complacent view. On the part of the mandarins there was a sustained adherence to the principle of territorial sovereignty and jurisdiction. As late as January 2, 1839, Captain Elliot, the chief su-

[1] Morse, *Intern Rel.*, p. 101.

perintendent, could see no prospect of having his anxiety relieved by a change of attitude on the part of the local government on the question of jurisdiction over the British merchants in China, for on that day he wrote to Viscount Palmerston:

My own anxiety on this subject will be more explicable, when I inform your Lordship, that till I am differently instructed, I should hold it to be my duty to resist to the last, the seizure and punishment of a British subject by the Chinese law, be his crime what it might; and crimes of the gravest character have lately been of every day probability.[1]

And Captain Elliot had just cause to feel perturbed   For hardly had his dispatch reached England when Commissioner Lin in March, 1839, ordered away the Chinese servants from the British factory, cut off their supplies, and placed them in a state of siege, for the sole purpose of enforcing obedience to the Chinese law against the opium traffic.[2]   Again, half a year later, on July 7, when Lin Wei-hi, a Chinese, was killed by English sailors in a riot on the Kowloon side of the Hongkong anchorage, " occasioned by their attempt to obtain spirits to drink," the commissioner lost no time in demanding the unconditional delivery of the English offenders for trial.   He declined even to consider the proposal of the British superintendent to hold a joint investigation "congenial to the customs of both nations" and place the murderer, when found, "on his trial according to the laws of his own country, before the Honorable [Chinese] officers;"[3] and he refused to accept the superintendent's subsequent invitation to send

[1] 29 *Br. and For State Papers* (1840-1841), 920,
[2] Davis, *China and the Chinese,* p 134
[3] 30 *Br. and For. State Papers* (1841-1842), 12.

deputies to attend a trial on board a British ship scheduled to take place on August 12. Captain Elliot proceeded with his trial without any Chinese representative and sitting as judge, he undertook, after much hesitation, to convict five sailors of riot and assault, and sentenced them to pay a fine and undergo a period of imprisonment in some prison in the United Kingdom.[1] But these proceedings only further strengthened the determination of the commissioner, who, seeing that mere verbal demand would not produce the desired surrender of the British culprits, went so far to enforce the territorial jurisdiction as to move down to Heungshan, midway between Canton and Macao, with 2000 troops to compel delivery. It is, of course, true that the British superintendent and the British merchants, in the face of an imminent attack by the commissioner, and the food supplies to Macao having been cut off, simply left China by embarking on board the ships on August 26,[2] and retained to the last the offenders whose surrender was demanded of them; but at the same time, so far as the question of principle is concerned, there is no room for doubt that the Chinese authorities uncompromisingly upheld their own sovereign jurisdiction, not only refusing to recognize, but persistently and, as in this case, forcibly resisting, any infringement of it by the British.

This was the last case of homicide involving British

[1] In holding this "court of justice" and sentencing his offending countrymen, Captain Elliott was not at all sure if he did not thereby exceed his authority, and he subsequently considered it necessary to plead his conscience in justification of his proceedings —30 Br. and For. State Papers, 25 In fact, it appears that "the sentence of imprisonment was never carried into effect, the government deciding that the authority vested in the superintendent did not give him jurisdiction over the person and liberty of the subject."—Morse, Intern. Rel, p. 238.

[2] Capt. Elliot to Vt. Palmerston, Aug. 27, 1839; 29 Br. and For State Papers (1840-1841), 1038.

subjects, which occurred before the outbreak of hostilities between China and Great Britain in the autumn of 1839, and the controversy which arose out of it was not different from that which had attended previous cases of a similar character. The situation on the question of jurisdiction over British subjects in China, more particularly during the half a century down to the eve of the opium war, may therefore be summarized as follows: On one hand the British merchants, with the aid of the East India Company prior to 1834, and with the official countenance and support of their Government after that year, openly, violently and stubbornly refused to submit themselves to the Chinese jurisdiction, especially in cases of grave crimes committed by any one of them; and on the other, the Chinese rulers manifested an equally strong determination and a like readiness to resort to all means in their efforts to overcome the contumacy of the British and to subject them to the control of Chinese law and authority. Between these two views and policies, there was obviously a broad gulf of difference—too broad to be bridged by peaceful compromise; and controversy and clash were naturally rife. As in the case of the other vexatious questions between the two countries, right having failed to prevail, the question of jurisdiction over British subjects in China was to be settled only by the arbitrament of might.

When the two countries were engaged in *bello flagrante* there was of course no opportunity for re-considering the question of extraterritoriality; but when the vanquished sued for peace, the victor did not fail to avail herself of the occasion to extract as many concessions of rights and privileges as she desired. In his instructions [1] of February 20, 1840, to Admiral G. Elliot and Captain C. Elliot, pleni-

---

[1] Morse, *Intern. Rel.*, p. 628, appendix B.

potentiaries appointed to treat with the Chinese Government, Lord Palmerston stated that the British Government was willing to accept, " as full reparation for the affront offered to the British Crown by the indignities put upon Her Majesty's Superintendent, and by the outrageous proceedings adopted towards Her Majesty's other subjects in China," and " as security against their occurrence, the cession of one or more Islands on the Coast, to be fixed upon by the Naval Commander and the Superintendent, as eligible to be occupied as stations at which Her Majesty's subjects trading to China might reside in safety, under the protection of British authority ; and from whence they might securely carry on their commercial intercourse with the principal Ports of the Coast of China ;" but that the British Government would forego the permanent possession of any island on the Chinese coast, if the Chinese Government consented, in lieu of any cession of territory, to give by treaty security and freedom of commerce to British resident in China. His lordship then stated what the " principal stipulations of such a Treaty ought to be," one of which was to the effect that commodities introduced into China by British subjects against the prohibition of Chinese laws and lawful goods smuggled into China by them without any duty being paid upon them might be seized and confiscated, " but that in no case shall the Persons of British Subjects be molested on account of the importation or the exportation of Goods." Another principal stipulation was thus stated:

That the British Superintendent of Trade, or Consul-General, shall, if ordered to do so by his own Government, be at liberty to make Rules and Regulations, and to establish Courts of Justice, for the government of British Subjects in China ; and that if any British Subject shall be accused of any offence or crime, he shall be tried by the Tribunal which may be established by the Superintendent or Consul-General for such a purpose; and that his punishment, if he be found guilty, shall be left to the British Government or its authorities.[1]

In the draft treaty accompanying these instructions, an article providing for the establishment of British courts in China and for the trial and punishment of British offenders by such courts, concluded with this clause: "And, in general, all causes and suits in which British subjects in China shall be defendants, shall be tried by the above-named tribunals."[2]

§ 7. *Concession of Extraterritorial Rights to British Subjects at Nanking, 1842*

Although it is thus seen that the cession of an island and the conclusion of a commercial treaty were intended to be alternatives, yet in the peace negotiations which took place at Nanking, Sir Henry Pottinger, who had superseded the earlier plenipotentiaries for Great Britain, obtained both of them. In addition to the cession of Hongkong, it appears that Sir Henry also secured the freedom of commercial intercourse, including the privilege of extraterritoriality for British subjects within the dominions of China. It is true that the treaty of peace signed on H. M. S. Cornwallis at Nanking, August 29, 1842, did not expressly provide for the enjoyment of such a privilege by British subjects; but at the same time there are substantial grounds for believing that the concession was granted by the Chinese peace commissioners at Nanking as part of the price paid for the restoration of peace and friendship.

In the first place, article XIII of the General Regulations, conceding the principle of extraterritoriality to Great Britain, expressly refers to certain correspondence ex-

---

[1] Morse, *Intern. Rel*, p. 629. [2] *Ibid.*, p 300.

changed at Nanking.   The language of the article in part reads:

Regarding the punishment of English criminals, the English Government will enact the laws necessary to attain that end, and the Consul will be empowered to put them into force; and regarding the punishment of Chinese criminals, these will be tried and punished by their own laws, in the way provided for by the correspondence which took place at Nanking after the concluding of the peace.[1]

Secondly, long before the general regulations were signed or published by the plenipotentiaries of the two nations, it appears to have been understood in England that the concession of extraterritoriality in favor of British subjects in China had been granted by the Chinese Government at the end of the war.   On March 17, 1843, a little over three months after the treaty of Nanking with its accompanying dispatches from Sir Henry had arrived in London (December 10, 1842), the Marquis of Lansdowne stated in the House of Lords

that he wished to impress upon Her Majesty's Government the necessity of legislating even during the Session, for the purpose of creating such an authority in that country as was absolutely necessary; in his opinion even an imperfect act would be better than none at all.   In 1838 the then Government proposed a bill for the purpose of establishing a Court at Canton but it was strenuously opposed by a right hon. Baronet now high in Her Majesty's Council, upon the ground that the Chinese government had given no authority for it, and would not recognize it.   That ground was now removed, for the expediency of such a tribunal had been recognized by the Chinese authorities.[2]

[1] *Treaties between China and Foreign States*, i, p. 196.
[2] 67 Hansard (1843), 1077.

And it appears further that the advice of the Marquis of Lansdowne was not unheeded. On August 3, 1843, when the general regulations could not have as yet reached England with the means of communication in vogue at the time, Viscount Gordon introduced in the House of Lords a bill entitled " An Act for the better Government of Her Majesty's Subjects resorting to China," which became an act of Parliament on August 22, 1843,[1] authorizing the Superintendent of British Trade in China to make and enforce laws for the control of British subjects in the dominions of the Emperor of China. Indeed within four weeks after the treaty of Nanking and the accompanying correspondence arrived in London, new Orders in Council began to be issued putting into full operation the court of justice created under the act of 1833.

The third ground for believing that the concession of extraterritoriality was obtained by Great Britain at Nanking at the end of the war, is that the general regulations embodying the extraterritorial provision were not only in substance a mere confirmation and amplification of certain principles of commercial intercourse already agreed upon between the plenipotentiaries of the two countries at the scene of the peace negotiations, but also were considered and understood at the time as forming a part of the treaty of peace. They were signed by Sir Henry Pottinger and Commissioner Kiying, probably on June 26, 1843, the day on which they met and exchanged the ratifications of the treaty of Nanking, but certainly on or before July 22, in the same year, when they were published by the two plenipotentiaries simultaneously in separate proclamations.[2] These regulations were put into effect at Canton imme-

---

[1] 6 & 7 Vict , c. 80.

[2] For the text of the proclamations, see 31 *Br. and For. State Papers* (1842-3), 138; *Parl. Papers*, 1844, vol. 51, p. 348

diately after their publication, and at the other four ports
a little later. In the British document, together with the
import and export tariffs, which "have been; after the most
searching scrutiny and examination, fixed and finally agreed
upon," they were designated as "a Commercial Treaty, stipulated for in the Definitive Treaty of Peace signed at Nanking on the 29th of August, 1842." [1]   Again, the fact that
these regulations were first officially printed intact with the
treaty of peace, although they were subsequently also appended to the supplementary treaty of October 8, 1843,
after being incorporated into its second article to avoid
any possible misunderstanding, seems likewise to show that
they were considered at least by the British to be a part
thereof. [2]

Moreover, certain questions put by the Earl of Clarendon
to the Earl of Aberdeen, Secretary for Foreign Affairs, as
to the character of the regulations, in the House of Lords,
on February 6, 1844,—when the text of the supplementary
treaty was yet on its way to England—seem directly to
bear out the point which is under consideration. After
expostulating on the importance of the treaty of peace and
the necessity of having it perfectly understood, the Earl
of Clarendon said, with reference to the regulations, that
they appeared to him

[1] Sir Henry Pottinger, in his proclamation of July 22, 1843, declared
that "at the same time it is his duty . . . to distinctly intimate, that he
is *determined*, by every means at his disposal, to see the provisions of
the Commercial Treaty fulfilled by all who choose to engage in commerce with China, and that in any case when he may receive well-
grounded representations from Her Majesty's Consuls, or from the
Chinese Authorities, that such provisions of the Commercial Treaty
have been evaded (or have been attempted to be so), he will adopt the
most stringent and decided measures against the offending parties."—
31 *Br. and For. State Papers* (1841-1842), 138, *Parl. Papers*, 1844, vol.
51, p 348.

[2] See *Parl. Papers*, 1844, vol. 151, pp. 329-338.

to be formed most carefully with a due regard to the customs of the Chinese, and with a view to prevent those insults and frauds on their side, and the quarrels and disorders on ours, by which the intercourse between the two nations had been so frequently interrupted. These regulations, he apprehended, must be considered as part of the Treaty; because in the second article of the Treaty they were referred to, and thus formed an integral part of it. But as this was nowhere positively affirmed, it was desirable to know what was understood and intended by Her Majesty's Government, whether British subjects were bound to obey those regulations, and whether Her Majesty's representatives in China had authority to enforce those regulations, as a portion of the Treaty engagements between the two countries?[1]

To this interpellation the Earl of Aberdeen said that

the regulations to which his noble Friend referred had been drawn up jointly by Sir H. Pottinger and the Chinese commissioners, and therefore certainly might be taken as a part of the Treaty.[2]

In view of these grounds it may be safely said that the principle of extraterritoriality was formally conceded by China to Great Britain, for the first time, not in the general regulations of July 22, 1843, still less in the supplementary treaty of October 8, 1843, but in 1842 at Nanking at the close of the opium war; although prior to that time, as has been shown, the British merchants had from the outset claimed and assumed the privilege, and although later the British Government had set up in China a system based upon the principle, in both cases in spite of the discountenance and opposition of the Chinese authorities. And the concession of extraterritoriality was, to use the language of the Earl of Clarendon, " one of the most important of the whole Treaty [of Peace]."[3]

[1] 72 Hansard (1844), 263.   [2] *Ibid.,* 266.   [3] *Ibid.,* 263.

§ 8 *British Legislation and Orders in Council of 1843 on Extraterritorial Jurisdiction in China*

It now remains to review briefly the extraterritorial legislation adopted by Parliament for application in China and the executive measures taken by the Crown in pursuance thereof, during the period between the conclusion of the treaty of Nanking, August 29, 1842, and for convenience' sake, the signing of the treaty of Wanghia between China and the United States, July 3, 1844, in order to see to what extent the extraterritorial system which Great Britain had originally erected in China without sanction of the law of nations and in defiance of the Chinese Government, and the recognition of the principle of which, had ultimately been wrung out from the Chinese Emperor only by force of arms, was reorganized and set into renewed operation. In carrying out this proposed survey it is desirable to follow as closely as possible the chronological order, as it is only thus that the process of perfecting the machinery of British extraterritorial jurisdiction in China may be clearly understood.

By an Order in Council of January 4, 1843,[1] it was ordered that the court of justice with criminal and admiralty jurisdiction, as appointed by the act of 1833 and established by an Order in Council of December 9, 1833, " shall henceforth be holden in the island of Hongkong; and that the same shall have and exercise jurisdiction for the trial of offences committed by Her Majesty's subjects within the said island and within the dominions of the Emperor of China, and the ports and havens thereof, and on the high seas within 100 miles of the coast of China.". The chief superintendent appointed in pursuance of the act of 1833 was required to hold the court. By the same Order

[1] 31 *Br. and For State Papers* (1842-1843), 1373.

all other provisions of the Order in Council of December 9, 1833, were confirmed.

Another Order in Council of February 24, 1843,[1] prohibited British subjects from resorting for commercial purposes to any other ports in China than the five opened by the treaty of Nanking, " or than may be in the occupation of Her Majesty's forces." Any British subject, upon conviction of a breach of this direction in any British court of record or vice-admiralty, was made liable to a penalty, not exceeding £100, or to imprisonment, for a term not exceeding three months; and all proceedings held under this Order, "shall be, as far as circumstances will permit, in conformity with the law of England."

On August 3, 1843, as will be recalled, a bill was introduced in the House of Lords for the purpose of improving the machinery for the government of British subjects in China. It was passed by the Lords on August 11 and by the Commons on August 17, without debate in either place;[2] and it became an act of Parliament on August 22.[3] The preamble of the act made no reference to the treaty of Nanking's including the general regulations, but recited the act of 1833, and then continued:

Whereas, for giving full effect to the Purposes of the said Act, it is necessary that Provision be made for the Establishment from Time to Time of Regulations for the Government of Her Majesty's Subjects resorting to China, and it is expedient that such Regulations should originate with some local Authority cognizant of the actual Circumstances and Exigencies of such Her Majesty's Subjects, and of the Trade carried on by them in China, etc.

[1] *Op. cit.*, 1374.

[2] 75 *Journal of H. Lords*, 570 *et seq.*; 71 Hansard (1843), 536, 908, 986.

[3] 6 & 7 Vict., c. 80.

It then enacted in the first section:

' That it shall be lawful for Her Majesty . . '. to authorize the
Superintendent' of the Trade of Her Majesty's Subjects in
China (so long as such Superintendent shall be also the Governor of the Island of Hong-Kong) to enact, with the Advice
of the Legislative Council of the said Island of Hong-Kong,
all such Laws and Ordinances as may from Time to Time be
required for the Peace, Order, and Good Government of Her
Majesty's Subjects being within the Dominions of the Emperor of China, or being within any Ship or Vessel at a Distance of not more than One Hundred Miles from the Coast of
China, and to enforce the Execution of such Laws and Ordinances by such Penalties and Forfeitures as to him, by the
Advice aforesaid, shall seem fit.

Section 3 provided:

That it shall also be lawful for Her Majesty . . . to ordain,
for the Government of Her Majesty's Subjects . . . [within
the aforesaid jurisdiction] . . . any Law or Ordinance which
to Her Majesty may seem meet, as fully and effectually as
any such Law or Ordinance could be made by Her Majesty
in Council for the Government of Her Majesty's Subjects being within the said Island of Hong-Kong.

In pursuance of this new act, Sir Henry Pottinger, who
had been appointed Governor of Hongkong on April 6,
preceding, was confirmed by a commission of August 26,
1843,[1] in his previous appointment to the office of chief
superintendent of British trade, and was empowered by
another commission [2] bearing the same date to exercise the
powers and authorities vested in his office by the first
section of the act of 1843.

[1] *Parl. Papers*, 1844, vol. 51 [556]; 31 *Br. and For. State Papers*
(1842-1843), 1233
[2] *Ibid.*

By an Order in Council of October 2, 1843,[1] it was directed that if any law or ordinance made in pursuance of the act of August 22, 1843, "shall be in any wise repugnant to, or at variance with" the Orders in Council of December, 1833, January 4, 1843, and February 24, 1843, "then such law or ordinance, so long as the same shall be in force, shall be obeyed and observed, anything in the said recited Orders in Council contained to the contrary in anywise notwithstanding."

An ordinance made by the Governor of Hongkong on January 24, 1844,[2] provided, in the first article, that "the law of England shall have the same force, virtue, power and effect over Her Majesty's subjects within the dominions of the Emperor of China, or within any ship or vessel at a distance of not more than one hundred miles from the coast of China, in all matters whatsoever, whether civil or criminal, that it has over Her Majesty's said subjects within Her Majesty's Colony of Hong-Kong." Article 2 authorized the courts in Hongkong to exercise over British subjects in China or within 100 miles from her coast the same power, jurisdiction and authority in criminal and civil matters, that they had or should have in Hongkong. By Article 3 British subjects brought before the courts of Hongkong for having committed crimes in China or in her stated neighborhood were precluded from objecting to the jurisdiction of such courts; and by article 4 Macao was to be considered as within the dominions of the Chinese Emperor for the purposes of the ordinance.

In order to carry into effect the ordinance of January 24, 1844, Sir Henry Pottinger enacted another of February

[1] 31 *Br. and For. State Papers*, 1237.
[2] *Parl. Papers*, 1844, vol. 51 [556]; 32 *Br. and For. State Papers* (1843-1844), 870.

28, 1844,[1] the first article of which provided that " Her Majesty's Consuls shall, within the limits of the ports in China where they may be officially resident, possess the same jurisdiction, power and authority that is now or shall always be possessed by any Court of Judicature at Hong-Kong, save always as is hereinafter mentioned and excepted." By the fourth article it was provided " that the said Consul shall have full power (if he thinks fit to use the same) to adjudicate upon and determine alone, and in a summary way, all misdemeanors and other minor offences, which shall appear to him not to deserve a greater punishment than he is hereinafter authorized to inflict, and also civil suits and actions, wherein the sum claimed shall not exceed 500 dollars, and which shall not be founded on any libel, trespass and other personal wrong." The next article made consular decisions liable to revision by the Supreme Court of Hongkong. By the sixth article the consul was given " power and authority to sentence any person committing any misdemeanor or other minor offence, to pay a fine to Her Majesty, her heirs and successors, not exceeding 200 dollars, and to suffer imprisonment for any period not exceeding two months, and in case of nonpayment of any fine to suffer a further imprisonment not exceeding two months in lieu thereof, or until the same shall be paid." The ninth article conferred upon the consul " full power to grant probates of the wills, and letters of administration to the estates of Her Majesty's subjects dying or leaving property within the limits of such port as aforesaid."

For the purpose of more effectively enforcing observance of the treaties between China and Great Britain, an-

[1] Parl. Papers, 1845, vol 51, China; 32 Br. and For. State Papers (1843-1844), 871.

other ordinance of April 10, 1844,[1] was made, of which the first article declared certain specified parts of the treaties[2] to be ordinances for British subjects in China and within 100 miles from her coast, and to have the same force and effect as if they had been severally enacted in the ordinance. The second article gave the British superintendent of trade and British consuls in China " full power and authority to enforce the due observance of the said Treaties," to inflict all fines and penalties provided therein, to levy the same by all means on the property of the offender or of the ship to which he belonged, and to commit him to prison in default of paying the penalty. Article 3 provided that

the said Superintendent of Trade and Consuls, in addition to inflicting the said fines or penalties, shall possess full power and authority to arrest and detain all persons offending against the provisions of the said Treaties, and the ships or vessels owned, commanded, or navigated by such persons, and to imprison such persons until they shall find proper security for their good behaviour, or shall demand to be sent to Hong-Kong.

Where the law of England or the treaties themselves did not provide any penalty for an infringement of certain provisions in the latter, the superintendent and the consuls were authorized by the fourth article to punish such infringement by a fine not exceeding 200 dollars to be levied in the same manner as other fines. In cases of flagrant offences against the treaty provisions, the superintendent was empowered by the fifth article to inflict and enforce on the offender double the amount of any fine or penalty

---

[1] 32 *Br. and For. State Papers* (1843-1844), 881.

[2] Arts. 1, 2, 4, 6, 9, 10, 11, 12 of the supplementary treaty, and all the general regulations.

which the consuls were authorized to inflict, and in default of payment, to commit him to prison for double the term of imprisonment in lieu thereof.

In an Order in Council of April 17, 1844,[1] after reciting the Chinese Courts of 1843 and stating:

And whereas [by the Foreign Jurisdiction Act of August 24, 1843,][2] it is among other things enacted that it is and shall be lawful for Her Majesty to hold, exercise, and enjoy, any power or jurisdiction which Her Majesty now hath, or may at any time hereafter have, within any country or place out of Her Majesty's dominions, in the same and as ample a manner as if Her Majesty had acquired such power or jurisdiction by the cession or conquest of territory: And whereas Her Majesty hath power and jurisdiction in the dominions of the Emperor of China:

it was ordered that British consuls and vice-consuls resident in China

shall severally in the districts within which they may respectively be appointed to reside, have and hold all necessary power and authority to exercise jurisdiction over British subjects within such districts as aforesaid, for the repression and punishment of crimes and offences by them committed within the dominions of the Emperor of China, and for the arrangement and settlement of all and all manner of differences, contentions, suits, and variances that may or shall happen to arise between them or any of them; and shall moreover have power and authority, as far as in them lies, to compose and settle all and all manner of differences, contentions, suits, and variances that may or shall happen to arise between British subjects and the subjects of the Emperor of China, and between the subjects of any foreign Power, and which may be brought before them for settlement.

[1] *Parl. Papers*, 1844, vol 51 [556]; 32 *Br. and For. State Papers*, 895.
[2] 6 & 7 Vict, c. 94.

By the same Order in Council British consuls and vice-consuls in China were given authority to cause any British subject charged with any crime committed in China, the cognizance of which appertained to them or any of them to be sent for trial to the colony of Hongkong. It was further ordered that the chief justice of Hongkong " shall, when duly required by the said Superintendent, proceed to the dominions of the Emperor of China, and shall have power and authority within the said dominions to inquire of, try, determine, and punish any crimes or offences committed by British subjects within the said dominions."

This Order in Council, of April 17, 1844, was the last measure taken by the British authorities before the conclusion of the treaty of Wanghia, July 3, 1844, between China and the United States, to perfect the machinery of British extraterritorial jurisdiction in China, the next step of importance being the ordinance of November 20, 1844,[1] made by Sir J. F. Davis, Governor of Hongkong, and Chief Superintendent after February 9, 1844, " for the better administration of Justice in the Consular Courts, and to establish a Registration of British subjects within the dominions of the Emperor of China;" which empowered British consuls and vice-consuls to compel the attendance of British witnesses under the penalty of a fine; to summon, in more grave cases, two or not more than four British subjects to act as assessors to assist them in the trial, but not in the decision, of such cases; and to deport from China any British subject, twice convicted of any crime in the consular court and unable to find sufficient and good surety for his future good behaviour; and which also provided for the compulsory registration of every British subject in China under the penalty of being refused the protection of the British Government in any difficulties in which he might be involved.

[1] 32 *Br. and For. State Papers*, 886.

§ 9. *Caleb Cushing's Theory of Extraterritoriality*

After what has been said above, it is scarcely necessary to remark that the generally accepted notion that Caleb Cushing, by negotiating the treaty of Wanghia, July 3, 1844, introduced extraterritoriality into China, is totally destitute of foundation. It is undoubtedly true that the provisions on the subjects found in the first American treaty have the merit of clearness in definition and analysis, but it is equally true that as to the principle, they contain nothing which may be called original. At the time when Mr. Cushing signed his treaty, Great Britain through her plenipotentiary, Sir Henry Pottinger, had, at the end of a long and expensive war and as a result of it, wrung from China a reluctant and unprecedented consent to the broad doctrine of extraterritoriality, and had, in pursuance of that express consent, set up a comprehensive and potent machinery for the exercise of jurisdiction over her subjects in China. Moreover, she had, even before the war, claimed and assumed the privilege for her subjects, in defiance of the Chinese Government. Indeed, the American plenipotentiary, in preparing his draft of the treaty, had the full benefit of consulting the texts of those already concluded by Sir Henry,[1] and, as will be presently seen, he himself acknowledged that in asking for the privilege of extraterritoriality for his own countrymen in China he was influenced by the example of Great Britain

There is, however, one point in connection with the study of the origin of the extraterritorial jurisdiction in China which calls for something more than a passing notice—a point, by the way, which may have accounted for the erroneous conception just noted. In his despatch to the

---

[1] On April 1, 1844, Mr. Cushing requested Viceroy Cheng to send him full copies of the treaties negotiated with Great Britain, and his request was readily acceded to.—14 *Chinese Repository* (1845), 361.

Secretary of State at Washington, July 5, 1844,[1] transmitting a copy of the treaty he had just concluded, Mr. Cushing enumerated among the "peculiar provisions" those by which "all Americans in China are to be deemed subject only to the jurisdiction of their own government, both in criminal matters, and in questions of civil right," and stated that he would "have occasion to enter into these subjects somewhat in detail." That occasion he found on September 9, 1844, when he sent to Secretary of State Calhoun a lengthy communication,[2] in which he expressed himself as being "solicitous" to call attention to the extraterritorial provisions he had inserted in the treaty of Wanghia, and endeavored, with an undisguised sense of triumph and pride, to justify the application of the principle of extraterritoriality to China on what he conceived to be principles of international law. At the outset, he had of course to lay down and consider certain postulates. He observed that the general question of extraterritoriality was very imperfectly understood: that "among the elementary writers on the law of nations, the most approved, —such as Vattel and Klüber,—omit to place in a proper light the all-important fact, that what they denominate the law of *all nations*, is, in truth, only the international law of Christendom." He pointed out that the practice of consular jurisdiction was initiated by the Italians who traded to the Levant; there being no security given by the Mohammedan rulers for the lives and property of Christians committed to their authority, these Italian traders formed themselves into separate communities and placed over each of them a consul, who was to exercise over it the same magisterial functions which were performed by similar offi-

[1] 14 *Chinese Repository* (1845), 555.

[2] S. Ex Doc. 58, 28 Cong., 2 Sess., 4; H Ex. Doc. 69, 28 Cong, 2 Sess, 5.

cers in their native countries — Pisa, Genoa, and Venice. Just at this period Europe itself had similar usages; the northern conquerors allowed the vanquished to be governed and tried by their own separate laws. Later the development of the state system on the continent resulted in the gradual disappearance of extraterritorial jurisdiction, while in non-Christian countries the practice continued. The inferences which Mr. Cushing drew from these circumstances were:

The extended power of foreign consuls, still maintained by Christian States as against Mohammedan States was the original fact; the limited power of foreign consuls within the Christendom itself is the new fact, or the innovation, which the several States of Christendom have established and asserted in favor of each of the completeness of its respective domain and sovereignty.

This fact, according to Mr. Cushing, was " the result and the evidence of the superior civilization, and respect for individual rights consequent thereon, which prevails in Christendom," thus ensuring personal security to every foreigner, and thereby dispensing with the necessity of exemption from the local jurisdiction; while " in semi-barbarous Mohammedan states, on the contrary, no Christian feels safe in subjection to the local authorities; and there, accordingly, each Christian state asserts for its subjects more or less of exemption from the authority of the local sovereign."

The propositions he next laid down were these:

In truth and fact, the subjection of foreigners in all criminal matters, and in most civil, to the local jurisdiction, and the consequent limitation of the power of consuls, is the general fact in the states of Christendom.

In states non-Christian, on the other hand, the general fact is the exemption of Christians from the local jurisdiction.

Great Britain was cited by the American envoy as an example to show that in no part of Asia, Africa, or America, so far as he remembered, she had ever admitted the subjection of her people to the local authorities, unless the local authorities were Christian; they being, with one or two exceptions, either European colonies or new states formed of such colonies; through the instrumentality of consuls or trading companies and factories, the British Government always secured this exemption; and he added that "such has been the practice of all the other states of Christendom, in their commercial relations and intercourse with the non-Christian states of Asia and Africa." In his opinion, the principles of territorial jurisdiction, to which even consuls were subject, they being exclusively commercial officers,

apply to the international intercourse of no states but those of Christendom. For, in regard to the various Mohammedan states . . . I conceive that the universality of the practice anterior to treaties, and still more when confirmed in signal instances by treaties, of conceding to Christian foreigners exemption from the local jurisdiction, renders such a practice a part of the law of nations, as against them just as much as in the same way the opposite rule has come to be the doctrine of the law of nations within the limits of Christian states.

Having thus established to his own satisfaction that extraterritoriality for foreigners in Mohammedan countries became part of international law as against them, Mr. Cushing stated that "all the reasons of the thing, which dictate the assertion of such a right in behalf of Christian foreigners in the Mohammedan states, apply with equal force to the pagan states of Asia and Africa;" and he forthwith proceeded to discuss the case of China. He said:

Questions of jurisdiction have arisen frequently in China:

and these questions have not been without difficulty, arising from the peculiar character of that empire, and the want of clear and fixed ideas on the subject among Europeans as well as Americans.

Nothing, it would seem, corresponding to our law of nations, is recognized or understood in China. I had some evidence of this in the progress of my own intercourse with the Chinese authorities; and there is abundance of public facts to the same effect.

He cited certain examples, such as the treatment of the British embassies under Lord Macartney and Lord Amherst, and observed that they evinced " utter ignorance or at least disregard, of the law of nations as understood in Europe." At the same time he admitted that the Chinese Government " never failed to assert " " a complete and exclusive municipal jurisdiction over all the persons within the territory and waters of the empire," and that while claims for surrender of European offenders had been sometimes successfully resisted, it " has also been acquiesced in sometimes by vessels belonging to various European states." After referring to the cases in 1780, 1784, and 1821, he continued:

In all these cases, the Chinese enforced a reluctant submission on the part of the foreign residents, by stopping or threatening to stop all trade. And the foreign residents were the less able to defend themselves against the claims of the Chinese, from not having any distinct perception of the true principle of public right which governed the subject.

Europeans and Americans had a vague idea that they ought not to be subject to the local jurisdiction of barbarous governments, and that the question of jurisdiction depended on the question whether the country were a civilized one or not. And this erroneous idea confused all their reasonings in opposition to the claims of the Chinese: for it is impossible to deny to China a high degree of civilization, though the civilization

is, in many respects, different from ours. . . . And while re-
pudiating the jurisdiction of the local authorities in China,
Europeans and Americans failed to perceive that rejection of
that jurisdiction implied the claim and admission of the jurisdiction of their own government.

Mr. Cushing then commented on Captain Elliot's proceedings in 1839 and remarked that in firmly resisting the surrender of certain English sailors charged by the Chinese
with homicide and in himself taking jurisdiction of the
case, the captain " had a right conception of the true point
of this question; adding that " so far as concerned Great
Britain, the whole matter was definitively settled by the late
treaties, which secured to British subjects in China perpetual exemption from the local jurisdiction, as elsewhere
in Asia, and exclusive subjection to the laws and authorities of their own government." Reverting to his own
mission to China, he stated:

I entered China with the formed *general* conviction that the
United States ought not to concede to any foreign state,
under any circumstances, jurisdiction over the life and liberty
of any citizen of the United States, unless that foreign state
be of our own family of nations—in a word, a Christian state.

The states of Christendom are bound together by treaties,
which confer mutual rights and prescribe reciprocal obligations. They acknowledge the authority of certain maxims
and usages received among them by common consent, and
called the law of nations, but which, not being acknowledged
and observed by any of the Mohammedan or pagan states,
which occupy the greater part of the globe, is *in fact* only the
international law of Christendom. Above all, the states of
Christendom have a common origin, a common religion, a
common intellectuality; associated by which common ties,
each permits to the subjects of the other, in time of peace,
ample means of access to its dominion for the purpose of

trade, full right to reside therein, to transmit letters by its mails, to travel in its interior at pleasure, using the highways, canals, stage coaches, steamboats, and railroads of the country, as freely as the native inhabitants. And they hold a regular and systematic intercourse as governments, by means of diplomatic agents of each residing in the courts of the others, respectively. All these facts impart to the states of Christendom many of the qualities of our confederated republic.

How different is the condition of things out of the limits of Christendom! From the great part of Asia and Africa individual Christians are utterly excluded, either by the sanguinary barbarism of the inhabitants, or by their phrenzied bigotry, or by the narrow-minded policy of their governments; to their courts, the ministers of Christian governments have no means of access, except by force, and at the heads of fleets and armies. As between them and us, there is no community of ideas, no common law of nations, no interchange of good offices; and it is only during the present generation that treaties (most of them imposed by force of arms, or by terror) have begun to bring down the great Mohammedan and pagan governments into a state of inchoate peaceful association with Christendom.

To none of the governments of this character, as it seemed to me, was it safe to commit the lives and liberties of citizens of the United States.

In China, I found Great Britain had stipulated for the absolute exemption of her subjects from the jurisdiction of the empire: while the Portuguese attained the same object through their own local jurisdiction at Macao. And, in addition to all the other considerations affecting the question, I reflected how ignominious would be the condition of Americans in China, if subjected to the local jurisdiction, whilst the English and the Portuguese around them were exempt from it.

I deemed it, therefore, my duty for all the reasons assigned, to assert a similar exemption in behalf of citizens of the

United States. This exemption is agreed to, in terms, by the letter of the treaty of Wanghia. And it was fully admitted by the Chinese in the correspondence which occurred contemporaneously with the negotiation of the treaty, on occasion of the death of Shu Aman.

By the treaty, thus construed, the laws of the Union follow its citizens, and its banner protects them, even within the domains of the Chinese empire.

Here is then Mr. Cushing's theory of extraterritoriality. Stripped of all verbiage, it comes to this: The practice of extraterritorial jurisdiction had been an original and universal fact in Europe, Asia, and Africa; with the evolution of the modern state in the first-mentioned continent, it disappeared and there developed a common law of nations with its doctrines of equality and territorial sovereignty, of which Christian states alone should be the beneficiaries, inasmuch as it was a creature of Christendom; while in the Mohammedan countries the practice continued to be observed as a usage, and was subsequently confirmed by treaties. This being the case, extraterritoriality should be considered as a rule of international law, as against these countries. The pagan states were as much non-Christian as the Mohammedan, and to them, therefore, the same rule of exemption of Christian foreigners from the local jurisdiction should be applied. In the case of China, although she had, prior to the war with Great Britain, always claimed and exercised jurisdiction over foreigners within her empire, yet such contention and practice were against "the true principle of public right which governed the subject," and the general acquiescence on the part of Europeans and Americans in the enforcement of the local jurisdiction upon them was due solely to their ignorance of that principle. Moreover, as manifested by her pursuance of the policy of seclusion, she had no knowledge whatever of the law of nations as understood in Christendom. Therefore, the proper rule of intercourse applicable to China in her relations with the subjects of Christian nations was, according to the international law of Christendom, that of their exemption from the territorial jurisdiction.

In following, however, Mr. Cushing's excursus on the origin and theory of extraterritoriality and his arguments in support of the application of that theory to China, it can scarcely fail to be perceived that the premises upon which he built his conclusion, however true they may have been of Europe and the Levant, with both of which he was undoubtedly familiar, were hardly true of China. In the first place, the original fact, found in western history, of extended consular jurisdiction and the domination of personal law among aliens has no parallel in Chinese history. China had already developed into a well-organized political entity when foreigners began to penetrate into her territory; and there is no evidence to show that prior to her modern treaties, alien law had ever been permitted to prevail among strangers within her empire to the prejudice of the supreme law of the land. In the second place, the analogy which the American envoy drew between Mohammedan countries and China, and upon which he based his application to the latter of the doctrine of extraterritoriality which had been persistently practiced by the former, was again inexact. It was true enough in Mohammedan states that religion determined one's status, that faith in the Koran was the fountain and foundation of all rights of liberty and property, and that those who followed a different creed had no status before their law and rulers. But in China no such disabilities were imposed on the members of exotic sects; there spiritual belief was not taken as the criterion of one's rights; persons of all religious persuasions were protected by one law and ruled over by one sovereign.

In short, the necessity for the exemption of foreigners from the local jurisdiction which existed in Mohammedan countries by reason of the religious basis of their law and institutions, did not arise in China, where foreigners, as a rule, were never subjected to disabilities on account of their faith in alien creeds.

With regard to Mr. Cushing's statement of China's ignorance of the law of nations as understood in Europe, it may be admitted that as the result of the absence, after the commencement of the modern era, of direct and free intercourse with western nations, she was unacquainted with many of the rules and principles which regulated the relations between the nations of Christendom; yet at the same time it is to be remembered that seclusion had not characterized her disposition toward foreign countries and their subjects in the earlier centuries, and that it had been subsequently chosen by her as the proper policy to pursue, it will be recollected, only when it had become, according to her lights, necessary to the integrity of her empire and the security of her interests. If the American envoy could have recalled in his mind the difficulties and dangers which China had experienced as the result of her earlier unrestricted intercourse with western nations and their subjects, it is probable that he would have withheld his stricture on this score and rendered an entirely different opinion.

On the other hand, if Mr. Cushing's intention, in entering into the extended discussion of the theory of extraterritorial jurisdiction in the Levant and of its application to China, was merely to justify his taking the initiative to insert two extraterritorial provisions in his own treaty, it would have been sufficient for him simply to point to the example of the British treaties as a precedent. By war Great Britain had succeeded in coercing China to relinquish, in favor of the British Government, her rightful jurisdiction over the British subjects within her territory; and concessions of rights, such as this, wrung out of one nation by another in consequence of the successful application of force, constituted, as they still do now, a lawful prize of victory, inasmuch as force was then as now a lawful means for any nation that chose to employ it. The United States, whose commercial interests in China were as extensive as those of Great Britain, could not, as it would be "ignominious," bear seeing British subjects in China more favorably treated by the Chinese Emperor than its own citizens; and the American negotiator of the treaty of Wanghia might well have rested content with placing the extraterritorial provisions of his making on such a simple ground as that of equality of treatment, as he might have thus escaped the onus of justifying theoretically a principle which was not applicable to China.

But one significant circumstance, however, appears to be that Mr. Cushing's instructions on the question of jurisdiction over United States citizens in China did not leave him as much discretion as he needed; that in demanding, of his own initiative, and obtaining the privilege of exemption from the local jurisdiction in favor of his countrymen in China, he probably apprehended that in so doing he had run counter to the wishes of his Government and consequently felt the necessity of explaining his action on some broader and loftier ground than that of a solitary precedent established by the arms of another nation. What the wishes of the United States Government were on the question may be easily gathered from the following passage taken from President John Tyler's letter [1] to the Emperor of China, July 12, 1843, of which Mr. Cushing as "envoy extraordinary and minister plenipotentiary of the United

[1] S. Ex Doc. 138, 28 Cong, 2 Sess, 8.

States of America to the Court of Peking," [1] was the official bearer:

The Chinese love to trade with our people, and to sell them tea and silk, for which our people pay silver, and sometimes other articles. But if the Chinese and the Americans will trade, there shall be rules, so that they shall not break your laws or our laws. Our minister, Caleb Cushing, is authorized to make a treaty to regulate trade. Let the people trade not only at Canton, but also at Amoy, Ningpo, Shanghai, Fuchau, and all such other places as may offer profitable exchanges both to China and the United States, provided they do not break your laws nor our laws. We shall not take the part of evil doers. We shall not uphold them that break your laws.

The emphasis here laid upon the indispensable condition to the prosecution of trade of observance of the territorial laws undoubtedly indicates a strong desire on the part of the United States Government to leave the conduct of its citizens in China to be regulated by the Chinese law; and if it is said that the passage was probably prompted by a wish on the part of President Tyler to intimate that his country would not undertake to protect its merchants from the consequences of engaging in illegal traffic, such as that of opium, the statement only further strengthens the inference as to the desire of the American Government. It

---

[1] This first American embassy to China was organized after Congress had made in January, 1843, an appropriation of $40,000 (H. Jour., 27 Cong., 3 Sess, 605), recommended by President Tyler in a special message of December 30, 1842 (H. Ex. Doc. 35, 27 Cong, 3 Sess.), " for the compensation of a commissioner to reside in China, to exercise a watchful care over the concerns of American citizens, and for the protection of their persons and property; empowered to hold intercourse with the local authorities, and ready, under instructions from his Government, should such instructions become necessary and proper hereafter, to address himself to the high functionaries of the Empire or, through them, to the Emperor himself."

is possible that Mr. Cushing had no opportunity of apprizing himself of the contents of the presidential epistle, but then he received from Daniel Webster, Secretary of State, May 8, 1843, instructions [1] about the proposed treaty which appear to point clearly in the same direction as to the intentions of his Government on the question.   In one place the instructions read:

You will state in the fullest manner the acknowledgment ot this Government, that the commercial regulations of the empire, having become fairly and fully known, ought to be respected by all ships and persons visiting its ports; and if citizens of the United States, under these circumstances, are found violating well-known laws of trade, their Government will not protect them from the consequences of their own illegal conduct.

Again, in the closing paragraph there is this clause:

It is hoped and trusted that you will succeed in making a treaty such as has been concluded between England and China [of August 29, 1842]; and if one containing fuller and more regular stipulations could be entered into, it would be conducting Chinese intercourse one step further towards the principles which regulate the public relations of the European and American States.

And there can scarcely be any doubt that the recognition of China's plenary jurisdiction over aliens within her territory would have been a more regular stipulation, and made China's foreign intercourse a nearer approach to the public relations of Europe and America, than its complete divestiture.

Moreover, the records of the time do not show that the United States merchants in China had expressed a firm de-

---

[1] S. Ex. Doc 138, 28 Cong., 2 Sess., 1.

sire for their exemption from the local jurisdiction On the contrary, it appears that they were fully disposed to submit themselves to the control of Chinese law as a matter of course. The surrender of the offender in the case of Terranova in 1821, and the declaration of intention they made on that occasion always to abide the territorial law, have already been noted.[1] Besides, in a memorial of May 25, 1839,[2] addressed by eight American merchants at Canton to Congress at Washington, requesting their Government " to establish commercial relations with this empire upon a safe and honorable footing," the only demand relative to the question of jurisdiction was:

6th. That until the Chinese laws are distinctly made known and recognized, the punishment for wrongs committed by foreigners upon Chinese, or others, shall not be greater than is applicable to the like offence by the laws of the United States or England; nor shall any punishment be inflicted by the Chinese authorities upon any foreigner, until the guilt of the party shall have been fairly and clearly proved.

In fact even this proposal appears to have been thought as unwise by other Americans in China. For in a later memorial[3] to Congress signed by thirty-six merchants of Boston and Salem, Mass., it was stated:

While the undersigned would advocate strongly the sending of a national force to China, for the protection of American commerce from illegal aggression, they would deprecate the delegation to its commander, or to any other person at this time, of any powers to interfere in the contest between Eng-

[1] *Supra*, p. 54.

[2] Read in Congress, January 13, 1840, H. Ex. Doc. 40, 26 Cong, 1 Sess

[3] Referred to House Committee on Foreign Affairs, April 9, 1840, H Ex. Doc. 170, 26 Cong., 1 Sess.

land and China, or to enter into any diplomatic arrangement whatever.

They would represent, that the character, laws, and customs, of the Chinese nation, are so little understood, that, even granting our right to demand a change in their foreign policy, it would be unwise to authorize an envoy to negotiate with them until the whole subject had been examined and considered in our national councils with all procurable information before them.

And in view of these two memorials, the portions quoted above from President Tyler's letter to the Chinese Emperor and Mr. Webster's instructions to Mr. Cushing, emphasizing the duty of the American citizens in China to observe the territorial laws, appear to be all the more significant, since it is not improbable that these documents were drawn up in accordance with the opinion, and to meet the desires, of those most closely concerned in the matter—the United States citizens in China.

Nor would it be altogether forcing the point to say that as a concession of privilege, the extraterritorial provisions in the treaty of Wanghia were not of as much importance as the American negotiator appears to have attributed to them, inasmuch as England, in obtaining extraterritoriality as well as other rights for the British subjects in China in 1842, avowedly, had not sought for exclusive privileges; and as China, having once been compelled by force to yield the principle of territorial jurisdiction to one foreign nation, had apparently been prepared to accord equal treatment in this respect, if she had not actually done so at the moment when Mr. Cushing reached China, to all others that were then represented commercially at Canton. Queen Victoria, in her speech before Parliament, February 1, 1844, said, " Throughout the whole course of my negotiations with the Government of China, I have uniformly disclaimed the wish for any exclusive advantage;"[1] and the Earl of Aberdeen, when asked in the House of Lords, on February 6, following, whether the omission of a provision to this effect in the British treaty was "purely accidental", replied that it had always been the desire of the Government that the privileges acquired by Great Britain "should be extended to all nations alike;" that although it did not appear in the first treaty, he had no doubt that a clause had been inserted in the supplementary treaty signed by Sir Henry Pottinger and the Chinese commissioner, although the text had not been transmitted to England; and that, further, to show how justified was Her Majesty in declaring what had been the principle with regard to the negotiations with China he had only to quote a paragraph from his instructions of November 4, 1841, to Sir Henry, to the effect " that he should constantly bear in mind, that we sought for no exclusive advantage, and demanded nothing which we were not willing to see enjoyed by the subjects of all other states." [2]

On the part of China, it appears that after the general regulations embodying the privilege of extraterritoriality for Englishmen in China were concluded, imperial edicts were issued, granting " to all foreign Countries whose Subjects, or Citizens, have hitherto traded at Canton the privilege of resorting for purposes of Trade to the other four Ports of Fuchow, Amoy, Ningpo and Shanghai, on the same terms as the English." [3] Besides, in a note to Mr. Cushing, April 19, 1844,[4] in reply to his proposal to

[1] 32 *Br. and For State Papers* (1843-1844), 1.

[2] 72 Hansard (1844), 267.

[3] Article VIII, British treaty of Oct. 8, 1843. *Treaties between China and Foreign States*, i, p 204.

[4] 14 *Chinese Repository* (1845), 364.

proceed to Peking and negotiate a separate treaty for the
United States, Viceroy Ching stated:

At present, the trade of every country with China is harmon-
ious, and every point relating thereto is properly adjusted,
which was accomplished when the imperial commissioner
Tsiyeng [Kiying], in conjunction with the present acting
governor, deliberated upon and settled with the English plenipotentiary, Pottinger, repeatedly discussing them until we
had arranged and fully agreed upon them all.   The consuls of
every nation were, moreover, to act in every particular according to this same arrangement.   Henceforth, China and
foreign nations would be at peace, gladness and prosperity
would be without limit, and joyful contentment everywhere diffused.

   Let your excellency, in order to prove this, take the several
regulations which I, the acting governor, on that occasion,
promulgated, and again with your country's consul, Forbes,
examine the former general regulations with those which were
subsequently agreed upon, and carefully look over them all,
and he will then know that our august emperor tenderly
cherishes men from afar, and that whatever would be of advantage to the merchants of every nation has certainly been
done to the utmost.

In a word, according to the viceroy, whatever had been
granted to the British subjects in China was also enjoyable
by citizens of the United States, and therefore, to use his
own expression, " it is useless, with lofty, polished, and
empty words, to alter these unlimited advantages " [1]

   In truth, in the case of Sue Aman, which occurred on
June 16, 1844, five days before the negotiations on the
treaty of Wanghia were opened, in which a Chinese by that
name was killed by an American at Canton, although Mr.
Cushing notified the American consul that he thought it

---

[1] 14 *Chinese Repository* (1845), 357.

desirable to inform his countrymen that he would " refuse at once all applications for the surrender of the party who killed Sue Aman," [1] no demand for his delivery appears to have been made, but, on the contrary, the local authorities appear to have considered that the American consul should himself decide the case in accordance with the new regulations of trade. It is true that in Viceroy Ching's letter to Mr. Cushing, June 18, 1844,[2] as translated by E. C. Bridgman, Chinese secretary, there is this clause: " But it has been ascertained that the native Aman was shot in the space before the factories by an American; and the said consul should himself know that he ought immediately to make a full inquiry into the matter, and deliver up the real murderer, that the case may be equitably judged, and no untoward event arise out of it." Yet the same paragraph containing the clause concludes with this statement:

The people are highly irritated against the offender, and it is impossible but that they have constant debates among themselves until they are revenged.   The said consul, knowing the feelings of the people for times past, should inquire closely into the affair and *himself decide it quickly*, that it do not become in the mouths of the people an occasion for collision. I hope you will by no means delay, as it is for this that I send this important statement.

The viceroy's language here conveys rather the idea of complaint against procrastination on the part of the consul in proceeding against the offender than a positive demand for the latter's surrender for trial by the Chinese authorities.   And this would seem to be borne out also by the remaining correspondence on the case.   On June 24,

[1] Mr. Cushing to Consul Forbes, June 22, 1844, *ibid*, 525.
[2] 14 *Chinese Repository* (1845), 488.

1844, Mr. Cushing sent a brief note[1] to the viceroy, Kiying, as follows:

I assure your excellency that I deeply regret what has occurred. I have caused to be instituted a careful inquiry into all the facts of the case, and shall take every step in my power to see that full justice be done in the premises, feeling most solicitous that harmony and good understanding may continue to exist, as well between the people of our respective countries as between their governments.

In reply to this, the viceroy on June 28, 1844, observed:[2]

Since your excellency has already transmitted orders to the resident consul, Forbes, that he make thorough inquiry into the matter, and report to you, it is to be seen that it will be conducted according to equity and right. But it is important that both sides be equally satisfied, in order to cause the minds of the people to submit; . . . If there is one particle of heavenly goodness, let this business by all means be judged on equitable grounds, so that there be no room for cavilling remarks (in future). Then will it be easy to protect and guard; and by the power of right thus operating, our mutual feelings for each other will become as they were formerly. I think that your excellency, too, is of the same opinion as this.

And in his letter of August 8, 1844,[3] acknowledging receipt of Mr. Cushing's report of the settlement of the case by the consul in accordance with his own directions,[4] Viceroy Kiying simply observed that the provincial treasurer

---

[1] 14 *Chinese Repository* (1845), 490.

[2] *Ibid*, 492.   [3] *Ibid.*, 532.

[4] On July 11, 1844, six American residents of Canton, who were summoned by the consul in pursuance of Mr. Cushing's order, "having heard the evidence placed before them, are unanimously of opinion that the killing was a justifiable act of self-defence."—*Ibid*, 526.

had already transmitted a communication from Consul Forbes, in which it was pointed out that Daniel, who killed Sue Aman by accident, had been delivered over to Cushing "to be returned to his country, to be dealt with according to its laws; and that the treasurer had examined and ascertained that this is in accordance with the treaty."

Finally, the unusual expedition with which the treaty of Wanghia was concluded, the whole course of the negotiations occupying scarcely two weeks, seems also to lend support to the proposition that in all probability the Chinese authorities considered the question of jurisdiction over the foreigners within their territory to have been settled once for all in their earlier negotiations with Sir Henry Pottinger, the British plenipotentiary.

CHAPTER X

PROTECTION UNDER THE EXTRATERRITORIAL JURISDICTION

§ 1. *Criminal Matters Involving Chinese and Aliens*

THE preceding section on the origin of the extraterritorial jurisdiction in China has made it clear that the essence of extraterritoriality, as claimed by Great Britain and as finally granted by China, consists in the exemption from the jurisdiction of the local authorities and the submission to that of one's own nation specially erected within the territory. It now remains to compare the provisions in the principal treaties in which China has conceded this broad principle of jurisdiction, to consider the manner in which, and the means with which, the treaty powers put this principle into practice, and to see to what extent aliens are thus protected or exempted from the operation of Chinese laws.[1]

In studying these problems, let us take up first the question of crimes and their punishment. The thirteenth of the general regulations of trade, July 22, 1843, which were subsequently incorporated *in toto* in the supplementary treaty with Great Britain of October 8, 1843, was the first explicit statement of the principle of extraterritoriality granted by China. As has already been seen, it provided that the punishment of English criminals should be left to the English Government which would enact the laws

[1] For all treaty provisions quoted or referred to in this section, see *Treaties between China and Foreign States*, which alone is consulted unless otherwise indicated.

necessary to attain that end, and which would empower its consuls to put them in force. But while the credit for taking the initiative and establishing a precedent must be awarded to the British compact, it is the American treaty of July 3, 1844, which defined for the first time with lucidity, fulness and precision, the principle of extraterritorial jurisdiction in China. Article XXI of this treaty provided:

Subjects of China who may be guilty of any criminal act towards citizens of the United States shall be arrested and punished by Chinese authorities according to the laws of China, and citizens of the United States who may commit any crime in China shall be subject to be tried and punished only by the Consul or other public functionary of the United States, thereto authorized according to the laws of the United States; and in order to the prevention of all controversy and disaffection, justice shall be equitably and impartially administered on both sides.

The broad principle thus stated was taken by France as the basis of a similar provision in her own treaty with China concluded at Whampoa, October 24, 1844. Article XXVII of the French compact read:

Si, malheureusement il s'élevait quelque rixe ou quelque querelle entre des Français et des Chinois comme aussi dans le cas où durant le cours d'une semblable querelle un ou plusieurs individus seraient tués ou blessés, soit autrement les Chinois seront arrêtés par l'autorité chinoise, qui se chargera de les faire examiner et punir, s'il y a lieu conformément aux lois du pays. Quant aux Français, ils seront arrêtés à la diligence du consul, et celui-ci prendra toutes les mesures nécessaires pour que les prevenus soient livrés à l'action régulière des lois françaises, dans la forme et suivant les dispositions qui seront ultérieurement déterminées par le gouvernement français.

Il en sera de même en toute circonstance analogue et non prevue dans la présente convention, le principe étant que, pour le répression des crimes et délits commis par eux dans les cinq ports, les Français seront constamment régis par la loi française.

It will be noted that the statement of the principle of extraterritoriality, as respects crimes committed by Frenchmen, is, if not more explicit, certainly more emphatic still than that which was found in the American treaty. It is, however, not so broad: the application of the principle was evidently intended to be limited to crimes and delicts committed by Frenchmen " dans les cinq ports;" while by the terms of the United States treaty it was stated with sufficient comprehensiveness to cover any crime committed " in China " by citizens of the United States. The restrictive phrase in question was later replaced perhaps intentionally by the words " en Chine " in Article XXXVIII of the French treaty of Tientsin, June 27, 1858.

Another point of difference between the two articles quoted respectively from the first American and the first French treaty may be noted. Whereas the former article stipulated that Chinese subjects guilty of any criminal act towards United States citizens shall be " arrested and punished by the Chinese authorities and that citizens of the United States guilty of any crime in China shall be subject to be " tried and punished," not " arrested and punished," by authorized functionaries of their own nation, the latter, while leaving Chinese offenders to be arrested by Chinese authorities provided: " Quant aux Français, ils seront arrêtés à la diligence du Consul, etc." In other words, while United States citizens guilty of a crime in China might be arrested by Chinese authorities, this right seems to have been relinquished by China as regards French criminals. The difference is borne out in later compacts with the two countries, which remain in force to-day. Article XXXVIII of the French treaty, June 27, 1858, reproduces Article XXVII of the treaty of Whampoa, with one modification already noted above, and not concerning the point now under consideration; on the other hand, Article XI of the American treaty signed June 18, 1858, expressly confirms the retention by Chinese authorities of the right recognized by the treaty of 1844, to arrest Americans committing crimes in China. This has been done by leaving out, in the second treaty, the word " arrested " in the clause as to Chinese offenders found in the first treaty, namely, " shall be arrested and punished by the Chinese authorities," and also by adding a new clause, which, by the way, is reciprocal by its terms, providing: " arrests in order to trial may be made by either the Chinese or the United States authorities."

The line of cleavage drawn, perhaps unconsciously, on the question of arrest of foreigners committing criminal acts in China, is traceable in the treaties with other powers. Article XXI of the first American treaty was copied almost literally in that with Norway and Sweden, March 20, 1847, and in the British treaty of June 26, 1858. Similarly, the treaties with Russia, June 1-13, 1858, with Portugal, August 13, 1862, with Spain, October 10, 1864, with Japan, July 21, 1896, contain no provision which requires their respective subjects, accused of a crime in China, to be arrested only by the functionaries of their own nation. On the other hand, in harmony with the French treaties, which deny China the right to arrest French offenders in China, are those with Germany, September 2, 1861, with Denmark, July 13, 1863, with Belgium, November 2, 1865, with Italy, October 26, 1866, with Austria-Hungary, September 2, 1869; with Brazil, October 3, 1881, and with Mexico, December 14, 1899.

It must be pointed out, however, that the discrepancy in the treaties referred to as to the exercise by Chinese authorities of restraint upon foreign persons applies only in places open to foreign commerce   Where subjects of treaty powers charged with a crime perpetrated in open ports, have escaped into the interior, or where they commit criminal acts in the interior, or in treaty ports where their nation is not represented, the treaties generally provide that the accused shall be arrested, taken custody of, and conducted by the Chinese local authorities to the nearest place where their consul resides, for trial and punishment.[1]

§ 2. Civil Matters Involving Chinese and Aliens

As regards disputes between Chinese and foreign subjects in China, the provisions of the treaties concluded with foreign powers are generally similar in language and meaning.   Article XIII of the general regulations incorporated into the supplementary treaty with Great Britain, October 8, 1843, prescribed two modes of settling mixed controversies, which are still followed to-day.   Although this article along with the remaining provisions of the

---

[1] By article xiii of the treaty with Japan, September 13, 1871, which was abrogated by that of Shimonoseki, April 17, 1895, it was provided, however, that subjects of each contracting party in the dominions of the other, when accused of a crime committed therein, should be arrested by the local authority, and if resisting capture with weapons of a murderous nature, might be slain in the act without further consequences beyond communicating a report of the killing to the consul; that those subjects guilty of a crime, if at a port, should be jointly tried by the consul and the local authority, and if in the interior, they should be tried and dealt with by the local authority with an official report to the consul, that in cases where a subject of one contracting party, in the dominions of the other, collected persons to the number of ten or more, conspiring to create disorder, he should be tried jointly by his consul, or solely by the local authority, according as the crime was committed in the port or in the interior; in either case, however, the execution was to be performed at the scene of the commission of the offence

general regulations was abrogated by the treaty of June 26, 1858, its contents were repeated in identical form in article XVII of the latter compact which reads:

A British subject having reason to complain of a Chinese must proceed to the Consulate and state his grievance. The Consul will inquire into the merits of the case and do his utmost to arrange it amicably. In like manner, if a Chinese have reason to complain of a British subject, the Consul shall no less listen to his complaint and endeavor to settle it in a friendly manner. If disputes take place of such a nature that the Consul cannot arrange them amicably, then he shall request the assistance of the Chinese authorities, that they may together examine into the merits of the case and decide it equitably.

Thus the two modes of settling disputes between Chinese and British subjects are amicable arrangement through the the Consul and prosecution of a suit to be examined and decided by the authorities of the two nations. The same system is provided in the treaties with France, Russia, Germany, Belgium, Italy and Austria-Hungary.

The American treaty of 1858 reproduces with no material change the articles contained in the treaty of 1844 on the subject of civil disputes between Chinese and Americans in China. Article XXIV reads:

When there are debts due by subjects of China to citizens of the United States, the latter may seek redress in law, and on suitable representation being made to the local authorities through the Consul, they will cause due examination in the premises and take proper steps to compel satisfaction. And if citizens of the United States be indebted to subjects of China, the latter shall seek redress by representation through the Consul or by suit in the Consular court.

Seeking redress by representation through the Consul is here distinguished from that by suit in the Consular Court

and constitutes a third mode of settling mixed controversies.
Again, article XXVIII, after determining the manner in
which the officers of one contracting party may be addressed by subjects or citizens of the other, provides:

And if controversies arise between citizens of the United
States and subjects of China which cannot be amicably settled
otherwise, the same shall be examined and decided conformably to justice and equity by the public officers of the two
nations acting in conjunction.

Of the three ways of disposing of disputes between
Chinese and foreigners in China, amicable settlement
seems to be the simplest and works well in communities
where the foreign element does not form a considerable
portion in the local population.   An American Consul at
Hankow once stated:

Several cases have been brought to me by Chinamen for
breach of civil contract by Americans—for non-payment of
wages claimed and for moneys due in various ways.   As the
official of the defendant, I have, in every separate case, been
enabled to bring matters to a satisfactory settlement by conference and advice without the necessity of any formal trial.[1]

Very often civil disputes between subjects of treaty
powers and Chinese are settled by correspondence between
the proper consul and the local authority; and it may be
said that consular representatives do not always show a
readiness to hold a court for hearing a civil suit against one
of their nationals, where there is a chance of otherwise
terminating it   In a recent case of collision, in which a
Russian steamer negligently ran into and sunk a Chinese
junk, thereby causing the loss of two lives, the vessel, and

[1] Mr. Sheppard to Mr. Seward, U. S. Minister to China, August 26th,
1879, *For. Rel*, 1879, p. 224.

a cargo valued at 500 taels, this attitude of disinclination to give a judicial hearing was conspicuously manifested by the Russian Consul at Hankow.. Although the local authorities repeatedly urged the holding of a court to try the defendant in the presence of a Chinese deputy, the consul declined the request with equal persistence and insisted that the $900, left at the customs house by the defendant as security for paying damages should be accepted as ample compensation for the losses sustained by the owner of the junk, and as a definitive settlement of the case, though nothing was provided for the family of the victims. The scanty indemnity was, however, finally accepted by the Chinese for the reason that " the case had been pending for a long time." [1]

Who shall decide mixed cases between Chinese and foreign litigants? This question once arose out of the ambiguous language employed in the provisions of nearly all the early treaties. The British treaty of 1858, for instance, provides in the last part of article XVI that " justice shall be equitably and impartially administered on both sides," and in the next article the XVII, that in mixed cases which cannot be amicably arranged the consul, " shall request the assistance of the Chinese authorities that they may together examine into the merits of the case and decide it equitably." [2]   On the interpretation of these clauses

[1] New collection of *Treaties and Conventions* (Russia), 28. This is a Chinese collection called Sin-Chuan-Yah-Chang-Ta-Chien and contains, in seventy-two volumes, nearly all the important texts, down to the date of its publication, of treaties, conventions, memorials, notes, despatches and other papers related to China's relations   The collection is being kept up-to-date by the addition of yearly volumes.

[2] The two clauses quoted above are found, word for word, respectively in articles xvi and xvii of the treaty of July 13, 1863, with Denmark, but their purport in the latter document is clearly indicated by the immediately preceding article, namely, the xv, which, after providing

opinion was divided. Some claimed that in a case of complaint by a Chinese against a British subject the assistance of the Chinese authorities required, extended only to the examination of evidence and exercise of an oversight at the trial, the consul alone having the power to form and render a judgment; others, on the contrary maintained that in any mixed case between Chinese and British subjects, the officers of both nations were required to hold a joint trial and jointly formulate a decision, in other words, both to be judges of the case In accord with the latter opinion was the chief justice of the British Supreme Court at Shanghai in the celebrated case of collision in 1875 between the Chinese junk Kin-tsai-fah and the English steamer Kwang-tung. A motion asking the court to declare null and void a judgment made by the English consul at Fuchow and the Taotai of that circuit acting conjointly was refused by the chief justice who declared that the trial had been conducted in accordance with article XVII of the Treaty of Tientsin.[1] This view of the article in question does not appear, however, to have been sustained by the British Government; on the contrary in the Chefoo Convention of September 13, 1876, concluded by China and Great Britain there was this declaration.

It is [further] understood that so long as the laws of the two countries differ from each other, there can be but one principle to guide judicial proceedings in mixed cases in China, namely, that the case is tried by the official of the defendant's

for the exemption of Danish subjects from the Chinese jurisdiction in controversies between themselves and in those between them and subjects of foreign powers, reads: "But if in such controversies Chinese subjects be parties involved, the Chinese authority shall be assessor in all proceedings, as in the cases provided for by articles xvi and xvii of this treaty."

[1] North China Herald, February 11th, 1875.

nationality: the official of the plaintiff's nationality merely attending to watch the proceedings in the interests of justice. [If the officer be dissatisfied with the proceedings, it will be in his power to protest against them in detail.] The law administered will be the law of the nationality of the officer trying the case. This is the meaning of the words, hui tung, indicating combined action in judicial proceedings in Article XVI of the Treaty of Tientsin, and this is the course to be respectively followed by the officers of either nationality.

The views thus stated in the Chefoo Convention are in unison with those held by many other treaty powers as regards similar provisions in their own treaties with China In a memorandum of October 4, 1879, prepared by Mr. G. F. Seward, American minister at Peking, were reviewed the instructions of the State Department at Washington and the opinions of Mr. Cushing as negotiator of the treaty of Wanghia and later as Attorney-general of the United States, which all agree in upholding the principle that the court of the defendant's nationality alone has the right to adjudicate a mixed case.[1] The same was subsequently embodied in article IV of the Treaty of November 17, 1880, between China and the United States. It is now expressly provided also in article IX of the treaty of 1881 with Brazil, article XXI of the treaty with Japan and article XIII of the treaty of 1889 with Mexico. In respect of the remaining treaty powers, probably with one exception,[2] if they

---

[1] *Foreign Relations*, 1880, p 146.

[2] This is Russia. So far as article 11 of the treaty of Kuldja, July 25, 1851, goes, it appears to be rather in accord than at variance with the rule, for it reads:

"Les marchands des deux Empires feront entre eux le commerce d'échange et régleront les prix librement et à leur gré Il sera nommé, pour surveiller les affaires des sujets russes, un Consul de la port de la Russie, et pour les affaires des commerçants chinois, un functionnaire de l'administration supérieure de l'Ili. En cas de collision entre

have not adopted the principle by express declarations, they appear to observe it uniformly at least in practice. It may, therefore, be stated as a rule that mixed cases between

les sujets de l'une et d'autre Puissance, chacun de ces agents décidera selon toute justice les affaires des ses nationaux."

But the subsequent treaties with Russia seem to contain different provisions Article vii of the Treaty of Tientsin, June 1-13, 1858, reads:

" Toute affaire entre les sujets russes et chinois dans les ports et villes ouverts sera examinée par les autorités chinoises de concert avec le Consul russe ou l'agent qui represente l'autorité du Governement russe dans l'endroit "

Article viii of the Treaty of Peking, Nov. 2-14, 1860, is a little more explicit. After authorizing the settlement of commercial disputes by arbitrators chosen by the parties themselves, it continues:

"Les contestations qui se rapportent point à des affaires de commerce entre marchands telles que litiges, plaintes, etc, sont jugées de consentment mutuel par le Consul et le chef local, et les délinquents sont punis d'apres les lois de leur pays."

Article x of the same treaty declares that in the examination and decision of the affairs on the frontier the article just quoted shall be conformed to, while as to criminal cases involving the subjects of both powers, article vii of the Treaty of Tientsin is to be followed.

The Treaty of St. Petersburg, Feb. 12-24, 1881, summarizes the mode of settlement to be followed in mixed civil disputes as follows:

" Toutes les affaires qui surgiront sur territoire chinois, au sujet de transactions commerciales ou autres, entre les ressortissants des deux États, seront examinées et réglées d'un common accord, par les Consuls et les autorités chinoises.

"Dans les litiges en matiere de commerce, les deux parties pourront terminer leurs differends a l'amable, au moyen d'arbitres choisies de part et d'autre. Si l'entente ne s'établit pas par cette voie, l'affaire sera examinées et réglées par les autorités des deux États."

In practice the mixed-court system, as distinguished from the court of the defendant's nation, is known to be followed along the conterminous frontiers of Russia and China. There cases of controversy between Russian and Chinese merchants accumulate with exceeding rapidity, and to dispose of them once for all a mixed court, presided over by a representative of each nation specially appointed for the purpose, is held once every three years in Eli and Tahcheng (Tarbagatai). The law administered is not that of either nation, but the customs of the locality in which a given case originated. Whatever

Chinese and foreign subjects in China are heard and determined by the authorities of the defendant's nation, an officer of the plaintiff's nation being entitled to be present to watch the proceedings, and examine and cross-examine witnesses, and, if dissatisfied with the judgment rendered, protest against it in detail.

The assessor or assessors to be sent by China to attend the trial of a mixed case in which the plaintiff is a Chinese must be Chinese authorities as designated in the Russian, French and English treaties concluded in 1858. Although article XXVIII of the American treaty of the same year employs the term " public officers of the two nations " instead, the United States Government has interpreted it to mean Chinese authorities, where assessors to represent China are to be sent to an American court trying a mixed case, and the Chinese Government appears to have acquiesced in the interpretation. This question once arose directly in a collision case at Tientsin in 1875, in which a Chinese brought a suit in the United States consular court at that port to recover damages against an American steamer. The customs taotai deputed, as assessors to represent him, two Chinese officials and Mr. Twinem, a British subject serving China as customs commissioner. Mr. Sheppard, the consul, while admitting the Chinese assessors, refused to receive Mr. Twinem in that capacity.[1] On receiving a report of the case, the Department of State at

decision the mixed tribunal renders is final. This *modus vivendi* has proved satisfactory as well as successful. In 1903 over 1,700 cases were definitely adjudicated by this triennial mixed court sitting in Eli, within the short period of one month. Since 1905 the same system has been extended to Kashgar, where, prior to that year, mixed cases had been accumulating for nearly two decades —*Memorial to the Emperor by Ma, Military Governor of Eli*, 1904, 3 new collections (Russia), 34.

[1] Mr Avery to Mr. Fish, June 23, 1875, *For. Rel.*, 1875, part i, p 347.

Washington approved the action taken by the consul at Tientsin, giving the following reasons:

It is quite clear that these provisions, [in the four principal treaties concluded between China and foreign powers in 1858], among other things, were intended to secure the attendance of a Chinese official of position and influence on the occasion of a trial of this nature who might not only watch over the interests of his own countrymen, and assist in a proper manner therein, but whose standing, intelligence and rank would serve as an assurance to his countrymen of the justice of the judgment which might be rendered.

The precise official designated was not named, because within the limits I have referred to it might well be left to the Chinese authorities to choose such person as might from time to time be best fitted to attain the desired end.

A foreigner, however, and a person of inferior position, although attached to a branch of the Chinese service, such as Mr. Twinem, complies with none of the requisites, is in no respect a public officer of the Chinese nation within the meaning of the treaty, and his presence could not secure the intended purpose.

Mr. Seward's refusal to allow Mr. Twinem to sit was proper and his course on the question seems to have been dignified and judicious.[1]

§ 3. *Cases between Aliens*

Thus far in this section the question of extraterritorial jurisdiction has been treated only as relates to matters, civil and criminal, in which both Chinese and foreign subjects are interested, particularly to those mixed cases in which the former are plaintiffs and the latter defendants; it being preferable to discuss more thoroughly in another

---

[1] Mr. Cadwalader to Mr. Avery, Aug. 16th, 1876, *For. Rel.*, 1875, part I, p. 400

section those cases which are brought by a subject of a treaty-power against a Chinese.

With regard to controversies in China in which Chinese subjects are not involved, the principle which China observes is that of non-interference Questions of rights, whether personal or of property, arising in China between subjects of the same treaty power are subject to the jurisdiction and regulated by the authorities of their own government. Those occurring in Chinese territory between the subjects of two different powers are disposed of in accordance with the provisions of treaties existing between them.[1] In such cases the general practice is that they are arranged officially by the consuls of both parties without resort to litigation; but where amicable settlement is impossible, the principle of jurisdiction followed is the same as in those between China and a foreign power, namely, that the plaintiff follows the defendant into the court of the latter's nation.

§ 4. *Extraterritorial Courts in China*

The ordinary machinery provided by each treaty-power for the exercise of jurisdiction over its own subjects in China consists of consular Courts, each presided over by a consul who, by virtue of the powers conferred on him by the laws of his nation and subject to the limitations therein provided, hears and determines cases between his nationals and those in which the latter are defendants.   Some powers

---

[1] The earliest provisions exempting foreigners in China from the territorial jurisdiction as regards controversies arising between them are article xxv of the American treaty of 1844, substantially reproduced in article xxvii of the treaty of 1858, article xxxix of the treaty of 1847 with Sweden and Norway, and article xv of the British treaty of 1858. The last-mentioned article provides for exemption only in cases between British subjects, no reference being made to cases between them and other foreign subjects.

authorize their diplomatic representatives at Peking, also, to hold courts and sit in judgment on their respective subjects, the jurisdiction thus exercised being either original or appellate.   Appeals from the consular courts of some countries run also to their adjacent colonial or home courts. Thus, for instance, appeals from the judgments of French consular tribunals in China are, in pursuance of laws which still remain in force, brought to the Court of Appeals of Saigon.[1]   The consul's and minister's courts, however, do not take jurisdiction in all cases occurring in China in which their nationals are defendants; where grave crimes are committed on Chinese soil by the subjects of certain treaty powers, the offenders cannot be tried and published in their consular courts or the court of their minister; they are required, after a summary inquiry, to be sent to their own country for such purposes   This procedure applies particularly to Russian and Spanish culprits in China.[2]

[1] De Clercq and De Vallet, *Guide pratique des Consulates* (2 volumes, Paris, 1898), 2, p. 600.   Prior to the issuance of the Order in Council of March 9, 1865, appeals from the judgments of British consular courts in China were brought to the Supreme Court of Hong Kong.—J. W. Norton-Kyshe, *History of the Law and Courts of Hong Kong, including consular jurisdiction in China and Japan* (2 vols., London, 1898), 2, pp 76-80.   Prior to the enactment of the act of March 3, 1891 (26 Stat. at L. 826, sec 4) appeal from a judgment of an American consular court or the court of the American minister at Peking, in a matter which, exclusive of costs, exceeded $2,500, was allowed to the circuit court for the district of California; but the act creating the circuit courts of appeal took away the appellate jurisdiction from "circuit courts" and incidentally left the litigants in consular courts in China without a higher tribunal to appeal to in more important cases.—F. E. Hinckley, *American Consular Jurisdiction in the Orient*, Washington, 1906, p. 49.

[2] Russian Treaty of Nov. 2-14, 1860, article viii; Spanish Treaty of Oct. 10, 1864, art. xiii.   A clause in the latter article provides for the sending of Spanish offenders in China to Manila for trial and punishment, but of course it has not applied since the cession of the Philippines to the United States in 1898; no new provision, however, is known to have been made in place of it.

There are, however, in China at present two foreign courts which are of a different nature and constitution from those of the consular courts and the courts held severally by the foreign ministers at Peking. Under the Order in Council of October 24, 1904,[1] there has been established in China a court officially entitled " His Britannic Majesty's Supreme Court for China and Corea." It is presided over by a judge and a number of assistant judges, respectively appointed by warrant under the royal sign manual. Any two judges sitting together constitute " the full court."

The new supreme court, like its predecessor, has in all matters, civil and criminal, an exclusive original jurisdiction for and within the district of the consulate of Shanghai, but, in other consular districts, it exercises an original jurisdiction concurrent with the jurisdiction of the " Provincial (British Consular) Courts."[2] It is thus evident that the British consul or consular-general at Shanghai is, under the new order in council, relieved of judicial functions which he had to perform theretofore, and the performance of which is still required of his colleagues in other parts of China. In this respect the British consulate at Shanghai forms a class of its own as compared to all the other consulates in the Chinese Empire. Further, the British

[1] This order in council is very comprehensive. It is a veritable code. It repeals ten previous orders in council relative to China, Japan and Corea, including that of March 9, 1865, which established the Supreme Court of Civil and Criminal Judicature for China and Japan; but it consolidates much of their substance with its own systematic whole. It contains nine parts, namely: (1) preliminary and general; (2) constitution and powers of courts (Supreme and provincial) ; (3) criminal; (4) civil matters; (5) procedure, criminal and civil; (6) mortgages and bills of sale; (7) foreign subjects and tribunals; (8) regulations miscellaneous. The complete text of the China and Corea Order in Council, 1904, as it is officially cited, is found in Hertslet's *China Treaties*, ii, pp. 834, 889

[2] *China and Corea*, Order in Council, 1904, articles 21 and 23.

Supreme Court may of its own motion order a case in a provincial court to be transferred to and tried by, itself, and such removal may be effected upon the report of a provincial court or upon the application of any party to the case.[1] Appeals in criminal matters are allowed to the Supreme Court from any British court in China, but no appeal from a decision of the Supreme Court can be brought to His Majesty, the King, in Council except by special leave of His Majesty in Council.[2] In civil matters any party in an action involving the amount or value of $25 or upwards, in a provincial court, has the right to appeal to the supreme court; and when an action involves the amount or value of $5,000 or upwards, either party may appeal from the supreme court to His Majesty in Council.[3]

The other notable exception to the uniform judicial machinery maintained by treaty powers in China is " The United States Court for China " created by the act of Congress, June 30, 1906.[4] The court has a judge, a district attorney, a marshall, all of whom are appointed by the President with the advice and consent of the Senate.

It is required to hold its sessions at Shanghai, as its seat, but also one session, at least, in Canton, Tientsin, and Hankow. It has exclusive jurisdiction in all cases and judicial proceedings whereof jurisdiction might, at the date of the act, be exercised by United States Consuls and ministers by law and by virtue of treaties between China and the United States, except in civil cases where the property involved in the controversy does not exceed five hundred dollars in United States currency, and in criminal cases

---

[1] *Op. cit*, art. 25.

[2] *Ibid*, arts 85, 86, 87

[3] *Ibid*, arts. 113, 114, 115, 116, 117.

[4] 34 U. S. Statutes at Large 814, c. 3934.

where the punishment for the offense charged cannot exceed by law one hundred dollars' fine or sixty days' imprisonment, or both.   From all judgments of the consular court, either party has the right of appeal to the United States Court for China.[1]   Appeals from judgments and decrees of this court lie to the United States circuit court of appeals of the ninth judicial circuit and thence to the Supreme Court of the United States.[2]

The number of foreign courts in China is necessarily large, each treaty power maintaining its own tribunals. In a port where thriving commerce has built up a foreign community of considerable size and numerous nationalities, there will generally be as many kinds of consular courts as there are states maintaining treaty relations with China. When it is remembered that, besides consular courts, there exist the Chinese courts, which will be studied in a later section, and the special foreign courts, which have just been described, the complexity of the situation as regards the administration of justice among Chinese and foreign subjects in China becomes easily comprehensible.   As early as 1879, complaint was made of the clumsy judicial structure in Shanghai, then far less important, as regards the value of its foreign interests and the number of treaty powers represented there, than it is now.   " The multiplicity of courts established in Shanghai," wrote the United States Consul, " may be fairly said to constitute the most cumbersome system of judicature known to exist in any considerable commercial center in the world." [3]

---

[1] Act of June 30, 1906

[2] *Ibid.*, s. 3

[3] Mr Bailey to Mr. Seward, Sept. 15th, 1879. *Foreign Relations,* 1879, p. 229.

§ 5. *The Law administered to Aliens*

In cases where a subject of a treaty power commits an offence in China, against whomsoever it may be, a Chinese, a foreigner of another power, or one of his own nationals, and against whatever it may be, treaties, laws, regulations or local customs, the law administered, as regards the mode of trial and the means of punishment, is invariably that of the offender's nation. In other words, the law applicable to a given crime committed in China, varies with the nationality of the culprit. For instance, a Frenchman guilty of an offence in any part of the Chinese Empire, is subject only to the penalties prescribed by the laws of France for such offence; an American, to those of the United States; a Mexican to those of Mexico. What the criminal law of a given nation is, or consists of, as regards crimes committed by its subjects in China, depends, of course, upon the law-making power of that nation.

In the case of British subjects committing criminal acts in the dominions of the Chinese Emperor, it is provided, as a general principle, in the China and Corea Order in Council, 1904, that subject to certain other provisions in the same order, British criminal jurisdiction in China "shall, as far as circumstances admit, be exercised on the principles of, and in conformity with, English law for the time being, and with the powers vested in the courts of Justice and Justices of the Peace in England, according to their respective jurisdiction and authority." [1] Certain acts of Parliament are declared to apply and to be administered in China, and in addition to these laws and the orders in council relative to China, the British minister at Peking is also empowered to make regulations which, when approved and published in the proper manner, have effect as

[1] Art. 35 (2) Hertslet's *China Treaties*, ii, p 849.

if contained in an order in council, and are enforceable by forfeiture, fine, and imprisonment. Such regulations may be made for any of the specified purposes, one of which is to secure " the observance of any treaty for the time being in force relating to any place or of any native or local law, or custom, whether relating to trade, commerce, revenue, or any other matter.[1]

Similarly, the statutes of the United States provide that the laws of the United States, where necessary and suitable, shall be extended over all citizens of the United States in China and four other countries therein mentioned, and over all others to the extent that the terms of the treaties, respectively, justify or require; but that in all cases where such laws are inappropriate or inadequate, the common law and the law of equity and admiralty shall be applied and that,

if neither the common law, nor the law of equity or admiralty, nor the statutes of the United States furnish appropriate and sufficient remedies, the minister in those countries, respectively, shall, by decrees and regulations which shall have the force of law, supply such defects and deficiencies.[2]

The act of June 30, 1906, creating a United States court, confirms these provisions except, as regards China, in one respect. The said act omits all mention as to the power of the American minister in China to make regulations for the purpose of supplying local needs and its language seems to imply that such power may not again be exercised.[3]

[1] Art. 155 (b), *ibid*, p. 884.

U. S. Revised Statutes, s. 4086.

[3] " Sec. 4. The jurisdiction of said United States Court, both original and on appeal, in civil and criminal matters, and also the jurisdiction of the Consular Courts in China, shall in all cases be exercised in conformity with said treaties and the laws of the United States now in force in reference to the American Consular Courts, and all judgments

In matters of a civil nature arising in China between a Chinese and a foreigner, the early treaties provide that they shall be examined and decided by the authorities of the two nations acting in conjunction, " conformably to justice and equity." [1] These terms, of course, are not helpful in determining what the law applicable to a given controversy is, since they are obviously used in their generic, not technical sense. The Chefoo agreement of 1876 declares that " the law administered will be the law of the nationality of the officer trying the case." [2] While doubt is sometimes entertained as to whether this declaration was not intended to apply solely to criminal cases, since it was avowedly made to explain the meaning of article XVI of the British treaty of 1858, which makes provision for criminal matters only, the American treaty of 1880, in article IV, should remove all uncertainty on the question, inasmuch as the same clause found therein is expressly declared to apply to " controversies " Furthermore, from the fact, already pointed out in the preceding pages, that the officer trying a mixed suit must be an officer of the defendant's nation, it must follow that the law to be applied in such a case, according to the Chefoo agreement, is necessarily the law of the defendant's nation   This rule, simple as it may seem, would prove perplexing enough, even if China and every treaty power had

and decision of said Consular Courts, and all decisions, judgments and decrees of said United States Court shall be enforced in accordance with said treaties and laws. But, in all such cases when such laws are deficient in the provisions necessary to give jurisdiction or to furnish suitable remedies, the common law and the law as established by the decisions of the Courts of the United States shall be applied by such court in its decisions and shall govern the same, subject to the terms of any treaties between the United States and China."—34 U. S. Statutes at Large, 814, c. 3934.

[1] Articles xxiv of the Treaty of 1844 and xxviii of that of 1858, both with the United States

[2] Section II (iii).

provided a complete code of laws covering every possible subject of controversy and every probable combination
of facts; for even then difficult questions would arise as to
which party to the suit is the real defendant, in order to
determine who shall try it and what law shall be applied.
But the laws in force dealing with the countless aspects
of the civil relations between Chinese and foreigners, and
also between the subjects of the different powers in China,
seem far from being sufficiently comprehensive to fulfil all
purposes. In one or two cases, the treaties provide the law
for a specific subject.

Thus, in regard to the rights and obligations of Chinese
shareholders in British joint stock companies and vice versa,
article IV of the British treaty of September 5, 1908, declares that both the Chinese and British courts shall respectively enforce compliance, when a suit is brought for
such purpose, with the charter of incorporation or memorandum and articles of association of such companies,
which the shareholders, on becoming such, whether Chinese
or British, must be held to have fully accepted; and foreign subjects in China accepting and operating a mining
concession from the Chinese Government under the mining
rules, are held to have consented to observe such rules, and
the courts of their nation will enforce them in respect of
questions arising out of the concession [1] But in a great
number of other matters, constituting causes of action between the subjects of different powers, the courts and
counsel on both sides must be under difficulties in ascertain-
ing what laws are applicable to them. For instance, the
question of what law governs real property owned by foreign subjects in China, whether the Chinese law which will
be the *lex loci rei sitae,* or that of the owner's nation, has

[1] British Treaty of Sept. 5th, 1902, art ix, United States Treaty of
Oct. 8, 1903, art. vii.

caused much embarrassment among the legal practitioners in the country. One writer observes:

The rights and property of a British subject in China can be assailed only in His Britannic Majesty's Court where the law of England is administered. But does the fact that a British subject owns land in China of itself invest that land with all the characteristics of land in England? It has been tacitly assumed that it does, and lawyers employ the English form of conveyance in transferring land. But the assumption is contrary to the theory of English law, which is that the law which governs the land is the *lex loci rei sitae*, that is, in this case, the law of China, and is completely at variance with a recent decision of the Privy Council on an appeal from the court of Zanzibar, where a similar system of extraterritoriality prevails. In that case it was held that the law which the British court administers as to land in Zanzibar is the lex loci, and that the British court must take judicial cognizance of that law. If this decision applies to China, (and there is no reason why it should not,) then the law under which land is held in China by British subjects is Chinese law; and what Chinese law is, beyond an intricate code of punishments and penalties, few would dare to say. The fact is that the lawyers in Shanghai and other treaty ports in China, do not really know what the law applicable to land held by British subjects and other foreigners, really is.[1]

§ 6. *Application of their own law advantageous to Aliens*

With reference to the question of the law applied in criminal and civil matters occurring in her dominions, China, as has already been indicated, is like mediaeval Europe. Foreigners going there are by treaty entitled to bring with them their personal laws, that is, the laws of

[1] A. M. Latter, barrister-at-law at Shanghai, "The Government of Foreigners in China," 19 *Law Quarterly Rev.* (1903), 316-325.

their own country; and generally speaking, they are governed by such laws. In cases arising between two subjects
of the same treaty power there is no question as to the law
to be applied to it; it is always the law of their own nation.
In a case between the subjects of two different powers including China, the personal law of the defendant, who is
generally supposed, at least in theory, to need more protection than the other party in the case, prevails. Now
what advantages do the foreigners derive from the application to them while in China of their personal law? It
may perhaps be difficult to show the relative merits of the
different systems of law of the treaty powers in respect of
the benefit which the application of one system confers
upon the defendant in a given case over that of another;
but, as regards the laws of the treaty powers on one hand,
and the Chinese law, as it stands to-day, on the other, there
can scarcely be any doubt that the difference between the
two resolves in favor of those who are exempt from submission to the latter system of jurisprudence. An English
lawyer in Shanghai observes:

There is no doubt that the extraterritorial system in China
places the foreigner in a far better position than he would be
in, had the treaties never been made, and the complaints of
foreigners living in Japan, now that the treaties have expired,
illustrate the truth of this statement.[1]

Another authority, a Chinese jurist learned in the Western jurisprudence as well as in that of his own country,
expounds the question under consideration with much
lucidity. He says:

The dissimilarity and inequality in the punishments inflicted
on offenders in mixed cases will at once be apparent if we
take for an example the case of homicide. Supposing a for-

---

[1] Latter, *op. cit.*

eigner is killed in an affray by a Chinese, the latter will have
to suffer death in accordance with Section 290 of the Penal
Code, which provides that " all persons guilty of killing in an
affray, that is to say, striking in a quarrel or affray, so as to
kill, though without any express or implied design to kill,
shall, whether the blow was struck with the hand or the
foot, with a metal weapon, or with an instrument of any kind,
suffer death by being strangled after the usual period of confinement." But if the case is reversed, that is to say, if a
Chinese is killed by an European or an American, the accused
will not in any case be sentenced to death. In all probability
he will be sentenced to a longer or shorter term of imprisonment, according to circumstances, or perhaps let off with
a fine. If the Chinaman is killed in play or purely by accident, no American or European court will convict the killer.
But it is a very different matter with a Chinaman, if he should
be the killer, in such a case. The consequences are serious
as he is surely to be convicted under Section 292 of the Code,
which reads: "All persons playing with the fists, with a stick,
or with any weapon or other means whatsoever, which can be
made the instrument of killing, and thus killing or wounding
some individual, shall suffer the punishment provided by the
law in any ordinary case of killing or wounding in an affray;
otherwise any person, who, being engaged in an affray by mistake, kills or wounds a bystander, shall be punished in the
same manner, that is, shall suffer death by being strangled."

Now let me take a civil case. Suppose a foreigner is sued
by a Chinese merchant for the recovery of a debt of $10,000.
The case naturally comes up before the consul of the country
to which the foreigner belongs. The Chinese merchant has
to produce strong evidence in support of his claim in order to
obtain a judgment in his favor. Even then he is not sure
that he can recover his money. If the foreigner has any
goods, or any other kind of property that can be seized, the
Chinese merchant may perhaps be able to get possession of
them and have them sold to satisfy his claim. But it is more
likely that there is nothing he can levy on. In that case he

has no further remedy. According to the law of some nations, a judgment-debtor cannot be put into jail. Furthermore,
a foreigner who owes other people money and is unable to
pay his debts in full, can either go into bankruptcy under the
insolvent law, or make a general assignment for the benefit
of his creditors. If he resorts to either course in a straight-
forward manner without fraud, his whole indebtedness is
wiped out, no matter how much or how little his creditors may
get back in the settlement; henceforth, he can engage in business again without any old debts hanging over him.

Now let us see what a Chinese can do, or rather cannot
do, when he is unfortunate enough to run heavily in debt.
All that he can do is to call a meeting of his creditors and
offer to settle with them on an equitable basis. But if any
of his creditors refuse to accept his terms there is no Chinese
court or insolvent law that can give him relief. If a judgment is obtained against him by a foreigner in a suit brought
for the purpose, his property will be seized. If that does not
realize enough to pay his debt in full, the property of his wife
and children and frequently of his parents and brothers also,
is distrained. In the meantime he is arrested and put under
confinement until the full amount he owes the foreigner is
satisfied. Let me give you a case in point. I have in mind a
respectable Chinese merchant I knew, who on account of his
reckless but perfectly legitimate speculation in business, had
the misfortune of becoming insolvent. Among his creditors
was a foreigner, who, through the consular representative of
his country, brought a suit against him He was summoned
to appear before the proper Chinese magistrate and as the
amount of the claim was not disputed, he was at once confined in the yamen. In the meantime all his property was
seized and sold, but it did not realize enough to pay the full
amount of the judgment debt. I learned subsequently that
he was kept in jail for several years and could not regain
his liberty until his relatives came forward and helped him to
pay all that he owed to the foreigner.

It may be urged, on the other hand, that, in the case just

cited, the parties were dealt with according to the laws of their respective countries, and that, if the parties had all been Chinese, they would have received exactly the same treatment. This, I admit, is indeed true. But the fact remains that for the same offence committed in China, different punishments are imposed according as the offender is a foreigner or a Chinese. A Chinese offender is severely dealt with in accordance with the law of the land, but a foreign offender is tried by a different code, which is more lenient in its provisions, and receives far less punishment for the consequences of his misdeeds." [1]

It may be suggested, however, that the disadvantages to which Chinese defendants in mixed cases are subject at present, as the result of the severity of Chinese laws as compared with those of foreign nations, could be removed by the Chinese Government, by providing in statutes that Chinese defendants in such cases should not be liable to undergo punishments or penalties, or to pay damages, greater than those prescribed for similar cases by the laws of the plaintiff's nation. Such a law cannot be impugned on the ground of discrimination; on the contrary, it could be upheld on principles of reciprocity and fairness. In criminal cases, it may probably be difficult of application by reason of the peculiar character as well as of the diversity of foreign laws, or undesirable from the standpoint of the Chinese ruling authorities, as the differentiation may diminish the deterrent effect of Chinese punishments; yet in civil matters, such as suits for damages or for recovery of debt, such difficulties or considerations do not seem to be inevitable, at least not to the same extent, and some such protective law, as has been indicated, may be profitably adopted in the interest of justice to Chinese defendants in mixed cases.

[1] Dr. Wu Ting Fang's Address before the New York State Bar Ass'n, January 15, 1901. 63 *Albany Law Journal* (1901), 49-54.

CHAPTER XI

THE EXTENT OF THE EXTRATERRITORIAL JURISDICTION

THE jurisdiction which a treaty power exercises in China extends over all the subjects and all the property belonging to them, subject to certain limitations which will presently be discussed. Of the two kinds of subjects of jurisdiction, namely, person and property, the former is more completely exempt from the territorial jurisdiction than the latter. The personal jurisdiction of consular courts is so extensive that even foreign employees in the service of the Chinese Government are not beyond its reach. Where British subjects in the Chinese Customs Service, for example, commit a tort on another person, they may be sued in the British consular court in the district where they reside or in the British Supreme Court at Shanghai, as the case may be, and the process of either tribunal can compel them to appear before it and answer for their acts, even though such acts were done by them officially in the service of the Chinese Government, and have been adopted by the latter as acts of state; although when such justification is pleaded and proved, they are not holden civilly liable.[1]

[1] This was substantially the opinion given by Earl Russell, Secretary of Foreign Affairs, to Sir F. Bruce, minister to China, August 14, 1863, after consultation with law officers of the Crown, in the case of Bowman v. Fitzgray The suit was brought originally in the British consular court at Shanghai in 1862 against the defendant, for seizure of goods, as a Chinese custom officer, and on the question of jurisdiction being raised, the plaintiff applied for and obtained from the Supreme Court of Hongkong a writ of mandamus directing Mr. Medhurst, the British consul, to try the case. Thereupon Prince Kung, on the part of the Chinese Government, protested against the procedure, and the matter was ultimately referred by Sir F. Bruce to Earl Russell, who

                                                                 193

In a criminal case the accused foreign employee in the
service of the Chinese Government is no less subject to the
jurisdiction of his consul; he is bound to resign his position
and appear before the proper consular court to plead, though
his plea of official authority and governmental approval for
his acts, when it is proved, entitles him to an acquittal.[1]
The question was once directly raised in the case of Edward Page, a British subject, employed in the Imperial
Maritime Customs at Canton, who on October 26, 1880,
shot and killed a Chinese, while attempting to smuggle
goods into the country.   Page, when arraigned in the
British Supreme Court upon an indictment charging him
with murder and with manslaughter, pleaded to the jurisdiction of the court because, declaring that while he was not

forthwith rendered the opinion as above stated —*Parl. Papers*, China
No 3 (1864), 31, 32, 94. A similar view of the question, as regards
citizens of the United States in the service of the Chinese Government
committing torts, was expressed by Mr. Angell, American minister at
Peking, in the despatch of April 30, 1881, to Mr. Blaine, Secretary of
State. "In civil cases," stated he, "if the defendant pleads and proves
that his act is official and approved by the Chinese Government, I think
his plea should cover him   But even in such cases he should appear
before the consul and plead and prove his official authority for his act"
—*For. Rel.*, 1881, p. 257

[1] Mr. Hitt, Acting Secretary of State at Washington, in his instructions to Mr. Angell, Minister at Peking, August 16, 1881, stated:
"The regulation, the substance of which is given in your despatch,
namely, that if any foreign employee of the Chinese customs kills or
wounds any person, he shall at once resign his place and report to the
consul of his nationality within whose jurisdiction he resides, and that
if the consul acquits him or decides that there is no cause for trial,
such employee may resume his station with full pay during the time,
since his resignation, appears to be a just and reasonable one.
"If in such a case the consul found that the employee killed or
wounded a man in the discharge of his official duty, and under such circumstances as that he, if tried by a Chinese tribunal, would be held
guiltless, or such as would, under the laws of the United States, make
the act justifiable or excusable, it would be the duty of the consul to
discharge him "—*For. Rel*, 1881, p. 286.

guilty, his acts on the occasion under consideration were official, and had been examined, approved, and ratified by the Tsungli Yamen as acts of state. Chief Justice French, however, decided that the defendant must plead, which he did, and after trial he was acquitted.[1]

It is perhaps unnecessary to state that the extraterritoriality accorded by China to subjects of treaty powers is not limited as to locality: it is coextensive with the confines of the Empire. Wherever a subject of a foreign power may go within the Chinese dominions he brings with him his right of exemption from the territorial jurisdiction. In fact many of the treaties now in force expressly provide that a foreign subject committing an offense against the law in any part of the community shall be handed over to the nearest consul of his nation for punishment, but, in the language of the British treaty of 1858, "he must not be subjected to ill usage in excess of necessary restraint." An American diplomat commenting on the article in 1858 stated:

This rendered into plain language means that the foreigner who commits a rape or murder a thousand miles from the sea-board is to be gently restrained, and remitted to a consul for trial, necessarily at a remote point where testimony could hardly be obtained or ruled on.[2]

Nevertheless this has been the procedure in practice.

On the same ground of the grant by China of entire jurisdiction over subjects of the treaty powers in her territory, it was declared as early as 1864 by another American minister at Peking, that "the Chinese Government cannot withdraw a consul's exequatur."[3]

[1] *For Rel.*, 1881, p. 257.

[2] Mr. Reed, Minister to China, to Mr. Cass, Sec of State, July 29, 1858, S. Ex. Doc. 30, 36 Cong., 1 Sess., p. 382

[3] Mr. Burlingame's instructions to United States Consuls in China, June 15, 1864, *Dipl. Cor.* 1864, pt. iii, p. 426.

CHAPTER XII

Limitations of the Extraterritorial Jurisdiction

§ 1. *Limitations founded on treaty stipulations*

THE limitations upon the exercise of the extraterritorial jurisdiction in China spring from many sources, one of which is treaty stipulations. For an example, while foreign property is considered inviolable by Chinese authorities, and subject only to the jurisdiction of the courts of the owner's nation, ships and goods belonging to a foreign merchant may, under existing treaties and regulations, be seized and confiscated by the Chinese customs officials for breach of the established revenue laws of the Empire, without being entitled to any countenance of protection from the Government of the owner's state.

When, however, the act of which a merchant at any port is accused is not one involving the confiscation of ship or cargo, but is one which by treaty or regulation, is punishable by fine, then it is necessary to cause a complaint to be entered in the consular court of the merchant's nation, and the consul will try the case and the customs commissioner is entitled to take his seat on the bench and conduct the case on behalf of the prosecution. Where a specific fine for the offense is prescribed by the treaty or regulations, the consul is bound, on conviction, to give judgment for that amount, the power of mitigating the sentence resting with the Chinese superintendent or commissioner.[1]

[1] Rule vi of the Customs Rules of May 31, 1868, Hertslet's *China Treaties*, ii, pp. 655, 657.

[318

An attempt made in 1862 by the Chinese customs authorities at Ningpo to fine an American vessel for breach of the port regulations was made the subject of a vigorous protest by the United States Minister at Peking. This was the case of the Bark Agnes. The ship put into the port of Ningpo with a cargo and Captain King duly paid the duties and obtained a permit to unload his goods. He landed a part of them after sunset, which was against the port regulations, and upon the local officer's attempt to stop him, he used rough language. Thereupon, the superintendent of the customs, afterwards sustained by the local Taotai, ordered the portion that had been already landed to be seized and placed a prohibition on the landing of the remainder until the Captain had apologized and paid a fine of 300 taels. The matter was subsequently referred to Peking. In his note to Prince Kung, December 15, 1862, Mr. Burlingame, the American Minister, made a strong protest, stating as follows:

Now, the undersigned does not deny the right of the Chinese Government to enforce its revenue laws by the seizure and confiscation of that property which is found after the owner has violated the law, as when goods have been smuggled; but he does deny the right of the Chinese authorities to punish or fine citizens of the United States under any circumstances. That can only be done, according to Article XI of the treaty, by the United States consul. In this case the Captain, after the duties were paid and the permit granted, was entitled to land his cargo. If, in landing it, he violated the port regulations, then only so much could be seized as was landed contrary to law; that which had not been landed was where it had a right legally to be.

Then referring to the action of the superintendent and the Taotai, Mr. Burlingame continued:

All this was an infringement of the jurisdiction of the United States consul, clearly wrong, and renders the wrong-doers responsible to the Captain for any damages he may have suffered by such illegal proceedings.

He then has to request that Your Highness will at once instruct the officers at Ningpo to remove the prohibition from the vessel, to restore to the captain his rights, and to compensate for whatever loss he may have been subjected to by these illegal proceedings.

The undersigned engages that the United States consul at Ningpo shall enter into a full examination of the conduct of the captain, and punish him for any improper act he may have committed.[1]

In his reply of December 27, 1862, Prince Kung seems to have fully accepted the American Minister's arguments, for he observed that "although the custom-house had a right to send a tide-waiter on board of her to superintend the landing, it had none to seize upon any goods or impose a fine of 300 taels;" and that the prohibition laid by the custom-house on the landing of the remaining goods in the "Agnes" was also wrong. Instructions, it was further stated, had accordingly been sent to the Provincial authorities to examine the case, and "if no attempt to smuggle, and, indeed, nothing besides landing cargo after sunset can be laid to the charge of the vessel, then to withdraw at once the prohibition, and by no means exact any fine from the captain."[2]

---

[1] *Dipl Corr*, 1863, pt ii, p. 845

[2] *Ibid* With reference to the objection of the Chinese Government to Section 3 of the United States anti-opium law of February 23, 1887, Mr. Denby in his despatch to Mr. Bayard, May 14, 1887 states:

"I agree that the clause (in Section 3) is antagonistic to the fourteenth article of the treaty of 1858, if opium is 'a contraband article of merchandise.'

"Under the said article contraband merchandise is to be dealt with exclusively by the Chinese Government. But it has never been admitted

§ 2. *Limitations founded on international law.*

The exercise by Treaty-Powers of exclusive jurisdiction, civil and criminal, over their subjects in China is limited by the rules of international law, which are observed by states in their mutual intercourse. Thus in a case where offenses are committed in China by nationals enrolled on the articles of a foreign ship, in conformity with the established usage among maritime powers, the jurisdiction of the court of the nation to which the vessel belongs may prevail over that of the court of the offenders' nation. For instance, the circular of the Department of State at Washington, under date of June 1, 1881, states:

In China and Japan the judicial authority of the consuls of the United States will be considered as extending over all persons duly shipped and enrolled upon the articles of any merchant vessel of the United States, whatever be the nationality of such persons, and all offenses which would be justiciable by the consular courts of the United States, where the persons so offending are native born or naturalized citizens of the United States employed in the merchant service thereof, are equally justiciable by the same Consular Courts in the case of seamen of foreign nationality.[1]

Whether in the case supposed the jurisdiction of the Court of the ship's nationality is exclusive of, or concurrent with, that of the Court of the offender's nation, the question seems to be settled; though it would be exclusive, if the offenses were committed on the high seas. In an interesting case, which arose in July, 1906, the decision of the

by my predecessors, and is distinctly disaffirmed by me, that a citizen of the United States can be tried for any offense and personally punished except by his own consul." *For Rel.,* 1887, p. 211.

[1] G H. Scidmore, *United States Courts in Japan,* p. 228.

Danish Consular Court at Shanghai seems to indicate that Denmark would, in the case supposed, consider the jurisdiction of the two courts to be concurrent, though the American consul held a contrary opinion, possibly on the sole ground that the offense in that case was committed on the high seas, which was not certain.

The facts of the case in 1906 were these: Two firemen of the Danish steamer Indian were arrested in Shanghai by the municipal police, on a charge of larceny of £64 19s. 6d. from a passenger on board, when the vessel was somewhere between Nagasaki and Shanghai. When brought before the Danish consul, one of the accused declared that he was a Norwegian and the other that he was an American; whereupon the consul declined to entertain jurisdiction and remanded the offenders to their respective consuls. The American consul declared that he could not see how he had jurisdiction over Eastman, the American, since his name was on the articles of a Danish ship. For the same reason the Norwegian consul declined to try Nielson, the Norwegian.[1] The reasoning of the American consul's decision was that it was a well-defined principle of international law that a vessel while upon the high seas was to be regarded as a part of the country whose flag she bore, that all offenses and crimes against the laws of the country were accordingly cognizable by its tribunals alone; and that the crime with which the prisoner was charged having been committed on the high seas, and while he was one of a crew of a foreign vessel, the American consul could take no jurisdiction over him.[2] The two prisoners were brought before the Danish court again, and on August 8, 1906, Mr. T. Raaschon delivered an opinion, part of which follows:

[1] 80 *North China Herald* (1906), 267.
[2] *Ibid.*, p. 282.

Since the offense complained of is a breach of the common criminal law and is outside the class of offenses punishable under the maritime law, and since it was found, when this case was previously before this court, that the theft, if committed, took place in Chinese sea territory, where the Treaty-Powers have jurisdiction over their nationals, the case was considered to be one of concurrence of jurisdiction; namely, of jurisdiction of territory and jurisdiction of flag. In such cases the instructions for Danish consuls are to give precedence to the authority having jurisdiction of territory and the accused were therefore handed over to their respective consulates. These, however, declined jurisdiction; the Danish courts as the authorities of flag must deal with the case.

The consul then stated that his court, being a treaty court, was ordinarily only competent in cases against its own nationals; and that the case should have been sent to the home courts or a special authority for his court asked for; that he had chosen the latter course and had obtained the necessary authorization to proceed to deal with the case. The prisoners were accordingly tried, convicted on evidence, and sentenced to ten and twenty days' imprisonment respectively.[1]

Another limitation springing from international law on the exercise of extraterritorial jurisdiction by a Treaty-Power in China operates in the case of its subjects being engaged, under obligation of contract entered into in time of peace, in the military operations carried on by a third power[2] at war with China. Apropos of the threatened attack of Formosa by Japan in 1874, Mr. Hamilton Fish,

---

[1] *North China Herald* (1906), p 358

[2] Most Treaty-Powers, notably the United States and Great Britain, prohibit their subjects in China, under the penalty of capital punishment, from taking part in or aiding a rebellion against the territorial Government.

Secretary of State at Washington, in his instructions of August 26 to Mr. Seward, consul-general at Shanghai, stated that should a citizen of the United States already in the military service of Japan, join the proposed hostile attack, he would do so not as an American citizen, but as a soldier in the army of one of the belligerent nations; that the United States would take no notice as against the attacked party, should he be killed in battle in the ordinary course of civilized warfare; and that in case of his being taken prisoner, it " would not exact more in his behalf than that no unusual or inhuman punishment be inflicted upon him, and would only watch and require that as prisoner of war he be treated according to the accepted rules of civilized warfare.[1] It may be added that from the strictly legal point of view, even this claim for humane treatment the United States would have been excluded from making since, in such a case, Japan alone would have been the rightful claimant.

§ 3. *Limitations founded on statutes*

The extraterritorial jurisdiction thus modified by treaty stipulations and the transcendent rules of international law, so far as its exercise by the foreign courts in China is concerned, is again limited by statutes. The jurisdiction of such courts is altogether statutory, and therefore it extends only so far as is, expressly or impliedly, authorized by the laws of their respective states Whatever is not so placed within their competency is not justiciable by them, though the matter might be one entirely within the scope of the treaty grant of extraterritorial jurisdiction. In his circular note to British Consuls in China, November 22, 1844, Sir

[1] *For. Rel.*, 1874, p 332. The same opinion was expressed by Mr. Fish in his instructions to Mr. Williams, chargé d'affaires at Peking, July 29, 1874, *ibid.*, p 300.

John F. Davis, Chief Superintendent of British Trades, after stating that the right of the British Crown to exercise any jurisdiction in China " is strictly limited to the terms in which the concession is made," continues to observe:

The right depends, in the next place, on the extent to which the Queen, in the exercise of the powers vested in Her Majesty by Act of Parliament, may be pleased to grant to Her Consular Servants, through Her Majesty's superintendent in China, authority to exercise jurisdiction over British subjects; and therefore the ordinances which may from time to time be issued are the only warrants for the proceedings of the consuls, and exhibit the rules to which they must scrupulously adhere.[1]

In the case of Walter Jackson, an American citizen, who had escaped from British justice at Hongkong into Shanghai, the proposal of the American consul at the latter port to hold extradition proceedings and deliver him up to the Hongkong authorities was discountenanced and disapproved by the State Department on the ground, among others, that no authority was given by the laws of the United States to any consular officer to exercise such a power.[2]

§ 4. *Limitations founded on policy*

Besides the limitations born of treaties, international law, and statutes, the extraterritorial jurisdiction exercisable by consular courts in China may be subjected to a diminution or disability in respect to subjects of their own nationality, who might be justiciable by them, but who on account of their incorrigible conduct, have been voluntarily

[1] *Parl Papers,* 1847, xxxx, China, no 795, p. 38.

[2] Mr. Hunter, Assistant Secretary of State, to Mr. Seward, consul at Shanghai, August 31, 1874, *For. Rel.,* 1874, p. 338; Mr. Cadwalader, Acting Secretary of State to Mr Seward, Oct. 23, 1874, *ibid*, p. 347.

abandoned by their own Government on grounds of policy, to be dealt with by the territorial authorities. A case of this kind occurred in 1865. General Burgevine, an American citizen, who had in 1862 been placed by the Chinese Government in command of an Imperial army to suppress the Taipung Rebellion, was charged with disobedience to orders from Peking, and Prince Kung, in his note to Mr. Burlingame, January 25, 1863, expressed himself as being of opinion that " Burgevine, being now a Chinese subject, and having offended against the law of the country, certainly ought to be arrested and punished in accordance with the law of China ";[1] although the Prince, on protest of the American Minister, abandoned this view for a time. Subsequently, however, when Burgevine, after having been once expelled from the country in consequence of his having taken part in the rebellion against the Government, stealthily returned to China in 1865, rejoined the insurgents, and was captured as a prisoner, Prince Kung refused to give him up, alleging that Mr. Burlingame had yielded all claim over him if he should again be taken in the Emperor's dominions.

Thereupon, on June 26, 1865, Mr. Williams, the American chargé d'affaires at Peking, reported Burgevine's second capture to the State Department, and recommended that the prisoner be yielded to the Chinese Government for the reason that " the example will deter others from trespassing so far on the rights of Americans as to stir up sedition, trusting to the want of witnesses and other legal proof to escape condemnation."[2] This recommendation was accepted though in guarded language by the Government of the United States, as on November 6, 1865, Mr. Seward, Secretary of State, wrote to Mr. Williams as follows:

[1] *Dipl. Corr*, 1863, pt. ii, p. 866.
[2] *Dipl. Corr.*, 1865, pt. ii, p 452.

In reply, I have to inform you that the President is of opinion that the offender Burgevine may, upon a just conviction, be left to the Chinese custody without being reclaimed by the United States representative. But this is to be understood to rest upon our voluntary consent upon the grounds of national honor, and not upon Chinese right under treaty stipulations.[1]

From the practical point of view, this was not a case of honor but one of necessity; honor is not a sufficient ground upon which to base the abandonment of a right; on the other hand, it is necessary that he who is permitted by his own country to enter the military service of a foreign nation, should be subjected to the jurisdiction of that nation. But before Mr. Seward's instructions were put into execution, however, Burgevine met with death by the accidental capsizing of the boat in which he was being transferred to Fukchau, and the matter was thus dropped; although it must be added that in notifying Mr. Williams of this fact, on September 1, 1865, Prince Kung did not omit to observe that Burgevine himself being " a man, who, by his frequent connections with the rebels, had, as you formerly remarked, acted so as to lose the countenance of his own country. It would have been right, therefore, to have regarded him as amenable to the laws of China." [2]

§ 5. *The jurisdiction primarily personal*

It has been said in a preceding section that as a rule the jurisdiction exercisable by a Treaty-Power in China extends over all the subjects as well as over all the property belonging to them. This extent of the jurisdiction, however, is its own limitation; it is primarily personal. Except as regards foreign members of the crew of a national ship,

[1] *Dipl Corr.*, 1865, pt. ll, p. 462
[2] *Dipl. Corr.*, 1866, pt. i, p. 471.

the jurisdiction of a consular court in China cannot under the treaties extend over persons other than the subjects of the nation to which it itself belongs.

The doctrine of assimilation, which prevails in Mohammedan countries whereby an alien, whether his own government has treaty relations with the territorial sovereign or not, is considered to be entitled, as against the exercise of jurisdiction over him by the local authorities, to the protection of the consulate in whose registry he has made an entry, is not recognized at all in China. Nor does the system of protegés exist there. During the Franco-Chinese war the Russian consul at Shanghai had certain Frenchmen arrested in that port actually brought before him for hearing, although his authority, as conferred by France and recognized by China, was limited to the use of good offices in behalf of French citizens.[1] But with the possible exception of Russia, the treaty powers have uniformly observed the essentially personal character of the extraterritorial jurisdiction as accorded them by China.[2] Great Britain and the United States, for example, both of which have upheld the doctrine of assimilation in Mohammedan states, disclaim such practice in China.[3] Sir Frederick W. A. Bruce, British Minister to China, in his circular instructions to British consuls within his jurisdiction, May 16, 1864, says:

[1] 4 Moore, *Intern. Law Digest*, 606.

[2] See *infra*, sec 18.

[3] See on this point the interesting case of Koszta (3 Moore, *Intern. Law Digest*, 820-854), in which this doctrine of assimilation was invoked by the United States Government as the main support of its argument in the conduct of its agents, who threatened to use force in order to secure the release of Koszta, who had been arrested in Smyrna by the Austrian consul and placed in custody on board the Austrian brig-of-war "Huszar"

According to the laws of most countries a man cannot, without the permission of his government, withdraw himself from his national and submit to a foreign authority, and the attempts by the consul to exercise any such jurisdiction might lead to serious protests on the part of other governments; moreover, Her Majesty's government has not empowered her agents in China to accept any such jurisdiction over foreigners or Chinese, and it is not expedient or politic to advance any such claim. The subjects of other nations, if entitled to buy lots, must be dealt with exclusively by their national consuls, if they are subjects of Treaty-Powers; and if they are subjects of non-treaty powers, it is for the Chinese government to devise a means of making them obey the law. Her Majesty's consuls acquire no valid rights over them by reason of their living on a lot leased from the Crown, or in virtue of any engagement they may personally enter into. Should there be any attempt to exercise jurisdiction over a foreign lessee against his will, the legality of the proceeding could not be sustained.[1]

This view of the limitations of the extraterritorial jurisdiction in China continues to be entertained by the British Government to-day. Hall has observed that while the Orders in Council relative to the exercise of British jurisdiction in the Ottoman dominions, Persia, Morocco, Muscat, Tripoli and Siam, still recognize the existence of a class of protected persons, consisting of either natives of the territory or other persons not British subjects, " it has not been the practice to give protection in China and Japan, and in the Order in Council affecting those countries, no mention is made of protected persons; jurisdiction is restricted to British subjects." [2]

---

[1] *Dipl Corr*, 1864, pt. iii, p. 380.

[2] *Foreign Jurisdiction of the British Crown* (Oxford, 1894), pp 137-139

The United States Government has on several occasions made known its view of the personal character of the jurisdiction conferred on the treaty powers by China. In his instructions of July 25, 1872, to Mr. Low, Minister to China, as to the nature and extent of the protection to be extended by United States representatives to Swiss citizens in that country, who were without their own national representatives there, Mr. Fish, Secretary of State, said:

> The protection referred to must necessarily be confined to the personal, unofficial, good offices of such functionaries. Although when exercised to this extent merely, this can properly be done only with the consent of the Chinese Government, and that consent must not be allowed to imply an obligation on the part of a diplomatic or consular officer of the United States in that country to assume criminal or civil jurisdiction over Swiss citizens, or to make himself or his government accountable for their acts.[1]

When later in the same year Mr. Fish was apprised of the conduct of Mr. Jewell, the American consul at Canton, who undertook to try in his consular court a citizen of New Granada (now known as Columbia) on a criminal charge, he sent new instructions to Mr. Low, January 8, 1873, similar in principle to those he gave as to Swiss citizens, but with even greater emphasis. He said:

> Mr. Jewell had no authority whatever to entertain jurisdiction of the case. That he should have fallen into the commission of such an error, with the laws of the United States, the consular instructions and the existing treaties between the United States and China all before him, seems unaccountable. The reasons assigned by the consul for his action can have no influence or weight in establishing as right a proceeding that is per se wrong. Under the laws of the United States juris-

[1] 4 Moore, *Intern. Law Digest*, 602.

diction in a criminal case cannot be conferred by consent even in one of the established courts of record of the country. Much less is this the case with the consular court, which is a tribunal of limited and inferior jurisdiction, possessing only such powers as are expressly conferred by acts of Congress in conformity with the provisions of existing treaties.

The waiver of their authority in the matter by the Chinese officials invested the consular with no new or additional powers. He is not an officer of that government, and he can derive no authority from it, directly or indirectly, which will give validity to any official action of his, when such action is not warranted by the laws of the United States or his instructions from this Department. Neither can the jurisdiction assumed in this case rest upon the consent of the accused. It would be unreasonable to demand for a prisoner the right not only to select but to create a tribunal for the trial of his own case; but the objection rests on still higher grounds, and in the interest of the accused himself, lest through ignorance or mistake he may misconceive that interest.

The court before which a criminal trial is proceeding will not, as a general rule, permit the prisoner to waive any substantial right secured to him by law, and never without fully advising him of the consequence of his action.

The principles of criminal law and practice are so well settled and so universally recognized in American and English jurisprudence, that any further discussion of them is deemed wholly unnecessary.

In Oriental countries, where, in order to preserve to citizens of the United States, as far as possible, the personal rights recognized as belonging to them in their own country, it is found necessary to have these rights and the privileges that pertain to them precisely defined by treaty stipulation, it becomes all the more necessary that officers of the United States resident in those countries should, in the exercise of their functions, confine themselves strictly within the powers guaranteed by treaty stipulation and regulated by settled principles of public law. Such a course on their part will not only tend to prevent unpleasant complications, but do much to secure·from the people of those countries respect for the rights of American citizens resident therein.

Your course in bringing this matter to the attention of the Department at the earliest moment is commended.   The action of Mr. Consul Jewell is disapproved and he will receive information of such disapproval directly from the Department.[1]

Again, during the Chino-Japanese war, Japanese in China, as well as Chinese in Japan, were placed under the friendly protection of United States representatives.   In his instructions[2] to Mr Denby, Jr., chargé in Peking, August 29, 1894, as to the precise nature of the protection to be extended to Japanese in China, which instructions *mutatis mutandis,* were sent on the same day to Mr. Dun, Minister at Tokyo, in relation to the protection of Chinese in Japan, Mr. Gresham, Secretary of State, said:

By consenting to lend its good offices in behalf of Japanese subjects in China, this Government cannot assume to assimilate such subjects to citizens of the United States, and to invest them with an extraterritoriality which they do not enjoy as subjects of the Emperor of Japan.   It cannot assume to hold them amenable to the laws of the United States nor to the jurisdiction of our minister or consuls: nor can it permit our legation or our consulates to be made an asylum for offenders against the laws from the pursuit of the legitimate agents of justice.   In a word, Japanese subjects in China continue to be the subjects of their own sovereign, and answerable to the local laws to the same extent as heretofore.   The employment of good offices in their behalf by another power can not alter their situation in this regard.

Accordingly, when the American consul-general at Shang-

[1] *For. Rel.*, 1873, pt. i, p 139.
[2] 4 Moore, *Intern. Law Digest*, 601-603.

hai refused to give up to the Chinese authorities two Japanese spies who had been arrested in the French concession by the French consul at the instance of the Chinese prefect and delivered to him by the consul, Mr. Gresham instructed Mr. Denby by telegraph that the consul-general should not have received them and was not authorized to hold them, but that they should be surrendered to the Taotai at Shanghai unconditionally.[1] This was done.[2]

In fact the jurisdiction of a consular court in China is so primarily personal that in a suit brought before it by a foreign subject against one of its own nationals it has no control over the plaintiff beyond the amount of money deposited by him as security for costs,—which for obvious reasons cannot be large. Take a concrete example. A Chinese sues a British subject in a British court whose power is limited to and extends only over the defendant and the Chinese plaintiff perjures, it cannot punish him, nor can it commit him for contempt of court; he can be prosecuted or punished only in a Chinese court and according to Chinese laws. Again, if the suit is brought on a claim for moneys due, and the defendant has no defense but sets up a counterclaim of equal or greater amount, the court cannot entertain the counterclaim, however obvious its validity may be; the reason being that a counterclaim is a claim against a man of another nationality and must be tried by the court, and according to the laws of that nationality.[3]

[1] *For. Rel.*, 1894, pp. 100-108.

[2] *Ibid*, p. 115.

[3] A. M. Latter on " The Government of the Foreigners in China," 19 *Law Quarterly Review* (1903), 316-325.

§ 6. *The Jurisdiction as to criminal matters is punitive, not*
preventive

Since very early times opinion has been divided as to the
precise scope of the clause, now found in the treaties of all
nations maintaining relations with China, which confers
upon these nations extraterritorial jurisdiction over their
own subjects in China in criminal and penal cases. As may
be surmised, the point of dispute centres about the meaning
and purport of the common clause which provides that subjects of a given treaty power, who may commit any crime
in China shall be tried and punished by the Consul, or other
public functionary authorized thereto, according to the laws
of that power. It will be impracticable to review here the
arguments advanced in support of one side or the other,
but the whole controversy may be summarized by saying
that it lies between a too narrow and a too broad construction of this important provision.

The question is undoubtedly fraught with difficulties un-
foreseen by the early western negotiators. Their attitude,
particularly that of the staunch advocate of extraterritoriality in China, the negotiator of the American treaty of
1844,[1] was simple and not unintelligible. They were familiar, through learning or experience, with the practice of
Christian foreigners in Mohammedan countries, where religion constitutes the sole test of a person's liberty and
rights; and when they saw that China, like Turkey, for instance, was not a Christian state, they naturally inferred
that she could not have the same scruples of truth, faith and
humanity which the nations of Christendom in their times
were believed to observe. Coupled with this want of confidence in China, based on the difference in religion, was
their natural lack of acquaintance with, hence appreciation

---

[1] See *supra*, chap. ix, sec. 9.

of, the real character of the Chinese institutions, law, and civilization; and the two deficiencies combined produced on their minds the resultant unsympathetic attitude toward the local systems of government and administration. This absence of sympathy naturally approached contempt when they observed, according to their own lights, the crude procedure followed in the trial of criminal cases, the unproportionate punishments meted out to the guilty, and the cruel manner in which sentences of death or imprisonment or corporal punishment were executed. In a word, their understanding of China was that she was not a country, to use the phrase of an English jurist, within " the circle of law-governed nations." If they could have done it they perhaps would have preferred to have nothing to do with such a country. But the bait of a lucrative trade was too tempting for their own nations to resist, and therefore they were obliged to find some way in which their commercial aspirations might be attained without at the same time suffering from the otherwise unavoidable consequences of their presence in the Chinese territory, and of their contact with the Chinese people. Hence originated in their minds the idea of introducing the artificial system of extraterritoriality into China. That the early negotiators intended that the device thus initiated should be of limited application in a small number of seaports seems to be a more reasonable view than that it should subsequently be extended to all parts of the Empire. Under the circumstances it would have been little short of a marvellous exhibition of prophetic power to foresee that the extraterritorial jurisdiction would have to be exercised on a great scale, such as it is, and that it would withal bring forth complicating questions, such as it has, as to its extent and scope.

If the early negotiators thought of the question of the scope of jurisdiction at all, they probably took this view:

that the territorial sovereign might enact any laws he was pleased to, but the enforcement of them, so far as their own nationals were concerned, would have to be effected by their own authorities. This attitude was in entire accord with, and eminently conducive to, their desire to secure for their nationals both the privilege to trade and a way to escape the crude and cruel forms of procedure, punishment, and execution of sentences in the Chinese system of law. It would be unreasonable, on the other hand, to attribute to these early sponsors of extraterritoriality in China an intention to withdraw their countrymen from all allegiance to Chinese laws, and to constitute them on Chinese territory, so to speak, into petty states, sovereign and independent with reference to the Emperor of China. Such an intention could not be reconciled with their purpose to establish foreign trade in China on a permanent footing; rather it would have defeated that purpose As has been seen in Chapter 6, China, during the pre-conventional period, always claimed and generally exercised the right to regulate trade within her territory; could it then be reasonably expected by the early negotiators that when she entered into treaty relations with their respective states, granting them extraterritorial jurisdiction over their subjects, she was willing entirely to forego the right of regulation where the trade affected foreign subjects or interests?

It is equally improbable that the early western negotiators intended to plant in China an extraterritorial jurisdiction which should go beyond the scope of that which then prevailed in Turkey, the home of judicial extraterritoriality. There it was only in cases between themselves that the Franks, or Christian foreigners, were entitled to be judged by their respective ministers and consuls Where natives were involved, whether as plaintiffs or defendants, jurisdiction was reserved in the old capitulations to the local

tribunals. In crimes and offenses committed by foreigners
against natives, as well as in civil causes between natives
and foreigners, Turkish courts, until very recently, had exclusive cognizance, with the guarantee that a consul or consular dragoman of the foreigner's nation was present. Indeed, when the United States Minister at Constantinople
in 1868 contested under the fourth article of the treaty of
May 7, 1830, between the two countries, the right of the
Ottoman authorities to take jurisdiction over two American
citizens whom they had arrested on a charge of an offense
committed in Syria, the Porte replied that the claim was
based upon an erroneous translation of the article in question and that the words " they (American citizens com-
·mitting an offense in the Ottoman Empire) shall be tried
by their minister or consul, and punished according to their
offense," were not to be found in the Turkish text. Other
cases, notably that of Stephen P. Mirzan, in 1879, have
since arisen and the United States representatives have exercised jurisdiction over the American citizens concerned,
but they have in each case elicited a protest from the Sub-
lime Porte. It may be added that although the word " try "
is used in the eighth article of the Belgian treaty of 1838
with Turkey, no case has as yet arisen under it.[1]

Furthermore, the language of the clause in question
seems to show that the western negotiators, in employing
it, did not entertain such extravagant notions as have been
attributed to them. Take, for an example, the specific
clause in the American treaty of 1844, which introduced the
system of extraterritoriality into China. The phrase, "citizens of the United States who may commit any crime in
China," necessarily implies that there were laws already in
force in China defining crimes, that is, describing certain

[1] Van Dyck, *Capitulations of the Ottoman Empire* (Washington,
1881), pp. 19-22, 28-29.

acts to be prohibited, and prescribing penalties for them and the manner of enforcing them. The words following the phrase, namely, "shall be subject to be tried and punished only by the Consul or other public functionary of the United States thereto authorized according to the laws of the United States," obviously mean, on the one hand, to exempt American offenders from the penalties and the manner of enforcing them, prescribed in the Chinese law, and on the other, to subject them to such mode of trial and such penalties as are provided by the laws of their own nation for the corresponding crime.

As to that species of local laws which are generally designated by the name of police regulations, not even diplomatic officers nor vessels-of-war are exempt from them. They, like aliens of non-official character, are also required to observe them. It would therefore seem extravagant to contend that foreigners in China are under no obligation to respect such laws enacted by the territorial sovereign.[1]

· In short, the consideration which must have animated the minds of the early negotiators in seeking from China the privilege of extraterritoriality; the usages then observed in the Ottoman Empire, the birth-place of the extraterritorial jurisdiction; the language of the provisions in the treaties between China and foreign states conferring this privilege on their nationals; and the recognized limitations on immunities accorded to diplomatic officers and public vessels all seem, in a fair view, to support the interpretation that the jurisdiction of the treaty powers over their citizens or subjects in China, is, as respects crimes and offenses, punitive and not preventive.[2] Extraterritoriality in

---

[1] See Moore, *Intern. Law Digest*, secs. 254, 255.

[2] Secretary of State Bayard, in his despatch to Mr. Young, Minister to China, March 11, 1885, observes: " In China . . . foreign powers

China as well as elsewhere is but a metaphorical term. It does not denote that aliens who are entitled to enjoy this privilege, though they remain in the territory, are actually to be held as though they were outside of it. To be precise, the term implies only exemption from process of the local courts, not exemption from obedience to the local laws.

With reference to the treaty powers themselves, it may be said that extraterritoriality entitles them to exercise so much authority over their nationals in China as is necessary to enforce effectively, by judicial methods, the laws declared to be in force by the Emperor of China. What the content of this authority consists of, may be easily comprehended; it includes only the power to regulate, for the purpose of enforcing territorial laws upon their own subjects or citizens in China, questions concerning the machinery of their courts, the law of procedure, the mode of trial, the rules of evidence, the incidence of responsibility, the measure, degree, kind and manner of punishment, and other kindred matters.[1] The sovereign power of legislation, on the other hand, remains in the Emperor of China unimpaired.[2] He may

have an extraterritorial jurisdiction, conferred by treaty. This jurisdiction is in no wise arbitrary but limited by laws, and is not preventive, but punitory." *For. Rel.*, 1885, p. 160

[1] " The foreigner in China is amenable only to his own courts as far as mode of trial extends and measure of punishment" Mr. Denby, Minister to China, to Mr. Bayard, Sec. of State, Oct. 9, 1886. *For. Rel*, 1886, p. 96.

[2] Mr. Seward, United States Minister to China, in his despatch of March 16, 1880, to Mr. Evarts, Secretary of State, observes:

" My own view is that we cannot deny the right of the Chinese Government to make rules and regulations affecting all matters within their sovereignty, but that we may scrutinize all rules and regulations made or proposed by them which affect our nationals, and object to them, if we find them in contravention of treaty stipulations, or suggest their withdrawal or modification if they appear burdensome. . . .

" The question of principle involved is an important one, and has

make any law that he sees fit for the purpose of maintaining the public peace and order, of preserving the decency and morals of the people, of promoting the welfare of his country, or for any other legitimate purpose. He may, for instance, lay a property tax on all property holders in his dominions for the purpose of raising revenue; or, as was suggested in the Tsungli-Yamen's circular note to the powers, March, 1878,[1] close a street to public passage. All these laws have a binding effect throughout the territory to which they are intended to apply, and the Chinese authorities are under obligation to administer them to all persons within their scope They may collect from a foreign property-owner his share of tax, and may prevent any foreigner from traversing the closed street. Only if the foreign property-owner refuses to pay his tax, the Chinese authorities cannot compel him to do it except by entering a complaint in the proper consular court of his nation; and if the foreign pedestrian persists in violating the law prohibiting passage through the specified street, the Chinese authorities cannot chastise him for defiance but must send him to the consular court of his nation for such punishment as the laws of his nation may have provided for such a case.

Nor is it difficult to see that China must of necessity be the sole judge of what laws are desirable or needed for her country, regardless of persons. For if the various treaty-powers were to transcend the limits of their power sanctioned by treaty by making substantive laws, as distinguished from adjective laws, for their subjects in China, not

occasioned a great deal of discussion and unpleasant feeling both in this Empire and in Japan I cannot doubt, however, the correctness of my own view. I have acted upon it ever since my arrival in this capital, and shall continue to do so unless instructed to the contrary by yourself." *For. Rel.*, 1880, p. 239

[1] *For. Rel.*, 1880, p. 177.

only would such assumption of power be a confounding of jurisdiction with sovereignty, but the laws on a given subject made by the different treaty-powers having as they do different interests to subserve, might be so conflicting and even contradictory as to destroy their practical value, on the one hand, and on the other, to paralyze China's efforts to promote her own welfare, and even endanger her state life.

As a matter of fact there is, in practice, no question as to the obligation on the part of the subjects of treaty-powers to observe Chinese laws on all matters where such laws have been, so to speak, adopted by the laws of these powers, so that what is punishable under the former is also punishable under the latter. The question arises where the doing of a certain act by any person in China is prohibited or required by a Chinese law under penalty of punishment, but not so prohibited or required generally or specifically by the laws of the treaty-powers as respects their own subjects in China. In such a case what must be done by the powers concerned and their subjects in China? The answer seems obvious from what has already been said. The foreign subjects, by reason of the protection which they receive from the Emperor of China while residing in his territory, are obliged to observe his laws, whatever they may be, and the treaty-powers, by virtue of their treaty right of exclusive control over the persons of their subjects in China, are under an implied obligation to enforce the laws upon such subjects by measures adequate for the purpose.[1] For to disclaim the

---

[1] In his circular to British consuls in China, November 22, 1844, Sir J. F. Davis, Chief Superintendent of British Trades, states that the Christian Powers, in taking advantage of the concession of extra-territoriality made by the Emperor of China, "are bound to provide as far as possible against any injurious effects resulting from it to the territorial Sovereign," and that "as the maintenance of order and the repression and punishment of crime are objects of the greatest im-

duty of foreigners in China to observe the territorial laws
would be, to say the least, an admission that there exists a
right without a corresponding obligation; while to deny
the obligation of the treaty-powers to enforce upon their
subjects in China all Chinese laws, except those from which
foreign subjects are exempted by specific and express provisions in the treaties, would be tantamount to asserting that
the interests of the few subjects of a treaty-power in China
should override the interests of the entire Chinese nation,

portance in every civilized community, it is obligatory upon Christian
Powers . . . to provide as far as possible for these great ends."—*Parl.
Papers*, 1847, xxxx, China, no 795, p 38.

Mr. Seward, the American Minister at Peking, makes the following
significant observation in his Memorandum of October 4, 1879:

"In actual practice it comes to this: That foreigners are bound to
observe the laws of the Empire so far as they conform to the laws of
their own country It is an offense against China to commit a murder
on Chinese soil . . . The person so offending may be arrested by the
Chinese, and they have the right to demand that he shall be tried and
punished: in the words of the treaty, 'impartial justice shall be done
in the premises'.

"This principle may be carried further, and it may be said that we
are bound to provide remedies in cases where the Chinese Government
declares unlawful certain acts which are not in themselves criminal
but which become so in consequence of enactments made for the
public advantage. It cannot be said that throwing ballast overboard in a
stream is in itself an offense against China, but the throwing overboard
of a ballast in a stream when it is prohibited by Chinese law, must be
considered an improper act, an offense against the nation, and, as such,
we are under obligation to provide a remedy, either by acknowledging
the validity of the law, adopting it, so to speak, for ourselves, or by
enacting a law of our own to meet the case"—On this point, see *For.
Rel*, 1880, p. 146.

The British Minister in Peking is now empowered by Article 155 of
the China and Corea Order in Council, 1904, to make regulations having the force of law, among others, for the purpose of "securing the
observance of any treaty for the time being in force relating to any
place or of any native law or custom, whether relating to trade, commerce, revenue, or any other matter."—Hertslet's *China Treaties*, ii,
p. 884.

and that the treaty-powers should be supreme judges of what the laws of China should be.

Suppose, for an example, China enacted a law prohibiting public derision of any religion in China; now if foreign subjects in China were not under obligation to observe Chinese laws, the over-zealous Christian missionaries would more often than not pay no regard whatever to the enactment, but would continue to abuse their freedom of preaching the gospel by denouncing all non-Christian religions; although when their indiscrete utterances should bring down upon themselves an outbreak of popular indignation and violence, they would at once charge the local authorities with a failure to protect them efficiently.[1] Suppose, again, China enacted a sanitary law for observance by all persons throughout her dominions; now if the treaty-powers were at liberty to determine whether they would enforce them upon their subjects in China, the result might easily be foreseen. One power might consider the law to be too exacting, another, unnecessary at all. Under such circumstances how could the law be enforced with the good effect which it was intended otherwise to produce? Suppose, once more, a Chinese law was enacted with a view to the maintenance of the public peace, prohibiting on Chinese territory the fighting of duels with dangerous weapons; if the treaty-powers were free to determine for themselves whether or not they would enforce it upon their own subjects in China, it is possible that some of them, which still consider such fighting as a manly art or an honorable way of settling private differences, would not make any effort to enforce it.

[1] In fact public derision by a British subject of any religion established or observed within China is now punishable by imprisonment or fine or both under Article 76 of the China and Corea Order in Council, 1904.—Hertslet's *China Treaties,* ii, p 862.

There is another view which serves to bring out more clearly the obligation of foreign governments having relations with China, to compel their subjects in China to observe Chinese laws. These governments may be considered the chosen agents of the Chinese Emperor to apply his laws to specific groups of persons in his dominions, namely, their respective subjects in China; for whatever jurisdiction they exercise over their subjects in China, they do so only by virtue of the consent of the Emperor expressed in treaties. In appointing them to this task the Emperor also invests them with exclusive authority to select for themselves the manner and means of performing that task, and at the same time pledges himself not to revoke this authority without their consent. Now why does the Emperor do this? What is the principal consideration for this valuable concession of power? There can be no doubt that he assigns away this power in trust, with the tacit understanding that it will be exercised in good faith for the purpose for which it is conceded, which is the effective enforcement of his laws against those persons over which the power extends. It is equally certain that in accepting the concession of power, which goes with the task, foreign nations understand it to be a legacy of trust and that they are expected to discharge that trust while enjoying the power thus conferred upon them. For if there were no such obligation implied in the concession there would be no reasonable ground on which the concession could be upheld; it would, on the contrary, amount to this absurdity: that the Emperor made the concession for the purpose of rendering himself unable in the future to prevent foreign subjects in his territory from violating his law with impunity, and that foreign states, under the pretense of protecting their subjects from the harshness and cruelties of the Chinese law, accepted the concession in order that the Emperor might be so disabled.

and their subjects might, by violating his laws without
check, bring harm to his nation.[1]

[1] The view that the concession of extraterritoriality by the territorial
sovereign or foreign powers is essentially an application of the theory
of agency in private law and has been suggested or intimated by several eminent authorites.

Mr. Fish, Secretary of State, in his instructions to Mr. DeLong,
December 20, 1870, states:

"A report made to Congress by my predecessor, Mr. Seward, shows
that it has been the habit of this Department to regard the judicial
power of our Consular Officers in Japan as resting upon the assent of
the government of the Kingdom, whether expressed by formal convention or by tacit acquiescence in the notorious practice of the Consular Courts. In other words, they were esteemed somewhat in the
same light as they would have been if they were constituted by the
Mikado with American citizens as judges, and with all the authority
with which a Japanese tribunal is invested in respect to the native subjects of Japan, to the extent that our Government will admit a jurisdiction understood to be extremely arbitrary. They were, so to speak,
the agents of a despotism, only restrained by such safeguards as our
own Government may interpose for the protection of citizens who
come within its sway."—Cited in Scidmore, *United States Courts in
Japan*, p. 226.

Professor John W. Burgess, of Columbia University, after reading
the case of Ross (140 U. S. 453), makes this observation ·

"It seems to me evident . . . that the principle here involved is
simply that of an immunity granted by the territorial sovereign of
Japan to the citizens of the United States while sojourning in Japan.
It is probably true that this practice of consular jurisdiction in foreign
lands is a relic of the medieval idea that law is personal—that is,
racial or national—and follows the individual wherever he may go.
But the modern principle is that law is territorial, and that all de-
partures from this principle are the exceptions which make the rule
manifest. We must, therefore, reconcile the existence of these exceptional immunities with the principle of territorial sovereignty; and
this can be done only by regarding all authority exercised within the
sphere of the immunity as proceeding from, and administered for,
the territorial sovereign, but administered by the countrymen of the
party or parties concerned, and administered according to such
methods as they or their home government may devise"—14 *Political
Science Quarterly* (1899), 9,

Professor Charles H Huberich, of Stanford University, with
reference to the case In re Tootals' Trust (33 Ch Div. 532), states:

"It is quite immaterial that the Chinese law provides that per-

What measures are to be adopted, what methods are to be
pursued, what agents are to be authorized for carrying out
the purpose—these questions must, under the treaties, be left
to the discretion of the foreign powers.   They may proceed against their subjects violating Chinese laws in the
form of a criminal prosecution or in that of a civil suit for
damages; they may by law prescribe fine or imprisonment
or both, as penalty for a breach of such laws; in a word,
they may do anything which is necessary to compel their
subjects to observe the territorial laws.   They may even so
exercise this discretionary power vested in them by treaty

sons of British nationality shall be governed by the rules of law
prevailing in England, or by such laws as may be enacted and made
applicable to them by the English authorities.   The English law is
operative in Shanghai as to certain persons and certain transactions
only because it is permitted and adopted by the territorial sovereign "—" Domicile in Countries Granting Extraterritorial Privileges
to Foreigners," 24 *Law Quarterly Review* (1908), 440-444.
    Again:
"In respect of all matters which private international law refers
to the law of the domicile he would be governed by the Chinese
law, the law of the territorial sovereign.   The law to which he
would be subject would be none the less the law of China because
it provides that persons of British and American nationality shall
be governed by such laws as their respective countries may enact
to govern their nationals in China   The Legislative power of China
extends to all persons and things within the territorial limits of the
Empire; the British Parliament in legislating for British nationals
in China acts merely under a delegation of authority.   Such laws
are operative within the territory of China only because China
recognizes them as part of the law of the land."
    Justice Albert M. Spear, delivering the opinion of the Supreme
Judicial Court of Maine in the case of Mather *v.* Cunningham
makes this dictum:
"Although the Emperor had suspended some of the Chinese laws
and permitted the extension of American law to the territory, yet
the source of the law was the Emperor, who had never released his
sovereignty over the soil (of Shanghai) "—74 *Abl. Rep.* (1909),
809, 814

as to determine for themselves in a case of breach of
Chinese law, by one of their subjects, which of them shall
be held responsible for the act of breach.   Take an example
for illustration.   In his memorandum on the extraterritorial jurisdiction, October 4, 1879,[1] Mr. Seward, United
States Minister to China, observes that the Chinese con-
ceptions of right and obligation are different from those
prevailing in the West; that under Chinese law a parent
may be punished, not only for the offense of his child, but
also because he has not so instructed him that he would not
offend; that a person who has lost property by theft may be
punished for not having kept such watch over his property
as to prevent its loss; and he concludes: " It would be idle
to say that in such and similar cases foreigners offend
against the native law, and that it is the duty of the foreign
court to punish them."   This objection seems unnecessary
when it is pointed out that the question involved in the two
supposed cases, is merely one of the incidents of responsibility for a given act of crime or offense.   The obvious
intent of the Chinese law in the one case, is to prevent the
commission of offenses by children and in the other, is to
prevent thefts.   In such cases the treaty-powers are not
obliged to punish the persons designated in the Chinese
law; they do not have to punish the parent for the offense
of his child or for not instructing him to abstain from committing it, nor do they have to punish the owner for having
had his property stolen, if they believe that, by reason of
the peculiar nature and the different frame of mind of their
own people, the mere punishment of the child committing
the offense would be sufficient to deter him, and others of
his age, and that the mere punishment of the thief would be
sufficient to discourage stealing in the future.   China's su-

[1] *For. Rel*, 1880, p. 146.

preme interest in such cases is that offending by children and stealing property shall not be committed on her territory again, by whomsoever it may be. In other words, the treaty-powers are under obligations to enforce upon their subjects in China every territorial law in force, so that the intent and purpose of the law shall not be defeated with reference to such subjects; as to the manner and means of · compelling such observance by their subjects, the powers are by treaty entitled to exercise their own discretion.[1] ·

[1] This question of the extent and limitations of extraterritorial jurisdiction was once raised in Japan, also, in connection with the hunting regulations which the Japanese Government had enacted in 1873 and sought to have enforced upon all persons within Japanese territory. The basis of the discussion between Japan and the United States was the clause in Article VI of the treaty concluded between the two states, July 29, 1858 (superseded on July 17, 1899, when the treaty of November 22, 1894, went into effect), granting extraterritorial jurisdiction on American citizens in Japan. The language of the clause relative to jurisdiction in criminal cases was similar to that of the like article in the treaty between China and the United States concluded in the same year, on June 18. The clause provided:
"Americans committing offenses against Japanese shall be tried in American consular courts, and when guilty shall be punished according to American law. Japanese committing offenses against Americans shall be tried by the Japanese authorities and punished according to Japanese law. The consular courts shall be open to Japanese creditors, to enable them to recover their just claims against American citizens, and the Japanese courts shall in like manner be open to American citizens for the recovery of their just claims against Japanese"
—Treaties and Conventions concluded between the United States of America and other Powers, 1777-1887, p 601. ·
The views of the United States Government as to the scope of the extraterritorial jurisdiction thus conferred on its citizens in Japan are worth quotation. On November 17, 1873, Mr. Bingham, American Minister to Japan, wrote to Mr. Fish, Secretary of State, as in the following language:
"I have the honor, in reply to your instruction No. 5, dated the 6th September, 1873, to say that, having examined, as therein requested the 'hunting regulations' referred to, I am of opinion that

nothing therein contained, when construed according to the manifest intent thereof, conflicts with the privileges secured by treaty to American citizens in Japan. It may not be improper for me to add in support of this opinion that I find nothing in the treaty of 1858 which in anywise denies to Japan the general power to legislate over all persons within her territorial limits by general laws, while article 6 of that treaty does, by necessary implication, in my judgment, declare that the government of Japan may by law define and prohibit offenses within her territorial limits, and that no person resident therein is privileged by any treaty to disregard and violate such general law. It is no answer to this to say that because there are certain privileges secured by treaty to the government and citizens of the United States, Japan may not, therefore, rightfully exercise general legislative power over all persons within her limits in all matters not expressly provided for in the text of the treaty. I am not unmindful, in considering this question, that by the sixth article of the treaty Americans committing offenses against Japanese are to be tried in American consular courts, and, when guilty, punished according to American law; but I submit that it does not result from this that the government of Japan may not by general law define and prohibit all crimes and misdemeanors against persons and property within her limits. There is nothing in the 'hunting regulations' that I can discover which can be construed to deny to American citizens the right to be tried for any breaches thereof before the American consular courts, and to be punished, upon conviction, according to American law. The penalties prescribed by the regulations can only be held to apply to Japanese subjects, while the prohibitions therein are obligatory upon all. This seems to me to be their intent, and so I understand they have been uniformly administered."—*For. Rel.*, 1874, p. 653.

To this dispatch Mr. Fish, on January 7, 1874, sent the following instructions:

"Your dispatch No. 17, of the 17th of November, 1873, in relation to the 'hunting regulations' recently promulgated by the government of Japan, has been received.

"Your views in relation to the character of these local laws and regulations, as containing nothing which conflicts with the privileges secured to American citizens resident in that country under existing treaty regulations between the United States and Japan, are entirely in accord with the views entertained by this Department.

"The right of the authorities of Japan to enact and promulgate laws for the government, security, and good order of its own people, cannot, of course, be questioned for a moment, and of the character and efficiency of these laws, the government must be the sole judge. Citizens of the United States resident in Japan are expected and required to observe and obey such laws in the same manner and to the same extent that the like obligations rest upon the subjects of that empire. In regard to the enforcement of these laws, and the imposition of penalties for their infraction, citizens of the United States have secured to them, by the provisions of existing treaties, the right of being tried in the consular courts of their own nation, established in Japan, and according to the mode prescribed by the laws of the United States, and are protected from the infliction of any other penalties than those prescribed or warranted by the laws of their own country. So long as these privileges are recognized and respected by the government of Japan, there can be no cause of complaint on the part of this government in relation to the promulgation of any municipal law or regulation which the legislative authority of that country may deem necessary to its public interest and welfare."—*Ibid.,* p. 658.

In the case of United States *v.* Middleton, decided in December, 1875, by the American court at Kanagawa, it was held that foreigners in Japan were exempt from obedience to Japanese laws only in so far as the treaties with Japan define such exemption; and that the law of Japan prohibiting hunting or shooting without license was binding upon citizens of the United States.—Scidmore, *United States Courts in Japan,* p. 223.

CHAPTER XIII

PORTS AND FOREIGN SETTLEMENTS

§ 1. *Treaty Ports*

. THE right of foreigners to reside in China for purposes
of trade is limited to certain localities. The British treaty
of August 29, 1842, confers this right upon British subjects
in Canton,[1] Amoy, Foochow, Ningpo and Shanghai. The
same right is enjoyed by Americans and Frenchmen under
the treaties of July 3, 1844, and October 24, 1844, respectively. In 1860 new ports were opened to foreign commerce in pursuance of treaties concluded with the United
States, Russia, France and Great Britain; and since then
the number of treaty ports has been greatly increased—increased nearly with every revision of the old treaties and
the making of new ones.

At any of the treaty ports subjects of treaty powers are
entitled to carry on their mercantile pursuits "without
molestation and restraint." For this purpose ground is set
apart by the local authorities in communication with the
proper consul; within this area foreigners are allowed to
rent buildings and lease land at current market rates, and
to build or open on property thus obtained houses, warehouses, churches, cemeteries,[2] hospitals, asylums, and

---

[1] This city was not immediately opened to foreign residence; under
the convention of April 4, 1846, and the agreement of April 6, 1847 the
British Government formally consented to the delay.

[2] The right of British subjects to erect churches and cemeteries at
Canton was expressly granted in the agreement of April 6, 1847.
Article 17 of the American treaty of 1844 and article 22 of the French
treaty of the same year resemble each other in substance except that
the latter adds *hospices* and *écoles* to the list.

schools. Article 3 of the American treaty of October 8, 1903, greatly enriches the content of the privileges which Americans have enjoyed in parts of China open to foreign residence and commerce. It reads:

> Citizens of the United States may frequent, reside, carry on trade, industries, and manufactures, or pursue any lawful avocation, in the ports or localities of China which are now open or may hereafter be opened to foreign residence and trade; and within the suitable localities at those places which have been or may be set apart for the use and occupation of foreigners, they may rent or purchase houses, places of business, and other buildings, and rent or lease in perpetuity land and build thereon.

The area set apart at a treaty port for residence by subjects of a treaty-power is known in China as a foreign settlement or concession   At an important commercial centre, such as Hankow and Tienstin, there are usually a number of these settlements, each representing a separate nationality   Most of these settlements are governed each by a municipal council elected by foreign taxpayers residing within the concession. The council administers the interests of the concession, issues regulations on all administrative matters, levies taxes, erects public works and roads, and maintains a police. For injuries to person or property sustained in consequence of its acts the council is suable in the courts of the nation of which the concession belongs and damages may be recovered out of the funds levied under the municipal regulations. In a word, the municipal council of a foreign concession practically discharges duties and incurs responsibilities which are usually attendant upon the municipality of a European or an American city. In certain recent settlements not yet organized into municipal-

ities the consul of the proper state assumes the administration directly.[1]

In Shanghai, one of the earliest places opened to foreign
trade and residence, the situation is somewhat different.
In 1845, the Taotai of Shanghai, in consultation with the
British consul, defined the limits of a British settlement,
in pursuance of article 7 of the supplementary treaty of
1843; a short time later the same step was taken by the
Taotai with the American consul under article 17 of the
American treaty of 1844; and in 1849, M. Montigny, the
French consul, requested the same Chinese authority to
give effect to article 22 of the French treaty of 1844, providing for the setting apart of a site for the residence of
French subjects, which request was promptly complied
with. By 1854 the interests in the maintenance of good
order were so great, and the municipal arrangements so insufficient, that all the consuls stationed in Shanghai met
together and drafted a joint code of regulations for an international settlement, which was proclaimed on July 5,
1854, by the consuls of Great Britain, France and the
United States. Under their regulations the three settlements were placed under one system of control and administration. In 1862, however, the French consul established
a separate municipal council and on July 11, 1866, the
French Government issued the " Code de Réglements d'organisation municipale," replaced on April 14, 1868, by the
" Réglement d'organisation municipale de la concession
française de Shanghai," which still remains in force.[2]

---

[1] Aug. Dauge, vice-consul de Belgique, De la condition juridique des
étrangers en Chine, 32 *Journal du Droit International Privé* (1905),
850, 853.

[2] The text of the code of 1866 will be found in 25 *Archives Diplo-
matiques* (1867), 447; that of the Réglement of 1868, in 34 *Arch Dipl.*
(1869), 631.

The British and American settlements were in 1854 combined into one.

In 1863, the American land-renters who had obtained a new settlement in 1862 voluntarily amalgamated with the British under the international settlement, and in March, 1866, the latter adopted a revised code of land regulations, which, with certain minor changes subsequently effected, remains the fundamental law of the Shanghai general foreign settlement or Anglo-American or international settlement, as the combined concession is variously called. Both the Réglement of 1868 for the French settlement and the regulations of 1866 for the general settlement were approved, September 24, 1869, on behalf of their respective Governments by the diplomatic representatives at Peking of France, Great Britain, North German Confederation, Russia and the United States so as to make them binding upon their respective nationals residing within either of the two settlements. The amendments to the regulations of 1866, adopted by the land-renters on May 27-28, 1869, and confirmed by the consuls on July 13, 1869, were likewise approved by the representatives of the aforesaid five powers on October 21, 1869.[1]

The municipal council in the international settlement at Shanghai is composed of nine members elected by the taxpayers once a year to administer the settlement. The council, on account of the cosmopolitan character of the settlement which it represents, is not amenable, in its corporate capacity, to the court of any one state, but may be sued before a special tribunal, composed of three consuls, chosen annually by the consular body at Shanghai. Correspondence

---

[1] Hertslet's *China Treaties*, ii, pp. 665-666 The text of the regulations and by-laws of 1866 with amendments will be found in *ibid*, ii, pp. 666-687.

with the Chinese authorities regarding the affairs of the municipality is carried on by the dean of the consular body.

In general, the municipal ordinances and regulations of the various foreign settlements in China are binding upon all persons, foreign or Chinese, who choose to reside therein, their consent to observe them being inferred from the fact of their residence in them. Obedience to these ordinances and regulations by subjects of a treaty-power residing within a given settlement is enforcible in the proper consular court when such ordinances and regulations have been previously approved by that power through its representative at Peking.[1]

---

[1] In 1881 the municipal council of the Shanghai international settlement brought an action before the American consular court against Mr. F. Reid to compel payment of taxes levied under the municipal regulations of 1866. The defendant denied the validity of these regulations but the court gave judgment for the plaintiff on the grounds that the regulations in question had been approved by the American minister and that therefore they had the force of law upon Americans, and that by his voluntarily establishing his residence within the settlement and thereby taking advantage of its good order and government the defendant had also made himself liable to pay his share of the municipal taxes. (Opinion of Consul-General O. N. Denny in this case will be found in *For. Rel*, 1882, p. 130.)

The question as to the authority of the American consul-general at Shanghai to enforce the ordinances of the municipality against citizens of the United States was again raised in 1887, and Mr. Bayard, Secretary of State, in his instruction to Mr. Denby, minister to China, admitted that it was "not without difficulty". He said that the statutes of the United States did not provide for the enforcement of such ordinances and the power conferred by them upon the minister to "supply defects and deficiencies" in the statutes as to the furnishing of appropriate remedies, "by decrees and regulations", meant "the power to regulate the course of procedure and the forms of judicial remedies rather than any general legislative power for the definition of offences and the imposition of penalties for their commission." He, however, was able to sustain the authority of the consul-general to enforce the ordinances of the municipality upon American citizens residing therein by the following course of reasoning:

In the case of Chinese violating municipal ordinances,

"The municipality of Shanghai is understood to have been organized by the voluntary action of the foreign residents of certain nationalities, or such of those residents as were owners or renters of land, for the purpose of exercising such local powers for the preservation of the orders and morals of the community as are usually enjoyed by municipal bodies. In the United States, where government is reduced to a legal system, these powers of local police rest on charters granted by the supreme legislative authority of the state; but it is not difficult to conceive of a case in which a community outside of any general system of law might organize a government and adopt rules and regulations which would be recognized as valid on the ground of the right of self-preservation, which is inherent in people everywhere.

"In this light may be regarded the municipal ordinances of Shanghai. The foreign settlement not being subject to the laws of China, and the legal systems of the respective foreign powers represented there being not only dissimilar *inter se*, but insufficient to meet the local needs, it became necessary for the local residents interested in the preservation of peace and order to supply the deficiency.

"American citizens residing in Shanghai enjoy, in common with other persons composing the foreign settlement, all the rights, privileges, and protection which the municipal government affords, and as they go there voluntarily, and presumptively for the advancement of their personal interests, they may reasonably be held to observe such police regulations as are not inconsistent with their rights under the laws of the United States. It is true that this reasoning is not conclusive as to the strict legal authority of the consul-general of the United States to enforce such regulations; but, taken in connection with the fact that at present American citizens in Shanghai are not subject to any judicial control except that of the consul-general of the United States, it affords a basis upon which his enforcement of the municipal regulations may be justified

"It is important to observe that the jurisdiction of consuls of the United States in China is very extensive, including not only the administration of the laws of the United States, and the law of equity and admiralty, but also of the common law. The consular courts have, therefore, what the courts of the United States generally have not—common law jurisdiction in criminal cases. It is true that this jurisdiction is difficult, indeed incapable, of exact definition, but it implies the power to enforce rules which are not to be found on the statute-book of the United States, and which can be ascertained only by the application of the general principles of the common law to special cases and conditions. In respect to matters of local police, a fair meas-

generally applicable to all or specially applicable to them alone,[1] they are handed over to the proper Chinese authorities.

As a rule, the population of a foreign settlement consists mainly of Chinese subjects, who move to reside therein for the security and protection which it affords. They are permitted to reside in the concessions, but generally, they may not hold land in them. As a matter of fact, however, a large part of the real estate in the concessions is owned by Chinese, and this is effected through the use of borrowed foreign names.[2] Chinese property holders in a foreign concession are not represented in its municipal council, though they contribute by far the largest share to the revenue of the municipality. In the international settlement at Shanghai three Chinese delegates are elected annually by the various Chinese commercial bodies, not to represent them in the council, but in order that the council may have some authorized person to consult with concerning the affairs of the Chinese communities. Notwithstanding these serious disabilities, however, Chinese families continue to immigrate into the concessions for residence; and this steady

ure and definition of the law may be found in the regulations adopted by the municipality in aid of and supplementary to the general juridical systems of the foreign powers. Such a process, while maintaining the peace and order of the community, tends to consolidate the local administration of law "—Mr. Bayard to Mr. Denby, March 7, 1887, Appendix to 3 *Wharton's Digest of International Law,* 852, sec. 67.

[1] As an example of such special ordinance may be cited article 23 of the land regulations of 1902 for the British concession at Hankow, which provides:

" All Chinese passing through or in the concession after 6 P. M. in the winter and 8 P. M. in the summer, until daylight, must be provided with lighted lanterns, under a penalty of being handed to His Britannic Majesty's Consul-General for transmission to the native authorities "—Hertslet's *China Treaties,* ii, p 801

[2] *Journal du Droit International Privé* (1905), 853

influx of Chinese elements has been a favorite argument with the foreign powers in their chronic claims for an extension of the territorial limits of their several settlements.

The legal status of the foreign settlements within the treaty ports must be next considered. The importance of discussing this question arises from two facts: first, foreign travelers have shown an aptitude to judge things by external appearances and consider a foreign settlement with its impressive foreign police "un petit état dans l'état"; and secondly, in every settlement in China there is an element in the foreign population, including sometimes its most influential members, who on one hand are ever ready to combat the exercise by China of her territorial rights within the settlement, and on the other, never cease to clamor for rights, and advocate measures, which are, to say the least, inconsistent with the provisions of treaties.

·The foreign settlement in any treaty port does not represent a transfer or lease of the land included therein to the sovereign of the power for the accommodation of whose subjects it is set apart by China. A settlement is established, not to confer upon its occupants new rights of jurisdiction, but only to give them a place of residence within such a space as to enable them to enjoy the advantage of living together. The land encompassed in the settlement remains Chinese territory, subject to China's sovereign rights. The legal position of the foreigners residing within the concession is the same as that of those residing without it. Foreign holders of real property in a concession are required to pay a land tax to the Chinese Government.

Chinese residents in it are equally subject to the control of Chinese authorities as their compatriots situated in other parts of the country, and owe the same measure of allegiance to the Chinese sovereign. If the foreign municipal council exercises any authority therein, it does so by virtue of the permission expressly given it by the Chinese Government in the land regulations under which such council is organized, or in special proclamations issued by responsible authorities; in either case it exercises an authority delegated by the Chinese Government; and such authority is exercised only for municipal purposes.[1]

The foregoing are a few propositions deduced from a number of opinions given by authorities who have had to deal with the question under consideration, either as declarations of general principles on the matter or in settlement of actual cases bearing directly upon it. Of these the more important ones may be reviewed here with profit.

The first important occasion for discussing the status of the foreign concessions arose in 1862 when the Taotai of Shanghai, hard pressed for revenue to pay for the defensive measures taken against the approach of the Taiping rebels, proposed to lay a graduated capitation tax on all Chinese subjects and, on July 5, requested the assistance of the British Consul, Mr. Medhurst, to ascertain the number of

---

[1] Unreasonable assertions of authority by the municipal authorities of the foreign concessions, however, are not unknown in China. An amendment to the rules of 1869 for the mixed court of Shanghai, published June 13, 1901, by the American, British and German consuls-general, provides that a foreign assessor should sit in the mixed court in all cases including those to which Chinese alone were parties. One of the amendments to the same rules proposed by the consuls-general in Shanghai states that, "the warrants issued by the Mixed Court for the apprehension of Chinese residing in the International Settlements of Shanghai must always be signed and sealed by the senior Consul-General." Such assertions of authority are undoubtedly contrary to the intentions of those who laid the foundation of the international municipality at Shanghai on the avowed principle of "exclusive jurisdiction of China over Chinese, and of each foreign nation over its subjects," and cannot stand for a moment the test of treaty stipulations, which are the criteria as well as the bulwark of the rights of foreigners in China.

Chinese residents, particularly those in foreign employ, in the British settlement.[1] On July 16, the consul declined to render the assistance requested of him; he admitted the right of the Chinese authorities to impose on their own subjects any tax not interfering with rights of foreigners secured by treaty;

but as regards those natives who reside within these limits [continued the consul] I am not in a position to recognize such a right, as it has been a matter of understanding for years past between the local authorities and this Consulate that the jurisdiction of the former over their own subjects living within these limits shall only be exercised through and with the consent of the British consul, and with the large Chinese population now depending on our protection and sharing our interests, it would be inexpedient to allow of any departure from this rule.[2]

The matter was subsequently referred to the British minister at Peking, Sir Frederick W. A. Bruce, who, on November 5, 1862, gave the following instructions in reply to the inquiry:

In reply to your despatch of the 14th August last, requesting my advice as to the proposals made by the Taotai for the taxation of Chinese subjects within the limits of the so-called British Concession, I have to observe that there is nothing in the Treaties which warrants me in interfering in any way in such questions. The Taotai is entitled to levy taxes as he pleases: and as long as he merely seeks to impose taxes on persons resident in the Concession, which are paid by those in the City and suburb, I see no reason for objecting to it at a time when it is our interest as well as that of the Chinese that the Government shall not be deprived of its resources.

[1] *Parl. Papers, China*, no. 3 (1864), p. 10.
[2] *Ibid.*

A heavy responsibility will rest on the Consul of any port should his action in such matters lead to the disbanding or mutiny of the highly-paid force under foreign officers which the Chinese have embodied by our advice.[1]

On being apprised of the question Earl Russell wrote to Sir Frederick on April 8, 1863, stating that Her Majesty's Government entirely concurred in his views and approved his instructions to the consul, and adding,

The lands situated within the limits of the British Settlement are without doubt Chinese territory, and it cannot reasonably be held that the mere fact of a residence within those limits exempts Chinese subjects from fulfilling their natural obligations.[2]

In 1863 the legal position of the foreign concession at the treaty ports was again considered in connection with the proposed reorganization of the municipality at Shanghai. On motion of the United States minister, Mr. Anson Burlingame, the foreign representatives at Peking met in conference and agreed to a number of principles, upon which the reorganization of the foreign settlements in Shanghai should be based. These are:

1. That whatever territorial authority is established shall be derived directly from the Imperial Government through our Ministers.
2. That such shall not extend beyond simple municipal matters, roads, police and taxes for municipal objects.
3. That the Chinese not actually in foreign employ, shall be wholly under the control of Chinese officers, as much as in the Chinese City.

[1] *Parl. Papers*, China, no. 3 (1864), p. 11
[2] *Ibid.*, p. 30.

4. That each Consul shall have the Government and control of his own people, as now: the municipal authority simply arresting offenders against the public peace, handing them over, and prosecuting them before their respective authorities, Chinese, and others as the case may be.

5. That there shall be a Chinese element in the municipal system, to whom reference shall be made, and assent obtained to any measure affecting the Chinese residents.[1]

It was upon these principles that the chief municipality at Shanghai was rebuilt. The authority of the territorial sovereign over it is expressly acknowledged in article 28 of the Shanghai Land Regulations of 1866, as revised in 1869, which provides that amendments and doubts as to the construction of these regulations "must be consulted upon and settled by the foreign consuls and local Chinese authorities, subject to confirmation by the foreign representatives and Supreme Chinese Government at Peking." [2]

The attempt made by a British consul at one of the new ports in 1864 to exercise jurisdiction over leased land in defiance of the non-concession doctrine as propounded by the foreign representatives at Peking led to "another full and frank exchange of views on the subject" between the ministers of Great Britain and the United States at Peking. In his circular instructions to the British consuls in China, May 16, 1864, Sir Frederick states:

I am anxious to prevent misapprehension as to the jurisdiction that may be claimed by British authorities within the limits of settlements formed at the ports of China on land leased by her Majesty's government for the purposes of trade. The lease to the British government gives no jurisdiction over

[1] Sir F. W. A. Bruce, to foreign land-renters of Shanghai, Aug. 6, 1863, *Parl. Papers*, China, no. 3 (1864), p. 146.

[2] Hertslet's *China Treaties*, ii, p. 678.

the territory itself. The land remains subject to the sovereignity of China, and no further jurisdiction can be exercised over British persons and property within it than can be exercised over them at any open port where there has been no special lease of land for their benefit. For the authority exercised in Her Majesty's name is derived from the treaties with China, and is not affected in any way by the grant of a lease.[1]

This view was shared by other foreign representatives then in Peking, and the latter in entertaining it were supported by their respective Governments.[2]

The Government of the United States, whose minister at Peking, Mr. Anson Burlingame, like Sir Frederick, was vigorously opposed, to use his own language, "to all pretensions of jurisdiction over persons or territory under the name of concession," binds itself in the following solemn engagement:

His Majesty the Emperor of China, being of the opinion that, in making concessions to the citizens or subjects of foreign Powers of the privilege of residing on certain tracts of land, or resorting to certain waters of that Empire for purposes of trade, he has by no means relinquished his rights of eminent domain or dominion over the said land and waters, hereby agrees that no such concession or grant shall be construed to give to any Power or party which may be at war with or hostile to the United States, the right to attack the citizens of the United States or their property within the said land or waters, and the United States for themselves hereby agree to abstain from offensively attacking the citizens or subjects of any Power or party or their property with which they may be at war on any such tract of land or waters of the said Empire.

[1] *Dipl. Corr.*, 1864, pt iii, p. 380.
[2] Mr. Burlingame to Mr. Seward, May 21, 1864, *ibid*, p. 379

It is further agreed that, if any right or interest in any tract of land in China has been or shall hereafter be granted by the Government of China to the United States or their citizens for the purpose of trade or commerce, that grant shall in no event be construed to divest the Chinese authorities of their right of jurisdiction over persons and property within said tract of land, except so far as that right may have been expressly relinquished by Treaty.[1]

Another proof of the fact that the grant by China of land for the purpose of making a foreign concession does not carry with it a transfer of the territory or of jurisdiction therein, is that the opposing belligerent powers in the past wars to which China was not a party, though they both maintained the so-called concessions in China, uniformly observed the neutrality of the territory included within these concessions and refrained from attacking each other there. In times of civil disturbances in China the parties to the strife have generally avoided the foreign concessions in carrying on their hostilities, simply as a matter of policy. In a war with a foreign power or pending its outbreak, China may close the treaty ports for defensive purposes, no matter how many foreign concessions they may contain within, though there is an obligation on her to remove the obstructions as soon as the necessity which occasioned their planting ceases to exist.[2]

The nature of the international and French settlements in Shanghai may be further inferred from the fact that title deeds to land [3] situated therein are not required to be

---

[1] Article 1 of the supplementary treaty of Washington, July 28, 1868.

[2] The failure on the part of China promptly to remove the obstructions in the Canton River after the conclusion of the war with France in 1885 led to a protest from the United States. On this question, see *For. Rel.*, 1884, pp. 64, 84; *ibid*, 1886, p. 95.

[3] The right of foreigners to own landed property in China is not

registered in the British or French consulate, but that registration in the consulate of the holders' nationality is held to be sufficient to establish their validity.   In the early days of the two settlements the English and French consuls, as a matter of fact, claimed territorial jurisdiction over the settlements and required all foreigners desiring to hold land therein to apply to them respectively; but the American consul refused to comply with the requirement and insisted on title deeds being issued to United States citizens through the consulate of the United States.   On the adoption of the joint code of land regulations in 1854 the representatives of Great Britain abandoned " without reservation all their previous pretensions to any exclusive rights or jurisdiction over their respective settlements." [1]   In fact, prior to 1898, sites in the French settlement were held under title deeds issued by the Taotai or under deeds of lease transferred directly from the original Chinese owners without all such deeds being necessarily registered in the French consulate. In that year, in the case of the three lots situated in the French settlement held by Thomas Hanbury, a British subject, under title deeds issued by the Shanghai Taotai in 1861 and registered in the British consulate, the French consul, on inspecting the deeds, pronounced them to be irregular on the ground that they were not registered in his consulate in accordance with the principle of *locus regit actum* in international law.[2]   Mr. Hanbury, through his

provided in any of the treaties, though it is practically enjoyed by them; the American trea'y of 1903 gives citizens of the United States the right to lease land " in perpetuity " within places " set apart for the use and occupation of foreigners."

[1] Memorandum by Act. Consul-General Brennan on the legal status of the French Settlement, *Parl. Papers*, China, no. 1 (1899), p. 268.

[2] French Consul at Shanghai to Mr. Hanbury, June 18, 1898, *Parl. Papers*, China, no 11 (1899), p. 224.

agents, refused to register his land in the French consulate, and this refusal was upheld by the British minister at Peking.[1]

When later in the same year, the French authorities asked the Chinese Government for an extension of the French settlement in Shanghai, the British Government, evidently having the Hanbury case still fresh in memory, openly opposed the proposition and bent all its energies to defeat it. It instructed its minister at Peking to remind China of her undertaking of February 9-11, 1898, as to the non-alienation of the Yangtze region, and warned her that compliance with the French demand would be " a violation of the rights of this country [Great Britain]." [2]

To compel the voice of the British Government to be heard, Lord Salisbury, on December 21, 1898, advised the Admiralty to send a third ship-of-war to Nanking, whither two British war-vessels had already been despatched " with a view to affording moral support to the Viceroy in resisting the French demands." [3] The British Government, however, ultimately withdrew its opposition to the French

[1] Sir C. MacDonald to Marquis of Salisbury, Aug 22, 1898, *Parl. Papers*, China, no. 1 (1899), p 267.

[2] Marquis of Salisbury to Sir C MacDonald, Jan 3, 1899, tel., *Parl. Papers*, China, no. 1 (1899), p. 341. Another of the reasons given by the British Government for opposing the original French demand for a settlement extension was that if the proposed extension were made certain British property would thereby be included in it, and that Great Britain " cannot agree that any British property should be given over to be administered by the French." The same circumstance arose in connection with the granting of a concession in Hankow by China to Russia and France. These difficulties led to the notification to China by Great Britain that it " will not in future allow the property of British subjects to be included in any concession granted to a foreign power, unless with the consent of the owners." —*Parl. Papers*, China, no. 1 (1900), pp. 191, 193

[3] *Parl. Papers*, China, no. 1 (1899), p. 330

demand, which had meanwhile been reduced to a much smaller area than it had originally asked for—but on what conditions? The opposition was withdrawn only after the French minister had agreed to forward, and had forwarded, to the French Consul-General in Shanghai the following instructions:

1. All deeds to British property are to be registered in the British Consulate;

2. All municipal Regulations are to be submitted for the approval of the British minister at Peking before they can be enforced on British subjects.

3. All titles to British property which are declared in order by the British Consul-General are to be considered so by the French authorities.

And in his note to Mr. Cambon, French ambassador at London, July 17, 1899, Lord Salisbury expressed himself as being prepared to instruct the British minister at Peking to support a French application for an extension of the French settlement in Shanghai within specified limits on the condition that the three rules quoted above " shall be strictly observed." It was further added in the note that the same rules were " to apply as regards British-owned property in the French concession at Hankow."

As to the limits of treaty ports the question remains doubtful in many cases. In pursuance of a common provision in the earlier treaties the limits of the ports for customs purposes are generally defined for the convenience of vessels entering them, as well as for the protection of revenue leviable on imports. But as to the boundaries of the ports on land, the matter is not settled. With reference to the likin, which may not be collected within the limits

---

[1] *Parl. Papers*, China, no 1 (1900), p 193

of a treaty port,[1] the Chefoo Convention of September 13, 1876, provided that " Sir Thomas Wade agrees to move his Government to allow the ground rented by foreigners (the so-called concessions) at the different ports to be regarded as the area of exemption from likin; " but the additional article of July 18, 1885, declares that this question " shall be reserved for further consideration between the two Governments," which so far as is known, has not yet taken place definitively.

For purposes of residence and trade[2] the limits of an open port would seem to be determined by, and co-extensive with, the limits of the foreign concession, or concessions as a whole, situated within it   The point was raised and so decided in a case arising in 1897. By the sixth article of the treaty of Shimonoseki, April 17, 1895, Hangchow, among others, was opened to the trade and residence of Japanese subjects " under the same conditions, and with the same privileges and facilities as exist at the present in open cities, towns and ports of China."   In the fourth article of the treaty of commerce and navigation, July 21, 1896, concluded in pursuance of a provision in the treaty of Shimonoseki, it is provided that Japanese subjects may reside and carry on trade " in all the ports and towns of China which are now or may hereafter be opened to foreign residence and trade," and that " within the localities at those places which have already been or may hereafter be set apart for the use and occupation of foreigners, they are allowed to rent or purchase houses, rent or lease land, and

[1] The exemption of the Settlements in Shanghai from likin taxation was stipulated for in an agreement concluded in 1876 between the Tsungli Yamen and the German minister.—67 New Coll. (General), 3.

[2] Under Article 12 of the British Treaty of Tientsin, June 26, 1858, however, British subjects may build or open houses, warehouses, etc., at the ports or at other places. See infra, sec. 16.

to build churches, cemeteries and hospitals." In the summer
of 1897 the Tsungli Yamen represented to Mr. Denby,
United States minister, that an American had established,
in violation of treaty, an office in the city of Hangchow,
outside of the Japanese concession, and asked him to direct
his national to remove from the said city. Mr. Denby replied that he was unable to see any reason why, under the
treaties, the said American, or any other foreigner, had not
the right to reside in Hangchow, this right of residence
being " secured by the sixth article of the Shimonoseki
Treaty as to the four towns which were opened by that
treaty." [1] Subsequently, however, the American minister
learned that the Japanese Government did not regard the
aforesaid treaty as conferring on Japanese the right of residence at Hangchow and Soochow beyond the limits of the
Japanese concessions; that England and other powers
would acquiesce in the contention of China that foreigners
should establish their business premises within the concessions designated for them at these cities; and that he
deemed it " inadvisable for this legation to insist on privileges under Japanese treaties which the Japanese themselves waive and which are not asserted in behalf of the
citizens of the other powers." [2] Meanwhile all the
issues of the question were made, as stated in Mr. Sherman's instructions to Mr. Denby, November 30, 1897,[3]
" the occasion of an exhaustive examination by the Solicitor of this Department, with the conclusion that the circumstances would not warrant insistence by this Government
upon a contention for the unrestricted residence of Ameri-

[1] Mr Denby to Tsungli Yamen, Aug. 4, 1897, *For. Rel*, 1897, p. 75.
[2] Mr. Denby to Mr. Sherman, Aug. 30, 1897, *ibid*, p. 76
[3] *Ibid.* For the opinion of Mr. Penfield, the solicitor, see *ibid.*, p 77.

can citizens outside of those foreign concessions [at Soochow and Hangchow]." [1]

In view of this conclusion come to by the United States on the question, derived, as it is stated, from "a fair and reasonable construction" mainly of the restrictive clause in the fourth article quoted above of the Japanese treaty of 1896, it is significant to note that substantially the same clause is stipulated in the third article of the treaty concluded by the United States with China at a subsequent date, namely, October, 1903. From this stipulation, and the fact that the restriction contained therein is declared to be applicable to all the ports or localities of China "which are now open" as well as to those which "may hereafter be opened" to foreign residence and trade, it seems as though the United States Government had, for purposes of residence and trade, at least, assented to the view persistently urged by the Chinese Government that the limits of an open port correspond with the limits of the foreign concession or concessions in their entirety established within it, save, perhaps, the general reservation under the most-favored-nation clause.

The question of the limits of the open ports has frequently been raised also in respect of matters of likin taxation and the Chinese authorities have as often adhered to their well-known view. Take a recent case for example. In 1905 a quantity of British-owned merchandise was subjected to the likin imports within the walled city of Changsha and thereupon the British minister complained of the action to the Waiwu Pu on the ground that Changsha had been opened to foreign commerce, and asked it to instruct the Governor of Hunan to the effect that the Chinese city within the wall was part of the port and that no likin could

---

[1] This conclusion seems to be in accord, also, with a recognized canon of construction, which is *expressio unius est exclusio alterius.*

be levied on foreign goods protected by the proper passes; but the Waiwu Pu replied that,

> According to its real meaning the word port does not include the moat or area within the city wall. If the Chinese officials and people are unwilling to have foreign merchants settle outside the limits of a port, they have some grief at heart, namely, that China is not allowed to exercise jurisdiction over foreign subjects within her territory. If in accordance with article 12 of the Anglo-Chinese treaty of commerce of 1902 extraterritoriality is relinquished, there will then be no objection to according foreigners the liberty to live wherever they may please.[1]

The same view as to the limits of the treaty port was held by the Governor in 1907 in the case of Kau Ching-tong, the Chinese representative of a Japanese firm, who was arrested in Shanghai outside the limits of the foreign settlements, on a charge of violating a Chinese law relating to the transport of tribute rice. The Japanese consul-general saw fit to interpose himself in the case, and in his communication to the Governor of Chekiang, under whose order the prisoner had been arrested, he argued against the legality of the arrest from the rules for the mixed court of Shanghai regulating suits and cases within the foreign settlements, and from " an established rule," to use his own language, " that the boundaries of every port open to foreign commerce extend in all directions 100 li from the Settlements." The reply of the Governor to these extravagant contentions was:

> Since the facts of Kau Ching-tong's case arose in the inland and his arrest was made within the Chinese jurisdiction, the rules for the mixed court in the foreign settlements have nothing to do with the case.

[1] 7 *New Collection* (Gr Br.), 3

Again article 6 of the treaty of commerce and navigation (of July 21, 1896) provides that Japanese may travel to the interior under passports but that in ports open to foreign trade they may go on excursions without passports, to a distance not over 100 Chinese li, and for a period not over five days. This is a general rule found in the treaties made by China with the foreign nations. It refers only to the case of a foreigner going out on an excursion and does not mean that the ports open to foreign trade themselves extend in all directions 100 li beyond their actual limits. Yet your communication states that "in accordance with the established rule the limits of a port open to foreign trade extend 100 li from the foreign Settlements in all directions." Such a rule I have never heard of heretofore. Your explanation seems to lack clearness. Moreover, it seems to be quite irrelevant to invoke the special rule regulating the excursions of foreigners in a case of the arrest of a Chinese subject within Chinese jurisdiction.[1]

§ 2. Ports voluntarily opened by China

In recent years China has of her own will and initiative opened a number of places in the various parts of her country to commerce, under conditions entirely different from those according to which certain ports have been established by treaty. The boundaries of a voluntarily opened port are fixed by imperial decree, and within them foreign merchants of all nationalities and Chinese merchants are permitted to lease ground without distinction. However, "the control of all affairs therein," as is provided in the renting and building regulations for the port of Chinan Fu, opened by China voluntarily, "shall pertain entirely to China; foreigners must not interfere."

To the assertion by China of a distinction between

[1] For correspondence relative to the case, see 40 *New Collection* (Japan), 1 *et seq.*

treaty ports and those opened by her own action, the powers have taken exception. They maintain that the treaty stipulations as to the former are equally and fully applicable to the latter. The first important case arose in 1899 when the customs commissioner at Santuao, opened by China herself, announced that in addition to the treaty tariff duties, wharfage dues, at the rate of two per cent on customs duties, would be collected for municipal purposes, in harmony, as the commissioner stated, with the practice at the treaty ports, where a similar tax is levied by the foreign municipal council or collected, as in Tientsin and Shanghai, by the customs and handed over to the councils of the nations concerned for their use.[1] The British representative at Peking, however, had a different opinion: he considered the proposed tax to be " objectionable on principle," and pointed out to the Tsungli Yamen at an interview that such an addition to the tariff was " unauthorized."

The subject was then brought up before a meeting of the foreign representatives on June 9, 1899, and the British chargé d'affaires stated that " to allow the imposition of this tax . . . would amount to the admission of the contention now being raised by the Chinese authorities, that to such ports as Woosung, Chinwangtao, and Santuao, which have been voluntarily opened by China, the stipulations as to treaty ports are not necessarily applicable, and this admission would but open the way for any further duties and taxes which the Chinese authorities at such ports might wish to impose on foreign commerce."[2] All the foreign representatives present, except the German chargé d'af-

[1] M. von Tanner, Customs Commissioner, to Viceroy Hsu of Fukien and Chekioug, May 24, 1899, *Parl. Papers,* China, no. 1 (1900), p. 251.

[2] Mr. Bax Ironside to Marquis of Salisbury, June 10, 1899, *Parl. Papers,* China, no. 1 (1900), p. 211.

faires, agreed with this view and pronounced the proposed tax as being illegal. The objections were recorded, and on November 2, the doyen of the diplomatic corps at Peking sent a note to the Tsungli Yamen, stating that while the foreign representatives were disposed to consider any opportunity of levying an additional tax, which was moderate and just, they could not admit that a higher tax might be imposed on commerce and navigation than had been fixed by the treaties; and that consequently the surtax of two per cent on customs duties established at Santuao would not be fair without the consent of the diplomatic corps. The note concludes with this sentence: " C'est une question de principe." ¹ Lord Salisbury, on August 26, 1899, in approving Mr. Bax Ironside's views and actions on the question, added the following instructions:

> No distinction can be admitted by Her Majesty's Government between ports opened by treaty or arrangement with a foreign Power and those declared open by the initiative of the Chinese Government.²

§ 3. Leased Ports

Within the territory leased by China to certain powers, except Port Arthur, foreigners generally are also entitled to reside and carry on trade. The precise position of foreign merchandise in such leased ports depends primarily upon the nature of the relationship in which the territory encompassed within the ports stands with the sovereign of China.

By the convention of March 6, 1898, the Emperor of China leased Kiaochow to Germany for ninety-nine years, " reserving to himself all rights of sovereignty (*alle Rechte der Souveränität*) in a zone of 50 kilom. (100 Chinese li)

---

¹ *Parl. Papers*, China, no 1 (1900), p. 406.   ² *Ibid.*, p. 276

surrounding the Bay of Kiaochau at high water," within which area is situated the leased port; and specifically he further " reserves to himself the right to station troops within that zone, in agreement with the German Government, and to take other military measures. As to the question of jurisdiction, the convention provides that " the territory leased to Germany cannot, prior to the expiration of the term of the lease, be administered by China but it is to be left to be governed by Germany, in order to avoid conflicts " [1]   The Chinese residents in the leased territory are entitled to enjoy the protection of the German Government, " provided they conduct themselves in conformity with law and order."   Chinese ships of war and merchant vessels are to be treated in the same manner as those of other nations friendly to Germany.   In the convention of March 15-27, 1898, respecting the lease of Port Arthur and Talienwan to Russia for twenty-five years from the date of signature,[2] it is stipulated that " the lease is under no circumstances to infringe upon the rights of the Emperor of China as sovereign owner of the territory leased." [3]   It is

---

[1] This is translated from the original Chinese text. The German text would read in English. " In order to avoid the possibility of conflicts, the Imperial Chinese Government will not exercise supreme power (Hoheitsrechte) in the leased territory during the term of the lease, but will leave the exercise of the same to Germany. "Hoheitsrechte" is translated as " rights of sovereignty" in *Parl. Papers,* China, no 1 (1899), p. 69

[2] The lease of these two ports and certain adjacent territories with the rights and privileges appertaining thereto was transferred by Russia, with the consent of China, to Japan by article 5 of the treaty of Portsmouth, September 5, 1905; and the transfer was confirmed by China under article 1 of the treaty with Japan of December 22, 1905

[3] The passages of the Convention here quoted are translated from the original Chinese text. The English translation printed in *Parl Papers,* China, no. 1 (1899), p. 128, does not seem to have been made from the original Chinese or Russian text

further stipulated that Chinese committing offenses within the leased territory " shall be sent to the nearest Chinese authority to be punished according to law," in conformity with the arrangement provided in the Russian treaty of Tientsin (1860) ; that Talienwan, except a certain portion thereof, " is to be treated as an open port and merchant vessels of the various nations may enter freely;" and that Chinese and Russian war vessels are entitled to use the naval port of Port Arthur and the naval base in Talienwan to the exclusion of the war vessels of other powers. The convention of May 27, 1898, for the lease of Kwongchow-wan to France is similar to that for the lease of Kiaochow to Germany. The French convention stipulates that the lease is to last for ninety-nine years, and to enable the French Government to establish therein a naval station with a coaling-depot, but that " this establishment is not to affect China's rights of sovereignty over the added terri-tory," which " will be governed and administered during the ninety-nine years of lease by France, in order to avoid any possible conflict between the two countries " Within the leased territory Chinese people may continue to reside and carry on their business and occupations under the pro-tection of France as long as they respect her laws and regu-lations Chinese ships and those of other friendly powers " are to be treated in the leased territory as in the open ports of China," but the anchorage " is to be exclusively re-served for French and Chinese ships of war, the latter in the state of neutrality only." Finally, Weihaiwei was leased to Great Britain under the convention of July 1, 1898, " for so long a period as Port Arthur shall remain in the occupation of Russia." [1] Within the leased ground

Since Port Arthur now does not remain in the occupation of Russia, the lease of Weihaiwei would seem to have expired by its own limitation.

" Great Britain shall have sole jurisdiction;" but it was also agreed that within the walled city of Weihaiwei Chinese officials shall continue to exercise jurisdiction except so far as may be inconsistent with naval and military requirements for the defense of the territory leased; and that, further, " Chinese vessels of war whether neutral or otherwise shall retain the right to use the waters herein leased to Great Britain."

Such were the provisions of the conventions of lease. The first question that arose about foreign subjects within the leased territory was: Were they entitled to continue to enjoy therein the rights of extraterritorial jurisdiction which they had enjoyed prior to the execution of the lease? It might have been expected that the lessee powers were not anxious to admit such a jurisdiction within the territory they had leased from China; and the other European states, not having large interests in China, were naturally indifferent. The two powers which were most concerned in the solution of the question were Japan and the United States; and these held contrary opinions on the subject. The Japanese Government maintained that jurisdiction was an essential part of sovereignty and could not pass with a mere lease, that sovereignty over the leased territory having been expressly reserved by China, jurisdiction over such territory remained where it had been, and that the jurisdiction which Japan had by treaty acquired over her subjects and their property in China could not be affected by China's treaty with a third power. In holding this view Japan, in 1899, solicited the support of the United States Government; but the latter, apparently not having as yet conceived the policy which its Secretary of State, John Hay, announced in his circular telegram of July 3, 1900,[1] to the surprise of the world, decided to pursue a

[1] "We adhere to the policy initiated by us in 1857," reads the tele-

different course. Accordingly, it declined to share the view held by Japan, and on February 3, 1900, Mr. Hay informed Mr. Conger, minister to China, of the conclusion which the Department of State, on advice of its solicitor,[1] had reached on the subject, namely,

That the intention and effect of China's foreign leases having apparently been the relinquishment by China during the term of the leases and the conferment upon the foreign power of all jurisdiction over the territory, such relinquishment and transfer of jurisdiction would seem also to involve the loss by

gram, "of peace with the Chinese nation, of furtherance of lawful commerce, and of protection of lives and property of our citizens by all means guaranteed under extraterritorial treaty rights and by the law of nations The policy of the Government of the United States is to seek a solution which may bring about permanent safety and peace to China, preserve Chinese territorial and administrative entity, protect all rights guaranteed to friendly powers by treaty and international law, and safeguard for the world the principle of equal and impartial trade with all parts of the Chinese Empire"—*For. Rel*, 1901, appendix ix, p. 12.

[1] The opinion rendered by the solicitor of the Department of the State, January 27, 1900, quotes in full articles 21, 24 and 25 of the American treaty of 1844, articles 11 and 24 of the treaty of 1858, and article 4 of the treaty of 1880; makes a brief but scarcely complete summary of the conventions of lease with Great Britain, Russia, and Germany, respectively, and then continues:

"As it is expressly stipulated in the leases that China retains sovereignty over the territory leased, it could doubtless be asserted that such territory is Chinese territory and that the provision of our treaties with China granting consular jurisdiction are still applicable therein. But in view of the express relinquishment of jurisdiction by China, I infer that the reservation of sovereignty is merely intended to cut off possible future claims of the lessees that the sovereignty of the territory is permanently vested in them."

Here follows the statement which is substantially identical with that contained in Mr. Hay's instructions to Mr. Conger, and already quoted above. The opinion closes with this: "All of the powers, with the exception of Japan, have acquiesced in this view, and their consuls accredited to China will not attempt to exercise jurisdiction in any of the leased territory."—*For. Rel.*, 1900, p 387.

the United States of its right to exercise extraterritorial consular jurisdiction in the territories so leased; while, as you remark, as these territories have practically passed into the control of peoples whose jurisprudence and methods are akin to our own, there would seem to be no substantial reason for claiming the continuance of such jurisdiction during the foreign occupancy or tenure of the leased territory.

Mr. Hay, therefore, asked Mr. Conger, if he found the western powers to be of the same opinion as to their own consuls in similar situations, to instruct the United States consuls in districts adjacent to the foreign leased territories, " that they have no authority to exercise extraterritorial consular jurisdiction or to perform ordinary non-judicial consular acts within the leased territory under their present Chinese exequaturs."

As against these views of the United States it may not be difficult to argue that the leases made by China as provided in the several conventions do not alter the nationality of the territory leased nor necessarily mean " the relinquishment by China during the term of the leases and the conferment upon the foreign power (in each case) of all jurisdiction over the territory." Specific and substantial rights of jurisdiction over Weihaiwei, and of use of all the leased territories and waters for military, or naval purposes, or for both, are expressly reserved by China in the several conventions along with the uniform reservation of her general rights of sovereignty over such leased territories and waters.

Nor will it be difficult to urge that the intention of the leases was the reverse of what has been attributed to them by the Government of the United States. As far as China is concerned, it could not reasonably be claimed that she intended to concede more than the language of the several conventions of lease explicitly provides. It must be remembered that China made these leases of territory, not out of her own pleasure or free will, but under threats of immediate invasion. She was a victim at once of foreign aggression and international jealousy. The operations of the German marines and troops on the coast of Shangtung Province, the demonstrations of the British squadron in the Gulf of Pe-Chili and those of the French fleet in the Bay of Kwangchow-wan are well-known as a matter of history. As regards the lease made to Russia, the circumstances under which it was granted were no less pressing. In his telegraphic report to the Marquis of Salisbury, March 24, 1898, Sir C. MacDonald, the British minister at Peking, stated:

I saw Yamen this afternoon. They said that Russian Government has informed them that they cannot consider question of Port Arthur and Talienwan apart, and insist on lease of both places being granted to Russia before the 27th March, failing which Russia will take hostile measures. Chinese Government are therefore forced, against their will, to give way.[1]

It would, therefore, be nearer the truth to say that the intention of China, in granting the leases to the four powers, was, not to relinquish " all jurisdiction " over the leased districts, but to concede as little of it as possible. At any rate, the conventions of the leases should not be liberally interpreted, as they seem to have been by the Government of the United States, it being a generally accepted rule of the law of nations that international servitudes on national territory, of which character the leases in question undoubtedly are, must be strictly construed against the state or states enjoying them.[2]

[1] *Parl. Papers*, China, no 1 (1898), p 53.
[2] " These [the servitudes enumerated] and such like privileges or disabilities must, however, be set up by treaty or equivalent agreement;

Again, if the intention of the lessee powers be inquired into, it will be found to have been, not to acquire the leased districts as part of their respective national dominions and therefore to exercise absolute control over them for all purposes, but only for military and political purposes. In other words, the territories and waters leased had been coveted by the lessee states on account of their strategic value, and for the gain of prestige and influence which would come to them as the result of their military control of these important strongholds. That such was the intention of the lessee powers would seem to be clear from the text of the conventions of lease themselves, in each of which the purpose of the lessee state is expressly declared to be the obtainment for its troops of the right to passage through the leased districts or the establishment of a naval base or a coaling station within them for the use of its fleet. This is particularly true of the lease of Port Arthur and Weihaiwei. Russia wanted to have Port Arthur solely for its strategic value and Great Britain objected to its possession by Russia for that very reason. The British Government was willing to let Russia lease Talienwan as an ice-free commercial port, but as to her proposal to acquire Port Arthur, it employed every pacific means within its control to defeat it.[1] It was only when the British Gov-

---

they are the creatures not of law but of compact   [Here follows an enumeration of customary servitudes.]   In their legal aspects there is only one point upon which international servitudes call for notice. They conform to the universal rule applicable to 'jura in re aliena'. Whether they be customary or contractual in their origin, they must be construed strictly. If, therefore, a dispute occurs between a territorial sovereign and a foreign power as to the extent or nature of rights enjoyed by the latter within the territory of the former, the presumption is against the foreign state, and upon it the burden lies of proving its claim beyond doubt or question."—W. E. Hall, *International Law* (5th, Oxford, 1904), p. 159

[1] " Her Majesty's Government on their part would not regard with

ernment found the resources of its diplomacy exhausted and its efforts still unsuccessful in frustrating the Russian project that it felt the necessity of occupying Weihaiwei, a port equally valuable as Port Arthur in strategic position, at the expense of China, in order to maintain the so-called balance of power at Peking.[1]   In short, the intention of the four European powers in leasing the territories in question was, evidently, to acquire military control over them so as to preserve their relative positions in China, and not to take them as an outright cession and during the

any dissatisfaction the lease by Russia of an ice-free commercial harbor, connected by rail with the trans-Siberian Railway which is now under construction   Questions of an entirely different kind are opened if Russia obtains control of a military port in the neighborhood of Peking. Port Arthur is useless for commercial purposes, its whole importance being derived solely from its military strength and strategic position, and its occupation would inevitably be considered in the East as a standing menace to Peking and the commencement of the partition of China. The military occupation or fortification of any other harbor on the same coast or in the Gulf of Pechili would be open to the same objections with almost equal force."—Marquis of Salisbury to Sir N. I. Conor, March 22, 1898, tel, *Parl Papers*, China, no. 1 (1898), p. 52.

[1] On March 25, 1898, when the lease of Port Arthur was known to have been made to Russia by China, Lord Salisbury telegraphed to Sir C. MacDonald the following instructions: " Balance of power in Gulf of Pechili is materially altered by surrender of Port Arthur by Yamen to Russia. It is, therefore, necessary to obtain, in the manner you think most efficacious and speedy, the refusal of Weihaiwei on the departure of the Japanese   The terms should be similar to those granted to Russia for Port Arthur. British fleet is on its way from Hong Kong to Gulf of Pechili "—*Parl. Papers*, China, no. 1 (1898), p 54.

Apprehensive, however, lest Germany might feel its commercial interest in Shantung jeopardized by the British occupation of Weihaiwei, Lord Salisbury, on March 26th, authorized Sir F. Lascelles, British Ambassador at Berlin, by telegraph, to explain the reasons to the German foreign office and added: " We do not wish to interfere with the interests of Germany in that region   The action, in our opinion very regrettable, of Russia with respect to Port Arthur, has compelled us to take the course we are now pursuing "—*Ibid.*, p. 54

term of the leases to stamp them with their own national
character, nor, again, to alter the status of foreigners
within such territories as guaranteed by the treaties between China and their respective states.

On the contrary, with respect to the lease of Port Arthur
and Talienwan, the intention of Russia was expressly
stated to be to leave the leased territories as integral parts
of the Chinese dominions, and to confirm rather than to
diminish the treaty-rights of foreigners within them. At
the very outset of the Russian proposal to lease from China
Port Arthur and Talienwan, Great Britain, while objecting
to the leasing of Port Arthur on account of its being
" notoriously useless for commercial purposes," stated to
Russia through her ambassador at St. Petersburg that the
British Government attached " supreme importance . . .
to the maintenance of all rights and privileges secured to
Great Britain by their existing treaties with China," and
solicited of her declarations in the nature of an assurance
that these rights and privileges would be respected by
Russia in the event of her obtaining a lease of the two
aforesaid places. In response to the British representation
the Russian Government seems to have made certain declarations which were even of a broader scope than those
desired by Great Britain. As summarized later by Lord
Salisbury,

These declarations are to the effect that Port Arthur as well
as Talienwan, shall be open to foreign trade like other
Chinese ports; that Russia has no intention of impairing the
sovereignty of China; and that she will respect all the rights
and privileges secured by existing Treaties between China
and other foreign Powers—a pledge which not only includes
equality of commercial treatment, but also the right of foreign
ships of war to visit ports which, though leased to Russia,
are still to remain integral portions of the Chinese Empire.

The despatch,[1] of which the passage just quoted forms a part, was read by Sir N. O'Conor, the British ambassador at St. Petersburg, to Count Mouravieff, the Russian minister for foreign affairs, under instruction from Lord Salisbury, and a copy of the same was also left with the minister, within four days after Russia had announced to the powers her lease of Port Arthur and Talienwan and, without making any reference to the use she was to make of Port Arthur, the opening of Talienwan to foreign commerce. In a note of March 22 (April 3),[2] acknowledging receipt of the note of April 1, from Sir N. O'Conor, embodying the instructions of March 28, from Lord Salisbury, Count Mouravieff briefly reviewed the conversations which he had had with the British ambassador on the question of the lease, and while disclaiming any declaration on his part of the purpose of insuring the opening of Port Arthur to foreign commerce, confirmed his previous statements as to the intention of Russia, in taking the lease, to preserve the territorial integrity of China and the rights of the powers guaranteed by treaties with China. His language is worth quoting:

You asked me whether in taking Port Arthur and Talienwan on lease, Russia intended to maintain the rights of sovereignty of China, and to respect the Treaties existing between that Empire and other States. I answered in the affirmative, and I added that we hoped, moreover, to obtain the opening of the port of Talienwan, which would offer great advantages to all nations. Now that the negotiations with China have brought about the desired result, all that is entirely confirmed. The substitution of the Russian usufruct for possession by China of Port Arthur and Talienwan has not affected in any way the interests of the other Powers in those regions; quite

[1] *Parl. Papers*, China, no 1 (1898), p. 56.   [2] *Ibid*, p 64.

on the contrary, thanks to the friendly agreement arrived at
between the two great neighboring Empires, a port hitherto
closed is open to the trade of the whole world, and placed under exceptionally favorable conditions, as it is destined to be
connected with the great line of the Siberian Railway.

Then follows the most significant statement:

As regards all other points, the respect for the sovereign
rights of China implies the scrupulous maintenance of the
status quo existing before the lease of the ports which have
been conceded.

Here, then, is a voluntary explanation by an interested
party to the convention for the lease of Port Arthur and
Talienwan, March 15-27, 1898, of the intent and purport
of the clause contained therein reserving China's rights of
sovereignty over the leased territories, an explanation
which seems to have escaped the notice of the State Department at Washington, or perhaps was not available to
it in 1900.

Furthermore, the same note states:

Your Excellency having observed to me that men-of-war
and merchant ships are, in certain cases provided for by the
Treaties, admitted even into the closed ports of China, I answered that accordingly this facility would be assured to them
by the Regulations in force.

It follows that Port Arthur will be open to English ships
on the same conditions as it has always been.

It would seem also that by admitting this right of foreign
ships to visit Port Arthur as well as Talienwan, Russia
made its intention in taking the lease still more manifest as
being not to curtail the rights of foreigners in the leased
districts, but to preserve the status quo existing before the
lease, and implicitly admitted the contention of Lord Salis-

bury that the ports in question, "though leased to Russia, are still to remain integral portions of the Chinese Empire."

In view of these circumstances it is significant that subsequently, when a Japanese subject was arrested at Port Arthur upon suspicion of being a military spy and Japan declined to admit the right of Russia to exercise jurisdiction over the prisoner, the Russian Government readily yielded to Japan and ordered that the subject be delivered to Japanese authorities.[1] It is equally significant that when, subsequent to the consummation of the lease of Port Arthur and Talienwan, the Russian legation at Peking issued a circular note to the other legations in the Chinese capital, stating that passports of foreigners going to these two places should be previously revised by a Russian consulate in China, the Russian Government, on being informed of the measure, instructed its representative in Peking to revoke the measure announced, the reason for this order of revocation apparently being that under the treaties between China and foreign powers passports are required only for extended journeys into the interior.[2]

§ 4. Ports of Call

Foreign vessels are also permitted to carry on a limited traffic at certain localities along the great rivers designated as ports of call. Six places on the Yangtze River have been opened as such ports under the Chefoo agreement of September 13, 1876, subject to certain regulations therein

---

[1] F. E. Hinckley, *American Consular Jurisdiction in the Orient* (Washington, D. C., 1906), p 177.

[2] With reference to this question Lord Salisbury instructed Sir C. MacDonald by telegraph, June 2, 1898, that he "should, in acknowledging receipt of the circular from the Russian Chargé d'Affaires, call attention to the fact that, under Article IX of Treaty of Tientsin, passports are required for extended journey into the interior only."—*Parl. Papers*, China, no. 1 (1899), p. 111.

outlined and four on the Wèst River under the agreement with Great Britain of February 4, 1897, under the same regulations as those on the Yangtze River; while the treaty of Shimonoseki, April 17, 1895, provides that steam navigation for vessels under the Japanese flag for the conveyance of passengers and cargo shall be extended to the places on the Yangtze River from Ichang to Chungking and on the Woosung River and the Canal from Shanghai to Soochow and Hangchow, subject to the rules and regulations in force governing the navigation of the inland waters of China by foreign vessels.

With reference to the places it declares to be ports of call, the Chefoo agreement stipulates that

these places being all places of trade in the interior, at which, as they are not open ports, foreign merchants are not legally authorized to land or ship goods; steamers shall be allowed to touch for the purpose of landing or shipping passengers or goods; but in all instances by means of native boats only; and subject to the regulations in force affecting native trade.

It also provides that

produce accompanied by a half-duty certificate may be shipped at such points by the steamers, but may not be landed by them for sale.

It further provides that

foreign merchants will not be authorized to reside or open houses of business or warehouses at the places enumerated as ports of call.

According to a list revised to April, 1911, by the British legation at Peking, there are in China twenty-five ports of call and sixty-eight places opened to foreign trade by treaty or by Imperial decree.[1]

[1] (a) Treaty ports and places opened by China to foreign trade:

§ 5. *The Legation Quarter in Peking*

The right of the diplomatic corps in Peking to fortify
for defensive purposes the quarter which it occupies and
that of each legation to establish a permanent guard for its
own security were demanded of China in the joint note of
the Powers, December 22, 1900,[1] as one of the conditions
necessary for the resumption of friendly relations.　This
as well as the remaining conditions was accepted by the
Chinese plenipotentiaries in their communication of January 16, 1901,[2] under imperial sanction　The final protocol
of September 7, 1901, in article VII confirms this acceptance, and provides further that

the quarter occupied by the legations shall be considered as
one specially reserved for their use and placed under their
exclusive control, in which Chinese shall not have the right to
reside, and which may be made defensible.

Aigun, Amoy, Antung, Canton, Changchun, Changsha, Chefoo, Chinan, Ching-wang-tao, Chinkiang, Choutsun, Chungking, Chutsychie,
Dairen (Dalny), Fakumen, Feng Huang Cheng, Foochow, Hailar,
Hangchow, Hankow, Harbin, Hun Chun, Ichang, Kiao-chau, Kirin,
Kiukiang, Kiungchow (or Hoihow), in Hainan, Kong Kung market,
Kongmoon, Kowloon (port of entry for Canton), Kuangchouwan,
Lappa (port of entry for Canton), Liao Yang, Lunchingtsun, Lungning, Newchwang (or Yingkou), Ningpo, Ninguta, Paitsaokou, Pakchow, Mandchourie (Manchuli), Mengtze, Mukden, Nanking, Nanhoi (or Pei-hai), Samshui, Sanhsing, Santuao (or Funing), Shanghai,
Shasi, Siminting, Soochow, Swatow (or Chao Chow), Szemao, Tatung-kou, Teng-yueh (Momein), Tiehling, Tientsin, Toutaokou, Tsitsi-har, Tungchiang-tsu, Weihaiwei, Wei-hsien, Wenchow, Wuchow,
Wuhu, Wusung, Yochow.

(b) Ports of call:

1 On the Yangtze, for passengers and cargo, Hokou, Luchikou,
Nganking (Anking), Tatung, Wu-Sueh

2 On the Yangtze, for passengers, Hwangchow, Hwang-tze-kang,
I-chang (not to be confounded with Ichang the Treaty Port), Kiangyin.

[1] Hertslet's *China Treaties*, ii, p. 1167.　　　　[2] *Ibid.*, p. 1171.

Under subsequent arrangements the total strength of the legation guard at Peking has been fixed at 2000 men furnished by the leading Powers.

Within the quarter thus established reside the members and servants of the foreign legations, their guards, and a number of foreigners, most of whom are employed in the service of the Chinese Government or are carrying on a limited trade. There are also a few provision stores and a hotel. Since, however, the quarter is established primarily for the use and security of the foreign legations it cannot be considered as a place open to foreign trade generally.[1]

The policing and general administration of the Legation Quarter are entrusted to a municipal council instituted and controlled by the diplomatic corps. Each legation contributes to the expenses for the administration of the quarter in proportion to the surface-area which it occupies within it [2]

[1] Article X of the commercial treaty with Japan, October 8, 1903, provides that "in case of and after the complete withdrawal of the foreign troops stationed in the province of Chili and of the Legation guards, a place of international residence and trade will be forthwith opened by China itself". By annexes 6 and 7 to the treaty the contracting parties agree to certain principles as to the control and administration of the proposed international place of residence and trade which are in accord with those governing places opened to foreign trade by China voluntarily. An interesting point of the agreement is that when the place is established, "the foreigners who have been residing scattered both within and without the city walls shall be required to remove their residence thereto and they shall not be allowed to remain in separate places and thereby cause inconvenience in the necessary supervision by the Chinese authorities;" and that, again, those who do remove before a fixed period "shall not be entitled to compensation" for the land and buildings held by them and taken by the authorities.

[2] *Dipl Rev* (1906), no. 16, pp 8-12; 32 *Jour. d. Dr. inter. privé* (1905), p. 854.

CHAPTER XIV

Travel and Passports

UNDER the rules made by the local authorities with the foreign consuls in pursuance of the provisions of the American and French treaties of 1844,[1] foreigners were accorded the privilege of going on excursions from the ports open to trade to a distance not exceeding 100 li, and for a period not exceeding 5 days. Beyond these limits they were forbidden to proceed. Notwithstanding the formal prohibition provided in the treaties, however, foreigners clandestinely penetrated into the interior of the country, where they were sometimes ill treated alike by the people and the authorities. Accordingly, in February, 1858, the British and French plenipotentiaries in China addressed an identical note to the chief minister of the council of state in which they pronounced the opinion that it was "almost impossible to execute this clause of the treaties" and stated that the right to travel in the Empire under proper passports delivered by their consuls and legalized by the Chinese authorities should be extended to foreigners.[2]

This right was formally granted by China to foreigners for the first time in article IX of the British treaty, June 26, 1858, which reads in part:

British subjects are hereby authorized to travel, for their pleasure or for purposes of trade, to all parts of the interior, under passports which will be issued by their Consuls, and

---

[1] Articles xxvii and xxviii, respectively.
[2] S. Ex. Doc 30, 36 cong., 1 sess., 164.

[390

countersigned by the local authorities. The passports, if demanded, must be produced for examination in the localities passed through. If the passport be not irregular, the bearer will be allowed to proceed. If he be without a passport, or if he commit any offence against the law, he shall be handed over to the nearest Consul for punishment.

A substantially identical provision was inserted in article VIII of the French treaty signed the following day, and it has since been copied in a number of treaties concluded with other foreign Powers.

The bringing of a passport is obligatory upon every foreign male adult traveler into the interior of the land,[1] except in the case of short excursions within the fixed limits. Failure to bring a passport makes him liable to be sent back to the nearest consulate of his nation for supervision or prosecution. Under article VI of the German treaty, March 31, 1880, German subjects discovered traveling in the interior without a regular passport may be taken back to the nearest German Consulate, to be restrained, and are " in addition to this, liable to a fine up to 300 taels." The only other treaty which contains a like provision is that with Japan concluded July 21, 1896.[2]

Traveling passports are issued by a consulate or the legation of the applicants' nationality, and are viséd either by the Waiwu Pu or the Governor of Peking, or the Provincial authorities. Article XI of the Austria-Hungarian

[1] The practice of the American legation is to issue only one passport for a married man with his family.

[2] The enforcement of the clause against traveling without passports would seem to be very difficult. Cases of its violation, especially by missionaries, occur frequently. In 1902 such a large number of foreigners were detected traveling in Northwestern China that the Waiwu Pu found it necessary to issue a circular note to the foreign legations reminding them of the existence of the treaty prohibition, and urging them to be more vigilant in enforcing it upon their own nationals.—8 Kuanghsu's *New Laws and Ordinances*, 49-51.

treaty, September 2, 1869, provides that " the Imperial and
Royal consul shall be careful to grant passports to respectable persons only.[1]   To the crews of foreign vessels the
provisions conferring the right to travel under passport are
generally declared to be inapplicable.   With passports foreigners may travel into the interior " for pleasure " or " for
purposes of trade."   The latter phrase means the bringing
of imported goods into the inland for sale or the purchase
of native produce there for shipment at a port.   The term
pleasure would seem to be susceptible of a very broad interpretation, but several kinds of enterprises, which may seem
to be pleasurable, have been declared not to be included
within its purport and meaning.   Thus hunting game is,
under the instructions of the Tsungli Yamen issued in
1876, not recognized as a pleasure, and passports issued for
that purpose will not be viséd.[2]   Purposes which are obviously not of a commercial or pleasurable character are of
course not recognized as giving the intending traveler the
right to passports.   In 1904 a passport viséd by the Hupeh
authorities was recalled by the Waiwu Pu for the purpose
of crossing out the words " for prospecting mines " con-

---

[1] In a note to Mr Reid, U. S. minister to China, June 6, 1858, Baron
Gros, the French minister suggested that the four powers in China
should adopt " a good system of passports," and that their diplomatic
agents or consuls should issue them to " persons offering all the guar-
antees desirable " and the latter should punish, without distinction,
every infraction of established regulations, to which the bearer of the
passport should bind himself in writing to submit.

Mr. Reid, in his reply of July 27, 1858, stated that Congress alone
could confer jurisdiction over American citizens in order to enforce
penalties for traveling in the interior without passports, and added:
" The granting by an American consul of passports to others than
American citizens is inadmissible; and here, also, in the opinion of the
undersigned, the consent of a party taking a passport would confer
no jurisdiction on a consular court."—S. Ex. Doc. 30, 36 Cong. Sess.,
392-393.

[2] 70 New Collection (General), 29.

tained therein. In 1905 the officials of Chekiang were instructed by the Waiwu Pu to strike the words "to investigate the Bhuddhist religion" from a passport presented by the Japanese Consul to be viséd by them.[1]   Taking surveys is likewise not a lawful enterprise to pursue while traveling in the interior under passports; and in 1908, upon the discovery of a party of Japanese students making topographical maps in Mongolia while ostensibly traveling under passports for pleasure, the Chinese board of foreign affairs issued a circular note to the foreign travelers in the interior to be prohibited, and at the same time sent restrictions to the provinces to act accordingly.[2]

Under the treaties foreigners may travel under passports to "all parts of the Empire."   To this comprehensive phrase there are two exceptions expressly provided in a number of compacts: traveling passports may not be issued for visiting the capital city of Peking for purposes of trade,[3] nor for places in insurrection for any purpose.   In a circular note sent to the foreign representatives in Peking in 1883 the Tsungli Yamen stated that thereafter passports issued by the legations and consulates in China to persons desiring to travel in the interior should, instead of vaguely stating "the 18 provinces," clearly designate the points to be visited and the route to be taken, in order to facilitate examination and render protection of the travelers easier, and it also requested their co-operation.   All the foreign legations assented to the proposal and acceded to the request except the American minister, who replied by stating that according to the laws of his country passports issued

---

[1] *Dipl. Rev* (1905), no 5, p. 8

[2] 8 Kuanghsu's *New Laws and Ordinances*, 51.

[3] The eighth of the Rules of Trade agreed upon by Great Britain, Britain, November 8, 1858, and the eighth of the rules annexed to the Danish treaty, July 13, 1863.

for traveling purposes usually specified three or four provinces which the applicants might propose to visit, and that
if a new passport was to be required for each trip to a place
in the interior there would be great inconvenience, especially to those who resided far away from the United States
legation.   Accompanied by a statement of the exceptions
raised by the American Minister, instructions were sent by
the Tsungli Yamen to the provincial authorities to see to
it that the new requirements were observed.[1]

Duly issued traveling passports, like the customs certificates and passes, are generally valid for a period of thirteen Chinese months, reckoned from the day of issue, at the
end of which period they must be returned to the authorities
who issued them.   In failing to comply with this requirement the bearers may be deprived of the privilege of applying for passports in future.   If passports are lost, new ones
may be obtained on application to the proper legation or
consulate; but if the declaration of loss is false, it renders
the declarant liable to be sent back to the nearest consulate
of his country for punishment, or for confiscation of the
goods, the transporting of which was the object of the trip
into the interior thus illegally undertaken.[2]

Foreign travelers under passports are not required to
report their arrival to the authorities of every locality they
reach on their way or to present their passports for examination; they are required to exhibit their passports only
when a demand to do so is made by the local authorities.

[1] 70 *New Collection* (Gen), 30-31

[2] See section 7 of the special stipulations annexed to the German
Convention of March 31, 1880, and also article vi of the Japanese
treaty of July 21, 1896. Article xiv of the British treaty of October
23, 1869, which was not ratified, limited the period within which passports were returnable to one year and Rule iv, annexed to the treaty,
gave one month's grace in addition Passports issued by the United
States legation are valid for two years.

At one time the Chinese Government sought to make it obligatory upon foreign travelers to deliver their passports for inspection at each place they should visit or pass through. Thus on November 10, 1893, the Tsungli Yamen sent a note [1] to Mr. Denby, the American minister and dean of the diplomatic corps, embodying the observation of the Taotai of Chingchow, Ichang, and Shihnan that since he entered upon the duties of his office, about eight months to date, there had been 199 foreigners traveling through his jurisdiction, that none of them had reported their arrival to the authorities therein, and that " should trouble occur to those who have not reported their arrival, the responsibility of giving protection to them should not rest on the shoulders of officials of the departments or districts." The Yamen observed in the note that " foreigners traveling with passports should report to the local authorities of the place on their arrival, to the end that due protection may be accorded them from time to time," and requested the minister of the United States to communicate with his colleagues, with a view to the consideration of the question presented and to the adoption of a feasible plan of action. Accordingly, the diplomatic corps held a number of meetings to consider the contents of the note, but " after mature deliberation " it came to the conclusion that it could not accede to the proposition of the Chinese Government. In a note to the Yamen, December 5, 1893,[2] conveying the decision of the foreign representatives, three reasons were given for it, namely, that the proposition was " impracticable " since " a heavy burden would be laid upon foreigners by such a rule, and the penalty suggested by the taotai for failure to comply with it, to wit, the forfeiture of protection, is by no means admissible "; that it was ex-

[1] For. Rel., 1893, p. 242.			[2] For. Rel, 1894, p. 153.

posed to an " insuperable " objection to wit, that it " would materially change the purport of the treaties; and finally that " it is questionable, also whether the proposed rule would accomplish any good purpose " since " the presence of foreigners in any locality in the interior is immediately known to all the population, the officials included, and ' travelers perfectly understand that, in case of trouble, they have the right to apply to the officials for protection and that it is the duty of the local authorities to protect them." The Yamen was not satisfied with these reasons and again urged the foreign representatives to put the requirements into effect, but its renewed efforts met with no more success than its initial attempt.[1]

Foreigners traveling in the interior of China with passports are under the treaties entitled to the protection of the authorities of all the places through which they pass but they have no right to demand from them *gratis* money and supplies. In 1869 two American citizens, traveling without passports from Canton to Kinkiang, posed as British officials and compelled a number of magistrates through whose districts they passed to settle their own accounts such as the expenses for hiring boats and carts. On being apprized of this case the Tsungli Yamen at once instructed the Governor of Kiangsi Province and

---

[1] Mr Denby himself entertained on the subject a view which was pronounced by the State department to be judicious, and which seems to be very fair. It is this:

" On the traveler's arrival at any departmental (chow) or district (hsien) city he might be required to report his arrival to the local magistrate, as well as the route which he proposes to follow on his departure therefrom.

" The traveler having given notice of his movements to the Chief Magistrates in the important cities, it would be their duty to notify all the subordinate officials, in the places through which the traveler would pass, of the fact that he was en route and there would be no excuse for a failure to afford protection."—*For. Rel.*, 1893, p. 241.

the Viceroy at Canton to reprimand those magistrates who had improperly paid the bills of the two American travelers and ordered the Taotai at Kinkiang to request the United States at that port to punish them for their misconduct.[1] The Yamen's instructions further state:

As to the future, when foreigners, whether on an official mission or for traveling, proceed to various parts in the inland, the local officials in the places which they traverse shall examine their passports and allow them to proceed. If the travelers be foreign officials, they may be taken good care of, but their traveling expenses shall not be paid by the local authorities.

In 1902 the Waiwu Pu issued general instructions to the provincial authorities enjoining them from supplying foreign missionary travelers gratis with funds, carts, horses, attendants and the like.[2] In 1903 a German sailor, traveling from Russia to Szechuan through Shensi, extorted from the local officials by threats of force money and provisions for himself and his horses, so successfully that, as he boasted himself, from the Russian border to Szechuan he had not spent a penny from his own pocket. The German minister, having read an account of the exploits of his countryman, inquired of the Waiwu Pu if it was correct and declared that German travelers in China were entitled to protection and not support by the local authorities. In his report,[3] as was asked of him, the Governor of Shensi stated that the account was true and added this explanation:

Because the officials at the various places did not understand how to handle foreign affairs and were ignorant of the existence of treaties, they suffered these cruel and insolent extortions. They should at once train themselves to prevent the recurrence of such cases. I have ordered that in future when-

---

[1] 70 *New Collection* (General), 29.   [2] *Ibid*, p 32.
[3] 16 *New Collection* (Germany), 24.

ever foreigners pass through the province on travel they are entitled only to protection assured them by treaty, and that they must not be furnished by the officials with money and supplies at public expense.   If foreigners attempt to extort money or demand supplies in violation of treaty stipulations, no matter what their nationality, the case should be immediately reported to me in order that I may notify the Waiwu Pu to request the minister of his country to take due action.

It may be observed that the treaties provide a more summary means of checking such illegal conduct on the part of foreign travelers in the interior than reporting the facts to their legation for action.   Any foreigner committing an offense in the interior, whether a violation of treaty provisions or a breach of peace, may be arrested, secured from escape, and sent to the nearest consulate of his country for punishment.   A vigilant exercise by the local authorities of this power expressly sanctioned by the treaties would seem to be adequate for the purpose of preventing the abuse by foreigners of the privilege of traveling in the interior.

CHAPTER XV

THE ALIEN MERCHANT IN THE INTERIOR OF CHINA

§ 1. *Sale of imported goods in the Interior*

THE right of the foreign merchant in China to carry on trade at the open ports generally has already been described in connection with the discussions of the status of ports and other places open to foreign commerce. In addition, the foreign merchant is under the treaties entitled to prosecute a limited trade in the interior of China. He may sell at an inland market foreign merchandise brought from a port or purchase Chinese goods there for transportation to a port.

If a foreign merchant desires to send his imported articles to an inland market he has the option of clearing his good of all transit duties leviable on the way by payment of a commutation transit tax or duty equal to one-half of the import duty in respect of dutiable articles, and two and half a per cent upon the value in respect of duty-free articles. On payment of either amount, as the case may be, a certificate is issued by the maritime customs, which entitles the goods to exemption from all further inland charges. If the merchant desires to accompany his imported merchandise into the interior he is required to obtain a passport for himself, as in all other cases of traveling in the inland. If he charters a boat or desires to use his own for the purpose of transporting the merchandise inland he is further required to obtain a river pass. Furnished with these papers he may proceed to the interior to sell his goods wherever he thinks fit.

§ 2. *Purchase of native produce for shipment to Chinese or foreign ports*

Where a foreign merchant desires to purchase Chinese produce or goods in the interior for transportation to an open port, it has always been necessary for him, since 1861,[1] to obtain through his consul a blank memorandum in three detachable parts, in each of which the merchant is required to state his nationality, the description of produce or goods to be purchased, the first barrier of entry outward, the date of their arrival there, and the intended port of shipment, and finally sign his own name to a statement contained therein in the nature of a declaration that he engages to pay the commutation transit duty leviable on the purchased articles at the barrier nearest to the port of shipment. On receiving a duplicate of the memorandum the maritime customs issues a transit certificate containing the name and nationality of the merchant and a description of the articles to be purchased, and entitling them, when the certificate is affixed with a seal by the first barrier of entry outward, to exemption from all charges whatever on the way to the last barrier behind the port of shipment. With these two papers the trip to purchase articles in the interior may be commenced by a Chinese agent of the merchant; if the merchant himself or one of his foreign agents undertakes the trip a traveling passport for purposes of trade is further necessary. So is a river pass if the merchant charters a boat or desires to use his own for conveying what he has bought to an open port. Meanwhile the customs taotai will give notice to the authorities of the first barrier of entry outward of the details of the trip being

---

[1] In this year Sir F. W. A. Bruce and the Tsungli Yamen entered into an agreement which formed the contents of the Regulations promulgated by the same British minister, October 30, 1861.—See 2 Hertslet's *China Treaties,* 633; for the instructions of the Yamen in pursuance of the agreement, see 67 *New Collection* (General), 35.

prosecuted.[1]   When the merchant or his agent arrives at this barrier with his purchased goods and presents the memorandum and the transit certificate, the authorities thereof are required to check up the goods with those described in the memorandum as to description and quality,[2] and if they find them correct they will affix the certificate with their seal and return it to the person in custody of the goods.   One part of the memorandum is retained by the barrier, another must be immediately forwarded to the maritime customs at the port of. shipment, and the third part sent at the end of ten days from the day of the presentation of the memorandum.· At the same time the merchant or his agent proceeds on his trip outward with his goods and the transit certificate, the latter to be presented for inspection and indorsement at every barrier he passes through.   When he arrives at the one nearest to the port of shipment the goods are valued by the customs officials sent from that port and on the transit duty being paid, they are allowed to be forwarded to the port.[3]

It is important to state, however, that native Chinese goods purchased by foreign merchants in the interior are entitled to the protection of a transit certificate only when they are *bona fide* intended for exportation to a foreign country; those similarly purchased for consumption or sale

[1] *New Collection* (General), 49-50.

[2] This rule has been strictly enforced since 1907 when the Superintendent of the Trade of the Northern Ports issued special orders to that effect under instructions from the Waiwu Pu. Prior to that time foreign merchants purchasing produce in the interior presented no goods for inspection at the first barrier of entry outward, notably at Changkia-kow, but merely exchanged a sealed certificate for the memorandum surrendered as a mere formality.—67 *New Collection* (General), 40.

[3] The form of the various papers necessary to be had for carrying imported goods into the interior and Chinese produce to a port will be found in 17 *Analytical Compilation,* 1 *et seq.*

in open ports are subject to all the barrier charges, leviable under Chinese regulations, from the place of purchase to the port of destination. Again, Chinese goods purchased in the interior and brought to a port for exportation under the protection of a transit certificate are further required, as also are Chinese goods purchased in open ports for the same purpose and free from transit taxation, to pay the tariff export duty before they can be exported.

§ 3. Treaty limitations upon the rights of the alien merchant in the Interior

The right of the foreign merchant to trade in the interior is limited to selling his imported merchandise and purchasing Chinese articles for transportation to an open port, under conditions which have just been described. From the language of the treaty provisions it seems that he may not buy articles of foreign origin in the interior and bring them out to a port nor may he sell at any place except in an open port the Chinese produce or goods he has purchased at an inland market. He is not allowed to tarry in the interior after he has sold his imported merchandise or purchased the needed articles of Chinese origin. He is prohibited to establish, anywhere outside of the places open to foreign trade, commercial houses or shops of any kind, including branch agencies conducted by foreign firms or merchants through Chinese subjects. The establishment· of permanent warehouses in the interior for the storage of articles purchased therein or brought thereto is likewise prohibited.[1]

[1] The prohibitions stated in the paragraph above are either necessarily implied from the confinement of the general right to trade to open ports in some treaties and expressly provided in others, such as article iii of the treaty with the Netherlands, October 16, 1863, and article xvi of the treaty with Portugal, December 1, 1887. Great Britain, in 1863, through its representative at Peking, expressed its

Prior to 1905 these prohibitions had been loosely enforced and as a consequence, many foreign trading establishments had clandestinely gained a foothold in the interior of China; but in that year there arose a case which gave occasion for the strict enforcement of the treaty provisions. One Vul-na-ro, an Italian subject, had opened a saloon in Shihkiachong in Chili, a place not open to foreign trade. When ordered to close up his house and remove from the place, the Italian trader appealed to his minister at Peking, who represented to the Waiwu Pu by stating that if Vul-na-ro's saloon was to be closed, all other foreign trading establishments in the interior should have been prohibited from the very beginning, and that the Chinese Government not having done so, it should compensate Vul-na-ro for the losses which might be sustained by him as the result of his compliance with the order of the local authorities to close up his saloon. The Waiwu Pu in its reply acknowledged its inability to see any reason for holding the Chinese Government liable to pay compensation, stated that Vul-na-ro would be given six weeks to wind up his accounts and leave Shihkeachong at the risk of his being arrested and sent to the nearest Italian Consulate for punishment; and added that similar orders had been issued to the provinces to have all the foreign trading houses or shops illegally established in the interior closed up and compelled to remove to open ports. Thereupon the

concurrence with the opinion of the Tsungli Yamen that under the treaties foreign merchants were not permitted to establish companies or warehouses in the interior, and instructions were accordingly sent by the Yamen to the provincial authorities.—For the instructions, see 67 *New Collection* (General), 35   The Japanese treaty of April 17, 1895, in article vi, confers for the first time upon Japanese subjects and, by virtue of the most-favored-nation clause, upon the merchants of other nations "the right temporarily to rent or hire warehouses" in the interior "for the storage of the articles so purchased or transported, without the payment of any taxes or exactions whatever."

Italian minister requested a settlement of the general question first and urged the Waiwu Pu not to proceed to close up Vul-na-ro's establishment lest there might arise " inconveniences." But the Waiwu Pu, apparently convinced of the correctness of its own stand in the matter, notified the minister that the Italian establishment in Shihkiachong, an inland place, was put up " obviously in contravention of the treaty stipulations," that the Chinese authorities could never consent to allow it, that the rule of limitation upon the right of foreign merchants to trade being applied to the subjects of all nations, the Italian merchants were not subjected to any discrimination by its enforcement upon them, that if it was closed by the authorities after the lapse of the period allowed him to remove, it would be a trouble invited by himself, that no inconvenience could arise out of the case, and finally that since China always transacted her international affairs in accordance with treaty provisions, there was " no need for negotiating a special arrangement on the question." [1]

§ 4. *Conditions under which the alien merchant may operate railways or mines in the Interior*

Independently of the treaty provisions, foreign merchants may, however, be allowed by special permission of the Chinese Government to establish their business in the interior. The Imperial Railway Regulations of 1904, by article 2, extend to foreign subjects or citizens the privilege of applying for an authorization to build railways in China, subject to the condition, applicable to them alone, that the foreign interests in a railway company organized under such authorization shall not exceed fifty per cent of its total capitalization.[2] Under article X of the Im-

[1] 33 *New Collection* (Italy), 3-4.
[2] For the text of the Railway Regulations, see 17 Kuanghsu's *New Laws and Ordinances*, 8.

perial Mining Regulations of 1907 subjects of treaty Powers, except certain classes of them,[1] are entitled to apply for permission to operate mines in China, in the interior as well as at the open ports, and to hold stocks in Chinese mining companies, subject to two primary conditions, namely that they shall observe Chinese laws, and that they may not purchase or otherwise own mining land in fee simple.

The language of the provision requiring foreigners operating mines in the interior to observe Chinese laws seems peremptory as well as emphatic.   It reads thus:

The subjects of treaty powers who voluntarily coöperate with Chinese subjects in mining enterprise shall be held to have thereby consented to observe Chinese laws, to submit themselves to the control of Chinese authorities, and to act in conformity with the Mining Regulations now in force or to be made in future, and other kindred laws, such as the Law of Companies.   They may be permitted to carry on the necessary operations only if they really observe (the foregoing requirements).[2]

[1] These are the following. (1) Buddhists, taoists, and members of missionary associations who pursue religion as a profession; (2) subjects of non-treaty powers and of powers which do not reciprocally accord the same privileges to Chinese subjects; (3) foreigners who do not observe the laws of China and those who have once been guilty of offences against the Chinese law or the law of their own country; (4) foreigners who are in the service of foreign Governments or of the Chinese Government; (5) those who have held offices under a foreign Government and have not definitely resigned them; and (6) those who may be denied the privilege by special order of the Chinese Government. Article 10 of the *Mining Regulations;* for the full text of which see 16 Kuanghsu's *New Laws and Ordinances,* 92; an English translation published in Tientsin, in 1907, under the title of "The Revised Mining Regulations and Supplementary Mining Regulations of China," though useful, does not seem to be as accurate as some readers may desire.

[2] *Mining Regulations* of 1907, article 49

Besides, foreign applicants for a permit to open mines in China are required to take out a testimonial from their consul "certifying their ability really to observe the Regulations and supplementary Rules made or to be made," and also give a bond "guaranteeing their constant observance" of the same.   When a permit to engage in mining enterprise is granted to a foreign merchant it confers upon him the status of a "mining merchant," entitles him to the especial protection of the local authorities, and exempts him, and him alone, from the application of those treaty provisions which require foreigners to obtain passports for travel into the interior, and which prohibit them in the same region to hold land, rent houses, establish trading companies or warehouses, and to do other similar acts.   In respect of all other foreigners, including those who desire to go into the interior for prospecting or working in mines, these provisions "remain in full force and without the slightest modification.[1]

It is interesting to note further the *modus operandi* provided in the Mining Regulations for dealing with litigation involving foreign "mining merchants" and crimes committed by them.   In the former case the usual procedure as prescribed in the treaties is to be followed; that is to say, such foreign merchants, when charged with a crime, shall be arrested, secured from escape, and transported to the nearest consul of his nation for punishment, only with this added proviso: that if the judgment rendered by the consul does not meet with the tacit approval of the Chinese authorities and satisfy the other mining merchants in the region wherein the offense was committed, then the subjects or citizens of the offenders' nation may not again be allowed to apply for a permit to open mines in the province.[2]

[1] *Mining Regulations* of 1907, articles 59 and 63.
[2] *Ibid.*, article 61.

In civil suits a more direct course of procedure is defined
in the Regulations. Whenever foreign merchants co-
operating with Chinese subjects in Mining enterprise in the
interior have monetary litigation with a Chinese or a subject of another country, affecting the private right of the
two parties, " the Chinese authorities shall decide it in accordance with the Chinese law and established rules ", except where the facts of the case are peculiar and not provided for in the laws and rules in force, in which case they
shall impartially settle it " according to the laws prevailing
in foreign states generally, and with due consideration of
the state of Chinese law." [1]

A system of appeal is likewise provided by the Regulations in cases concerning mining affairs. From the decision of the mining deputy in the district in which the
case has arisen the foreign litigant is expressly authorized
to appeal to the general mining bureau in the province;
if still dissatisfied, he may bring the appeal to the Provincial
Judge, the Governor, or the Viceroy, and thence to the
Ministry of Agriculture, Works and Commerce in Peking
as the final resort. It is also provided that " no minister
or consul of any nation may intervene." It is further provided that wherever appeal may be brought to, the case
" shall be decided according to the Regulations," that only
where it is one not covered by express provisions in the
Regulations " the mining laws of foreign states may
be cited as the basis of a decision ", and that even then
the rule cited " must not be contrary to the principles of
the Regulations." [2]

[1] *Mining Regulations* of 1907, article 60.
[2] *Ibid.*, article 62.

§ 5. *The question of the right of the alien merchant to invest in Chinese joint-stock companies established in the Interior*

May foreigners invest in Chinese joint-stock companies established in the interior of China other than those engaged in mining and railway enterprises? It will be remembered that the British treaty of September 5, 1902, by Article IV indirectly authorizes British subjects to invest capital in Chinese companies and that the corresponding article in the Japanese treaty of October 8, 1903, in like manner permits Japanese subjects conjointly with Chinese subjects, and vice versa, to " organize a partnership or company for a legitimate purpose; " in neither provision is there any limitation as to the locality of the companies or partnerships · organized or to be organized in China. Article LVII of the Chinese Law of Companies,[1] which was sanctioned and promulgated by an imperial decree of January, 1904, provides:

Subjects of foreign states who hold stocks in companies established by Chinese subjects shall be held to have consented to observe and conform to the Chinese Commercial Law and the Chinese Law of Companies.[2]

It is to be noted that the language of this provision, like that of the treaty stipulations referred to above, indirectly permits foreigners to hold interests in Chinese companies without making a distinction as to companies established in the interior and those in the open ports. ˙ Whether or not the distinction, not expressly provided in the article under consideration, should be recognized in the interpretation of its language, is a question which elicited a sharp difference

[1] For the text of this law, see 16 Kuanghsu's *New Laws and Ordinances.*

[2] *Ibid.,* p. 6.

of opinion in. 1906 between the Viceroy of the Kiangnan Provinces and the Board of Agriculture, Works and Commerce in Peking.

The Viceroy maintained that the article in question confers upon foreigners the privilege of holding stocks only in Chinese companies established in the ports open to foreign commerce and not in those located in the interior. In support of this proposition he assigned a number of reasons. Industries carried on in the interior of China affect the means of living of the Chinese people at large. In the course of negotiating the commercial treaty of 1902 with Great Britain Sir James L. Mackey, the British minister, insisted for a long period of time upon China's according British merchants the liberty to establish manufacturing companies in all parts of her empire and it was only after a most persistent refusal that the Chinese negotiators succeeded, finally, in limiting the exercise of that liberty to the open ports.[1] The privilege of holding stocks in Chinese manufacturing companies established in the interior is, moreover, the same as that of operating industries in the interior, inasmuch as foreign merchants could thereby not only share with Chinese merchants profits derived from such industries but could even, by reason of their investments, control such Chinese companies in the interior, or, by fraudulent combination with unscrupulous Chinese merchants, establish independent factories in the interior for themselves. Therefore, to interpret article LVII in

[1] The only reference to the subject is made in section 9 of article viii of the treaty which reads: "An excise equivalent to double the import duty as laid down in the Protocol of 1901 is to be charged on all machine-made yarn and cloth manufactured in China, whether *by foreigners at the Open Ports or by Chinese anywhere in China.* . . . *The same principle and procedure are to be applied to all other products of foreign type turned out by machinery, whether by foreigners at the Open Ports or by Chinese anywhere in China.*"

question so as to confer upon foreigners the privilege of holding stocks in Chinese companies located in the inland other than those engaged in mining and railway enterprises would be, on the part of China, to give away a right, which has not been asked of her or otherwise impaired, and which, on the contrary, has been carefully reserved to her by the British treaty of commerce of 1902.

The Board, on the other hand, entertains a contrary view of the subject. It admits the necessity of protecting Chinese capitalists engaged in industrial enterprises in the interior from foreign competition, but it holds that that necessity is fully met by the restrictive clauses in the various commercial codes limiting the proportion of foreign interests in Chinese companies. On the legal side of the question the Board holds that article IV of the British treaty of September 5, 1902, and the identically numbered article in the Japanese treaty of October 8, 1903, authorize the investment of foreign capital in Chinese enterprises without recognizing distinctions based upon the locality of their seat of establishment and that article LVII of the Law of Companies was enacted with due consideration of these treaty stipulations. It adds that the privilege of holding stocks in Chinese companies situated in the interior is different from, and does not carry with it, the privilege of operating manufacturing establishments in such region, and that if foreign stockholders in Chinese companies should, by fraudulent devices of one kind or another, gain full control of such companies or maintain independent factories in the interior, such foreigners will be prosecuted in accordance with treaty provisions.[1]

[1] For the correspondence on the question exchanged between the Viceroy and the Board, see 66 *New Collection* (General), 11-14.

CHAPTER XVI

The Christian Missionary [1]

§ 1. *Toleration and Preaching of Christianity*

In China, prior to the commencement of extensive intercourse with foreign states, religious toleration by the Government had been the rule and the interdicts occasion-

[1] The fourth of the "additional articles," concluded with the United States, July 28, 1868, provides "that citizens of the United States in China of every religious persuasion . . . shall enjoy entire liberty of conscience, and shall be exempt from all disability or persecution on account of their religious faith or worship in China." It is clear that under this article citizens of the United States in China have the right to profess and worship any religion they wish, but it does not seem clear that they have the right to preach any religion they like. According to the Chinese Government, at any rate, foreign missionaries of other creeds than Christianity not being expressly and specifically provided for in the treaties, can not be recognized by it as such, and are not entitled to the same measure of protection as is accorded to Christian evangelists.

The question was raised in 1905 by Mr. Yasuya Uchida, the Japanese minister in Peking, who represented to the Waiwu Pu that there were many Japanese Buddhist missionaries in China, preaching the teachings of Buddha and exhorting men to do good, and asked that they be protected to the same extent as were the Christian missionaries, citing in support of his request the most favored nation clause in the Japanese treaty of July 21, 1896. The Waiwu Pu declined to accept this view, stating that evangelization by Christian workers in China was expressly authorized by treaty, and that the clause cited by the minister referred only to privileges of a commercial nature, and had nothing to do with questions of missionary enterprise. In a later note the minister renewed his reference to the most favored nation clause and, after citing the twenty-ninth article of the treaty of June 18, 1858, between China and the United States and the fourth article of the treaty of July 28, 1868, between the same powers, argued that the

ally fulminated against the profession and preaching of exotic creeds had been the exceptions, brought about mostly by the indiscretion of their teachers. Not to speak of other foreign religions, Christianity itself had prospered in China since very early times, notably in the sixth and thirteenth centuries. Perhaps the most intolerant imperial edict ever issued against the Christian religion was that promulgated by Emperor Youngching, in 1724, and yet three years after, in the treaty concluded with Russia, he expressly engaged that " the Russians shall be permitted to exercise their religion with all its rites and to recite their prayers." [1] Indeed from 1724 to the middle of the nineteenth century, though imperial decrees were frequently renewed prohibit-

freedom of worship and the prosecution of missionary work granted in these provisions, were not limited to the Christian religion. Accordingly, he urged:

"Our Buddhist missionaries coming to China to promulgate the teachings of Buddha should enjoy the same protection as Christian missionaries. Hereafter if our Buddhist priests, the Chinese subjects who shall have taken up their faith, and their temples should be disturbed or injured, the Chinese Government should recognize its obligation severely to suppress the disorder. . . ."

The Waiwu Pu, however, stood firm in its position; and the policy which has since been carried out would seem to indicate that its view has prevailed. Thus in 1908 the Prefect of Hainghwa Fu, Fukien, declined the request of the Japanese consul to protect the Japanese missionary temple in Putien Hien; and in the same year, in response to a request for instructions from the Viceroy at Canton as to certain Japanese Buddhists found in Wemeichow Fu and Chaochow Fu, the Waiwu Pu stated that they could be protected only as traveling aliens. Subsequently, a Japanese Buddhist temple in Chenghai Hien was closed by order of the local authorities; another erected in the suburbs of the city met with the same fate; and a third established in Haikow, Hainan, was sealed up by order of the Japanese consul at Canton, issued in compliance with a request of the local authorities — For the correspondence between the Waiwu Pu and the Japanese legation on the subject, see 40 New Coll. (Japan), 24; for details of the instances cited, see Dipl. Rev. (1908), no. 2, p. 13.

[1] Treaty of Kiakhto, October 24, 1727, article v.

ing the teaching of the Gospel, and ordering the expulsion of Catholic missionaries, a great many of them remained in the interior of the country under sufferance of the local authorities, and the number of Chinese converts, about 300,000, continued to worship according to their new faith. It was also during this so-called period of persecution of Christianity—at the beginning of the nineteenth century—that the Protestant missionaries made their first appearance in China and established there a permanent footing for their evangelical enterprise.

In the treaties concluded with the United States and France in 1844, China may be said to have accorded western missionaries for the first time, formally though impliedly, the privilege of preaching their religion within her territory, since she agreed therein that American citizens and Frenchmen should be permitted to erect churches, schools and hospitals in the five open ports.[1] The imperial edict of February 20, 1846,[2] which revoked the previous injunctions against Christianity and permitted the teaching of its doctrines in the ports,[3] seems to lend support to the

---

[1] Article xvi of the American treaty and article xxii of the French treaty.

[2] It is said that this edict and others of like nature were issued by the Emperor in compliance with a request of France to that effect— Count de Courcy, Chargé in China, to Count Waleuski, French minister of foreign affairs, July 30, 1856, 13 *Revue d' Hist. Dipl.* (1899), 497. Article xiii of the French treaty, June 27, 1858, provides that "all that which has been previously written, proclaimed, or published in China, by order of the Government, against the Christian religion, is completely abrogated and remains invalid in all the provinces of the Empire."

[3] This and other edicts issued by the Emperor Taokuang did not permit the preaching of the Gospel in the interior. Accordingly, when M. Chapdelaine, a French missionary, was put to death by a Magistrate in Kwangsi in 1856, and Count de Courcy, the French chargé d' affaires, on July 25, 1856, complained of this offense to the imperial commissioner at Canton on the ground, among others, that "the free

statement. Full recognition of the liberty to preach and proselyte was not granted to Christian missionaries until 1858 when a simultaneous revision of their treaties with China afforded four powers a convenient opportunity for demanding it of her.

, The Russian treaty of June 1-13, the first of those concluded in that year, in article VIII, after stipulating for the protection of Chinese Christians, provides that

> The Chinese Government, considering missionaries as good men, seeking for no material advantage, will permit them to propagate Christianity among its subjects, and will not prevent them from moving about in the interior of the Empire. A certain number of missionaries leaving open towns or ports shall be provided with passports signed by the Russian Authorities.[1]

Under article XXIX of the American treaty of June 18, which is literally reproduced in the treaty of October 8, 1903, persons who peaceably profess, practice and teach the principles of Christianity " shall in no case be interfered with or molested." The eighth article of the British treaty of June 26 entitles persons doing the similar acts in like manner to freedom from interference, not in all cases, as is provided in the American provision, but when

exercise of this religion (of the Lord of Heaven) is formally authorized by the edicts of the Emperor Taokuang," the commissioner rejoined in his reply of August 20, 1856, that "the imperial edicts prescribed that the propagation of the Christian religion shall be authorized only in the five ports open to commerce, and that it shall be forbidden to penetrate into the interior of the Empire to preach that religion—this is, moreover, clearly stipulated in the treaty itself."— 13 *Revue d'Histoire Diplomatique* (189), 481, 488-9, 491-2.

[1] This is translated from the French translation said to be made from the Russian text and printed in *Treaties between China and Foreign States*. The Chinese text given in parallel columns therein does not altogether agree with the French version; for instance, the attributes predicated of missionaries are not stated at all in the Chinese text.

"not offending against the Laws" The French treaty signed on June 27, contains in article XIII the fullest provision [1] relative to the Christian missionary. It reads:

The Christian religion having for its essential object to make men virtuous, the members of all the Christian communions shall enjoy complete security for their persons, their property and the free exercise of their religious rites, and an efficacious protection shall be given to the missionaries who peaceably go into the interior, furnished with regular passports provided for in the eighth article.

It is thus seen that the presence of the western Christian missionary, as such, in the interior of China as well as in the open ports and the prosecution of evangelical work there are authorized by treaty and missionaries are entitled to the protection of the Chinese authorities.

§ 2. *Control and Protection of Missionaries*

However, troubles, whether of their own making or

---

[1] The sixth article in the Chinese text of the additional convention, October 25, 1860, is even more comprehensive as to the privileges of Christians and French missionaries, but it is to be added that the authoritative text of the convention is the French, in which the corresponding article provides for nothing beyond the restoration of confiscated property to the proper Christians. The translation of the Chinese text of the article reads:

"It shall be promulgated throughout the length and breadth of the land, in the terms of the Imperial Edict of the 20th of February, 1846, that it is permitted to all people in all parts of China to propagate and practice the 'teachings of the Lord of Heaven,' to meet together for the preaching of the doctrine, to build churches and to worship, further all such as indiscriminately arrest (Christians) shall be duly punished; and such churches, schools, cemeteries, lands, and buildings, as were owned on former occasions by persecuted Christians shall be paid for, and the money handed to the French Representative in Peking, for transmission to the Christians in the localities concerned. It is, in addition, permitted to French missionaries to rent and purchase land in all the Provinces, and to erect buildings thereon at pleasure."—Hertslet's *China Treaties.*

fomented by ignorant, intolerant, or wicked people, have
frequently befallen Christian missionaries in the interior;
popular riots, springing from one cause or another, have
repeatedly occurred in inland districts in which their persons and property have been the worst or the only victims—
sometimes threatening the friendly relations between China
and the Western states, and more often giving rise to complicated international questions.   With a view to the avoidance of such difficulties in the future the Chinese Government has more than once expressed its desire to have the
Christian Powers agree to place their missionaries in the interior within the control of the local authorities.   Thus,
following the settlement of the Yangchow riot in 1868,
Wan-tsiang, senior minister of the Tsungli Yamen, sent
to Sir Rutherford Alcock, British Minister at Peking, a
note dated June 26, 1869, in which he observed that the
principal cause of missionary trouble in the interior lay in
the fact that the western missionaries, taking advantage of
their immunities from local jurisdiction, sought indiscriminately to protect Chinese Christians, many of whom were
making their religion a pretext for extorting money from
honest people; that the reason why Confucianism and
Buddhism, also an alien creed, prospered in China without
encountering opposition and causing disturbances, was that
their followers and preachers were fully subject to the control of the authorities, and he urged that if the Christian
missionaries were similarly controlled " the result will be
that Christians and non-Christians will be placed on a just
level vis-à-vis each other, and trouble will not arise from
unexpected success ".   It is not known what Sir Ruther-

---

[1] *For. Rel*, 1871, p 110. A memorandum from Tsungli Yamen to
Sir R. Alcock, July 18, 1869, *Parl. Papers*, China, no. 9 (1870), 12, is
a note of substantially the same tenor; probably it is a translation of
the identical note with the date differently translated

ford said in his reply, which was made verbally, to these observations, but it seems more than probable that he did not concur in them.

The outbreak of the Tientsin massacre in 1870 revived the anxiety of the Chinese Government on the missionary question, and in February of the following year the Tsungli Yamen accordingly sent to the foreign representatives at Peking a circular note enclosing eight rules by which it proposed to regulate the conduct of the missionary and the relation between converts and non-converts. In the third rule it was stated:

Missionaries residing in China ought to conform to the laws and usages of the empire. They ought not to be permitted to set up an independent style and authority, nor should they resist the laws of the land, and oppose the orders of its magistrates; they should not assume power, nor encroach on the rights of others, injuring their reputations and causing scandal in the communities. They should not misuse or oppress the people, commit acts which lead men to suspect their designs, and provoke the indignant hatred of all classes; nor lastly, should they malign the holy doctrines of the Chinese sages, and thus arouse public resentment. Every missionary ought to come under the authority of the local magistrates, therefore, in all these respects.[1]

With reference to this rule as well as another following it Mr. Low in his note of March 20, 1871,[2] remarked that it appeared to him " entirely unnecessary," adding that missionaries had no right under the treaties to do the things complained of, and that any additional regulations to prevent such acts were " superfluous ". In the instructions

[1] Two translations of the Chinese note are printed in *For. Rel.*, 1871; one by the American legation on p 99, and the other by the British legation on p. 150.

[2] *For. Rel* , 1871, p. 107.

sent to Mr. Low, October 19, 1871, Acting Secretary of State Davis states that the idea expressed by the Yamen that it might become necessary so far as missionaries were concerned, to curtail some of the rights of American citizens granted by treaty, "cannot be entertained for one moment by the United States ".[1] The British Government was more emphatic in its refusal to accept the Chinese propositions. In the instructions sent by the foreign office in August, 1871,[2] to the British representative at Peking it was stated:

Her Majesty's Government cannot allow the claim that the missionaries residing in China must conform to the laws and customs of China to pass unchallenged. It is the duty of a missionary, as of every other British subject, to avoid giving offense, as far as possible, to the Chinese authorities and people, but he does not forfeit the rights to which he is entitled under the treaty as a British subject because of his missionary character.

The instructions added, however, that in withholding its assent to the proposed rules the British Government was not "actuated by any other motive than the wish to avoid embarrassing a question, already of sufficient difficulty, by cumbrous and impracticable regulations"; that as to British missionaries, if they behaved improperly, they should "be handed over to the nearest consul for punishment, like other British subjects, as provided in the treaty;" that if the consuls failed to afford redress in any instance the local authorities could appeal through the Imperial Government to the British minister in the ordinary course of international usage; that both the minister and the consuls were given extensive powers for maintaining the peace, order, and good government of British subjects in China,

[1] *For. Rel.*, 1871, p. 153   [2] *For. Rel.*, 1871, p 156.

and if these powers were inadequate the British Government " would readily increase them "; but that until the inadequacy was proved it " must decline to supplement the existing treaties by regulations which, although only intended to deal with a particular class of British subjects, would undoubtedly subject the whole British community in China to constant interference in their intercourse with the native population of a most vexatious description."

While the protection of Protestant missions and missionaries in China has always been left to their respective Governments, France, until very recently, persistently claimed to be the protector of Catholic missions in China. The French protectorate over Catholic missions in China commenced with the despatch of five Jesuit missionaries to the country by Louis XIV in 1685. Prior to this year Portugal, by virtue of a papal bull granted by Pope Nicholas V, January 8, 1454, which was renewed, with few interruptions, by the succeeding popes, had alone exercised the right of protection over Catholic missions in Asia; but after France undertook to assume the role of protector, Portugal was gradually compelled, by the waning of her influence and power in the Far East, to relinquish her religious prestige and position in favor of France, although as late as the beginning of the nineteenth century, she was still reluctant to give up the right to nominate bishops for Nanking and Peking as suffragans to the archbishop of Goa. After entering into formal treaty relations with China in 1844, France became more zealous of her position as protector of Catholic missions in the Chinese Empire and sedulously labored in their behalf, in order that the influence which flowed from her position might not be lost to her. Early in 1846, for instance, her first minister to China made a representation in behalf of Catholic missionaries and Catholic converts, in pursuance of which Emperor Tao-kuang issued

the noted Edict of February 20, 1846, removing all previous restrictions upon these foreign ecclesiastics and permitting Chinese subjects freely to embrace the Christian
religion.

Throughout the nineteenth century France was on good
terms with the Pope and was therefore alone entrusted by
the latter with the protection of Catholic missionary interests in the Far East. This privileged position of France
was not only favored by the Catholic ecclesiastics who
carried on their evangelical work in China but was undis-
puted by the Catholic states of Europe, though some of
them had occasionally attempted to withdraw their own
subjects from French protection on grounds of public
policy. Portugal, who had been the trusted guardian of
Catholicism in Asia, made no serious effort to revive her
lost title. In her unratified treaty of August 13, 1862, with
China, nothing was said of Portuguese missionaries; and
when the mission of Hainan was placed by the Pope in
1876 under the jurisdiction of the bishop of Macao, the
latter applied to the French consul at Canton for a passport for M. A. C. Garcez, a Portuguese missionary who
had been appointed to administer the affairs of the mission.[1]
The treaty of Peking, concluded between China and Portugal, December 1, 1887, which remains in force, contains
merely a toleration clause [2] which is found in most treaties
with other nations.

Austrian missionaries were also under the protection of
France. Although one of them endeavored in 1880 to
obtain through the British consul at Canton a passport with
accompanying documents, such as those delivered by the
French Legation, namely, the proclamation of February,
1862, and the decree of April 4, 1862, both of which
were considered as safeguards to foreign Catholic evan-

[1] H. Cordier, *Relations de la Chine*, etc., p. 637.   [2] Article lii

gelists in China, the Viceroy of the two Kwang Provinces rejected the application, and, on further request, granted only a Traveling Passport. In 1882 the same Austrian missionary applied for and received a French Passport.[1]

In 1868, M. de Quevedo, then Spanish minister in China, desiring to place Spanish missionaries within the protection of his legation, issued a circular to the consuls within his jurisdiction declaring that thereafter Spain would herself undertake to protect Spanish ecclesiastics in China and requiring the latter to surrender the French passports in their possession for those issued by the Spanish legation. This was opposed by the Spanish Dominicans in the Chinese Empire, and the French legation, after the lapse of a few years, resumed the issuance of passports to Spanish emissaries.[2]

During the Chinese-French war of 1884-5, the protection of the interests of France in China was entrusted to the Russian legation at Peking. But the Italian minister, M. de Luca, saw in the war an opportunity permanently to withdraw his nationals who were engaged in the propagation of the Catholic faith from the shelter of the French Catholic protectorate. In compliance with a request of some Italian missionaries, he personally went to Hankow and delivered to each Italian ecclesiastic a nationality certificate in order that he might not be mistaken by the Chinese for a Frenchman.[3]   Although M. de Luca, in his

---

[1] H. Cordier, *Relations de la Chine*, etc., ii, p. 638.   [2] *Ibid*, p 639.

[3] This was possible not only because there is a close resemblance in the physical appearances of the two peoples, but also on account of the fact that in the Chinese version of the passport issued by the French legation, the bearer, whatever his nationality, was indiscriminately and invariably described as a Frenchman although this point was left open in the French version, in order to be filled in as each case demanded. British passports all contain the phrase "a British subject" after the name of the bearer, just as the United States passports contain the phrase "a citizen of the United States" in the corresponding place

note of November 15, 1884, to the Tsungli Yamen, calling
upon the latter to instruct the Viceroy of the two Hu Provinces to affix his seal to the Italian nationality certificates
with a view to the assurance of protection to their holders,
did not raise the question of the French protectorate over
Catholic missions in China,[1] the ministry of foreign affairs
at Rome did not fail to make political capital out of the
action of the Italian minister at Hankow.   M. Mancini declared to the French Ambassador, M. Decrais, that he approved M. de Luca's conduct and that the Vatican was
grateful for the interest which the Royal ministry had
shown under the circumstances in Italian ecclesiastics.
This, however, was indirectly denied by the representatives
of the Vatican, who declared February 5, 1885, that instructions were about to be sent to the Italian missionaries,
inviting them to resort as exclusively as possible to the
good offices of the French bishop at Peking.[2]   The Italian
legation at Peking has since intervened more than once in
behalf of its nationals engaged in missionary work in
China, notably in the cases settled in Shansi Province in
1901.

Great Britain, who, though a Protestant state, counts
millions of Catholics among her subjects and has a large
number of representatives in the Catholic missions in China,
was particularly cautious to avoid any recognition of the
right, which France claimed, to protect all Catholic missionaries in the Chinese Empire so as to enable her to extend
it over those of British nationality.   In the fourth article
of the arrangement of March 15, 1899,[3] an official intercourse between Chinese local authorities and Roman Catholic missionaries, unofficially agreed upon between the

[1] H. Cordier, *Relations de la Chine*, etc., ii, p. 642.   [2] *Ibid.*, p. 644.
[3] Hertslet's *China Treaties*, ii, p. 1154

Tsungli Yamen and the French bishop of Peking, it was provided that "in grave cases concerned with Roman Catholic Missions, Bishops and Priests must request the Minister of the nation specially intrusted by the Pope with the protection of missionaries, or the consul of the nation, to arrange the affairs with the Tsungli Yamen or the local officials ".

With reference to this provision, Lord Salisbury instructed Mr. Box-Ironside in Peking, June 20, 1899, " to inform the Chinese Government . . . that where Bishops and Priests of British nationality are concerned, Her Majesty's Government cannot allow their affairs to be subject to the intervention of the officials of any Government other than the British Government, unless with the consent of her Majesty's Diplomatic Representative in special cases." [1]   The contents of this instruction were communicated to the Yamen, August 1, 1899.[2]

To China, the French protectorate over Catholic missions within her territory had proved generally disagreeable for the simple reason that France exercised this protection, as one of her own writers has observed, much less as a homage paid to religion than as one of the leading factors of French policy in the Far East.[3] The protectorate observes the same writer, was for a long time " pierre angulaire de notre politique dans l'Extreme Orient ".[4] England derived her strength in China from commerce, Russia from the extent of her territory and her propinquity to China, and France from religion. It was therefore natural that in 1885 China attempted, though unsuccessfully, to wreck the foundation upon which France had been planting and building her political influence within her empire, by seek-

---

[1] *Parl. Papers,* China, no 1 (1900), 149   [2] *Ibid,* p 324
[3] H. Cordier, *Relations de la Chine,* etc, ii, p 637
[4] *Ibid,* p 625

ing to establish direct relations with the Vatican   The occasion which inspired the Chinese Government to begin a campaign against the French religious protectorate was the delivery of a papal message to the Chinese Emperor early in 1885, when hostilities were still raging between France and China, expressing the Pope's appreciation of the Emperor's benevolent edict issued upon the outbreak · of the war, which promised protection to Christian missionaries of all nationalities, French as well as other; and asking His Majesty to continue this gracious policy toward the foreign ecclesiastics. Père Ginlanelli, who was entrusted by the court of the Vatican to deliver the message, when he passed through Peking on his way to a missionary post in Sheusé, was, through Sir Robert Hart, as his intermediary, given an imperial audience on April 8, 1885, at the close of which the papal epistle was handed to the Emperor. Two days later the Tsungli Yamen returned an official reply conveying the Emperor's appreciation of the Pope's letter and his good wishes for the head of the Church. All these proceedings took place at Peking without the knowledge of the French consul at Tientsien, France's sole representative in North China during the war, for he was not informed by Bishop Tagliabue in the capital until they became accomplished facts.

Undoubtedly, the Yamen considered this a good opportunity to open relations with the Holy See if not for the purpose of terminating French protection of missions in China, at least with the hope of avoiding in future the complication and difficulties which France appeared to be always ready to throw in the way of settling Catholic missionary cases, in order to make them serve her political ends. Li Hung-Chang, to whom the Yamen intrusted the task of carrying out the more or less secret project, at once appointed George Dunn, a British merchant, to proceed to Rome. Everything seemed to point to a successful issue of the campaign. The Pope appeared well disposed toward the proposal; he appointed Mgr. Agliardi as legate to China; and the latter accepted the appointment. England, Germany, Italy and even Belgium encouraged the court of Peking to persist in its course. Abroad, Cardinal Manning and the Archbishop of Westminster made common cause with Marquis Tseng, who was actively engaged in bringing about the subversion of the French protectorate. But all this, however, proved of no avail in the face of the subtle influence of diplomacy which the French Ambassador at the Vatican was able to exert over responsible authorities of the church. The latter were led to see that no single power was prepared to take the place of France in the protection of the Catholic interests in China. China herself could hardly be confided with the protection, the agents of the Church not being strong enough to check the possible reprisals of the Empire against Catholic missions. All of this meant that the Vatican would be obliged to ask for the joint protection of the European powers or to invoke the good offices of Italy, neither of which was desirable. The conclusion, as stated by the Archbishop of Tyre to Lefebvre de Beháine, the French ambassador, was: " le *statu quo* est de beaucoup préférable." [1]

The desire of the Chinese Government to establish direct relations with the Holy See was apparently also engendered by the opposition which France had set to its attempt to appropriate the site of the Pe Tang (Cathedral of the North) for the purpose of extending the palace garden in the capitol. This affair also serves to elucidate the Chinese

---

[1] Lefebvre de Beháine to French Foreign Ministry, September 9, 1885, H. Cordier, *Relations de la Chine*, etc., ii, p. 647. For a documentary account of the whole affair, see *ibid*, pp. 590-604, 645-648.

view of the character of the French protectorate over
religious missions. The property on which the cathedral
stood was originally granted to the Jesuits by Emperor
Kanghi, July 4, 1693, as a gift; it was subsequently built
upon by the missionaries with subvention granted by Louis
XIV. The cathedral was destroyed in 1827 when persecution
against Christianity was wide-spread, but was restored
to the Lazarists, who had succeeded to the Jesuits, through
the efforts of the French Minister, in pursuance of the
sixth article of the convention of Peking, October 25, 1860.
Under these circumstances it was contended that the cathedral was " most incontestably the property of France," that
" neither the Pope nor the Lazarists had any right over the
Pe-Tang." [1]   When the Tsungli Yamen proposed in 1874
for the first time to recover the property by purchase, the
French Government [2] as well as the missionaries absolutely
refused to consider the proposal.   For the time being this
uncompromising attitude caused much feeling but the death
of Emperor Tungchi put an end to the negotiations.   The
retirement of the Empress Dowager from the regency in
1885 made the resumption of extension work on the palace
park necessary, and negotiations were therefore made to
France for the recovery of the Pe-Tang site.   But before
the French consul at Tientsin, M. Ristelhueber, received
his authorization from his Government to negotiate a settlement, Li-Hung-chang, evidently encouraged by the prospect of having a papal representative accredited to the court
of Peking, effected a secret agreement, through his agent,
Mr. Detring, with M. Favier, procurator of the Lazarist
mission in Peking.   By the terms of this agreement, which

[1] H. Cordier, *Relations de la Chine*, etc., ii, pp 611-612.

[2] At the laying of the corner-stone of the new cathedral, May 1, 1865,
M. Berthemy, the French minister, is said to have declared: " C'est la
France qui la pose, malheur à qui y touchera."—Cordier, ii, p. 605

was to take effect upon ratification by the Emperor and the Pope, the mission was to relinquish its rights over the Pe-Tang and, in return, to receive a new site in Sichankow and 350,000 taels for purposes of construction.   When Consul Ristelhueber was informed of the conclusion of this agreement, there was an outburst of feeling on the part of the French authorities both toward Mr. Favier and Li Hung-chang, but the latter stood firm in his position for a time.   Li contended, in effect, that the property had been given by Emperor Kanghi to the Jesuits as an act of grace, that the interposition of the French legation on the occasion of its restoration to the missionaries was accepted only in execution of the Peking convention of 1860, and that the Emperor had the perfect right to retake it when he needed it for other purposes, especially when due compensation was promised the occupants.   Further, an arrangement was about to be made with the Pope for the settlement of all missionary questions with him directly, of course, including the ratification of the Favier-Detring convention; in this arrangement there would be no invasion of the traditional protection exercised by France over Catholic missions in China, but if the French Government opposed the conclusion of such an arrangement, China would be determined to confine herself to the execution, pure and simple, of article XIII of the treaty of 1858, which, according to the opinion of the eminent legists consulted on the subject, did not confer on France any right of international protection over religious missions in China. When, however, the Pope, as has already been stated, yielded to the influence of French diplomacy and resolved with fresh faith to continue to confide to France the protection of the interests of the Church in the Far East, Li Hung-chang was deprived of his most formidable weapon for coercing France to accede to the wishes of the Chinese

Throne on the subject of the Pe-Tang; and forthwith he changed his attitude. August 18, 1886, he, through Consul Ristelhueber, telegraphed to the President of France, stating that he had just been informed of the fact that France claimed certain rights over the Pe-Tang, by virtue of which the intervention and assent of the French Government were necessary for the retrocession of the establishment, and that he now wished to request the President kindly to ratify the Favier-Detring agreement. Three months later, November 18, Li wrote to M. Constans, the French minister, who had arrived in China meanwhile, declaring that the transfer of the Pe-Tang was simply demanded as an act of kindness from a friendly Government; that as to the opening of direct relations with the Pope, China never attached much importance to the coming of a papal delegate, and that "questions concerning missions will naturally continue to be treated, as previously, by France."[1] From this time on, the negotiations for the appropriation of the Pe-Tang followed a normal course. Li sent a formal request to M. Constans, November 22, to which the latter acceded on November 25. An imperial edict of December 3, 1885, ratifying the arrangement, expressed the Throne's appreciation of the successful termination of the affair by conferring an official title on Bishop Tagliabue, M. Favier, and Commissioner Detring, and by decorating George Dunn and Consul Ristelhueber. Favier and Dunn were each presented with a gift of 2,000 taels, besides. The Yamen sent to M. Constans, December 15, 1886, for transmission to Bishop Tagliabue, a little deed to the new site in Sichikow made out in the bishop's name. An agreement signed December 16, by the French minister and the bishop, declares that it remains understood between the parties that " the rights which the French Government pos-

[1] H. Cordier, *Relations de la Chine*, etc, ii, p. 615

sesses over the existing Pe-Tang are reserved and will be
carried over the site in Lichihow and over the buildings
which may be erected thereon." [1]   The final instruments
for the transfer of the Pe-Tang was signed December 14,
1887, by the representative of the Yamen on one part, and
by those of the French legation and the Catholic mission
on the other. [2]

It is clear that the Chinese Government did not consider
the protection of Catholic missions by France as a right
recognized by any treaty which it had concluded with her.
Cordier, on the other hand, has observed, agreeably with
the attitude and policy of the French Government, that
Article XXII of the treaty of Whampoa, August 25, 1845,
the first international compact between China and France,
was of "une importance exceptionelle," because it was
"une nouvelle confirmation du protectorat exercé sur les
missions par la France." [3]   This inference, however, could
not be sustained without straining the letter of the provision, inasmuch as the latter spoke of only "les Français"
as being entitled to establish churches, hospitals, asylums,
schools and cemeteries, and in the final clause the punishment of the guilty was stipulated only in case " des églises
ou des cimetières Français," not churches or cemeteries of
any nationality, were destroyed.

The thirteenth article of the treaty of June 27, 1858,
providing for the toleration of the preaching and embracing
of " the Christian religion," as admitted by Cordier, " ne
stipule pas toutefois notre protectorat sur les missions "[4]   As
to the sixth article of the Peking treaty of 1860, the same

[1] Cordier, *Relations de la Chine*, ii, p. 622.
[2] For a documentary account of the whole affair, see *ibid*, ii, pp
604-624.
[3] *Ibid.*, i, p. 17; ii, p. 626.
[4] *Ibid.*, ii, p. 626.

writer maintains, however, that the clause providing for the restoration of the confiscated property of Catholic missions "par .l'entremise du ministre de France" "marque bien la reconnaissance d'un droit."[1] This is, however, merely one interpretation of the effect of the clause. On the other hand, a different construction may be fairly upheld. The confiscations referred to had taken place at a period long before China's treaty relations commenced with France or any other Western nation except Russia. The restoration stipulated for was expressly declared to be based, not on any treaty, not even on that of 1844, but on a domestic law, the edict of February 20, 1846. Under these circumstances the restoration of the confiscated property might appropriately be considered as an act of grace on the part of China, and the interposition of the French legation was accepted merely as the safest and most convenient way of reaching the owners of the property. In short, the inference from the clause under consideration of implied assent on the part of China to the French protectorate over Catholic missions in China seems to be far from established beyond doubt or question.

But whether there was or was not any treaty sanction, express or implied, for the exercise by France of the right of protection over Catholic missions in the Chinese Empire, it is a fact that the right was repeatedly exercised and that such exercise does not appear to have been seriously questioned by the Chinese Government. On the contrary, the latter seems to have tolerated it in practice. In 1865, for instance, the Tsungli Yamen accepted the representation of M. Berthemy, the French minister, and granted to Catholic missions, as such, the privilege of acquiring real property in the interior. Again, often during the last half a century the French legation presented claims to

---

[1] *Relations de la Chine*, etc., ii, p. 626.

the Chinese Government, on various occasions, in behalf of Catholic missions regardless of their nationality, and they were paid without raising the question of their protection by France. Passports were also issued by the legation to Catholic missionaries of all nationalities residing in China, and they were honored by the Chinese authorities.

French protection of the Catholic interests in China has now ceased, however. In January of 1906, the French minister at Peking notified the Waiwu Pu that his Government had informed him of the law which the French National Assembly had enacted, ordering the severance of official relations between the state and the church, and had instructed him to declare that after the date of the note the French legation would take care only of cases affecting French missionaries and that those affecting missionaries of other nations should be referred to their ministers.[1] Accordingly when a German Catholic missionary, subsequently in the same year, applied to the French legation for a passport, the applicant was referred to the German minister.

§ 3. *Missionaries, as a rule, treated equally with other Foreigners*

In their own practice the foreign powers make no difference in the treatment of missionaries and those who pursue a different vocation. " The missionary is simply a citizen (or a subject) and the sacred character of his object and purpose does not enter into the question of the determination of his rights." [2]

While refusing to allow any of the treaty rights of their nationals to be diminished in respect of their missionaries,

[1] *Dipl. Rev.* (1906), no. 2, p. 6

[2] Mr. Denby, minister to China, to Mr. Bayard, Secretary of State, Oct 9, 1886, *For. Rel.*, 1886, p. 96.

the treaty powers generally seem to be equally scrupulous, with one notable exception, in abstaining from asking on behalf of such missionaries special privileges not enjoyable by others engaged in a different calling. The United States has been particularly vigilant in preserving the equal treatment of its citizens by China. In his instructions to Mr. Low, Minister at Peking, October 19, 1871,[1] Acting Secretary of State Davis states:

The President will see with deep regret any attempt to place a foreign ecclesiastic, as such, on a different footing from other foreigners residing in China. It is a fundamental principle in the United States that all persons, of every sect, faith, or race, are equal before the law. They make no distinction in favor of any ecclesiastical organization. Prelates, priests, and ministers can claim equal protection here, and enjoy equal rank in the eye of the civil law. The United States asks no more in China than they confer at home. Should the peace of the empire be disturbed by efforts from any quarter to induce or compel the government to confer unusual civil rights on foreign ecclesiasticals, you will make it plain that the United States have no sympathy with such a movement, and regard it as outside of the treaty rights which have been conferred upon the western nations. Should these demands, however, be complied with, this Government will then consider whether, under the thirtieth article of the treaty of 1858, a similar right will not at once inure to the benefit of all the public officers, merchants, and (other) citizens of the United States.

The view of the United States in a word, is this: "An American missionary, in the eyes of the law, is a citizen, no more.[2]

In a circular addressed by the British minister, Sir E.

---

[1] *For. Rel.,* 1871, p. 153

[2] Mr. Young to China Branch of Evangelical Alliance, March 28, 1885. *For Rel.,* 1885, p 167.

Satow, to British consuls in China, August 31, 1903,[1] it is pointed out

That missionaries are not accredited agents of the British Government, for the enforcement of the treaty (of Tientsin, 1858), and Article VIII. was not intended to confer upon missionaries any right of intervention on behalf of native Christians.

If a missionary has to complain on behalf of himself that his teaching is interfered with, or that a Chinese preacher or convert has been interfered with or persecuted, his proper course is to lay the facts before the Consul of the district in which he resides, who, after due examination, will make such representations to the Chinese authorities as the case may require.

A similar rule appears to be in force as respects German missionaries. In 1906 when one of them asked the Magistrate of Nankai Hien by direct correspondence to allot to his church certain property adjoining it, and the magistrate sent guards to survey the land and was about to grant the application, the German consul at Canton, on learning of the affair, immediately requested the Viceroy to stay the proceedings of the magistrate on the ground that any matter between missionaries of his country and the local authorities should be communicated to the Chinese officials through the consul and not directly by the interested persons. On the other hand, France seems to have always recognized a special position for her missionaries in China. They are, for instance, allowed to correspond directly with the local authorities on missionary matters and settle their own claims in less grave cases.

The policy of the Chinese Government has been to treat

---

[1] Hertslet's *China Treaties*, ii, p. 1181.

[2] *Dipl. Rev.* (1906), no. 14, p 4

foreign missionaries in the same manner as other citizens or subjects of the treaty-Powers. It recognizes no official character in them as missionaries, and enjoins on the local authorities not to accept intercourse with them on such footing. Pretensions were not infrequently advanced, and presumptuous acts done, by Roman Catholic missionaries, but they were usually discountenanced by the Chinese authorities. Thus the circular note of 1871 on the missionary question stated among other instances, that in 1867 a French bishop in Zechuen addressed the authorities of that province by despatches which he stamped with an official seal cast for that purpose, that another bishop in Kweichow presumed to send an official communication in terms of equality to the foreign office by the government post, and that another Romist missionary in Shantung had the boldness to style himself a suin-fu or governor; it characterized such acts as " unjustifiable and impertinent proceedings," and, as a means to deter their repetition, proposed in the seventh rule [1] the following:

The missionaries ought to observe Chinese customs, and to deviate from them in no respect; for instance, they ought not to make use of seals, the use of which is reserved for functionaries alone. It is not allowed them to send despatches to a Yamen, whatever may be their importance. If, however, for an urgent matter it should be absolutely necessary to write, they may do it; but taking good care not to speak of matters beyond the subject, and use, like people belonging to the class of literates, the ning-tieh (petition). When the missionaries visit a great mandarin, they must observe the same ceremonies as those exacted from the literates; if they visit a mandarin of inferior rank, they must also conform to the customary ceremonies. They must not unceremoniously go into the Yamens and bring disorder and confusion into the affair.

[1] For. Rel., 1871, p. 164.

The foreign governments addressed admitted the principles thus expressed, and declined to accept the rule itself only on the ground that sufficient remedies were already provided in the then existing treaties and regulations. In 1875 when a French priest addressed a " communication " on a certain subject to the magistrate of Icheng Hien in Kiangsu, it was reported to the Viceroy, who issued an order in which he made a statement to the following effect:[1] Priests are not officials. Whenever they have matters to complain of the local officials they should use the form of a petition or that of a letter. If the missionary's complaint is in the form of a " communication you shall notify the said missionary that hereafter he may not employ that form of correspondence again in order that the treaties may be conformed to." Again, in the circular note,[2] addressed by the Yamen to the foreign Powers in 1878 one of the things which, it was stated, " China cannot tolerate or submit to " was that " among the missionaries are some who exalting the importance of their office, arrogate to themselves an official status, and interfere so far as to transact business that ought properly to be dealt with by the Chinese local authorities."

An exception[3] to the policy maintained by the Chinese

---

[1] 6 *Analy. Comp.*, pt. iii, 19.   [2] *For. Rel.*, 1880, p. 177.

[3] Honors and courtesies have only occasionally been extended to missionaries; these acts are simply a matter of grace, and are not done frequently enough to make them exceptions.

In 1887, Bishop Tagliabue and M. Favier, both of the Cathedral of Pe-Tang in Peking, were granted by the Emperor the red button and the char blue button respectively.—24 *Mem. Dipl.* (1887), 133.

Again, in 1901, the Bureau of Foreign Affairs in Shansi was instructed by the Chinese Plenipotentiaries to have the provincial authorities and gentry welcome certain Protestant missionaries, who were about to go there to negotiate a settlement of the missionary cases in Shansi, and also to provide for them a residence and banquets, "in order to cause cordial feeling toward them."—61 *New Coll.* (Gen.), 27.

Government of equal treatment of missionaries and other citizens or subjects of the treaty Powers was the arrangement [1] made by the Tsungli Yamen with Fan-Kuo-hang (from Chinese), the Roman Catholic bishop stationed in Peking, and sanctioned by an Imperial decree of March 15, 1899. By the terms of this arrangement Roman Catholic bishops were to rank with Governors-General and Governors, provicars and head priests with treasurers, judges, and Taotais, and other priests with Prefects and Magistrates; Chinese officials were to return calls in accordance with the rank of the priest; bishops were required to furnish the provincial authorities with a list giving the names of " the priests deputed to transact international business with the Chinese officials;" the local officials, when applied to in regard to missionary cases " must at once discuss and arrange the affair in an equitable and friendly manner; and so forth." The arrangement, however. worked unsatisfactorily, the privileges it accorded the Catholic missionaries being frequently abused,[2] and on March

[1] For the Chinese text of the arrangement which consisted of five articles, see 61 *New Collection* (General), 24; for an English translation of it, see *Parl. Papers*, China, no. 1 (1900), p 142

[2] As an instance of the abuses, the case in Fukien, reported in a despatch which the Waiwu Pu received from the Viceroy of Min-Cho Provinces, May 4, 1906, may be noted. " In the city of Wheingnan," stated the Viceroy, "there has always been a Catholic church house inhabited by the French priest Shih Sing-hi, who ordinarily goes about in a small sedan-chair accompanied by a single attendant on horseback The people look upon his traveling in that manner as an ordinary event Suddenly, on March 11, 1906, there came from Amoy a Frenchman by the name of Ku, who pretends to have been appointed by his Government as Superintendent of the Roman Catholic missionaries in Fukien, Formosa, Tonking, and other places. He rode in a big sedan-chair carried by eight men, and his two companions, Priests Ngan and Shih, each rode in a chair carried by four men. These chairs were followed by more than ten small chairs and horses In front of them there were marshalls, gong-carriers, and a company of 200 guards armed with rifles When the procession was

12, 1908, the Throne, on memorial of the Waiwu Pu, repealed the law of 1899, which sanctioned the arrangement
by declaring it to be " no longer desirable or necessary ",
and ordered the provincial officials to accord Roman Catholic missionaries, in their intercourse with them, such rights
and privileges as should be in conformity with treaty
provisions.[1]

§ 4. *Residence and Property-Holding in the Interior*

In one important respect missionaries in China are placed
on a different footing from other classes of foreigners.
Apart from the privilege of sojourning and leasing property for temporary use anywhere in China,—a privilege
which is an incident of the treaty right to travel in the
Empire on passports, and which is, therefore, equally enjoyable to all classes of foreigners,—Christian evangelists,
as members of organized missions, are granted the treaty
right to rent and to lease in perpetuity, as the property of
such missions, buildings, or lands in all parts of the Empire,
for missionary purposes, and, by implication, the additional right of permanent residence in the interior, while as

entering the city gates the gong carriers beat their gongs and the
guards ordered a blank discharge to inspire awe, and' the neighboring churches fired salutes from their guns and rifles At this point
the minds of men were alarmed   It was only after the magistrate detailed soldiers to the scene that the people began to disperse.

"The next day these foreigners left the city in the same style.
When they arrived at Shentiennu the country inhabitants were panic-
stricken and fled, almost causing serious troubles."

It may be added that the Waiwu Pu promptly called the attention
of the French minister at Peking to the case, and requested him " to
consider the question and to instruct the French consul at Amoy to
investigate into the case and strictly to forbid its recurrence, in order
that the treaties may be observed and peace be maintained between the
Christians and non-Christians."—For the report and correspondence
about this case, see 10 *New Collection* (France), 34.

[1] 61 *New Collection* (General), 25

individuals, they are accorded, by the authorities of certain localities, similar liberties in respect to property and residence; whereas foreigners pursuing other vocations in China are allowed to enjoy neither. To appreciate the extent of the right and the character of the liberty, it is only necessary to study the origin and history of the differential treatment on this point maintained in China in favor of the missionaries.

The last clause of the sixth article of the Chinese text of the convention concluded between China and France. October 25, 1860, reads:

It is, in addition, permitted to French missionaries to rent and purchase land in all the Provinces, and to erect buildings thereon at pleasure.

It appears that for nearly a decade after the convention was concluded the clause was understood and viewed in the same light as the remaining provisions of the compact,—without betraying the least suspicion as to its authenticity or conclusiveness. Early in 1869, however, it was discovered that the clause was one " added to the Chinese version of the Convention which has no counterpart in the French text; and as Article III of the French treaty of 1858 stipulates that the French text shall in all cases govern,—whatever is not found in the French text cannot be held binding on either contracting party.[1] Indeed the dis-

[1] Sir R. Alcock to Earl of Clarendon, March 12, 1869, *Parl. Papers,* China, no. 9 (1870), 2 It is to be noted that Sir Rutherford does not appear to have been aware of the discrepancy as late as September 11, 1868, for under that date he wrote to Lord Hawley, stating that " it does not seem that any new clause of a Treaty is required to give to British missionaries the right they seek of purchasing land, and residing in all parts of the country. Article vi of the French Treaty is perfectly clear on that point, and what is acquired as a right for French missionaries, is equally acquired, by the favored nation clause, for the British, as I have recently had occasion to remind the Foreign Board."—*Parl. Papers,* China, no 2 (1869), 26

crepancy appears to be a pure interpolation in the Chinese text, there being "no similar words, no language, which by any construction, can seem to have been made the basis of the actual translation from French to Chinese.[1]

What the understanding of the French Government was, after the signing of the convention of 1860, as to the rights represented in the interpolated clause, it is not known; but in view of the fact that the sixth article of the French text of the convention clearly stipulated for the complete' restoration to their original owners of the confiscated Catholic establishments in the provinces, it is not unlikely that it understood the article, by implication, to permit Catholic priests, as members of missionary bodies, to resume the privilege, which they had enjoyed before the policy of persecution was enforced, of residing and purchasing property, in the interior of the Empire, for missionary purposes. At any rate, it appears from the terms of the arrangement[2] reached, February 20, 1865, between the Tsungli Yamen and M. Berthemy, the French Minister, that the privilege of holding property in the inland was then assumed by the contracting parties to have been in existence in favor of Catholic missions. The arrangement provided that where property was to be sold to Catholic missionaries the title deed was to state the name of the seller or person executing the transfer, and was to set forth that the property was to be held in common by the members of the local Catholic church; special mention was not to be made of any missionary or convert, so as to leave no doubt that the ground still remained Chinese soil. In its instructions to the Provinces, in 1865,[3] with reference

---

[1] Mr. Denby to Mr. Bayard, October 9, 1886, *For. Rel.,* 1886, p. 96.

[2] Incorporated in the Yamen's instructions to the provinces, 1895, 71 *New Coll.* (Gen.), 27.

[3] 71 *New Collection* (General), 26.

to the arrangement, the Yamen explained the reason for these restrictions and pointed out the limitations of the arrangement by stating:

The practice of building churches in the interior dates back from a very early period. Missionaries, however, are, after all, subjects of foreign nations; therefore, if they desire to purchase land for the purpose of building mission chapels thereon, the title-deed should only state that the land is sold to become the public property of the local Catholic church. If foreigners, in violation of treaty, attempt to purchase property in the interior for private ownership, this shall continue to be prohibited as heretofore.

In the same year the Superintendent of the Trade of Northern Ports, in ordering the local authorities within his jurisdiction to observe the terms of the arrangement, put forward his construction of it to the effect that no Chinese subject was permitted to lease or otherwise transfer his property to be used for missionary purposes without first obtaining an authorization from the local magistrates, "who in fact have generally refused to give it." The French legation considered this construction as an interpolation and repeatedly protested against its enforcement by the local authorities, especially by its notes of February 5, 1882, and August 31, 1888. Finally, on December 3, 1894, the Tsungli Yamen, in compliance with a renewed request of Mr. Gerard, the French minister, issued new instructions to the Viceroys and Governors of the Provinces to the effect that the prospective seller .of property to French Catholic missions in the interior should no longer be required to inform the local authorities of his intention to sell or to ask beforehand their authorization of the sale.[1]

[1] M. Gerard to M. Hanotoux, April 30, 1895, 128, *Arch. Dipl.* (1898), 305. For a French translation of the Yamen's instructions, see *ibid.;* for the Chinese text, see 71 *New Coll.* (Gen), 27.

Thus it is clear that so far as the Roman Catholic missionaries are concerned, they have, since a century ago, always been allowed to acquire, in conformity with the specified conditions, land situated in the interior, regardless of the question whether the power they are thus permitted to exercise is in the nature of a right or only a privilege. The Protestant missionaries, on the other hand, have had a great deal of difficulty in knowing what rights or privileges if any, they had and for that matter, they do not absolutely know what they have, with reference to residence and property holding in the interior of China. Their own view, as expressed by their representative in 1888, when it was feared lest the United States Government might " advocate the side of no right under the treaty," is that to do so " would be a severe blow," and that " better would it be if silence were adopted, in case a decision cannot be rendered on the other side." [1]

By conciliatory dispositions and prudent conduct a large number of them have succeeded in establishing a permanent foothold in inland places, and by purchasing and holding land in the name of their Chinese converts, as this was the only safe means in the early days, they have acquired a considerable amount of inland property   But opposition has frequently been encountered in their initial attempt to plant a missionary chapel in an uncultivated field while popular riots have taken place, time and again, in places where they have already established themselves, threatening dispossession and expulsion.   Under such circumstances it is natural that they have evinced a desire approaching anxiety, to know what their status in the interior is.

The view of the Chinese Government on the question

[1] Mr. Reid to Mr. Bayard, Secretary of State, May 24, 1888. *For. Rel.*, 1888, p. 325.

has been an easily intelligible one. It has always considered the establishment of a permanent residence, and the acquisition of real property in the interior by French missionaries as members of a local church, to be rights provided for by treaty; [1] and has deemed it only fair that what has been enjoyed by French missionaries should equally be accorded, with like conditions, to missionaries of other nationalities. Thus in 1887 the Emperor in exchange for the grounds of the Catholic cathedral gave to the Catholic mission a large and valuable tract of land within his capital, close to the Forbidden City, to be used for churches, schools, convents, hospitals and as the residence of the numerous clergy, and in addition, gave them 400,000 taels for the purpose of the mission. Again, in its note of February 19, 1897,[2] in reply to Mr. Denby's note embodying a draft [3] of five propositions made by the State Department of Washington as the best means to prevent the recurrence of anti-foreign riots, the Tsungli Yamen states:

Your Excellency proposes the following measures:
First. Recognition by the issuance of a formal declaration in an imperial decree that American missionaries have the right to reside in the interior of China. It may be observed that this right is provided for by treaty. Imperial decrees have already been issued commanding that due protection should be given to the United States citizens residing in China. . . .
Second. Your excellency states that the declaration in such decree should be that American missionaries have the right

---

[1] This may mean either the Berthemy convention of 1865 or the convention of October 25, 1860; the latter seems to be more likely the case, since the Chinese Government does not appear to have been aware of the discrepancy between the sixth article of the Chinese version, and that of the French text, of the convention of 1860, or to have ever contested the authoritativeness of the Chinese version.

[2] *For. Rel*, 1897, p 61.   [3] *For. Rel.*, 1896, p. 62.

to buy land in the interior of China; that they shall have all privileges of the Berthemy Convention, and that deeds taken by them shall be in the name of the missionary society or church which buys the land, as that society provides.

The princes and ministers beg to state that while the treaties between the United States and China do not provide for this, still the American missionaries should be treated in this matter the same as the French missionaries.

The Yamen's answer to the first proposition " is a valuable admission, as treaties, except the Berthemy convention, are silent on the question of residence in the interior." [1] As regards individual missionaries, the Chinese Government has not opposed or contested their enjoying the right, accorded missionary societies, of residence and of purchasing lands or houses in inland places; indeed, it has left the matter entirely to the dispositions of the local populace and the discretion of the local authorities. In no case where individual missionaries have, by the tolerance of the people and officials as well as by their own tact, established themselves in an inland district has the Government at Peking raised an objection; and where they have been denied admission, or dislodged, after having once been admitted, it has usually defended the action of the authorities rather on grounds of local inconvenience and popular animosity than on that of the non-existence of the right at the outset.

The general practice of the local authorities indicates that they have regarded the right of missionaries to reside permanently in the interior, and there to hold lands or houses, to be secured by treaty, and that in following out their view they, whether for want of a clear perception, or in pursuance of a studied policy, have not as a rule insisted upon the distinction between missionaries as members of an

<hr/>

[1] Mr. Denby to Mr. Olney, February 25, 1897, *For. Rel.*, 1897, p. 60.

organized body, and missionaries as individuals. It is true
that in 1868 the Taotai of Chefoo for instance refused to
set his seal to a deed of gift, sent to him by the British
consul, purporting to transfer to a British missionary title
to a temple situated in Chihia Hien, on the ground that
foreigners had no right to hold property in the interior;[1]
and, again, in 1881 the magistrate of Namhoe objected,
correctly or incorrectly, to the purchase by an American
missionary of land situated just outside of the walls of the
port of Canton, for two stated reasons: first, that the treaties between the United States and China did not allow citizens of the United States to buy land beyond the walls of
the port of Canton, and, second, that even if this was not
the right view of the treaties, still the missionary in question had no right to buy in his own name for the mission
society.[2] But such opinions as these are exceptional; by
far the more common view entertained by the local authorities has been in favor of the missionaries.

Thus take a few examples. In 1872 two American missionaries, of the Southern Presbyterian Church mission
took possession of a piece of land in Hangchow, 140 miles
from Ningpo, then the nearest port, purchased "in the name
of a friendly Chinese." The property stood on a hill fac-
ing the Yamen of the Provincial Treasurer, and buildings
were erected on it, which according to soothsayers, seriously disturbed the Yamen's free shui or geomancy. He,
understanding that the missionaries had obtained the property in exercise of their treaty-right, desired them merely
to exchange the land on the hill for another piece on the
plain. The proposal was accepted through the American
consul on condition of receiving a site of equal size, a sum

[1] *Parl. Papers,* China, no. 9 (1870), 1.
[2] *For. Rel*, 1881, p 283.

of $11,000 for the expenses likely to be incurred in making the exchange, a title-deed made out in the name of the mission and under the seal of the magistrate, and finally a proclamation to be issued by the lieutenant governor stating that the exchange was made voluntarily on both sides. These conditions were accepted by the Chinese, and in his communication conveying to the consul the fact of the acceptance, the Taotai of Ningpo—after quoting the twelfth article of the American treaty of 1858, which in fact authorizes residence and acquisition of property only at the open ports, and provides nothing for inland residence or the holding of inland property—observed that " according to his language, the treaty does not prohibit foreigners renting lands and building houses," and referring to the arrangement planned for making the exchange, added that " this seems to be for mutual harmony, and in accordance with the right principles." [1]   Again, in 1875 the committee for Foreign Affairs for the province of Fukien issued a special proclamation, which, after stating the principles of the Christian religion as declared in the treaties, apparently to give a reason for the " foreigners of every nationality conducting missionary operations in the interior of China," continues as follows:

In reference to foreigners obtaining land of the Chinese in the interior, under a perpetual lease, on which to construct chapels, the lease should be handed over by the foreigner concerned to his consul, and by him transmitted to the local authority for inspection, and in order to receive the official seal, and then returned to the foreigner.   And they are permitted to rent the premises of the people for use as chapels in all the cities, towns and villages as they may choose.   Let it be understood

[1] Taotai Koo to Consul Lord, Sept. 25, 1873, *For. Rel*, 1874, p. 239. For the remaining correspondence on the case, see *For. Rel.*, 1873, pt. i, pp. 118, 120, 122, 125, 127, 130, 135; *For. Rel.*, 1874, pp. 235, 237, 244.

that their renting buildings for chapels is, in all respects, the same as though the buildings were rented to merchants for shops, or to families as places of residence: the neighbors on either hand must not invent falsehoods, or raise objections, but must heed the treaties.

This proclamation is issued in order to fully inform you officials, seniors, soldiers, and common people that the purchase of premises, opening of chapels, and prosecuting of missionary work in all places by foreigners, is plainly specified in the treaty. If in any place a fraudulent sale is made, let full complaint be made to the local officials, and permit no local disturbance to the making of trouble.[1]

Mr. Avery, then minister at Peking, expressed the belief that " could such proclamations be issued in all the provinces . . . the number of missionary difficulties would soon be very small." [2] Six years later (1881), in another case, wherein American missionaries under the Presbyterian Board of Mission went to Tsinau Fu on traveling passports, there purchased, as usual, in the name of a Chinese Christian, a house situated by the side of the local college of literates, took possession of the property for six weeks and were then dispossessed by the literates for want of authentic deeds, the local officials willingly offered, at the suggestion of the missionaries, two locations from which the latter might select one in exchange for their original house, without raising the question as to their right of holding any property in the city.[3] In the same year the Southern Methodist Mission of the United States had already acquired property worth some $15,000 in Soochow; and upon its purchasing a new site in Yuenho Hien, and at the request of the missionaries, the magistrate thereof issued a special proclamation on December 31, 1881, in-

[1] *For. Rel.*, 1875, pt. i, p. 404.   [2] *Ibid.*, p. 402.
[3] *For. Rel.*, 1881, pp. 287, 291.

structing the constables and the people of that place " to
bear in mind that the renting or purchasing of land by
foreign missionaries for the building of houses in which
to preach the doctrines of Christianity, is in accordance
with treaty stipulations," and warning unprincipled persons
not to " take advantage of any cause to create disturbance in that vicinity " under pain of arrest and punishment.[1] The American chargé d'affaires, referring to this
proclamation, said:

This document is interesting and valuable, since it not only
shows a favorable disposition on the part of the Chinese
authorities towards our people, but admits a right which has
not been claimed by us under the treaties, *i. e.*, the right of
missionaries to purchase and hold for the use of their work
real estate at interior points in China.

When Chinese local authorities generally shall accept the
liberal position taken by the district negotiate at Soochow, we
shall be relieved of many delicate and complicated questions
which now vex the diplomatic relations of China and the
United States.[2]

On the part of the British Government much caution
has been exhibited in dealing with the question of permanent residence and acquisition of property by British missionaries in the interior of China.   To the argument advanced by the British missionary body in 1861, in support
of the action of two of its members in purchasing a property in Poklo, an inland district in Kwang-tung in the face
of opposition from the local gentry, that the right to make
such a purchase was conceded by the twelfth article of the
British treaty of 1858, which provided that " British subjects, whether at the ports or at other places " might buy

---

[1] *For. Rel.*, 1882, p. 132.

[2] Mr. Holcombe, chargé at Peking, to Mr. Frelinghuysen, Sec. of
State, Mar. 4, 1882, *For. Rel.*, 1882, p. 132.

land and build or open houses, warehouses, churches, etc., the representatives of the British Government in China replied by stating that the interpretation placed by them on the words " at other places " was not admitted; and when they took retreat under the favored nation clause and claimed the privileges believed to have been secured to the French missionaries by the sixth article of the French convention of 1860, they were given to understand that Her Majesty's Government was reluctant to insist upon the claim.[1]   In 1868 their position in the interior remained unimproved.   When, in that year, a British evangelist received, as a present from a Chinese family, to be used for missionary purposes, a temple situated in Chihia Hien Shan-tung, and sent the deed of gift to his consul to be stamped by the local authorities, the consul notified him, subsequently, that the Taotai of Chefoo refused to affix his seal to the deed and that he would not prosecute the claim any further.   The Committee of the Baptist Missionary Society thereupon communicated the facts of the case to the British foreign office and inquired whether British subjects have a right by treaty to hire, purchase, or receive as a gift, land or buildings in China, if natives were disposed to let, sell, or give." [2]   The question was referred to Sir Rutherford Alcock, the British minister at Peking, and on May 19, 1869, upon his advice, the Earl of Clarendon gave him the following instructions.[3]

I have to acquaint you that her Majesty's Government agree with you that it is not incumbent on them to insist in favour of British missionaries on the privileges conceded to Roman Catholic missionaries, and brave the consequences of doing so.

[1] *Parl. Papers*, China, no 5 (1871), 116.

[2] Rev. F. Trestrail to Lord Stanley, Dec. 8, 1868, *Parl. Papers*, China, no 9 (1870), 1

[3] *Parl. Papers*, China, no. 9 (1870), 4

But still less would they feel disposed to do so, when, as appears to be the case, the privileges claimed for the Roman Catholic missionaries rest on no sound foundation, but on an interpolation of words in the Chinese version alone of the French Treaty with China.

You will, therefore, not allow British missionaries to suppose that, in virtue of that interpolation, Her Majesty's Government can support their pretensions to any other privilege of residence and locomotion in China than British subjects in general may enjoy, and should it be necessary, you will warn them that if they seek to assert greater privileges they will do so at their own risk and responsibility, and must not expect any action or forcible interference on the part of Her Majesty's Government for their relief.

Early in April, 1870, the National Bible Society of Scotland renewed, in a memorial to the Earl, the claims previously advanced by other missionaries bodies, but received no better than the following:[1]

Her Majesty's Government is not prepared to insist on any such extended construction of the term " place " in the XII Article, as is suggested by the Memorialists. If the Article was subject to be construed in that sense, the limitation of trade to certain specified ports would have been superfluous.

Her Majesty's Government, whatever may be the claim asserted by the French Government in behalf of French missionaries, are not prepared to claim for British missionaries any other privileges than those that may be enjoyed by other British subjects.

In his circular of September 20, 1870,[2] Mr. Wade, British minister at Peking, instructs the British consuls in China that the reply decides two points:

[1] Mr. Hammond to Hon A. Kinnaird, Apr. 14, 1870, *Parl. Papers, China*, no 1 (1871), 170.

[2] *Ibid.*

1st. That, under Treaty, the British missionary body had no right of residence in China distinct from the right of any other British subject.

2nd. That, the right of British subjects to residence can be exercised only at the Treaty ports, or in their immediate vicinity.[1]

Mr. Wade further states that as the consul " is responsible for the control, and more or less for the protection of his port community," the safest rule for him will be that . . . " he is not at liberty to sanction permanent residence at points so distant, or so isolated, as to make it impossible to satisfy these obligations"; although he adds that in his opinion it would be " inexpedient that any position now occupied by a British mission inland should be . . . precipitately abandoned." Finally, Sir C. MacDonald, in his Despatch of March 17, 1898,[2] to the Marquis of Salisbury, positively declares that in view of the Berthemy convention of 1865, as modified in 1895, and the imperial decree of August, 1895, ordering the protection of all missionary establishments in China, he is of the opinion that " missionaries have the right to acquire property for the purposes of their mission in all parts of the Chinese Empire."

The Government of the United States appears to have been more desirous, or less disinclined, than the British Government to support the establishment of permanent

---

[1] The term " immediate vicinity" has been, in one notable instance, extended "at the Port of Kiukiang a manner to which it would perhaps be hard to find a parallel elsewhere in China" This is the case of the Kuling estate and the surrounding properties leased by the Chinese officials to individual foreigners, British, American, and Russian, for building sanatoriums and summer houses. The properties aggregate something like a square mile, and are located at distances ranging from about 6 to about 16 miles from Kiukiang, the port.—*Parl. Papers*, China, no. 1 (1903), 32.

[2] *Parl. Papers*, China, no. 1 (1899), 60.

residence and the acquisition of property by its missionaries in the interior of China.   The views which have been
iterated and reiterated, by the successive heads of the
American legation at Peking and the state department at
Washington, both in connection with actual cases and in
the abstract discussion of the general question, are substantially the same.   On one hand, it has never been denied
by them that the treaties which China has concluded with
the United States, or with any other foreign nation confer
no legal right upon American missionaries to reside permanently in the interior, and there to acquire and hold
real property; on the other, it has been claimed by them,
with equal persistence, that a permissive or prescriptive or
quasi legal right, as it is variously described, has accrued
to American missionaries in certain localities in China
where the authorities have, by express permission or tacit
acquiescence, allowed citizens or subjects of other foreign
Powers to be permanently located.   In such places equality
of treatment will always be insisted upon by the United
States in behalf of its own citizens.   In other localities,
where no tolerance has been accorded any foreigner to
settle, as a permanent resident, the United States leaves it
to the zeal, enterprise, and ability of the missionaries themselves to blaze a fresh field for their pious cultivation.   If
they meet with popular opposition, and fail in their attempt
to plant their outposts in new territory, the United States
Government regards it as a misfortune, but it does not
hold itself bound, as in fact it is not entitled under the
treaties, to claim for its own missionaries a privilege which
has not been enjoyed by those of other foreign states.
Should they succeed in establishing a permanent foothold
in a new locality with the knowledge, but without the opposition, of the people and the authorities, it countenances
the success with favor, beholds it with satisfaction, and,

on account of their self-denial and philanthropic motives, is disposed to congratulate, rather than to censure, them. It besides, considers it proper and advisable for its diplomatic and consular representatives to assist the missionaries in any reasonable effort to secure grounds for the prosecution of their business, although it maintains at the same time that they have no right to insist upon acquiring property in such new localities. In other words the effort on the part of the missionaries to establish a permanent residence in inland districts where no tolerance has previously been extended to foreigners other than as temporary sojourners on travel, as well as the primary securing of land or house property therein to enable them to carry on their proselytizing labors, must be their own individual acts. But wherever the American missionaries may be, in the interior as well as in the open ports, and in whatever character they may be there, whether as permanent residents or as passing travelers, the Government of the United States holds that they with everything appertaining to them are entitled to the protection of the local authorities, that if they transgress the law or usage of the place, they must be proceeded against according to treaty provisions, and that under no circumstances will it allow its citizens to be subjected to expulsion or ejectment by mob violence or without due process of law.

In a word, the United States Government, recognizing it to be "the inherent and inalienable right of man to change his home," is not disposed to discourage, still less to prevent, its citizens in China from settling in the interior of China, but will, on the other hand, remonstrate against the discontinuance of the right of residence and of holding property in inland districts when it has once been enjoyed by its own citizens or those of other foreign powers through the sufferance of the authorities; leaving it to the

Chinese Government and its agents to enforce, if they can, the restrictions provided in the treaties on the right of foreigners to reside and acquire property in China within the limits of the open ports—a restriction which is a usual, fair, and generally necessary condition of enjoying the privileges of extraterritoriality.[1]

It is to be noted, however, that so far as the missionaries who desire to acquire and hold property in the interior in the name of some organized missions, to which they belong, are concerned, the question has been settled by the fourteenth article of the American treaty of Shanghai, October 8, 1903, which provides:

Missionary Societies of the United States shall be permitted to rent and to lease in perpetuity, as the property of such Societies, buildings or lands in all parts of the Empire for missionary purposes, and, after the title-deeds have been found in order and duly stamped by the local authorities, to erect such suitable buildings as may be required for carrying on their good work.

As regards American missionaries in China belonging to no particular church or missionary society, they now stand where they have always stood. In his instructions to Min-

[1] The statement of the views of the United States Government given above is based on the following despatches and instructions: Mr Low to Mr Beebe, Jan. 15, 1873, For. Rel., 1875, pt i, p. 338; Mr. Avery to Mr De Lano, Dec 28, 1874, For Rel, 1875, pt. i, p. 334, Mr. Avery to Mr. Fish, June 1, 1875, For. Rel, 1875, pt. i, p. 332; Mr. Fish to Mr. Avery, July 30, 1875, For. Rel., 1875, pt. i, p. 398; Mr. Cadwalader to Mr. Avery, Aug. 11, 1875, For. Rel., 1875, pt. i, p. 399; Mr. Angell to Messrs Murray and Hunter, July 30, 1881, For. Rel., 1881, p. 289; Mr. Holcombe to Mr. Carrow, May 6, 1882, For. Rel., 1882, p 139; Mr. Frelinghuysen to Mr. Young, July 3, 1882, For. Rel., 1882, p. 142; Mr. Denby to Mr. Bayard, Oct 9, 1886, For Rel, 1886, p 96; Mr Denby to Mr. Bayard, May 19, 1888, For. Rel, 1888, pt 1, p 270; Mr. Bayard to Mr. Reid, July 17, 1888, For. Rel., 1888, pt i, p 325

ister Rockhill, March 22, 1906,[1] as to their right to acquire property in the interior of China, Secretary of State Root states that an examination by the department of the various treaties with China " clearly shows such a right to be legally non-existent ". They may claim in certain localities " an equitable or quasi legal right based upon custom "; and the circumstances under which, and the extent to which the department will support them in the obtainment of such a right are thus described ·

In meritorious cases, in which the circumstances were such as to give rise to no objection on other grounds than the unwillingness of China to consent to sales of land to Americans in the interior, this department would find great force in the argument that inasmuch as China, through her officials, has in numerous instances permitted the subjects of other nationalities to purchase land in certain localities in the interior, this Government may, with good reason, consider such purchases as precedents establishing the right of Americans, whether members or non-members of a missionary body, to make similar purchases.

It is to be pointed out that Mr. Low's views on the measure of protection to be extended to American property in the interior stand unsupported by the views of the department of state and of other American representatives at Peking. His views are thus:

2nd. If property be purchased and buildings erected thereon, and they should be damaged or destroyed by mob or other violence of the Chinese, the claim for damages would be an equitable rather than a legal one; and if the local, or the imperial, authorities should refuse to respond, upon the ground that the property was purchased in violation of treaty-rights, it is extremely doubtful if our Government would sanction any

[1] H. Ex Doc. 1, 59 Cong, 2 Sess, p. 277.

proceedings which might be instituted by its diplomatic or consular officers to collect it.

It was added, also, that property rented for permanent residence inland " would be subject to the same rules and liable to the same disabilities as purchased property." [1]

In purchasing or leasing land or houses in the interior the principles and rules which are provided by the treaties for similar acts in the open ports do not apply. In 1893 when the officials at Nanking promulgated a new rule requiring foreigners desirous of acquiring property, first to agree with the elders and gentry of the place, and then report to the authorities for an official survey of the ground, the department of state instructed Mr. Denby that " the adoption of such a measure at a treaty port would undoubtedly be a contravention of the treaty, being an interference by the local authorities, in advance, to prescribe initial negotiations otherwise than directly between the lessor and the lessee, but that he " cannot be expected to intervene in such action outside of the treaty ports," intimating, at the same time, a desire to know on what ground his notification was made to the Taotai of Nanking, through the acting consul, that the proposed rule would not be acquiesced in or acted upon by the legation.[2] In 1911, with a view to the avoidance of complications usually attendant upon foreigners acquiring property in the interior, the Waiwu Pu, after consultation with the foreign representatives at Peking, drew up six rules governing the matter, and sent instructions to the Provinces to enforce their observance. These rules are: (1) that property-owners shall be free to sell their property and the missions desiring to buy shall not coerce them to sell; (2) that the missions,

[1] *For. Rel*, 1875, pt. i, p. 338.
[2] Mr Gresham to Mr. Denby, June 5, 1893, *For. Rel*, 1893, p. 233

shall, before purchasing any property, consult the local officials and request them to make an official survey of the ground and ascertain the records: (3) that after the purchase is made, they shall apply to the authorities for a tax-deed; (4) that the property purchased shall always remain the property of the mission, and a tablet shall be erected to record its ownership; (5) that if the mission, after purchasing a property should sell it to Chinese, they are prohibited clandestinely to sell it to foreigners; (6) that the local authorities shall forbid the purchase of property in all cases where the property is purchased in the name of a mission, but not to be used for the purposes of the mission, or where it is to be used for foreign merchants for trading purposes.[1]

§ 5. *Prosecution of Secular Work*

The question of the right of the missionary to engage in secular work in the interior, though an important one, has not been seriously raised. The treaties are silent on the subject; they contain no provision which might be cited in support of a claim to such a right. In practice, however, all kinds of work are tolerated in the interior. The missionaries maintain printing establishments, bookbinderies, industrial schools, dispensaries, boarding houses for strangers; they are doctors, colporteurs, newspaper correspondents; they do washing and sewing; they manufacture and sell all kinds of furniture. It is, of course, understood that the profits of these various enterprises go to the general fund of the mission, and are used to promote religious purposes. In 1896 an American missionary at Tak Cheo, Kansuh, inquired of Mr Denby if he could lawfully engage in " agriculture, stock raising, or trading," as a means of support while laboring as a missionary among the Thibetan

[1] *Eastern Times,* Shanghai, April 19, 1911

border tribes." [1] The minister replied that he was unable
to draw a line between pursuits, such as those mentioned
above, already permitted by the Chinese authorities and
those proposed by the inquirer. In apprising the state department of his reply Mr. Denby observed that the question was one of first impression, and that in his view

If the particular enterprise engaged in any locality is not prohibited by the officials and is allowed to be prosecuted without
objection, it would finally be sanctioned by usage, and might
be entitled to protection of the treaty powers.

The department considered his views to be " discreet ".
It also expressed the opinion that while some of the secular
operations tolerated by the local authorities, such as the
manufacture of furniture, laundry, and sewing, were
" not, obviously, part of the privilege of residence," still if
they were for any reason opposed, the argument " might
be validly advanced, the case arising, that the residential
privilege embraces all normal uses to which the ground and
the belongings can be applied "; adding that " if attempt
be made at any time to restrict the existing usage, the proposition herein outlined would afford ground upon which to
base remonstrance and conduct suitable argument." [2]

[1] Mr. Simpson to Mr. Denby, Nov. 18, 1896, *For. Rel.*, 1897, p 106.
[2] Mr. Rockhill to Mr. Denby, March 29, 1897, *ibid*, p. 105.

CHAPTER XVII

PROTECTION OF ALIENS AND ALIEN PROPERTY

THE treaties generally provide for the protection of foreigners in China by the Chinese authorities. They are to be defended from insult or injury of any sort. If their dwellings or property be threatened or attacked by mobs, incendiaries, robbers, or other violent persons, the local officials are required to take the necessary steps for the recovery of the stolen property, the suppression of disorder and the arrest of the guilty parties, who are to be punished according to the law of the land. Some treaties contain express provisions to the effect that in such contingencies of danger to the persons or property of foreigners, the local officials, on requisition of the consul or without it, shall despatch soldiers to the scene of trouble for the purpose already mentioned.[1] In a few treaties it is also stipulated that the punishment of the offenders cannot prejudice the prosecution of suits against them, by the parties entitled thereto, to recover damages for the losses sustained.[2] But if the authorities, whose charge it is, fail to arrest the guilty persons, no other compensation can be required of the Chinese Government than the punishment of these authorities according to the laws of China.[3]

[1] See, especially, American treaty of June 18, 1858, art. xi; French treaty of June 27, 1858, art. xxxvi; Belgian treaty of March 2, 1865, art. xvii.

[2] See, especially, treaty with France, June 27, 1858, art. xxxvi; with Germany, Sept 2, 1861, art. xxxvi.

[3] See, especially, treaty with Denmark, July 13, 1863, art. xviii; with Spain, Oct. 10, 1864, art. xvi; with Belgium, Nov. 2, 1865, art. xvii; with Italy, Oct. 26, 1866, art. xviii; with Austria-Hungary, Sept. 2, 1869, art. xli.

The measure of protection provided by the treaties for foreigners in China is variously described as being special, full and entire, complete, or the fullest.   But in view of the treatment of foreigners in China, immediately antecedent to the commencement of the conventional period, and of the provision in the American treaty of 1844, reproduced in that of 1858, that citizens of the United States in China peaceably attending to their affairs are " placed on a common footing of amity and good will with subjects of China ", it would appear reasonable to suggest that the different terms employed in predicating the requisite measure of protection all mean the same thing: that foreigners in China shall be protected by the authorities to the same degree as Chinese subjects are; it, of course, being presumed that each country exercises a most vigilant care in protecting its own nationals.

In the protection of subjects or citizens of treaty Powers no distinction based on their whereabouts in China can be made.   The Chinese authorities are required equally to protect them, whether residing at the open ports or engaged in traveling or in missionary operations in the interior.   The British treaty of 1858 provides that the fullest protection is to be afforded to the persons and property of British subjects " wherever these shall have been subjected to insult or violence."   The American treaty of the same year stipulates for the protection by the local authorities of " all citizens of the United States of America in China."   The protection clauses in the treaties with other foreign states are clothed in similarly comprehensive terms.[1]

In actual practice the efforts of the Chinese Govern-

---

[1] It is interesting to note that while the thirty-sixth article in the French text of the treaty of 1858 stipulates for protection of French citizens without any qualification, the same article in the Chinese text mentions only " Frenchmen at the various ports open to foreign trade."

ment and local authorities to insure the safety of foreigners in China are not infrequently aided by their own Governments. Under normal conditions the security of the lives and property of the foreign residents or travelers in the interior depends, naturally and necessarily, upon the local authorities while those who reside in the open parts are under the immediate protection of the local police, Chinese or foreign, as the case may be, the consuls, and the Chinese authorities, supported by foreign as well as Chinese warships. When a popular outbreak occurs at an inland point where foreign persons or property may be in danger, it is not uncommon to see foreign gunboats dispatched to the scene of disturbance, if such access is possible, to assist the local authorities in carrying out protective measures;[1] and if the times become generally turbulent, as in

[1] The question of the right of foreign gunboats to visit inland points was somewhat warmly discussed in 1903 by the diplomatic and naval representatives of the United States in China. The United States gunboat "Villalobos," apparently on the initiative of her own commander, made a visit to Nanchang on Poyang Lake, which provoked a protest by the Taotai at Kiukiang on the ground, among others, that the presence of foreign armed vessels in an inland district might give occasion to bad men for making trouble. In an instruction to the commander of the "Villalobos," approving his visit, Rear-Admiral Evans, in command of the American Asiatic Fleet, also authorized him to state to the Taotai and other Chinese that the American gunboats "are always amply provided for dealing with 'bad men,'" and they would, without further instructions, "administer severe and lasting punishment" to them, should they indicate any desire "to pay other than proper respect to American life and property;" that the Chinese officials were expected to suppress all disorder and give ample protection to Americans, but that if they should fail to do so, the American gunboats would take in hand "the question of adequate and proper protection", and that "In order to satisfy ourselves that the various local authorities are properly [protecting Americans].... our gunboats will continue to navigate the Poyang Lake and the various other inland waters of China wherever Americans may be, and where, by treaty with China, they are authorized

the case of a civil or international war, it is not unusual on the part of the foreign legations and consulates to recall their nationals in the interior to open ports, where concerted measures are, in such cases, frequently taken by the

to engage in business or reside for the purpose of spreading the gospel "—*For. Rel.,* 1903, p. 87.

On being apprised of the substance of these instructions, and in referring to the protest of the Taotai, Minister Conger requested Rear-Admiral Evans to point out the provisions which gave the American gunboats the right to go wherever they pleased, in the waters of China, except on rivers leading to open ports. The Rear-Admiral, in his reply of August 11, 1903, stated that although he might be unable to point out any specific provision, as requested of him, in the treaties concluded between China and the United States, he considered that American gunboats, under the favored nation clause, were entitled to the same rights in the Poyang Lake and the neighboring waters which were exercised by the gunboats of various other nationalities for similar purposes; and that besides, he considered his duty to watch over and protect the lives and property of American citizens engaged in any lawful pursuit in China, and to keep himself informed of their conditions, and be ready instantly to send an armed force to wherever it was necessary.—*For. Rel.,* 1903, p. 88.

The question was finally referred to Washington, and Secretary of State Hay, in his reply of October 7, 1903, to the request of the Secretary of the Navy to make such comment as he might desire, observed:

" That the Department is inclined to the opinion that Rear-Admiral Evans is right in his contention that our gunboats may visit the inland ports of China, including those which are not treaty ports. Even if this right were not explicitly granted to us by treaty, Rear-Admiral Evans is unquestionably right in using it when like ships of other powers are constantly doing so His reasons for wishing to visit these places, as expressed in his communication of August 11, 1903, to Minister Conger, are absolutely convincing.

" This Department thinks, however, that article lii of the British treaty of 1858 with China, which is reproduced in article xxxiv of the Austro-Hungarian treaty of 1869 gives full authority for his course." —*For. Rel.,* 1903, p. 90 Here followed the text of the article in the British treaty, which, in part, provides that " British ships of war coming for no bestial purpose, or being engaged in the pursuit of pirates, shall be at liberty to visit all ports within the dominions of the Emperor of China."

Treaty-Powers for the joint protection of nationals, or to the Legation Quarter in Peking, which, by treaty, may be put in a state of defense. By special arrangements with the Chinese Government or the local authorities, foreign marines and troops were at different times in the past landed in the foreign settlements at the open ports to insure the safety of the foreigners and their property situated therein.[1]

It is also to be stated that in a crisis or civil commotion or anti-foreign outbreak, whether actual or apprehended, white foreign residents in the interior are willing to withdraw to open ports; they commonly leave their property behind in the care of the local officials, who are thus subject to an onerous responsibility and sometimes to practical difficulties, but who, as a rule prove equal to this extraordinary task. The procedure has often been followed. May 25, 1853, Mr. H. Marshall, United States commissioner to China, for instance, in response to an appeal from the American residents in Fuchow for the protection made

---

[1] Ex-Secretary of State Elihu Root, in his presidential address before the American Society of International Law, April 28, 1910, "The Basis of Protection to Citizens Residing Abroad" (4 *Am. Jour. of Intern Law,* 516), stated with reference to the landing of armed forces in a foreign country for the protection of their nationals: "Such a course is undoubtedly often necessary, but is always an impeachment of the effective sovereignty of the government in whose territory the armed demonstration occurs, and it can be justified only by unquestionable facts which leave no doubt of the incapacity of the government of the country to perform its international duty of protection. It leads to many abuses, especially in the conduct of those nationals who, feeling that they are backed up by a navy, act as if they were superior to the laws of the country in which they are residing and permit their sense of immunity to betray them into arrogant and offensive disrespect." The same practice, it may be added, also induces clamour on the part of the missionaries in the interior of China, often to the amazement even of their own Government, for the presence of gunboats at their missionary stations on seeing the slightest symptoms of trouble or disturbance.

in view of the then threatened approach of the Taiping rebels, gave them this order:[1]

You will cause an inventory of your property, real and personal, to be made out in due form, exhibiting, item, the value as estimated by two disinterested valuers. Should any emergency arise which immediately threatens your persons or property, you will deposit the said inventory or the duplicate with the chief local authority at Fuchow, and at the same time you cause seals to be placed upon your effects and upon your doors. You will then request the said chief local authority to place a military guard over said property for its especial protection, as the treaty provides. You will say to the chief local authority of Fuchow that these proceedings, on your part, are taken by my instructions to you, in order that there may be no mistake on his part of the intention of the United States to hold China responsible under the treaty to indemnify the American citizens for any loss or damage their persons may sustain by the lawlessness or violence of the subjects of China, and that he may regulate his actions accordingly.

The difficult position in which Chinese officials of Kiangsi Province were placed in 1900 by foreigners who left their property in their care was graphically described by British Consul W. J. Clennell of Kiukiang in his report,[2] on Kiangsi. He said:

It must be admitted that the position of the Chinese officials during the crisis was one of great difficulty. At a time of extraordinary public danger and excitement, with popular feeling roused to fever heat all over the country, with anti-foreign or anti-dynastic movements breaking out in more or less seri-

[1] H. Ex. Doc. 123, 33 Cong. Sess., 162. Instructions of a similar nature were issued by Mr. H. Marshall to the American Consulate of Canton, September 22, 1853, *ibid.*, p. 276.

[2] *Parl. Papers*, China, no. 1 (1903), i, 33.

ous rioting on every side, while the issue of the greater struggle in the North yet hung in the balance, and a large proportion of the populace, and even of the better instructed, sincerely believed in the Boxers' claim to invulnerability, or, at the least, supernatural assistance, while every day brought reports, true or false, of fresh alarms, and no one knew what the morrow might bring forth, or how far and how soon this province might be involved in the general upheaval, while trade was at a standstill, throwing thousands everywhere out of employment, in a season when drought had destroyed the harvest and caused widespread suffering, the officials had suddenly thrown on their hands for safekeeping an extraordinarily miscellaneous collection of private property, ranging from surgical instrument-cases to boxes of winter clothing, and from brood mares and Australian bulls to cats and dogs, not to mention the books and fittings of mission chapels, household furniture of all kinds, magic lanterns, pianos, and in fact almost every movable thing that can be named. In some cases, probably in most, careful inventories had been made out and filed in the Yamens, but this was by no means so in every instance.

Mr. Clennell also stated that foreigners on their return found that some articles were lost or stolen but that in some cases the stolen property, such as ponies and cattle, were recovered and in some, compensation was given. "As things were," he concluded, " and especially in view of the common belief that the evacuation would be a permanent one, wonder can only be felt that so small a proportion of the foreigners' possessions went astray ".

CHAPTER XVIII

SUBJECTS OF NON-TREATY POWERS

As has been stated in Chapter XII the protegé system which flourishes in Turkey, Morocco, and elsewhere, does not exist in China. The Chinese Government has always maintained its right of control over the subjects of non-treaty-powers within its territory, and the treaty powers have never contested the claim; on the contrary, by express declarations and consistent practice of abstention from interference in behalf of such persons in China, they have unquestionably recognized its validity. The protection which they have from time to time accordéd the subjects of non-treaty powers has been confined to the exercise of good offices, as the term is generally understood.

On the part of the Chinese authorities two courses of action have been pursued in the actual treatment of the subjects of nations maintaining no treaty relations with China. In the early years of foreign intercourse, though fully conscious of their unchallenged right to do it, they generally manifested a disinclination, due partly to their want of familiarity with the usages of the west and partly to the practical difficulty, in their minds, of distinguishing by sight the subjects of one western nation from those of another, to adopt regulations looking to the control of the persons of non-treaty powers. The fact that nearly all foreigners in China formed communities of their own, segregated from the Chinese world, as it were, also encouraged the Chinese authorities to think that special regulations for the purpose stated were unnecessary. The result of this policy soon proved its inexpediency. In the words of an American diplomat written in 1858, " there is an absolute immunity of the citizens of non-treaty powers. A Saxon, or Swede,[1] or Dane, or Prussian does as he pleases. He defies law, commits crime with impunity, refuses the payment of duties or debts." [2] Besides, designing merchants belonging to some one of the non-treaty powers, arrogated to themselves the title of consul, under cover of which they committed smuggling and other illegal acts. When under the majority of the treaties revised in 1858 foreigners of nations having treaties with China gained the right to travel in the interior, the Chinese Government began to see the danger of having subjects of non-treaty powers wander into all parts of the Empire unrestrained. Accordingly it laid the situation before the American minister and asked him for advice as to the control of such subjects, stating at the same time that it was " plain " that they " should not be placed on the same footing as the subjects of those nations having treaties." [3] The minister gave two practical suggestions: " Make treaties with such powers, small and great, as approach them [Chinese authorities] for that purpose " and " resolutely refuse to recognize these interloping officials [merchant-consuls of non-treaty powers]".[4]

During the last half a century the policy of the Chinese

[1] As a matter of fact, a treaty of peace, amity, and commerce was concluded between China and Sweden and Norway, March 20, 1847, but it may be that no consuls were appointed by the latter up to 1858.

[2] Mr. Reed to Mr. Cass, July 29, 1858, S Ex. Doc 30, 36 Cong., 1 Sess, p. 382

[3] Imperial Commissioners to Mr. Reed, Nov. 1, 1858, S. Ex Doc. 30, 36 Cong., 1 Sess., p. 314.

[4] *Ibid*, p 516.

Government appears to have been, on one hand, to grant a status to the subjects of non-treaty powers by according to them certain privileges which were enjoyed by the subjects of treaty powers, and, on the other, to place them within the more perfect control of the Chinese authorities. Thus take, for example, the right to trade. In 1861 the Tsungli Yamen instructed the superintendent of the trade of the southern ports to prohibit foreigners of non-treaty states to trade at any open port other than those situated along the coast.[1] The following year they were forbidden to trade at any port without first obtaining the consent of some recognized consul at that port to exercise his friendly offices in their behalf; failing which, in the phraseology of the instructions, " not only, they will not be allowed to trade there, but if they are maltreated or injured, the local officials will not hold themselves responsible." [2] But in recent times they are expressly authorized by imperial decrees to reside and trade, for instance, in the ports opened by China of her free will, as long as they submit to the laws and authorities of China.

The privilege of the subjects of non-treaty states to travel in the interior of China has undergone a similar course of development. In 1861, when there existed as yet no treaty relations between the Netherlands and China, a Netherlander, who had traveled to Peking under a passport issued by the Shanghai Taotai, was taken back to that city by order of the Tsungli Yamen, which at the same time sent instructions to the Provinces stating that " the subjects of non-treaty powers shall not be allowed to travel in the interior." [3] Subsequently, regular traveling passports were permitted to be issued to those foreigners whose nations

[1] 68 *New Coll.* (General), 34.   [2] *Ibid.*
[3] 70 *New Coll.* (General), 28.

had no treaties with China, but who were placed by their own Government under the friendly protection of some legation in Peking. This practice was recently discontinued. In 1908, on reference by the Hukuang Viceroy for a decision of the question raised by the Customs Taotai at Hankow whether regular passports might continue to be issued to Turkish subjects under the friendly protection of the German diplomatic and consular representatives in China, as when under the care of the French legation, the Waiwu Pu rendered this ruling:

We find that it has already been declared that subjects of non-treaty powers while on travel in China shall be treated in the same manner as Chinese are, and therefore passports need no longer be issued to them In all respects such subjects shall hereafter be looked upon as if they were Chinese, in order to safeguard China's right of jurisdiction.[1]

Under the instructions of the foreign office issued to the Provinces in 1909 there are provided, for subjects of non-treaty powers desiring to travel in the interior, special protection papers, which they may obtain on application, by themselves or through some consul willing to accord them the benefit of his good offices, to a commissioner of foreign affairs or a customs Taotai. The local authorities are required, " upon finding the papers to be proper, to extend to the holders due protection and look upon them as if they were Chinese subjects." [2]

Nor has China relaxed in the exercise of her jurisdiction over the subjects of non-treaty states In 1869 the Tsungli Yamen, apropos of a case of robbery committed by certain unknown foreigners in Chefoo, sent a circular note to the foreign legations at Peking stating that when

[1] 70 New Coll. (General), 33
[2] 11 Hsuen Tung's New Laws and Ordinances, 41.

persons of non-treaty powers committed crimes on land or water within the Chinese dominions, they should be arrested, tried, and punished by the Chinese authorities according to Chinese law; and the published replies of the American, British, and French representatives show that they all admitted the principle without question, although they made suggestions, also, looking to the mitigation of the rigor of the Chinese criminal law in cases where foreigners of non-treaty powers were defendants.[1]   Recently the Chinese Government has redoubled its efforts to safe-guard the rightful jurisdiction.   In the police regulations for the ports voluntarily opened by China to foreign trade it is uniformly provided that when foreigners whose Governments have no treaties with China violate the laws or regulations, or are sued in a civil action, the case shall be tried and adjudicated by Chinese authorities.[2]

An interesting case in which a subject of a non-treaty power was defendant, occurred in 1904, and was summarily dealt with by the Chinese authorities   Within four months of his stay in Peking this individual committed six grave crimes, such as assault and battery, highway robbery, and the like.   Strangely, the police department in the

---

[1] The American minister suggested that in such cases a foreign consul might be invited to assist in the trial by Chinese authorities. The British and French representatives reserved their right of interposing in behalf of those foreigners who asked for, and they consented to extend to them, their good offices. The French minister intimated also that in a case where a subject of a non-treaty state was defendant he "should not be subjected to unduly severe punishment, in order to avoid incurring the displeasure" of foreign nations. The English minister expressed "his hope that since the Chinese criminal code is exceedingly severe, the case may not always be decided according to Chinese law, lest it will violate the feelings of the foreign people."— 69 *New Collection* (General), 14-15.

[2] See, for example, articles 6 and 7 of the *Regulations for the port of Chinanfu*, 1904, H. Ex. Doc., 59 Cong., 2 Sess., p 166.

Chinese capital at the outset did not order his arrest but went about to ascertain his nationality, as he had refused to reveal it. The doyen of the diplomatic corps, the Austrian minister, stated that if the culprit refused to tell the truth about his own nationality, China might expel him from the country. It appeared, afterwards, however, that he was a Greek subject under the nominal protection of the French legation. When approached for information, the French minister stated that the Greek, being an inveterate criminal, had long been placed outside of the pale of French protection, and that he would not interfere at all, but leave him to be dealt with by other nations as they saw fit. Thereupon he was arrested by the local police and taken to Tientsin, where he was tried before Tan Shao-yi, then Customs Taotai at that port, convicted, his property worth about $320 was confiscated, and he himself sentenced to imprisonment with the proviso that he would be released as soon as some reliable foreign firm appeared to guarantee that he would, after release, immediately leave China and never return again.[1]

As may be gathered from what has been said at the beginning of the section, the fact that the subjects of a non-treaty power are placed by their own Government under the friendly protection of a foreign legation in the Chinese Capital, does not at all entitle them to the treaty exemption from the jurisdiction of Chinese Courts. In 1908 when the German minister represented to the Waiwu Pu that in compliance with Turkey's request the German Government had instructed him to act in behalf of the Turkish Government in matters arising between China and Turkey, the Waiwu Pu replied that the German minister would be recognized " as the intermediary between the two countries

---

[1] ɔ9 *New Collection* (General), 28-30.

so far as ordinary matters were concerned ", but that it wished to declare again that " subjects of non-treaty powers residing in China are subject, as heretofore, to the judicial power of China, and they will be treated in the same manner as Chinese subjects.   In a word, whatever the case may be, Turkish subjects will be dealt with as the subjects of other non-treaty states."   Instructions to this effect were also sent to the Provincial authorities.[1]

[1] 70 *New Collection* (General), 33.

CHAPTER XIX

CONCLUSION

FROM the foregoing chapters it seems clear that in spite of their frequent allegations that the Chinese are exclusive and anti-foreign, foreigners in China enjoy very many rights and privileges which are not accorded to aliens in other countries. Their persons, their dwelling houses, and, to a very large extent, their property are all invested with the immunities of extraterritoriality. It is true that this special status is guaranteed to them by treaties and they are therefore entitled to it; yet at the same time it may be said that their peaceful enjoyment of it has been made possible only by the favorable disposition toward them alike of the Government and people of China. Misfortunes have indeed befallen them sometimes as the result of official malfeasance or mob violence, but to what extent this fact is peculiar to China, is fairly an open question. On the other hand, the Chinese Government itself has, as a rule, shown a keen solicitude for their security in person and property, and has treated them with liberality and consideration. It was this favorable disposition toward foreigners as such which led China to accord them the privilege of unrestricted intercourse with her own subjects and place them on an equal footing with the latter even in early days before the conventional period; and although the rights and privileges which they now possess in China were secured at the outset with the aid of the sword, it was the same favorable disposition on the part of China toward aliens which has made possible not only the peaceful enjoyment of these rights and privileges but also the extension of the same with nearly every revision of the treaties. Instances of restrictive measures against foreigners are indeed not wanting, but these have been adopted rather for protection against their abuse of the extraordinary immunities which they enjoy rather than for the purpose of discriminating against them on the ground of their alienage.

Of the problems which have arisen from the intercourse between Chinese and foreigners in China, two have claimed the greater part of the attention of the Chinese Government and the Governments of the treaty powers. These are religion and commerce, being a natural outcome of the fact that the foreign element in China has always consisted mostly of missionaries and merchants. To take the former first, missionary cases, or church cases as they are called by the Chinese, have occurred with a discomforting frequency; chapels have been burned, missionaries killed or injured, and Chinese Christians have fallen victims to popular wrath. Many of these cases ended with disastrous consequences to China. Over a billion dollars have been paid, a number of strategic points of territory have been reliquished, the prestige of the nation has been seriously impaired, hundreds of officials, high and low, have been humiliated, and thousands of lives of a humbler order have been sacrificed. Yet curiously enough, hardly a single one of these has ever arisen out of a strictly religious controversy based on differences of the Chinese and foreign creeds. One and all, they appear to have taken birth in those defects of personal understanding and conduct, on one side or the other, accentuated by racial discrepancies, which would give rise to misgivings and conflicts everywhere as between individuals, or groups of individuals, of diverse races. To be precise, the so-called church cases are all traceable either to the ignorance of the masses which led them to lend a credulous ear even to the most fantastic stories about the doings of the foreign ecclesiastics, or to the excess of zeal or want of prudence on the part of the Christian missionary. At first, cases of this sort emerged mostly between the foreign missionary and the local people; later, between the latter and Chinese Christians, and recently, to the surprise of the non-Christian people, between Protestant and Catholic converts. The nation-wide feeling engendered by this phase of China's foreign intercourse has been intense, always approaching the pitch of indignation whenever any of the treaty powers sought to make political capital out of the unfortunate killing of one or two of its venturesome missionaries.

This question of church cases at one time reached, in fact, such a degree of importance that it was deemed advisable to insert a special provision in the British treaty of September 5, 1902, wherein Great Britain, undoubtedly appreciating the momentous character of the problem, agrees to join in a commission to investigate it and devise means for its solution, whenever such commission should be " formed by China and the Treaty Powers interested." [1] No such commission, however, has been formed as yet and, unless there be another outbreak of such serious cases as those taking place in 1891, 1895, or in 1900, which is very unlikely, it will probably never be formed in future, at least not with the question now under consideration as its principal object.

Fortunately few church cases occur now as compared with former years, and the number is growing less every year. Besides, not only have foreign nations in late years abstained from seizing upon missionary cases as a means

---

[1] Art. xiii, Hertslet's *China Treaties*, i, p. 183.

to attain their political ends, but some of them have taken steps to prevent a too frequent breach of the public peace by their own evangelists in China. Great Britain, for example, now prohibits by law, and under the penalty of imprisonment or fine or both, the public deriding, mocking, or insulting by a British subject of any religion established or observed in China;[1] and also enjoins its missionaries not to intervene in behalf of themselves in matters relative to the prosecution of missionary work or in behalf of their converts in any matter.[2] With such wise precautions as these; with the granting to Protestant missionaries in the American treaty of 1903 of a defined privilege of residence and property-holding in the interior, just as the same privilege was conferred upon Catholic missionaries in the Berthemy convention of 1865; with the increasing appreciation on the part of Chinese officials of the necessity of settling each church case as it arises and settling it, not to appease the mind of one party alone, generally the foreign party, but justly, to the satisfaction of both, so as to avoid adding grievance upon grievance in the view of the people and adding claim upon claim for redress on the side of the missionary, and finally with the rapid enlightenment of the Chinese masses and the growing regard on the part of foreign evangelists for the sensibilities and susceptibilities of the local populace, there is now every reason to hope that, although missionary cases may still occur now and then, the missionary question, as it has been understood, will soon cease to wear the aspect of exceptional importance which it has worn heretofore, and will retire to the place where it properly belongs, in the unofficial intercourse between Chinese and foreigners.

[1] China and Corea Order in Council, October 24, 1904, art. 76, Hertslet's *China Treaties*, ii, p. 862.

[2] Circular of Sir E Satow, British minister to Peking, to British consuls in China, August 31, 1903, Hertslet's *China Treaties*, ii, p. 1181.

The other problem, that of commerce, is intimately associated with the question of extraterritoriality. The needs of international commerce unquestionably require, on one hand, the untrammeled development of a promising market such as China doubtless affords, and, on the other, a more uniform and less artificial system of relationship between Chinese and foreign merchants than the one now prevailing under the extraterritorial jurisdiction. The appalling diversity of laws and courts needs to be replaced by a single and simple set of Chinese tribunals and Chinese laws, and the whole country needs to be opened up to the free resort and residence by foreign merchants, before foreign commerce in China can really attain the stage of development which is now hoped for by many persons interested in it. All this is undoubtedly perceived by the enlightened and far-sighted merchants of all nationalities.

But to accomplish this is not the task of China alone but the work of the treaty powers as well. So long as the latter, whatever tribute they may pay in words to China's growing desire to recover her jurisdiction over foreigners within her territory,[1] remain tenacious in the maintenance of the principle of extraterritoriality, it is unlikely that China will be anxious to level down the barriers which now stand in treaties between the open ports and the interior or to remove the restrictions, which are now found in her laws, upon the freedom of the foreign merchant to share in the unprecedented opportunities for trading and investment throughout the country. Purely from the prac-

[1] Great Britain, in the treaty of September 5, 1902, Japan and the United States, in their respective treaties of October 8, 1903, have each agreed "to give every assistance" to China's judicial reform and declared herself prepared to relinquish her extraterritorial rights "when satisfied that the state of the Chinese laws, the arrangement for their administration, and other considerations warrant her in so doing."—See Hertslet's *China Treaties*, i, pp. 182, 387, 575.

tical point of view it would seem inexpedient to permit alien commercial houses to be established broadcast in every part of the land when they are still invested with the immunities of extraterritoriality; for while missionaries in the interior, apart from their occasional demonstrations of exuberance of spirit in evangelical work, which have given birth to many an anti-missionary riot, have, as a class, been little impeachable in their private conduct, it would be entirely a different case with foreign merchants, for in their train there are apt to be characters of all kinds and grades. The desired freedom and free development of commerce can be fully obtained only by China and the treaty powers working together. It seems that their interests being intrinsically common, each may justly be expected to contribute her quota to secure their advancement. If China or any of the foreign states maintaining treaty relations with her is bent upon getting something for nothing, little can be done either for recovering territorial rights on one hand or for obtaining full commercial freedom on the other. Mutual forbearance and reciprocal concession are no less the best policy in the intercourse between nations than in the relations between individuals; and history has shown that few international questions of an important character have been peacefully settled without observing these apparently commonplace principles. In other words, intelligent co-operation alone can enable each to realize his legitimate object, whether jurisdiction or commerce.

If the signs of the time are read aright, such co-operation, however, seems to be forthcoming. Both China and the treaty powers have begun to realize that sound and smooth international relations between them, as between other states, must be built on sincere international goodwill, and their common delusions as to the inherent antagonism of Chinese and foreign interests are gradually giving way to a growing appreciation of the substantial identity of these interests. China, on one side, has in recent years opened up on her own initiative, a number of new places to foreign trade and has already set herself to the task of improving her mercantile system to meet the needs of foreign commerce. Many of the treaty powers, on the other side, have come to appreciate the capabilities and potentialities of the Chinese people and have begun to see the futility, perhaps the folly, of entwining international politics with international commerce; they are beginning to direct their energies into the broad and straight channels of legitimate and pure commercial development. In short, between China and the treaty powers there seems to be rising a feeling of community of interest, and evidence is beginning to crystallize of their willingness to co-operate for the purpose of attaining their common object.

From a larger point of view, not only commerce but peace, its best guarantee, will be promoted by the co-operation of the treaty powers with China, and this, too, seems to be perceived by the latter. The chronic riots and civic commotions in the past, which proved so disastrous to commerce, are traceable to the weakness of the former Central Government as its primary cause. But now the people of the nation have overthrown the worn-out régime of hoary antiquity and are erecting on new foundations a strong and efficient government. If, to the intelligent and intensely patriotic efforts of the Chinese people to regenerate their country, there are added the sympathy and moral support of the treaty powers, the rise of a powerful and progressive China will surely be hastened a hundred-fold. And China in progress and power means the Far East in permanent peace.

TOPICAL INDEX

(NOTE: Consult Analytical Table of Contents.)

Agnes, case of the Bark, 197

Arabs, early visits to China, 15

Assessors, in mixed cases, 177

Austria-Hungary, treaty with, 169

Assimilation, doctrine of, 206

Belgium, treaty with, 169

Benedict XII, 19

Brazil, treaty with, 169, 175

British, first visits to China, 25 ff.; early attempts to address the emperor, 41 ff ; court of justice establisl.ed in China, 95 ff.; proposed civil, criminal and admiralty courts of 1838, 112 ff.; war with China over opium, 129 ff ; extraterritorial rights conceded to, 133 ff.; legislation and orders on extra'erritoriality, 138 ff.; civil jurisdiction in China, 170 ff.; courts in China, 181 ff ; lease of Weihaiwei, 254

Buddhist, missionaries, 290, note.

Burgevine, General, case of, 204 ff.

Cadogan, case of the, 56

Canton, early trade at, 32, 34; trade arrangements at, 35 ff

Catholics. *See* Rome and missionaries.

Centurion, case of the, 67

Chefoo convention, 174, 186

Christianity, early papal embassies, 16, 19, early dissensions among missionaries, 29 ff ; persecution, 30 *See* Missionaries

Code, see Penal Code

Cohong, 35 ff., 43

Companies, joint-stock, rights of alien investment in, 286 ff

Consuls, early appointments for China, 46, *see* Jurisdiction

Courts. extraterritorial in China, 179 ff.

Criminal cases, early, 171 ff.; under extraterritorial jurisdiction, 194

Cushing, Caleb, theory of extraterritoriality, 146 ff.; mission to China, 156 ff.

Customs duties, internal, 277 ff.

Debts due aliens, early methods of liquidation, 43 ff.

Defence. case of the, 86

Denmark, treaty with, 169

Doris, case of the, 68

Dutch, first operations in China, 25

Earl of Balcarras, case of the, 78 f.

East India Company (British), early operations in China, 25; 36 ff.; 49 ff ; 66 ff ; 74; 95 ff., 117

East India Company (Dutch), 27

Emily, case of the, 54

Extraterritoriality, genesis of, in China, 62 ff.; concession to British, 133 ff.; Cushing's theory of, 146 ff ; concession to the United States, 146 ff.; criminal jurisdiction, 166 ff ; in leased ports, 255 ff.; in Turkey, 214 ff.; western ideas of, 216 ff.

France, treaties with, 167, 291; criminal jurisdiction in China, 167 ff ; and protection of Catholic missionaries, 297 ff. *See* missionaries.

Genghis Kahn, 15 f.

Germany, treaty with, 169 (1880); 269; lease of Kiaochow, 252 f.

Great Britain, *see* British

Gregory X, 16

Holy See, *see* Rome and Missionaries

Innocent IV, 15

International law, limitations of, on extraterritorial jurisdiction, 199

Japan, treaties with, 169, 175, 267; treaty of Shimonoseki, 170, note.

Jurisdiction, Chinese notions of, 47; early exercise over foreigners, 49 ff.; early attitude of aliens

Studies in History, Economics and Public Law

Edited by the

Faculty of Political Science of Columbia University

VOLUME XXII, 1905. 520 pp. Price, cloth, $3.50; paper covers, $3.00.
The Historical Development of the Poor Law of Connecticut.
By EDWARD W. CAPEN, Ph.D.

VOLUME XXIII, 1905. 594 pp. Price, cloth, $4.00.
1. The Economics of Land Tenure in Georgia.
By ENOCH MARVIN BANKS, Ph.D. Price, $1.00.
2. Mistake in Contract. A Study in Comparative Jurisprudence.
By EDWIN C. McKEAG, Ph.D. Price, $1.00.
3. Combination in the Mining Industry. By HENRY R. MUSSEY, Ph.D. Price, $1.00.
4. The English Craft Guilds and the Government.
By STELLA KRAMER, Ph.D. Price, $1.00.

VOLUME XXIV, 1905. 521 pp. Price, cloth, $4.00.
1. The Place of Magic in the Intellectual History of Europe.
By LYNN THORNDIKE, Ph.D. Price, $1.00.
2. The Ecclesiastical Edicts of the Theodosian Code.
By WILLIAM K. BOYD, Ph.D. Price, $1.00.
3. *The International Position of Japan as a Great Power.
By SEIJI G. HISHIDA, Ph.D. Price, $2.00.

VOLUME XXV, 1906-07. 600 pp. Price, cloth, $4.50.
1. *Municipal Control of Public Utilities. By OSCAR LEWIS POND, Ph.D. Price, $1.00.
2. The Budget in the American Commonwealths.
By EUGENE E. AGGER, Ph.D. Price, $1.50.
3. The Finances of Cleveland. By CHARLES C. WILLIAMSON, Ph.D. Price, $2.00.

VOLUME XXVI, 1907. 559 pp. Price, cloth, $4.00.
1. Trade and Currency in Early Oregon. By JAMES H. GILBERT, Ph.D. Price, $1.00.
2. Luther's Table Talk. By PRESERVED SMITH, Ph.D. Price, $1.00.
3. The Tobacco Industry in the United States.
By MEYER JACOBSTEIN, Ph.D. Price, $1.50.
4. Social Democracy and Population. By ALVAN A. TENNEY, Ph.D. Price, 75 cents.

VOLUME XXVII, 1907. 578 pp. Price, cloth, $4.00.
1. The Economic Policy of Robert Walpole. By NORRIS A. BRISCO, Ph.D. Price, $1.50.
2. The United States Steel Corporation. By ABRAHAM BERGLUND, Ph.D. Price, $1 50.
3. The Taxation of Corporations in Massachusetts.
By HARRY G. FRIEDMAN, Ph.D. Price, $1.50.

VOLUME XXVIII, 1907. 564 pp. Price, cloth, $4.00.
1. DeWitt Clinton and the Origin of the Spoils System in New York.
By HOWARD LEE McBAIN, Ph. D. Price, $1.50.
2. The Development of the Legislature of Colonial Virginia.
By ELMER I. MILLER, Ph.D. Price, $1.50.
3. The Distribution of Ownership. By JOSEPH HARDING UNDERWOOD, Ph.D. Price, $1.50.

VOLUME XXIX, 1908. 703 pp. Price, cloth, $4.50.
1. Early New England Towns. By ANNE BUSH MacLEAR, Ph.D Price, $1.50.
2. New Hampshire as a Royal Province. By WILLIAM H FRY, Ph.D. Price, $3.00.

VOLUME XXX, 1908. 712 pp. Price, cloth, $4.50; paper covers, $4.00.
The Province of New Jersey, 1664—1738. By EDWIN P. TANNER, Ph.D.

VOLUME XXXI, 1908. 575 pp. Price, cloth, $4.00.
1. Private Freight Cars and American Railroads.
By L. D. H. WELD, Ph.D. Price, $1 50.
2. Ohio before 1850. By ROBERT E. CHADDOCK, Ph.D. Price, $1.50.
3. Consanguineous Marriages in the American Population.
By GEORGE B. LOUIS ARNER, Ph.D. Price, 75 cents.
4. Adolphe Quetelet as Statistician. By FRANK H. HANKINS, Ph.D. Price, $1 25.

VOLUME XXXII, 1908. 705 pp. Price, cloth, $4.50; paper covers, $4.00.
The Enforcement of the Statutes of Laborers. By BERTHA HAVEN PUTNAM, Ph.D.

VOLUME XXXIII, 1908-1909. 635 pp. Price, cloth, $4.50.
1. Factory Legislation in Maine. By E. STAGG WHITIN, A B. Price, $1 00.
2. *Psychological Interpretations of Society.
By MICHAEL M. DAVIS, JR., Ph.D Price, $2.00.
3. *An Introduction to the Sources relating to the Germanic Invasions.
By CARLTON HUNTLEY HAYES, Ph.D. Price, $1.50.

VOLUME XLVI, 1911-1912. 623 pp. Price, cloth, $4.50.

1. [114] **The Ricardian Socialists.** By ESTHER LOWENTHAL, Ph.D. Price, $1.00.
2. [115] **Ibrahim Pasha, Grand Vizier of Suleiman, the Magnificent.**
By HESTER DONALDSON JENKINS, Ph.D. Price, $1.00.
3. [116] *The Labor Movement in France. A Study of French Syndicalism.
By LOUIS LEVINE, Ph.D. Price, $1.50.
4. [117] **A Hoosier Village.** By NEWELL LEROY SIMS. Price, $1.50.

VOLUME XLVII, 1912. 544 pp. Price, cloth, $4.00.

1. [118] **The Politics of Michigan, 1865-1878.**
By HARRIETTE M. DILLA, Ph.D. Price, $2.00.
2. [119] *The United States Beet-Sugar Industry and the Tariff.
By ROY G. BLAKEY, Ph.D. Price, $2.00.

VOLUME XLVIII, 1912. 493 pp. Price, cloth, $4.00.

1. [120] **Isidor of Seville.** By ERNEST BREHAUT, Ph.D. Price, $2.00.
2. [121] **Progress and Uniformity in Child-Labor Legislation.**
By WILLIAM FIELDING OGBURN, Ph.D. Price, $1.75.

VOLUME XLIX, 1912. 592 pp. Price, cloth, $4.50.

1. [122] **British Radicalism 1791-1797.** By WALTER PHELPS HALL. Price, $2.00.
2. [123] **A Comparative Study of the Law of Corporations.**
By ARTHUR K. KUHN, Ph.D. Price $1.50.
3. [124] *The Negro at Work in New York City.
By GEORGE E. HAYNES, Ph.D. Price, $1.25.

VOLUME L, 1912. 481 pp. Price, cloth, $4.00.

1. [125] *The Spirit of Chinese Philanthrophy. By YAI YUE TSU, Ph.D. Price, $1.00.
2. [126] *The Alien in China. By VI KYUIN WELLINGTON KOO. Price, $2.50.

VOLUME LI, 1912. 4to. Atlas. Price; cloth, $1.50; Paper covers, $1.00.

1. [127] **The Sale of Liquor in the South.**
By LEONARD S. BLAKEY, Ph.D.

VOLUME LII, 1912.

1. [128] *Provincial and Local Taxation in Canada.
By SOLOMON VINEBERG, Ph.D. Price, $1.50.
2. [129] **The Distribution of Income.** By FRANK HATCH STREIGHTOFF. (*In press*.)
3. [180] **To be announced.**

VOLUME LIII, 1912. 600 pp. Price, cloth, $4.00.

[131] The Civil War and Reconstruction in Florida. By W. W. DAVIS. (*In press*.)

The price for each separate monograph is for paper-covered copies; separate monographs marked, can
be supplied bound in cloth, for 50c. additional. All prices are net.*

The set of fifty-one volumes, covering monographs 1-131, is offered, bound, for $172: except that
Volume II can be supplied only in part, and in paper covers, no. 1 of that volume being out of print.
Volumes I, III and IV can now be supplied only in connection with complete sets.

For further information, apply to

Prof. **EDWIN R. A. SELIGMAN,** Columbia University,
or to Messrs. **LONGMANS, GREEN & CO.,** New York.

CPSIA information can be obtained
at www.ICGtesting.com
Printed in the USA
LVOW13s0010160418
573609LV00008B/164/P